T0244374

THE WISDOM OF THE ENLIGHTENMENT

Michael K. Kellogg

Prometheus Books

Guilford, Connecticut

(PB) Prometheus Books

An imprint of The Rowman & Littlefield Publishing Group, Inc.
4501 Forbes Boulevard, Suite 200
Lanham, Maryland 20706
www.rowman.com

Distributed by NATIONAL BOOK NETWORK

British Library Cataloguing in Publication Information Available

Library of Congress Cataloging-in-Publication Data

Names: Kellogg, Michael K., 1954– author.
Title: The wisdom of the enlightenment / Michael K. Kellogg.
Description: Lanham, MD : Prometheus, an imprint of Globe Pequot, the trade division of The Rowman & Littlefield Publishing Group, Inc., [2022] | Includes bibliographical references and index. | Summary: "From Descartes' assertion of 'I think, therefore I am,' to the philosophies of Enlightenment thinkers like Moliere, Spinoza, Voltaire, Hume, and Kant, this book charts the new and revolutionary philosophies at a time when progress seemed possible across the whole range of human knowledge and endeavor. In sweeping aside tired superstitions and applying a new scientific methodology, the Enlightenment ideas of progress through free exercise of reason ushered us into the modern world. This engaging and comprehensive survey of Enlightenment thoughts and thinkers is a celebration of the faith that all problems are solvable by human reason"— Provided by publisher.
Identifiers: LCCN 2021026080 (print) | LCCN 2021026081 (ebook) | ISBN 9781633887930 (cloth) | ISBN 9781633887947 (epub)
Subjects: LCSH: Enlightenment.
Classification: LCC B802 .K45 2022 (print) | LCC B802 (ebook) | DDC 190—dc23
LC record available at https://lccn.loc.gov/2021026080
LC ebook record available at https://lccn.loc.gov/2021026081

For Lucy

With thee conversing I forget all time,
All seasons and their change, all please alike.
—Paradise Lost, 4.639–40

CONTENTS

INTRODUCTION

From our perspective, the technology of the eighteenth century was crude, urban life uncomfortable, social welfare grudging and feeble, transport and communication cumbersome, diet inadequate, and medicine a gamble not worth taking. . . . Modernity was still struggling to be born. But men saw life getting better, safer, easier, healthier, more predictable—that is to say, more rational—decade by decade; and so they built their house of hope less on what had happened than on what was happening, and even more on what they had good reason to expect would happen in the future. [1]

Enlightenment—*Aufklärung* in German, *Lumières* in French—is more an idea than a period. But it is an idea that took hold in a particular historical context of revolutionary scientific advances, increasing economic and social freedom, rising literacy and prosperity, and a greater willingness to challenge authoritarianism in politics and religion. Samuel Johnson cautioned that "human life is everywhere a state in which much is to be endured, and little to be enjoyed." [2] But human life was already far removed from the "solitary, poor, nasty, brutish and short" state of nature famously depicted by Thomas Hobbes. The Enlightenment was a time when progress seemed possible across the whole range of human knowledge and endeavor. There were timeless truths to be discovered; there were vast opportunities to better the human condition; it was only a matter of sweeping aside tired superstitions and superannuated dogmas and applying the new scientific methodology to observed phenomena.

Choosing a beginning date for a book on the Enlightenment is no easy task. One might start with the Peace of Westphalia in 1648, which largely ended thirty years of devastating religious wars that had transmogrified into a continent-wide struggle for hegemony. Or one could pick 1643, the beginning of the seventy-two-year reign of Louis XIV, the "Sun King," in France, where—despite absolutism—the Enlightenment often seemed to shine brightest. My own choice, precisely because enlightenment is an idea rather than a period, is 1637, the year Descartes's *Discourse on the Method of Rightly Conducting One's Reason and Seeking the Truth in the Sciences* was published. Descartes sought to explain the physical world entirely in scientific terms—specifically, the mathematics of matter in motion. His "method of doubt" was to question all received truths that could not be placed on a firm foundation of innate ideas known directly by reason. He even sought to extend his method of "rightly conducting one's reason" to psychology, treating the passions as immaterial forces interacting in the human soul according to fixed laws.

Descartes's theories were challenged and refined, and his innate ideas largely rejected. But his methodology, however questionable in some respects, embodied a profound, touching, and almost giddy belief in the power of human reason to uncover truth, a belief shared by rationalists and empiricists alike. In his famous essay, "What Is Enlightenment?," the German philosopher Immanuel Kant, with whom I will end the book, wrote that "enlightenment is the human being's emergence from his self-incurred minority."[3] We must, he argued, learn to think for ourselves in matters of science, art, politics, and particularly religion, rather than accepting doctrines handed down over generations. "The public use of one's reason must always be free, and it alone can bring about enlightenment among human beings."[4] Reduced to a bumper sticker, the motto of Enlightenment thinkers could be "Progress Through Reason" or, even better, "Progress Through Freedom," for they advocated scientific, political, economic, and religious freedom, confident that reason would show the way.

Perhaps it was a naive belief, and it certainly had its detractors even in the seventeenth and eighteenth centuries. But the idea of progress through the free exercise of reason helped bring us into the modern world, and remains with us today.[5] Each thinker discussed in this book wrestled with that idea in his own way. Before we deal with particular writers, however, it is worth setting forth the main strands of Enlightenment thought, as well as the countertrends that called into question the Enlightenment faith that all problems are solvable by human reason.

THE SCIENTIFIC REVOLUTION

In 1687, Isaac Newton published his masterwork, *Principia Mathematica*. In it, he demonstrated that all physical phenomena, whether in the heavens or on earth, could be reduced to a handful of fundamental laws about space, time, mass, force, momentum, and inertia, all expressed mathematically. It was a stunning scientific achievement, arguably the greatest of all time, despite being bracketed eventually by general relativity for events on the largest scale and by quantum mechanics for events on the smallest scale. Certainly, it was viewed as such by Newton's contemporaries. An epitaph on Newton's grave by the poet Alexander Pope accurately captures the awe that greeted Newton's work.

> Nature and Nature's Laws lay hid in Night:
> God said, "Let Newton be!" and all was light.

Though the opposite of modest, Newton demurred: "If I have seen farther, it is by standing on the shoulders of Giants."[6] But he said this in a letter to Joseph Hooke, another brilliant scientist and Royal Society rival, who was short and had a twisted spine. Newton's famously gracious remark seems to have been deliberately slighting and cruel. He repeatedly minimized or ignored Hooke's significant contributions to physics, and even went so far as to "lose" Hooke's portrait when the Royal Society moved to larger quarters. Newton may have been the greatest scientist of all time, but he was not a nice person.

Regardless, taken at face value, Newton's comment was correct. The Scientific Revolution had many giants, starting with the great astronomers who tracked the motions of the planets and the stars, both for their innate fascination and to aid in maritime navigation. Since the second century, the Ptolemaic model placed the earth at the center of the universe. In 1543, just before his death, Nicolaus Copernicus proposed an alternative heliocentric model as a simpler, more elegant explanation of planetary motion. The superiority of that model was confirmed by Tycho Brahe's (1546–1601) meticulous observations, which paved the way for Johannes Kepler (1571–1630) to establish three basic laws of planetary motion, published between 1609 and 1616: the planets move in elliptical orbits with the sun as one of two focal points; each planet in relation to the sun sweeps out equal areas in equal times, indicating that the speed at which planets travel is in inverse proportion to their distance from the sun; and, finally, the time it takes for each planet to complete its orbit is proportional to the size of the orbit.

Galileo Galilei (1564–1642) rigorously studied the speed, velocity, and trajectory of falling objects, decisively refuting Aristotle's view that heavy objects fall faster than light ones. He also built cutting-edge telescopes, which showed that Venus, like the moon, has phases caused by its motion around the sun, further bolstering the Copernican model. The Ptolemaic system did not go quietly, however. The church wanted the earth to stand still, with man at the center of God's creation, and found support for that view in the Bible. The aging Galileo was forced to recant in 1633 under threat of torture. "E pur si muove" (And yet it moves), Galileo is said to have muttered. The anecdote is apocryphal, but the sentiment was sound. The church could make neither the earth nor scientific progress stand still. Fifty-four years later, Newton's *Principia* was hailed throughout Europe.

Other thinkers offered equally broad shoulders. Francis Bacon all but invented the scientific method. His *Novum Organum* in 1620 advocated observation, experimentation, induction, and quantification as the road to knowledge.

> Our [inductive] logic instructs the understanding and trains it, not (as common logic does) to grope and clutch at abstracts with feeble mental tendrils, but to dissect nature truly, and to discover the powers and actions of bodies and their laws limned in matter. Hence this science takes it origin not only from the nature of the mind but from the nature of things.[7]

René Descartes first articulated the mechanical view of the universe perfected by Newton, and invented analytic geometry, which allowed him to translate geometric shapes into coordinates. In order to track motion over time, Newton invented calculus—independently discovered by the German polymath Gottfried Leibniz, which of course led to a bitter quarrel, conducted mainly through surrogates, over who could claim priority. What could not be disputed was that calculus was an indispensable tool in the development of science. In a Newtonian universe, if you could know the position and momentum of every particle at a given moment in time, you could track mathematically their positions and momentums at every future point in time and retrace their positions and momentums at every past moment. Calculus was the language of an omniscient God, laying bare the past, the present, and the future.

The Scientific Revolution of course extended beyond physics and astronomy. As early as 1600, William Gilbert developed the laws of magnetic attraction and repulsion. William Harvey in 1628 demonstrated that blood circulates through the body, pumped by the heart muscle. Robert Boyle studied the behavior of gases and proved in 1662 that their volume is inversely proportional to the pressure imposed on them. That was the same year that the Royal Society was granted a royal charter by Charles II. The Parisian Académie Royale des Sciences followed in 1666, with a generous endowment from the king to support active research.

Antonie van Leeuwenhoek (1632–1723) used the increasing power of microscopes to reveal to the Royal Society in 1676 that a drop of water is teeming with microorganisms. The Royal Observatory was built at Greenwich that same year, along with its counterpart in Paris. Telescopes and microscopes joined mathematics as the great instruments of scientific progress. John Ray (1627–1705) undertook a massive catalog of life on earth, including separate volumes on fishes, insects, birds, and mammals. Carl Linnaeus (1707–1778), the father of modern taxonomy, published a *Systema Naturae* in 1735 that used two-word classifications (generic and specific) for each species. Christiaan Huygens (1629–1695) developed the wave theory of light. Ole Rømer (1644–1710) then calculated the speed of light with remarkable precision. Edmond Halley (1656–1742) vastly expanded our understanding of the size of the universe and tracked the elliptical orbit of comets around the sun, subject to the same laws of planetary motion established by Kepler. When "Halley's Comet" reappeared as predicted in 1758, it was a stunning and justly celebrated confirmation of Newton's work.

The list of examples can be multiplied, with advances in meteorology, electricity, and optics. Throughout the seventeenth and eighteenth centuries, there was a sense that nature's secrets were an open book for anyone with a gift for mathematics and a passion for observation and experimentation. Ignorance and superstition were in retreat. That optimism culminated in the quintessential Enlightenment project, the French *Encyclopedia*, or *Systematic Dictionary of the Sciences, Arts, and Trades*, published in twenty-eight volumes between 1751 and 1772. The aspiration of the *Encyclopedia* was to summarize the current state of knowledge across disciplines as a stepping-stone to further progress. Descartes had predicted that mathematical science would make men the "lords and masters of nature."[8] Certainly, it transformed our view of the world and the universe of which we are such a minute part. But, if anything, that reorientation sparked an even greater focus on humankind, whose exact nature still "lay hid in Night."

THE PROPER STUDY OF HUMANKIND

Alexander Pope had a gift for capturing the zeitgeist of the Enlightenment in rhymed couplets:

> Know then thyself, presume not God to scan;
> The proper study of mankind is Man.[9]

While others focused on the natural world, a number of philosophers were trying to use some of the same methods that were so fruitful in science to study human nature. The most influential of these attempts was John Locke's 1689 *Essay Concerning Human Understanding*, in which he argued, in direct opposition to Descartes's theory of innate ideas, that the human mind at birth is a blank page, or *tabula rasa*, upon which the world impresses itself in the form of sense impressions. These sense impressions are, so to speak, the elementary particles of the mind, which are gradually drawn together to form ideas. The human mind, for Locke, is a miniscientist, relying on observation and induction to gather knowledge of the world. Among the *philosophes*—the French vanguard of the Enlightenment—Locke enjoyed almost equal status with Newton.

The importance of Locke's empirical psychology, however, did not lie in the attempted extension of Newtonian mechanics to the association of ideas in the mind. What proved far more fruitful was his reorientation of scientific thought toward the study of humankind, both individually and collectively. Psychology, sociology, economics, natural law, and even education became recognized disciplines during this period. No one matched Newton's reduction of complex phenomena to a few laws of general applicability, though Adam Smith certainly tried. In that sense, the scientific method revealed its limitations where humans were in question. But that didn't mean that reason could not improve our understanding of human behavior and institutions and thereby lead to their improvement. As one of Voltaire's characters pronounced, with a surprisingly Candide-like optimism, "Le monde avec lenteur marche vers la sagesse" (The world slowly marches toward wisdom).[10]

The comparative sociology of the Baron de Montesquieu is a case in point. His 1748 masterwork, *The Spirit of the Laws*, extends far beyond a consideration of positive law to embrace the entire structure of government, including institutions, traditions, customs, and even manners. Montesquieu pioneered what we would now call comparative sociology. He recognized that human institutions and customs will vary from place to place. "Many things govern men: climate, religion, laws, the maxims of the government, examples of past things, mores, and manners; a general spirit is formed as a result."[11] Montesquieu saw no deliberate plan or social contract in the formation of society, as Locke had argued. Society was, in Montesquieu's view, an organic growth, a view later adopted by political conservatives such as David Hume and Edmund Burke.

Yet Montesquieu also argued in favor of certain general principles and aspirations that could guide this organic growth in a more progressive direction, toward individual freedom, peace among nations, and general prosperity. In particular, he advocated for a constitutional republic with a separation of powers (executive, legislative, and judicial) and a solid core of individual, inalienable rights—views that would strongly influence our founders. Montesquieu also argued powerfully for legal reform, including due process and humane punishments, at a time when judicial torture was still common and the list of capital offenses, at least in England, had expanded to include shoplifting and unlawfully cutting down trees. "Natural law" became the touchstone against which positive law was to be measured. Montesquieu accordingly took an uncompromising stand against slavery, which the Founding Fathers unfortunately did not follow. As Samuel Johnson would bitterly exclaim on the eve of the American Revolution, "How is it that we hear the loudest yelps for liberty among the drivers of negroes?"[12]

When Adam Smith published *An Inquiry into the Nature and Causes of the Wealth of Nations* in 1776, his good friend David Hume wrote to congratulate him: "I am convinced that since Montesquieu's *Esprit des Lois*, Europe has not received any publication which tends so much to enlarge and rectify the ideas of mankind."[13] It was an astute remark.

Montesquieu had already drawn a connection between increased liberty and increased prosperity. That insight drove Adam Smith's own pioneering work, in which he detailed the economic advantages of free trade, the division of labor, the deployment of private capital, and the invisible hand that allows self-interest to operate for the public good within a framework of free commerce. As those ideas gained currency, extreme state control of the economy lessened. Countries that had viewed trade as a zero-sum struggle for dominance came to realize that both sides could benefit. Protective tariffs, state subsidies, and monopoly franchises—all elements of what was then known as "mercantilism"—were still extant, but they were losing their stranglehold on commerce as the economic case against them grew more powerful.

A commitment to commerce, like the commitment to science, came to be seen as a means of human betterment. David Hume called merchants "one of the most useful races of men."[14] Voltaire echoed the sentiment: "Great men I call those who have excelled in the useful or the agreeable. Those who sack provinces are only heroes."[15] But it was Adam Smith who made the case that economic freedom and rising standards of living are firmly conjoined:

> The natural effort of every individual to better his own condition, when suffered to exert itself with freedom and security, is so powerful a principle, that it is alone, and without any assistance, not only capable of carrying on the society to wealth and prosperity, but of surmounting a hundred impertinent obstructions with which the folly of human laws too often incumbers its operations.[16]

Smith was not wholly laissez-faire. He understood that rampant self-interest must be checked by law and that a commercial society will invariably have losers for whom provision must be made. He also understood, more profoundly, that capital would impose constraints on labor that might come to seem like a form of slavery. But he felt that personal freedom requires, in the first instance, freedom from hunger and want, and that capitalism was the great engine of economic growth.

There is no question, moreover, that economic prosperity was both increasing and expanding, sparked by increased commercial freedom and innovations in the production of goods. Crop rotation and horse-drawn hoes made land more productive. The spinning jenny, invented by James Hargreaves in 1764, led to the industrialization of textile manufacturing in which England played an outsized role. Large smelters increased the demand for coal, which would fuel the steam engines and factories of the coming Industrial Revolution. Marine insurance diffused risk, just as stock exchanges allowed the formation of capital. Advances in navigation improved speed and safety in the shipping of goods. The development by John Harrison, a Yorkshire clockmaker, of a practical chronometer for use at sea finally solved the conundrum of how to measure longitude. All the maritime nations had been vying for such an advantage. England, an island nation, had the foresight to develop the strongest navy by far, a key to trade in the eighteenth century and imperial expansion in the nineteenth.

With access to foreign markets came a new range of amenities that gradually altered the rhythms and increased the ease of everyday life in matters large and small. Tea was introduced in England in the early 1650s. The first coffeehouses followed in 1652, where people could gather to read the first newspapers and discuss the events of the day. The first letter boxes arrived in 1653, along with the "penny post." Watches now had minute hands. As England moved gradually toward a money-based economy from a land-based one, checks made payments easier and more secure. Streetlamps and plate glass led to a literal form of enlightenment. Even the humble commode marked a significant improvement over the traditional, stand-alone chamber pot.

There were hopes that international trade would lead to other forms of international cooperation and thus a lessening of the deadly and destructive wars that had plagued the seventeenth century and carried over into the eighteenth. Immanuel Kant, in his remarkable essay "Toward Perpetual Peace," advocated that states band together in a kind of United Nations, all dedicated to peace, representative government, and the rule of law. It was a vain hope—then, and perhaps now—but captured something of the idealism of the age. Equally idealistic, but somewhat more successful, was the call for freedom of religion. Atheism was still not tolerated, but religious minorities endured less persecution. The philosophes and their fellow travelers (including Spinoza, Hume, and Kant) openly disparaged clerics, dogma, and meaningless rituals designed to gain divine favor. But they generally made clear—sometimes sincerely—that they were not antireligion. Deism, a belief in God based on secular reasoning rather than scriptural revelation, was their new form of worship.

Perhaps most important was a growing rejection of the doctrine of original sin, of man as inherently fallen. David Hume and Adam Smith argued that morality did not depend on divine commands to control a recalcitrant human nature, but was itself grounded in human nature. Men and women naturally share certain moral sentiments, such as tenderness to offspring, love, and friendship. We feel affection for others and wish to promote their good as well as our own. Neither Hume nor Smith was naive. Each recognized that selfishness is endemic. But cooperation with others is also part of our natural makeup, and our secular moral language and judgments depend on such sentiments. "It is sufficient for our present purpose," Hume wrote, "if it be allowed, what surely, without the greatest absurdity, cannot be disputed, that there is some benevolence, however small, infused into our bosom; some spark of friendship for humankind; some particle of the dove kneaded into our frame, along with the elements of the wolf and serpent."[17]

No one suggested—least of all Hume and Smith—that either human-kind or society could become perfectly altruistic or eradicate the many and varied iniquities driven by self-interest. But, with few exceptions—most notably Thomas Hobbes and, in his very different way, Jean-Jacques Rousseau—Enlightenment thinkers believed that moral and polit-ical progress could be made through the exercise of reason. What Hume called the "moral sciences"—political economy, psychology, sociology, and education—were all dedicated to that ideal.

Even history became a moral science. Voltaire's *Siècle de Louis XIV* (1751), Hume's *History of England* (1754–1762) and, most splendid of all, Edward Gibbon's *Decline and Fall of the Roman Empire* (1776–1789) used history as a backdrop for the study of man, society, manners, and morals. Their sweeping panoramas combined narrative mo-mentum with philosophical reflection. They sought both to amuse and to instruct.

It is commonplace to say that their histories read like novels. But we may want to reverse that judgment and note that the early novels read like case histories. The novel became another tool for the study and critique of society. Daniel Defoe's *Moll Flanders* (1722), Samuel Richardson's *Cla-rissa* (1748), Henry Fielding's *Tom Jones* (1749), and Laurence Sterne's wildly digressive *Tristram Shandy* (1759) were designed to instruct as well as to amuse. As we shall see, even adventure novels such as *Robin-*

son Crusoe (1719) and *Gulliver's Travels* (1726), disparate as they were from each other, were fraught with philosophical intent.

Libraries made such books accessible to an increasingly literate and burgeoning middle class. Concert halls throughout Europe resounded with the cantatas of Bach (1685–1750), the oratorios of Handel (1685–1759), the symphonies of Haydn (1732–1809), and the operas of Mozart (1756–1791). Music reached a height of perfection that has never been surpassed. As Peter Pesic notes in his history of polyphonic music, the Bach fugue was considered "a heightened exercise of human reason, feeling, and persuasion . . . suggesting an almost divine capacity."[18]

Painting, too, was undergoing a dramatic transformation led by the great Dutch masters, particularly the revealing character studies of Rembrandt van Rijn (1606–1669), the profoundly illuminated domestic scenes of Johannes Vermeer (1632–1675), and the rich, brooding landscapes of Jacob van Ruisdael (1628–1682). French art started to outgrow its baroque and rococo phases. Denis Diderot, a philosophe as well as an influential art critic, condemned mannerism and artificiality in painting and society alike. While retaining the neoclassical values of order, harmony, and proportion, Jacques-Louis David (1748–1825), in historical tableaux, and Jean-Baptiste-Siméon Chardin (1699–1779), in scenes of everyday life, each strove for greater naturalism and realism. In England, the landscapes of Thomas Gainsborough (1727–1788) and the portraits of Joshua Reynolds (1723–1792) were heavily influenced, respectively, by van Ruisdael and Rembrandt. Art was another means of studying the natural world and developing a greater appreciation of the complexities of human nature. Art, too, could reveal "a heightened exercise of human reason, feeling, and persuasion . . . suggesting an almost divine capacity." Of course, it could also reveal precisely the opposite, as William Hogarth (1697–1764) demonstrated, particularly in engraved series such as *A Harlot's Progress* and *The Rake's Progress*. Hogarth's art was a form of social criticism revealing the darker side of Enlightenment "progress."

THE ANTI-ENLIGHTENMENT

No era is one thing and one thing only. Inevitably there are countertrends. Hogarth's ironic use of the word *progress* insisted that too many people were being left behind by the Enlightenment project. For them, progress was a free fall into the abyss of poverty, disease, and crime. Even those who managed to find employment often earned less than subsistence wages and endured mind-numbing monotony as gradually increasing industrialization and the division of labor forced them to repeat a few simple operations over and over. The seeds of the French Revolution and Romanticism were already being planted by Rousseau, who argued that advances in science and technology, far from being unalloyed goods, were dramatically increasing inequality and alienation.

Absolute monarchs still reigned throughout Europe. Political freedom was an ideal rather than a reality. Indeed, for some it was not even an ideal. Thomas Hobbes argued that self-rule by the people was a recipe for chaos and mutual destruction. His classic description of the state of nature was a state of constant war in which the strong preyed on the weak:

> In such condition there is no place for industry, because the fruit thereof is uncertain: and consequently no culture of the earth; no navigation nor use of the commodities that may be imported by sea; no commodious building; no instruments of moving and removing such things as require much force; no knowledge of the face of the earth; no account of time; no arts; no letters; no society; and, which is worst of all, continual fear and danger of violent death; and the life of man solitary, poor, nasty, brutish, and short.[19]

For Hobbes, only despotic government could provide individual and collective security.

But the trade proved a poor one. The loss of freedom did not bring security. For a time, intellectuals pinned their hopes on supposedly enlightened monarchs such as Louis XIV in France (r. 1643–1715), Frederick II of Prussia (r. 1740–1786), Joseph II of Habsburg Austria (r. 1765–1790), and Catherine the Great of Russia (r. 1762–1796). But disillusionment soon set in. Absolute monarchs proved even more unruly than the people they ruled. They fought endless wars for small gains in territory and prestige, subjecting the populace to slaughter, displacement, and disease, and then requiring them to pay for the privilege through ruinous taxation.

The Peace of Westphalia in 1648 finally brought to an end nearly eighty years of war between Spain and the Dutch republics, as well as the German phase of the Thirty Years' War, which had cut the population of Germany nearly in half. But France continued to fight with Spain for another decade. France also had internal troubles after Louis XIV, in 1685, revoked the Edict of Nantes, which had guaranteed religious freedom for Protestant Huguenots. The Fronde was a series of civil wars between 1648 and 1653 pitting first parliament, and then aristocrats, against the absolute authority of the monarchy. Both efforts failed miserably. The French Revolution, when it came, would need to command a broader base of support.

Civil wars began in England in 1642 and largely ended with the execution of Charles I for treason in 1649. But Oliver Cromwell soon set himself up as another despot, the self-proclaimed "Great Protector." When he died, those who were tired of strict Puritan rule readily embraced the Restoration of Charles II, only to rebel again against his successor, the Catholic James II, in the Glorious (because bloodless) Revolution of 1688. Meanwhile, England suffered through the Great Plague of 1665 and the Great Fire of London in 1666, both chronicled with care by the diarist Samuel Pepys. To the average Londoner, it must have seemed a dark time indeed, though Pepys maintained his acute powers of observation along with an active sex life.

The War of Spanish Succession—which pitted a French Bourbon claimant against an Austrian Habsburg one—engulfed Europe from 1701 to 1714. Following the death of Charles II of Spain, England and the Dutch Republic joined a Grand Alliance to prevent the union of Spain and France under a single monarch. Philip of Anjou, the grandson of Louis XIV, was ultimately confirmed on the Spanish throne by the Peace of Utrecht in 1713 but on the stipulation that the crowns of Spain and France never be held by the same person. England got Gibraltar and Minorca in the bargain. But nothing was ever fully resolved, and wars over territory, the balance of powers, trade, and religion continued to make a mockery of the Enlightenment project of perpetual peace among a commonwealth of nations. There was even a global Seven Years' War, from 1756 to 1763, over burgeoning and highly profitable foreign empires.

Despite intellectual opposition, slavery flourished in those foreign empires. As many as twelve million Africans were torn from their homes and families, chained together, and marched to the nearest port, where they were forced into appallingly crowded and often unseaworthy ships. Those who survived worked on the tobacco, coffee, and sugar plantations of the Caribbean and the southern mainland of North America. The Netherlands, once a beacon of religious and intellectual freedom, the refuge of

Descartes and Spinoza, the home of Rembrandt and van Ruisdael, was the worst offender under the relentless brutality, cruelty, and greed of the Dutch West India Company.

War, poverty, slavery, inequality, miserable workplaces, and crowded slums were unimpressed with the Enlightenment project. And yet things were getting measurably better, whether or not it seemed that way to the average citizen. Literacy was rapidly increasing, and gross domestic product (GDP) was soaring in Great Britain and throughout Western Europe. Real progress was being made and, despite backsliding, would continue to be made in the coming centuries.

ELEVEN ENLIGHTENMENT THINKERS

Jean-Jacques Rousseau—who was regularly supported by one patron or another and who abandoned each of his infant children in turn while he wrote a treatise on child-rearing—argued that material prosperity is not worth its cost in human freedom and dignity. Rationalism and commercialism became terms of reproach wielded by those Romantics who emphasized self-expression, creativity, and the uniqueness of each individual. But the Enlightenment thinkers we will study did not ignore the seemingly intractable paradoxes of human life or the vast gap between the real and the ideal. For the most part, they were pragmatists as well as idealists.

René Descartes (1596–1650) is, by common consent, the first modern philosopher. He provided the philosophical foundations for a purely secular, scientific worldview based on the mathematics of matter in motion. He was also the first, but certainly not the last, to wrestle with the problems of free will and the role of God in a deterministic universe.

John Milton (1608–1674), in his great epic, *Paradise Lost*, delves into mysteries of the universe that are not captured in Descartes's worldview. In Milton's opinion, these mysteries give human life a meaning that a purely secular understanding cannot reach. His mythopoeic account of Satan's rebellion and the fall of Man intermixes epic struggles with a moving story of human innocence, sex, marriage, temptation, fall, recrimination, and reconciliation.

Jean-Baptiste Poquelin, known to us as **Molière** (1622–1673), has been called "the gravedigger of Descartes," and for good reason. Descartes posited an immaterial soul that retains free will and yet inexplicably interacts with the deterministic universe. In Molière, we have no absolute existence apart from the social and moral relations we have established. In our longing for intrinsic value, we continually disguise ourselves from one another and even from ourselves. Exposing those pretentions is the source of Molière's unique blend of comedy and tragedy.

Blaise Pascal (1623–1662) could not endure a purely secular existence built on transient social and moral relationships. He accepted the fact that we cannot reason our way to God. He even accepted the Enlightenment faith in reason as an instrument of human progress. But Pascal clung desperately to the notion of a transcendent, hidden God who is the source of all value and meaning in life and with whom we can somehow establish a direct connection beyond reason. "The heart has its reasons," he famously wrote, "which reason does not know."

Benedict de Spinoza (1632–1677) was reviled and ostracized as an atheist because he believed in an immanent God as embodied in nature, not a transcendent God who is separate from and intervenes in nature or otherwise performs miracles that disrupt the chain of cause and effect. *Deus sive Natura* (God or Nature): these are not two substances, Spinoza argued, but only one substance understood in its dual aspects. Einstein, when asked about his own religion, replied, "I believe in the God of Spinoza." The God of Spinoza is a way of looking at nature filled with wonder and awe and the sense of mystery urged by Milton. Spinoza took a similar approach to human beings. We are not composed of separate substances—mind and body—that inexplicably interact with each other. Humans can be described simultaneously in the vocabulary of cause and effect—of neurons firing and muscles contracting—and the completely separate vocabulary of emotions, intentions, thoughts, and desires. Neither form of speaking is privileged over or excludes the other. The latter vocabulary is the foundation of morality, which is based not on external rules but on a fuller understanding of our humanity.

The dual nature of human life is reflected in the novels of **Daniel Defoe** (1660–1731) and **Jonathan Swift** (1667–1745). *Robinson Crusoe* is an empiricist's bible. Defoe tells his story in a Lockean manner: impression by impression, piling up vivid concrete details into simple ideas that gradually form an increasingly complex portrait of one man's journey and the emotional and spiritual resources that sustain him. In the hands of Defoe and his successors, the novel is a means of psychological,

moral, and social understanding and, as such, an instrument of Enlightenment progress. Swift, in *Gulliver's Travels*, launched an opposing tradition, a satiric and ironic movement that is less interested in characters
than in types. It is a tradition that is skeptical of Enlightenment claims to
progress and takes a darker view of man and his institutions.

François-Marie Arouet, known to us as **Voltaire** (1694–1778) was the
gadfly of the *ancien régime*. For most of his eighty-three years, he was
Europe's most prominent advocate for religious tolerance, scientific
progress, intellectual freedom, and legal reform. He was a poet, playwright, historian, essayist, polemicist, and author of a number of *contes
philosophiques*, including the immortal tale *Candide*. All his writings
revealed unflagging energy, satirical wit, rapier-like prose, vast intelligence, and an astonishing range of interests. Perhaps he spread himself
too thin, but Voltaire captured and transformed the spirit of his age.

Samuel Johnson (1709–1784), like Voltaire, packed many lives into
his seventy-five years. He was a journalist, poet, playwright, and author
of a *conte philosophique* that stands comparison to *Candide* and *Gulliver's Travels*. He compiled a *Dictionary of the English Language*, prepared a scholarly edition of Shakespeare's plays, and wrote *Lives of the
Poets*. Most of all he was a talker—perhaps the most famous talker of all
time—as transcribed with painstaking care by James Boswell in his multivolume *Life of Johnson*. Yet it is as an essayist that Johnson most claims
our attention. He wrote of the "hunger of imagination"—our restless
quest for changed circumstances and new objects of desire, which finds
repose only in a deeper understanding of human nature. No moralist other
than Aristotle and Montaigne has offered us such a balanced and realistic
prescription for human flourishing. Despite the inevitability of sorrow,
loss, and failure, Johnson's message is ultimately optimistic: "It is necessary to hope, tho' hope should always be deluded, for hope itself is
happiness, and its frustrations, however frequent, are yet less dreadful
than its extinction."

David Hume (1711–1776) set out from a young age to destroy the
premise of previous philosophical inquiry: that we can use abstract reasoning to uncover the foundations of human knowledge and experience.
He attacked the innate ideas—self, substance, and causation—that Descartes made the basis of his mechanical universe. He sought to demonstrate that morality is grounded in neither reason nor religion, but in
natural human feelings of benevolence and kinship. He dismissed what

were then the standard arguments for the existence of God and condemned the "monkish virtues" that were the product of a morbid religious enthusiasm. Hume advocated for the autonomy of science, including social sciences such as psychology, economics, political science, and even morality. He rejected only the claim that they depend for their first principles upon reason or revelation. In the process, Hume gave birth to an entirely different approach to philosophy.

Immanuel Kant (1724–1804) wanted to rescue philosophy from Hume's skeptical assault on reason. Where Hume rejected all innate ideas, Kant argued that there are conditions necessary to experience, and hence we can know those conditions with certainty prior to and apart from experience, including a self that has the experience, an external world that is experienced, and the strict succession of events governed by cause and effect. Where Hume argued that morality arises naturally from the sentiments and affections of humankind, Kant argued that morality has a formal nature known to reason from which our categorical duties as humans necessarily follow. Where Hume rejected all arguments for the existence of God and immortality, Kant contended that God and immortality were necessary postulates to make sense of our moral duty. Kant set limits on reason to make room for faith, but he also, with equal if not greater vigor, set limits on faith to make room for reason. Kant thus drew a strict distinction between experience—things as they appear to us—and things as they are in themselves, about which we can have no knowledge but only faith.

There are other Enlightenment authors who could justly claim chapters of their own—notably Hobbes, Locke, Pepys, Leibniz, Montesquieu, Richardson, Fielding, Diderot, Adam Smith, and, of course, Rousseau himself, though he will find his proper place at the start of the next volume on Romanticism. But the writers chosen here provide the widest range for an exploration of the wisdom of the Enlightenment. And Kant marks, in a sense, both the last hurrah of reason and the end of the Enlightenment project to solve all problems through the use of reason.

Kant—who was a passionate admirer of Rousseau—said it was fundamental to the nature of humankind to have transcendental longings that can never be satisfied by empirical knowledge and thus to ask questions about God, freedom, and immortality that we cannot answer. The most basic such question was posed by Leibniz: Why is there something rather than nothing? It is a question to ponder while gazing out at the ocean or up at the stars. All the problems of science could be answered without getting us one step closer to answering that ultimate metaphysical question. For Kant, as for Milton and Pascal, it is in pondering the imponderables that we find meaning and value.

Yet, as other Enlightenment thinkers insisted, the advance of the material and moral conditions of life through science and the use of reason are what give us the freedom to make such inquiries. Natural science, political science, economics, moral theory, history, literature, even music and painting: all these disciplines were practiced with the ostensible goal to better understand humanity and to improve its condition. Much progress remained. But it is not an exaggeration to say that, in the seventeenth and eighteenth centuries, humans became somewhat more humane and civilization somewhat more civilized.

I

DESCARTES AND THE MECHANICAL UNIVERSE

Aristotelian Scholasticism met its end at the hands of René Descartes in a stove-heated room near Ulm, Germany, in the winter of 1619. Whether it was a drawing room or a library, we don't know. But we do know the weapon: mathematics. And, despite Descartes's best efforts to the contrary, theology itself was collateral damage.

Descartes's *Discourse on the Method of Rightly Conducting One's Reason and Seeking the Truth in the Sciences*, though written more than fifteen years later and greatly expanded upon in the subsequent *Meditations on First Philosophy*, recites the steps by which he arrived at a purely mechanical view of the universe. Cartesianism, as it quickly became known, provided the philosophical foundations for the Scientific Revolution of the seventeenth and eighteenth centuries that transformed our understanding of the world and our ability to harness natural forces for the betterment of humankind. Descartes is, by common consent, the first modern philosopher.

It is perhaps remarkable, then, that Descartes was so demonstrably wrong about two critical aspects of his philosophy. His arguments for the existence of God—arguments he thought necessary to place the basic laws of nature beyond doubt—were extremely weak, and his strong form of dualism—the separation of mind and body—is largely incoherent. But in philosophy, as in baseball, hitting safely in one of every three at bats will put you in the hall of fame. Descartes hit a massive grand slam on the issue that really counted, demonstrating that the physical world can be explained in terms of mechanics (matter in motion), which can in turn be expressed mathematically. It is an astonishing achievement, even if the bases were already loaded by Copernicus, Kepler, and Galileo.

One might immediately object that the laws of matter and motion and their mathematical expression are all scientific discoveries, not philosophical ones. They are, moreover, discoveries that we normally attribute to Galileo and Newton, rather than to Descartes. Those are both fair points. But we have to understand the historical context in which Descartes was writing to appreciate fully his contribution to Western thought. Medieval Scholasticism—with its Aristotelian references to "substantial forms" and "final causes," and its heavy reliance on scripture, revelation, and miracles in explaining the world—still dominated the schools. Descartes himself received a heavy, though fortunately not fatal, dose of it at the Jesuit college of La Flèche, where he spent eight years. In the end, he decided that the Scholastic portion of his education was worse than useless; it was affirmatively harmful in trying to think clearly about the material world. So Descartes resolved to start from scratch, abandoning everything he had been taught, starting with the application of reason alone and seizing only upon what he called "clear and distinct ideas" to build his account of the world. Mathematics provides the prototypes for such ideas. To understand the equation $2 + 2 = 4$ is immediately to grasp its truth. That the angles of a triangle always add up to 180 degrees might take a bit more thought but, once demonstrated, is equally self-evident. These are truths determined separately from, and are not dependent on, experience or experiments.

Descartes's central insight is that we can form equally clear and distinct ideas about matter and motion, and that we can express those ideas mathematically. The fundamental attribute of matter—its primary quality, as we now say—is extension. Material objects can be measured with precision by their extension in space (length, depth, breadth). The fundamental attribute of motion is a change of position in space. That, too, can be charted with precision. Descartes invented analytic geometry to turn matter and motion into algebraic equations and their corresponding coordinates.

Descartes did not have calculus, which was necessary to complete the mathematics of continuous change. That would be developed by Newton and Leibniz—each working independently of the other but both building on Descartes's analytic geometry. Yet Descartes was able to anticipate

Newton's basic laws of motion—that a body in motion will continue in a straight line unless acted on by some other body; that a body at rest will remain at rest unless acted on by some other body—from his articulation of the ideas of matter and motion.

In the process, Descartes established the mechanistic world picture that has dominated scientific thought ever since. Many of Descartes's specific scientific theories were displaced by Newtonian physics, which could be characterized as both the triumph and the demise of Cartesianism.[1] Newton was more systematic and comprehensive. He was able to reduce the material world to a handful of fundamental laws about space, time, mass, force, momentum, and inertia. In a Newtonian universe, if you could know the position and momentum of every particle at a given moment in time, you would be able to predict their position and momentum at every future point in time and trace their position and momentum at every past moment. You would, in short, be omniscient.

Newton was the greater scientist. But Descartes was the greater philosopher. The basic question Descartes asked was, "What must be true if we are to have any scientific knowledge about the world?" That is, what are the conditions that make such knowledge possible? Posing this question marked a fundamental shift in philosophy away from metaphysics (speculation about the fundamental nature of reality) to epistemology (theory of knowledge). Descartes believed that basic laws of matter and motion, like those of mathematics, are known directly by reason. Those laws are the foundations of scientific knowledge. Or, to make the point slightly differently, Descartes argued that these clear and distinct ideas are the necessary conditions for scientific knowledge; hence, they are the starting point for all scientific inquiry. Immanuel Kant would later call these ideas *a priori* synthetic propositions: propositions that are true about the world prior to our experience of the world because they need to be true if we are to have that experience.

Descartes was a devout Roman Catholic and, hence, always uneasy about how his philosophical and scientific views would be received by the church. He was part of what historian Jonathan Israel has called the moderate Enlightenment, which sought a synthesis of reason and faith.[2] Descartes repeatedly protested that, with the single exception of the Copernican movement of the planets around the sun (an issue on which he hoped the church would come to its senses), his natural philosophy was fully compatible with church teaching. Yet Descartes offers us a wholly nontheological account of the world. To be sure, Descartes contends that his account is guaranteed by God. But, at the end of the day, Descartes rendered God superfluous to our efforts to gain a scientific understanding of the world in which we live. He relied on reason alone to combat ignorance, irrationality, and superstition, and in the process swept aside scriptural revelation, miracles, the afterlife, and ecclesiastical authority. Descartes was thus a harbinger of the radical Enlightenment of Spinoza and others.

LIFE

René Descartes was born in the Loire Valley in France on March 31, 1596. His Catholic family was in the highest reaches of the Third Estate, on the fringes of the nobility. Both grandfathers had been doctors. His father, Joachim, was a lawyer and administrator.

Descartes had two older siblings who survived childhood, including a beloved sister, Jeanne. His mother died when he was barely a year old, and he was raised largely by his maternal grandmother, Jeanne Sain, after whom his mother and his sister had been named. Joachim remarried in 1600, but Descartes had very little contact in his youth with his stepmother or the four half siblings who were born in rapid succession. His relationship with his father appears to have been equally distant. Indeed, when Descartes published the *Discourse on the Method* and accompanying essays—a text that made him known throughout Europe—his father's only response was, "How can I have engendered a son stupid enough to have had himself bound in calf?"[3]

Descartes was a frail child, highly susceptible to the cold, and was allowed to stay late in bed even when he went off to school at the age of ten. He attended the distinguished Jesuit college of La Flèche in Anjou. La Flèche combined a classical with a Christian education: *humanitas* and *pietas*. The first five years were spent largely on Latin and Greek grammar, music, and the classics. All teaching, discussion, and even casual conversations with fellow students had to be conducted in Latin, except, presumably, for the courses in Greek. It was a rigorous education but not in the rigorous conditions still characteristic of many schools. There were no beatings, and Descartes was given ample time to sleep. He also had time to read widely and deeply in the classics beyond the prescribed curriculum.

Most students left after five years and pursued a professional course such as law, medicine, or theology. Their solid humanistic grounding was thought to be ideal preparation for such careers. Descartes remained at La Flèche for three years beyond the basic course, doing advanced work in mathematics, physics, and philosophy. One incident from his time there warrants mention. Henri IV, the first French king from the House of Bourbon, was a Protestant who converted to Catholicism in order to inherit the throne, reputedly with the words, "Paris is well worth a mass." He promulgated the Edict of Nantes in 1598, which guaranteed religious freedom to Protestants, thereby ending the religious wars that had riven France for decades. Henri was assassinated by a Catholic fanatic in May 1610. The fourteen-year-old Descartes participated in an elaborate ceremony at La Flèche, which involved the display and then burial of Henri IV's heart at the college. He saw firsthand the results of religious intolerance.

After La Flèche, Descartes apparently studied law and possibly also medicine at Poitiers. He was highly uncertain of his future career and flirted with many possibilities—law, medicine, and even the army—before rejecting them all. Descartes inherited several farms from his mother. He eventually sold them and invested the proceeds to support himself, modestly, as an independent scholar and a gentleman. He had no university connections and enjoyed no patronage until late in life, when it sadly would prove fatal.

As he explained in the semiautobiographical *Discourse*, Descartes had thrown himself into his studies at La Flèche and Poitiers in the hope and expectation of acquiring "a clear and certain knowledge of all that is useful in life."[4] Once completed, however, he realized he had fallen far short of that goal. "For I found myself beset by so many doubts and errors that I came to think I had gained nothing from my attempts to become educated but increasing recognition of my ignorance."[5]

He was pleased with the languages he learned at La Flèche, since they enabled him to read ancient Greek and Latin authors. He fully acknowledged both the charms of literature and the thoughtful judgments formed by ancient historians. "Reading good books," he wrote, "is like having a conversation with the most distinguished men of past ages—indeed, a rehearsed conversation in which these authors reveal to us only the best of their thoughts."[6] And yet he concluded that he had "already given enough time to languages and likewise to reading the works of the ancients, both their histories and their fables."[7] They excite the imagination but paint the world in a false light. They do not provide us with the stability of truth.

The same held for philosophy. It had been practiced for many centuries by the most brilliant minds and yet, Descartes lamented, "there is still no point in it which is not disputed and hence doubtful."[8] As for the various sciences, insofar as they borrow their first principles from philosophy (which Scholasticism surely did), he concluded "that nothing solid could have been built upon such shaky foundations."[9] Jurisprudence and medicine bring honor and riches to those who practice them, but are still full of "superstition and falsehood."[10] Descartes even eschewed theology because he considered the revealed truths of religion beyond our powers of understanding. Heaven, he concluded, is open to the ignorant no less than the learned, and left it at that.

The one subject in which Descartes delighted above all others was mathematics, "because of the certainty and self-evidence of its reasonings."[11] And yet he had no idea at that point in his life how to build "upon such firm and solid foundations" in seeking clear and certain knowledge of the world.[12] Accordingly, Descartes abandoned his studies in favor of experience. Sounding very much under the influence of Montaigne, Descartes wrote:

> Resolving to seek no knowledge other than that which could be found in myself or else in the great book of the world, I spent the rest of my youth traveling, visiting courts and armies, mixing with people of diverse temperaments and ranks, gathering various experiences, testing myself in the situations which fortune offered me, and at all times reflecting upon whatever came my way so as to derive some profit from it.[13]

In 1618, Descartes traveled to the Protestant portion of the Netherlands, where he enlisted as a volunteer in the army, along with other young nobles. The United Provinces, as they were then known, had broken off from Spain and its Counter-Reformation. Despite the fact that the United Provinces were Protestant and France was Catholic, the two countries had formed a loose alliance in opposition to Spain. But Descartes found army life tedious. He was more interested in his friendship with the scientist Isaac Beeckman, under whose guidance he studied geometry, the physics of falling bodies, optics, and hydrostatics. He even wrote a short treatise on the mathematics of musical intervals.

In 1619, Descartes left the army in the Netherlands and made a journey through Germany in the service of Emperor Maximilian of Bavaria. It was there, in the stove-heated room near Ulm, that he apparently had a nervous breakdown of some sort. Descartes would later describe the experience in terms of a series of dreams, the third of which embodied a divine vision of the mechanical universe reduced to its essentials of mathematics, matter, and motion.

In the ensuing nine years, Descartes traveled restlessly from place to place working on his scientific and philosophical ideas: two years back in France, followed by two years in Italy, and then back to France. He made significant progress in analytic geometry and on the law of refraction in optics. His most cherished project, however, was what he called *Rules for the Direction of Our Native Intelligence*. Descartes was attempting to find a method of thinking and investigating that could be applied to any and all subjects and that would allow the formation of "true and sound judgments about whatever comes before [the mind]."[14] It was not just a scientific method for which Descartes was searching, but a method for making progress in natural philosophy, a term that combines what we ordinarily think of as philosophy with the natural sciences. Descartes wanted to develop a firm and solid foundation for the natural sciences, and he considered that to be inevitably a philosophical project. Or rather, he saw no clear demarcation between philosophy and science. The broadest assumptions of the natural sciences are philosophical propositions that can be discovered directly by reason, applying the methodological principles he was developing. Descartes left his *Rules* unfinished. But he had found the project that would consume the rest of his intellectual life: a universal method of resolving questions of natural philosophy. Descartes's dream would become the world's reality.

Descartes returned to the Netherlands in 1628 and stayed there for most of the rest of his life, moving frequently among the cities and villages with a view, it seems, mainly to conceal his location from unwanted visitors. He had a few close friends, particularly Marin Mersenne in Paris, whom he relied on to keep him apprised of intellectual developments and to publicize his own writings. But Descartes was quarrelsome and reclusive to the point of paranoia, and he was quick to turn on those who criticized his work or on those he thought were taking credit for his ideas.

In 1630, he began work on a treatise to be known as *The World*. It was to be a fully mechanistic account of the universe, including the human body. The treatise was largely complete and ready for publication in late 1633, when Descartes learned that Galileo had been condemned for, and forced to recant, his teaching that the earth revolves around the sun, a proposition supported by the work of Copernicus and Kepler and also critical to Descartes's new physics. The reason for the condemnation was a passage in the book of Joshua, in which God, at Joshua's request, commanded the sun to stand still so that the children of Israel could defeat the Amorites in battle.[15] Galileo countered in vain that "the Bible . . . was not written to teach us astronomy."[16] Descartes surely agreed. But he left his work unpublished, partly from fear but mainly, it seems, because he was hesitant to break with the church so decisively. As he wrote to Mersenne in November 1633:

> I had intended to send you *Le Monde* as a New Year gift . . . but in the meantime I tried to find out in Leiden and Amsterdam whether Galileo's *World System* was available, as I thought I had heard that it was published in Italy last year. I was told that it had indeed been published, but that all copies had been burned at Rome, and that Galileo had been convicted and fined. I was so surprised by this that I nearly decided to burn all my papers, or at least let no one see them. For I couldn't imagine that he—an Italian and, I believe, in favor with the Pope—could have been made a criminal, just because he tried, as he certainly did, to establish that the earth moves. . . . I must admit that if this view is false, then so too are the entire foundations of my philosophy, for it can be demonstrated from them quite clearly. And it is such an integral part of my treatise that I couldn't remove it without making the whole work defective. But for all that, I wouldn't want to publish a discourse which had a single word that the Church disapproved of; so I prefer to suppress it rather than publish it in a mutilated form.[17]

The World was not published until 1664, well after Descartes's death, and Descartes turned his attention more toward the philosophical foundations of science.

In 1635, Descartes had a daughter with Helena Jans van der Strom, a servant in the home where Descartes had been staying the year before. Francine was baptized as a Protestant. It is not clear how often Francine and her mother visited Descartes, but they may have lived together for extended periods. Descartes was extremely fond of Francine and was affected deeply when she died of scarlet fever in 1640 at the age of five. It was a difficult year for Descartes. His father died a few months later, as did his sister Jeanne shortly thereafter. It was an even more difficult time in Europe generally. The Thirty Years' War between Catholic and Protestant nations was still raging. By the time it ended in 1648, with the Peace of Westphalia, eight million Europeans had died, either directly from the violence or from the plagues and famines that ensued. Yet Descartes's scientific and philosophic investigations seemed largely unaffected by the broader tragedy unfolding around him.

His *Discourse* was published in 1637, along with essays on geometry, optics, and meteors, each designed to illustrate his methodology as applied to a particular area of science. *Meditations* was published in 1641, along with six sets of objections solicited by Mersenne and Descartes's replies. Descartes was now both famous and infamous. He began to correspond with royalty, including Princess Elisabeth of Bohemia, who was interested in his work on the passions, and Queen Christina of Sweden, who was interested in philosophical questions and eager to attract scholars and artists to her court. Descartes also traveled to Paris, where he met with Thomas Hobbes, Pierre Gassendi, and Blaise Pascal, who were among the most prominent European intellectuals.

Descartes wrote two other significant works, *Principles of Philosophy* and *Passions of the Soul*. In 1649, at the urging of Pierre Chanut, the French ambassador to Sweden, he finally accepted an invitation from Queen Christina. It was an unfortunate decision, which he regretted the moment he arrived. It was a bitterly cold winter, even for Sweden, and the young queen wanted lessons in philosophy from Descartes at five o'clock in the morning, though he was accustomed to remaining in bed until eleven. Descartes nursed his friend Chanut through a bout of pneumonia, but he himself soon succumbed to the same infection and died on February 11, 1650. His body was later exhumed and transported back to France where, after several moves, it was buried a final time in the Church of Saint-Germain-des-Prés in Paris.

COGITO, ERGO DEUS EST: RADICAL DOUBT AND ABSOLUTE FAITH

Some medical schools welcome new students with a startling warning: "Half of everything we will teach you is false; we just don't know which half." It is a frank admission that, even in the twenty-first century, we must rely altogether too much on custom and surmise rather than on certain knowledge.

Yet medical care has made remarkable advances since the seventeenth century, when a proposed cure could easily prove more fatal than the disease. As Descartes explained:

> It is true that medicine as currently practiced does not contain much of any significant use; but without intending to disparage it, I am sure there is no one, even among its practitioners, who would not admit that all we know in medicine is almost nothing in comparison with what remains to be known, and that we might free ourselves from innumerable diseases, both of the body and of the mind, and perhaps even from the infirmity of old age, if we had sufficient knowledge of their causes and of all the remedies that nature has provided. [18]

To make this vision a reality, Descartes concluded, what we need most is a new method for all scientific inquiries, a method that would allow us to move beyond custom and surmise to genuine knowledge.

Descartes was convinced that our so-called knowledge of the world was riddled with falsehoods. But, like the new medical students, he didn't know which were the truths and which the falsehoods. He therefore resolved to reject all opinions that are not completely certain and indubitable. "I realized that it was necessary," he wrote, "to demolish everything completely and start again right from the foundations if I wanted to establish anything at all in the sciences that was stable and likely to last." [19]

Descartes accordingly adopted as his first rule "never to accept anything as true if I did not have evident knowledge of its truth: that is, carefully to avoid precipitate conclusions and preconceptions, and *to include nothing more in my judgments than what presented itself to my mind so clearly and so distinctly that I had no occasion to call it into doubt.*" [20] Descartes took mathematics as his model. The truths of mathematics, once properly grasped, cannot be doubted. Nor can they be disproved by experience. They are a starting point for understanding the world.

It is important to recognize, however, that Descartes is not suggesting that all scientific knowledge can be known by reason alone. How fast bodies fall, the exact paths of the planets through the night sky, the hydraulics of the circulation of blood, the refraction of light through various media: these facts all depend on observation. Descartes himself did a great deal of empirical research, including dissections and experiments in optics. Nor is he suggesting that scientific principles can be known with the certainty of mathematical propositions. What he is contending is that the fundamental principles of science—the conditions under which such knowledge is possible—must be established as a precondition of scientific progress. They are the foundation upon which all else is built, and if the foundation is shaky, the edifice will collapse.

There is a standard distinction drawn in histories of philosophy in the seventeenth and eighteenth centuries between rationalists and empiricists: those who rely on reason to understand the world, and those who rely on experience. It is an unhelpful divide, because even the most determined rationalist, of which Descartes was one, acknowledges that our specific knowledge of the world comes through the senses. And even the most determined empiricist, such as John Locke, acknowledges the critical role of reason in establishing truths about the world. In theory at least, whether you start with reason or experience, you should end up in the same place.

Descartes started with neither reason nor experience, but with doubt. He resolved, at least as a thought experiment, to "reject as if absolutely false everything in which I could imagine the least doubt, in order to see if I was left believing anything that was entirely indubitable."[21] First, he rejected the testimony of the senses. Philosophers since Plato had shown numerous ways in which our perceptions are unreliable and inherently flawed. Descartes went further, withholding judgment even as to whether he was awake or asleep and merely dreaming what he thought he could perceive. There are no sure signs to distinguish waking from sleep. "How often," he wrote, "asleep at night, am I convinced of just such familiar events—that I am here in my dressing-gown, sitting by the fire—when in fact I am lying undressed in bed!"[22] It is a lovely, Proustian moment: "Sometimes," the narrator Marcel would explain, "the candle barely out, my eyes closed so quickly that I did not have time to tell myself: 'I'm falling asleep.' And half an hour later the thought that it was time to look for sleep would awaken me; I would make as if to put away the book which I imagined was still in my hands, and to blow out the light."[23]

Descartes imagined that "some malicious demon" could be deceiving him and that there was no earth or sky, no matter, no colors or sounds; all external things were merely the delusions of a dream.[24] He flirted with the idea that this demon could delude him even about mathematical propositions.

In the face of such radical doubts, Descartes needed to find "just one thing, however slight, that is certain and unshakeable."[25] He found it in three Latin words: *Cogito, ergo sum* ("I think, therefore I am," or "I am thinking, therefore I exist"). However much I might be deceived, as long as I am thinking, I must be something. Even if I am deluded about all else, this deluded "I" necessarily exists. Descartes considered this truth "so firm and sure that all the most extravagant suppositions of the skeptics were incapable of shaking it," and he therefore accepted it as the first principle of the philosophy he was seeking.[26]

But what is this "I" that thinks? What do I know about it? Descartes here makes a remarkable leap from epistemology back to metaphysics: this thinking self—whose essential nature is solely to think—is separate and apart from his body. Thought requires no extension in space. It has no length, breadth, height, or other physical characteristics. "Accordingly this 'I'—that is, the soul by which I am what I am—is entirely distinct from the body, and . . . would not fail to be whatever it is, even if the body did not exist."[27] In other words, I know with certainty that I possess a soul, even if I am deluded about the existence of my body and the rest of the external world. Therefore, the soul is separate from and not dependent on the body.

We will discuss this immaterial "I" below. But for now, let us grant to Descartes that whatever else we might doubt, we cannot doubt that there is thinking going on. Which among those thoughts can we embrace as sufficiently clear and distinct to regard as true? That is Descartes's second great metaphysical leap—a leap straight into the arms of God. It is unclear who was the wit who first collapsed Descartes's argument into four Latin words: *Cogito, ergo Deus est* ("I think, therefore God exists"). Tom Stoppard used the line in his 1972 play, *Jumpers*, but it was in currency long before then. And it is not unfair as a dig at an argument that simply does not bear the weight Descartes places upon it.

Descartes's fundamental point is that the idea of God is the idea of a perfect being: infinite, all-powerful, all-knowing, and the creator of all that exists. The "I" that thinks is none of these things. "I" am an imperfect being and would therefore be incapable of forming the idea of such perfection unless that idea "had been put into me by a nature truly more perfect than I was and even possessing in itself all the perfections of which I could have any idea, that is—to explain myself in one word—by God."[28] As a variation on this point, Descartes contends that the very idea of God—as a perfect being—necessitates that God exists, because otherwise he would be lacking something and therefore would be imperfect. Since nothing can be added to his perfection, he must exist. The idea of a perfect being includes existence just as surely as the idea of a triangle includes the equality of its three angles to two right angles. Finally, as a backup point, Descartes argues that God is the original or ultimate cause of all things. If God did not exist, there would be an infinite regress of causation, which is impossible. If "I" exist, then God must exist, because without God I would not be. *Cogito, ergo Deus est.*

Once Descartes "establishes" the existence of God, the rest is easy. If God is perfect, he is not a deceiver, because any sort of trickery or deception implies imperfection: "the will to deceive is undoubtedly evidence of malice or weakness, and so cannot apply to God."[29] If God is not a deceiver, then I am not in a constant dream state, and what I experience as existing—at least in terms of the primary qualities of matter measurable by mathematical physics—does actually exist. That does not mean my intellect is flawless or that I cannot be mistaken in my perceptions and reasoning. But it means, according to Descartes, that what I perceive clearly and distinctly cannot be false. And from that premise, a "whole chain of other truths" about the natural world can be deduced.[30]

God becomes the guarantor not just of man's rational and sensible faculties but also of much of the system of physics already worked out by Descartes in *The World.* Einstein once said that the most incomprehensible thing about the world is that it is comprehensible.[31] For Descartes, it is God who gives man the ability to comprehend the functioning of the universe and to make predictions based on applied mathematics. God is the guarantor of the fundamental laws of nature, and those laws are knowable by reason.

The problem, of course, is that Descartes's arguments for God's existence, if we can even call them that, are extremely weak. They were freely criticized in Descartes's own day, and Immanuel Kant would systematically demolish them in the following century. But Descartes is not trying to convince us that God exists. He treats the existence of God as a given. "I cannot think of God except as existing," he writes.[32] The idea of God "is innate in me, just as the idea of myself is innate in me."[33]

Descartes's primary goal is to make his physics acceptable to the church by tying its validity to the existence and nature of God. Descartes had completed his physics treatise before he even wrote the *Discourse* and *Meditations*. But he withheld it from publication because it would have been unacceptable to, and likely condemned by, the church. If he can now show that his science is not just compatible with faith, but flows from the very idea of God, he will have turned the tables. His physics will be an act of piety rather than heresy. I don't doubt the sincerity of Descartes's faith, but what really matters to Descartes is legitimizing the physics itself, as he candidly admitted when he urged his friend Frans Burman not to devote "so much effort to the *Meditations* and to metaphysical questions. . . . They draw the mind too far away from physical and observable things, and make it unfit to study them. Yet it is just these physical studies that it is most desirable for people to pursue, since they would yield abundant benefits for life."[34]

It is therefore unsurprising that the church was unmoved by Descartes's demonstration. The God of the *Discourse* and *Meditations* is not the God of the Old or New Testament. He is an abstraction who guarantees the truth of the basic principles of physics known to man and measurable mathematically. It doesn't make sense to apply any additional attributes to this God, such as wisdom, goodness, anger, or justice. Descartes accepts their attribution, because he accepts the teachings of the church. But in terms of the course of the argument in these two works, God is little more than the mechanical universe itself and the laws that govern it. Such a God is superfluous as an answer to skepticism. As long as the mathematical method of pursuing the natural sciences works—and it works spectacularly well—that in itself is enough to demonstrate its validity. It is the "whole chain of other truths" that ultimately matters and that is most desirable for men to pursue. The deceiving demon and the undeceiving God are equally irrelevant to that enterprise. Even without a metaphysical foundation, the edifice does not collapse.

MATTER, MOTION, AND MATH

When Descartes shifts from metaphysics to the mathematics of matter in motion, he would appear to cross from philosophy into science. But the line of demarcation is by no means sharp. Descartes is still searching for a universal method for dealing with scientific questions. And the method he chooses, at least in its critical initial stages, has less to do with experimentation than with thought. In articulating the broadest principles of science, Descartes still relies on clear and distinct ideas, ideas that are underdetermined by sense experience and hence, he believes, "implanted . . . in our minds" by divine providence.[35] There is a gap between our perceptions and reality; clear and distinct ideas fill that gap and give us certain knowledge of reality and a pathway to scientific truth. But to reach those clear and distinct ideas, we must strip away all that is incidental and questionable in perception.

In his second meditation, Descartes gives the example of a piece of wax fresh from the honeycomb. It tastes of honey and smells of the flowers among which it was gathered. It is cold and hard with a definite shape, size, and color, and it emits a sound when rapped with a knuckle. We seem to perceive it clearly and distinctly. Yet, place that wax near the fire, and it is utterly transformed: "the residual taste is eliminated, the smell goes away, the color changes, the shape is lost, the size increases; it becomes liquid and hot; you can hardly touch it, and if you strike it, it no longer makes a sound."[36] None of the features by which we thought we knew it through the senses remain; the taste, smell, size, touch, and hearing have all been altered, and yet the wax remains. And we can imagine numerous further changes, such as forming it into a square or a ball or any other shape.

It must therefore be, Descartes concludes, that the true nature of the wax is revealed not to the senses or even to the imagination. The qualities I see, taste, smell, feel, and hear do not belong to the essential nature of the wax. The essence of the wax and all other bodies is perceived "by the intellect alone, and . . . this perception derives not from their being touched or seen but from their being understood."[37] Yet how are objects understood or perceived by the intellect? In terms of matter and motion— extension and position—both of which can be measured mathematically.

Descartes is drawing a sharp distinction between what we would call primary and secondary qualities. The primary qualities include "extension in length, breadth and depth; shape, which is a function of the boundaries of this extension; position, which is a relation between various items possessing shape; and motion, or change in position; to these may be added substance, duration and number."[38] All of those things can be measured mathematically and thus are subject to certain knowledge. They are the reality to be studied by science.

The secondary qualities are what I perceive with the senses: the colors I see, the sounds I hear, and what I smell, taste, and touch. Objects do not themselves possess these secondary qualities. These are effects on our brains caused by objectively existing differences in extension and motion.[39] Secondary qualities do not resemble real things, even though they are triggered in me by real things interacting with my senses.[40] That doesn't mean they aren't adequate representations for purposes of everyday life. But the real world is the world of mathematics and physics. The world as it appears to us is not real in the same sense even though, of course, it seems far more real to us.

In his work on optics, perception, and physiology, Descartes made significant strides toward explaining secondary qualities in terms of primary qualities. Variations in primary qualities affect what secondary qualities we perceive. But all scientific explanation must be in terms of primary qualities. Science requires us to abstract from the world as we perceive it to reveal the underlying reality known to the mind alone. That reality—what can truly be known with certainty—can be expressed mathematically. Using such a method, Descartes concludes, "it is possible for me to achieve full and certain knowledge . . . concerning the whole of that corporeal nature which is the subject-matter of pure mathematics."[41] As he explained to Mersenne, "my entire physics is nothing but geometry."[42] It is an astonishing anticipation of modern physics, which at its highest level is little more than a series of equations. Descartes was the first person to recognize the importance of mathematics in unifying apparently disparate sciences such as music, astronomy, mechanics, and optics. Science, in his view, is just the application of mathematics to matter and motion.

Descartes's achievement is all the more remarkable when seen in the context of what preceded and what followed it. Despite the Renaissance; despite the scientific advances of Kepler and Galileo; and despite the philosophical articulation of the scientific method by Francis Bacon in the *Novum Organum* and other works, the science of Descartes's day was still based largely on the work of Aristotle, which described the physical world in terms of "substantial forms" and "final causes." A substantial form or intrinsic trait is what makes an object what it is. A final cause is that for the sake of which something takes place, its aim or teleological purpose. For Aristotle, terrestrial motion is goal-oriented: a body engages in it to achieve some end consistent with its intrinsic nature, and once the end is achieved, the motion ceases.[43] For example, an object made of earth seeks its natural resting place on the earth (which is the center of the Aristotelian universe). The intrinsic qualities of an object thus explain its effects. Molière would later ridicule this view, in the context of medicine, when he had a physician explain that opium makes us sleepy because of its "soporific" quality. That is obviously no explanation at all. It simply repeats the effect for which an explanation is sought.

Descartes's physics, by contrast, is based on efficient, not final, causes. All physical change is to be explained by extrinsic, not intrinsic, factors. That is why Descartes's method provides such a powerful tool for advancing scientific knowledge. The fundamental principle of his treatise *The World* is that matter and motion alone are sufficient to explain all natural phenomena.[44] This is, if you will, a philosophical commitment, but it is one that has borne unique fruit in the natural sciences. All occult forces are eliminated in favor of a purely mechanistic account of the world. Macroscopic phenomena, including the nature and properties of light, are explained in terms of microscopic mechanical processes. And the same is true of celestial phenomena, which are governed, contrary to Aristotle, by the same fundamental laws of motion that govern terrestrial phenomena. That is why it was so critical to the system put forth in *The World* that the earth revolves around the sun like the other planets. Rather than abandon that bedrock principle, Descartes preferred not to publish. In his later work, he presented his system more obliquely. As he explained in a letter to Mersenne, "I hope that readers will get imperceptibly accustomed to my principles, and recognize their truth, before they notice that they destroy the principles of Aristotle."[45]

Descartes's specific scientific achievements will be remembered by only a handful of scholars of the history of science. He developed the law of refraction and anticipated, in rough form, Newton's laws of motion. Most important, he developed analytic geometry, which became a critical tool in applying mathematics to the natural world. But he also rejected atomism and adopted, instead, an odd form of infinitely divisible microcorpuscularianism from Beeckman, in which matter is continuous; there are no ultimate particles and no empty space or vacuum between particles. He also relied on a confusing account of vortices to explain the orbits of the planets.

Yet Descartes can still lay claim to be the father of modern science and the scientific worldview that held sway from Newton to Einstein. As one of the greatest historians of science, Stephen Gaukroger, concludes, "*Le Monde* presents a fully mechanist alternative to Aristotelian systems."[46] Descartes banishes Scholastic concepts and forms that do no explanatory work. The physical realm is purely reactive. Everything is to be explained in terms of matter and motion, measured mathematically. That new scientific paradigm formed the basic background for the great scientific advances from the seventeenth through the nineteenth centuries.

What Descartes fails to acknowledge, however, is that in his system God is just another Scholastic concept that does no explanatory work. Descartes insists on retaining a place for God as the creator and sustainer of the universe. But, in fact, God is absent from the mathematical equations that describe the physical world. God's agency is unnecessary to a purely scientific account of natural phenomena. The church was quick to recognize this absence, and placed Descartes's works on its rapidly growing Index of Forbidden Books in 1663.

Descartes's goal in the *Discourse* and *Meditations* was to bracket the physical world of matter and motion as a realm of purely scientific explanations, while at the same time establishing the separate realms of God and the soul. He succeeded spectacularly in the first task. But he failed to prove the existence of God. His assertion of faith can be accepted at face value. But the concept of God is superfluous to the study of the natural sciences; indeed, it is inimical insofar as religion purports to pretermit scientific demonstrations that, for example, prove the earth, like the other planets, revolves around the sun. But what about the "I" that thinks, which Descartes equates with the immortal soul? Is that also unproven and superfluous? That turns out to be a much trickier question.

THE GHOST IN THE MACHINE[47]

Aristotle explained motion in terms of intrinsic traits even for wholly inanimate objects. Descartes explained motion in terms of extrinsic traits even for animate creatures, including human beings. He proposed to apply to the physiology of organic life the same fully mechanistic explanations of matter and motion he used for material phenomena.[48] As Descartes postulated in his *Treatise on Man*, "I suppose the body to be nothing but a statue or machine made of earth," which walks, eats, breathes, and with "all those of our functions which can be imagined to proceed from matter and to depend solely on the disposition of our organs."[49]

Descartes was unable to provide the details of such an explanation beyond a rather crude discussion of the circulation of blood and the nervous system, or what he calls "animal spirits," which he defines as extremely small bodies that flare quickly, like "jets of flame," and are capable of moving the muscles.[50] He did not know enough biology or chemistry to show how digestion, growth, and other processes specific to life can be explained by the same physical laws that govern matter and motion in the inanimate world.[51] But his supposition that such an explanation is possible would become a staple of the new science of biochemistry in the nineteenth and twentieth centuries. For now, he was content to accept that God was fully capable of designing machines as intricate as human beings. The body, he concludes, is "a machine which, having been made by the hand of God, is incomparably better ordered than any machine that can be devised by man, and contains in itself movements more wonderful than those in any such machine."[52] We would call it evolution, of course, but the point is essentially the same. Humans are the most intricate and complex of nature's creations, but they are still subject to the same laws and principles that apply to all other physical bodies.[53]

In his capacity as a scientist, Descartes does not resort to "the soul" to explain the functioning of the human body. A strictly scientific account of life on earth does not require a soul, any more than it requires a God. And yet, Descartes insists, human beings are uniquely endowed with a soul imparted by God. Indeed, the existence of the soul, or mind, is the first principle of Descartes's philosophy, prior even to his clear and distinct idea of God. "I am . . . in the strict sense only a thing that thinks; that is, I am a mind, or intelligence, or intellect, or reason."[54] I can imagine myself without a body, but in the very act of so imagining I affirm the existence of the "I" that thinks.

For Descartes, the defining characteristic of any material substance is extension. The defining characteristic of the mind is thinking, and thought has no extension; the mind is therefore an immaterial substance.

"I am not that structure of limbs which is called a human body."[55] I am a thing that thinks. Descartes purports to be cautious in articulating what this "I" consists of. "I must be on my guard against carelessly taking something else to be this 'I', and so making a mistake in the very item of knowledge that I maintain is the most certain and evident of all."[56] Yet Descartes readily equates this "I" with "the soul by which I am what I am."[57] The soul is what makes me unique among all creatures on earth. The soul, he concludes further, is "entirely distinct from the body, . . . and would not fail to be whatever it is, even if the body did not exist."[58]

In short, I am not just a thing that thinks; I am also "a thing that doubts, understands, affirms, denies, is willing, is unwilling, and also imagines and has sensory perceptions."[59] That is a lot of freight to place on the immaterial "I," especially so when the Christian soul is packed in as well. We saw a large gap between the abstract God of Descartes—who serves as the guarantor and sustainer of the world of science—and the personal God of the Christian Bible. There is an equally large gap between Descartes's "I"—which began as an abstraction from the recognition that, even in doubt, there is thinking going on—and the moral, volitional agent that is the Christian soul.

Even setting that gap to one side, however, there are at least five problems created by Descartes's radical dualism, which posits both material substances (bodies) and immaterial substances (minds) that somehow interact with one another. Those problems have befuddled philosophers ever since.

First, there is no gradation. For Descartes, the mind or soul is an all-or-nothing thing. Either you have a soul with all its conscious powers or you are nothing more than an automaton.[60] According to Descartes, only humans have souls; animals do not. It follows from his premises that animals are purely machines with no thoughts or feelings whatsoever.[61] That is not a view we can readily accept. It runs contrary to our experience to suggest that a dog or a cat feels neither pain nor pleasure, and has no understanding or volition or sensory perceptions. I don't know about you, but my dog "is willing" to take walks and "is unwilling" to have his teeth brushed. He also, when he "perceives" that my suitcase is packed, "understands" that I am about to leave. And he manifests intense pleasure when I return. Yet those are precisely the traits that Descartes considers the hallmarks of a soul. Descartes treats the lack of language as dispositive proof that animals have no minds or souls. But, of course, modern research shows that a variety of animals do communicate with one another, and dogs communicate in clear ways with their owners (when they want to go out, or be petted or fed). Animals may be less complex and sophisticated organisms, with less developed brains than humans, but that seems a matter of degree, not of kind, as evolution has clearly demonstrated.

Second, Descartes creates a seemingly unbridgeable gap between my subjective experience and the outside world, between ideas and reality. Indeed, Descartes frankly admits that we cannot know what perceptible reality is really like. In Descartes's physics, as noted above, the only "real" (that is, mathematically measurable) qualities of the physical world are extension and motion, and we know them through mathematics. This abstract physical world contains nothing that resembles color, sound, smell, pain, or pleasure. Those are effects on our brains via the sense organs caused by objectively existing differences in extension and motion. Secondary qualities do not resemble real things, even though they are triggered in me by real things interacting with my senses. And they come into consciousness only through the activity of the mind. In a sense, then, we—our minds—create the perceptible world around us. The so-called empiricists, led by John Locke, will take the opposite tack, emphasizing the primacy of sense experience and reducing ideas to abstractions from those experiences. But for them, as for Descartes, sense experience still plays out in the internal, private theater of the mind, and reconstructing a known world from that private theater proves an impossible challenge.

Third, it is unclear how the mind, which is wholly immaterial, can cause effects in the material world and vice versa. How does the mind move the body? And how does the physical world create perceptions on the immaterial mind? Descartes suggests that the mind or soul is connected to the body by means of the pineal gland.[62] All sensations pass through the pineal gland to the mind, and the body is in turn moved by the mind as a result of the subtle movements of the pineal gland. But the indirectness of these effects—as if we were watching a screen and pulling levers in a control room—does not correspond to our experience, as Descartes is compelled to admit. "Nature also teaches me, by these sensations of pain, hunger, thirst and so on, that I am not merely present in my body as a sailor is present in a ship, but that I am very closely joined and, as it were, intermingled with it, so that I and the body form a unit."[63] Descartes cannot explain how this occurs. Yet without such an explanation, the mind is just a ghost in the machine of the body.

Fourth, Descartes insists that it is "certain that I am really distinct from my body, and can exist without it."[64] Thinking "does not require any place, or depend on any material thing, in order to exist."[65] But he does not give a coherent explanation of how the soul can exist outside the body. In the absence of sense organs, it cannot have any perceptual awareness. Divorced from the pineal gland, it cannot exercise volition even under Descartes's theory. Nor can it use language to communicate. Aquinas accepted the resurrection of the body at the final judgment. But Descartes rejects it, insisting that the soul is independent and can exist forever outside the body. When Homer, Virgil, and Dante depicted the underworld, they gave their "spirits" the shape of human bodies and allowed them to perceive and converse with one another. In a beautiful and moving passage, Odysseus rushes to embrace his mother, who had died while he was away at war. Three times he tries to hold her, and three times she flutters through his fingers. His mother attempts to console him as best she can:

> My son, my son, the unluckiest man alive!
> This is no deception sent by Queen Persephone,
> this is just the way of mortals when we die.
> Sinews no longer bind the flesh and bones together—
> the fire in all its fury burns the body down to ashes
> once life slips from the white bones, and the spirit,
> rustling, flitters away . . . flown like a dream.[66]

We can perhaps understand the concept of living forever. But we cannot understand the concept of continuing to exist, in any personal sense, without a body. Even our creative imaginings of the underworld require at least a spirit body.

Finally, there is the question of the compatibility of free will with the mechanical universe. If all movement has material causes, as Descartes's physics assumes, then there is no room for the spontaneous interjection of the mind into the material world. In order to make us moral agents, Descartes must insist that "the will is by its nature so free that it can never be constrained."[67] But, by his own account, the material world is a closed system subject only to the laws of cause and effect and the mathematics of matter and motion. Even if the soul can exercise free will, it cannot break that chain. Aquinas had a similar problem—to explain how free will is compatible with God's omniscience. Specifically, if God already knows what I am going to do before I do it, and God cannot be wrong, in what sense am I free to do otherwise? Aquinas devised an answer to that theological problem by distinguishing foreknowledge that an event will occur from mandating that it occur. That answer may or may not seem convincing. But Descartes had a much more serious problem, which was to explain how the soul can be free to exercise its volition when the body is governed by ineluctable mechanical laws.

The easy way to resolve these paradoxes, of course, is to reject the idea of any immaterial "substance" analogous to a physical substance but without the extension. Yet we still have to explain our language about thoughts, passions, and emotions. Some neurologists seek to trace and reduce all alleged "mental" states to specific states of the brain and the nervous system. Some behaviorists seek to trace and reduce all alleged "mental" traits to statements about behavior, both actual and likely. Ludwig Wittgenstein, the greatest philosopher of the twentieth century, rejected all such approaches in favor of the autonomy of our discourse about the mind. And, of course, many continue to have faith in an immortal soul that can exist independent of the body. The Cartesian debate continues.

Descartes's great contribution was not to provide definitive answers, but to pose all these questions in a way no serious thinker could ignore, yet none could fully resolve. They reduce perhaps to a single query: If the material universe is a closed system, subject to a purely scientific account, where is there room for the mind, the soul, and the spirit that make human life worthwhile? John Milton built his epic poem, *Paradise Lost*, around that very question.

2

JOHN MILTON AND THE PARADISE WITHIN

Of Man's first disobedience and the fruit
Of that forbidden tree whose mortal taste
Brought death into the world and all our woe
With loss of Eden till one greater Man
Restore us and regain the blissful seat
Sing Heav'nly Muse . . .[1]

Those are the opening lines of the greatest epic poem in the English language.[2] Milton takes as his subject the brief account in the book of Genesis of the creation of Adam and Eve, their joy in the garden of Eden, Eve's temptation by the serpent, and their banishment after eating forbidden fruit from the tree of the knowledge of good and evil. Milton expands that handful of verses into a work that is simultaneously cosmological in its mythology and intimate in its domesticity, a work that grapples with theological and philosophical issues but always returns to the promise and pathos of human experience.

Milton's models also intermixed epic struggles with intimate moments: Hector removing his helmet so as not to frighten his infant son on the battlements of Troy; Aeneas and Dido retreating to a cave during a storm to consummate their growing passion; and Odysseus forsaking immortality with the goddess Calypso in order to reunite with Penelope over the secret of the bed they had long ago shared. But *Paradise Lost* exceeds all of these in the starkness of the contrast and the intensity of its poetry. Milton gives us a myth not of the Trojan War or the founding of Rome—

which are decidedly human events, even if observed and influenced by the gods—but of the creation of the entire universe, of the glories of heaven, of Satan's rebellion against God, of the victory of God's son and the casting of the rebel angels into a hell of their own devising, where they give birth to Sin and Death, twin powers that will oppress men and women until the Second Coming. Yet embedded within that ur-myth is a very human story that recapitulates it in miniature: a story of innocence, sex, marriage, temptation, fall, recrimination, and reconciliation in a love that is somehow stronger and purer as, hand in hand, Adam and Eve face an uncertain future together.

I am not suggesting that *Paradise Lost* is a greater poem than *The Iliad*, *The Odyssey*, or *The Aeneid*. Far from it. Milton is admittedly an acquired taste. His diction is lofty, his word order inflected, his sentences lengthy, and his religious sentiments largely foreign to modern tastes. Samuel Johnson, who was repelled by Milton's radical politics and austere puritanism, famously wrote that "*Paradise Lost* is one of the books which the reader admires and lays down, and forgets to take up again. None ever wished it longer than it is. Its perusal is a duty rather than a pleasure."[3] Fair enough. But Johnson's dismissive epigram—"the want of human interest is always felt"[4] —is deeply misguided. To be sure, there are abstruse passages dealing with theology and metaphysics that fail to hold most readers' attention. And the detailed but plainly allegorical battles between the forces of heaven and the soon-to-be archfiends of hell do not grip us in the way that the heroic encounters in *The Iliad* and *The Aeneid* do. But the human interest in the story of Adam and Eve, and even in the character of Satan, the nihilistic antihero, is enormous and deeply stirring. And Milton's broader meditations on the origins of evil, divine providence, and human freedom give the poem a depth of resonance that, as Samuel Taylor Coleridge notes, is "the true occasion of all Philosophy."[5] Make no mistake; Milton, though rarely analytical, is every bit as philosophically profound as Descartes—perhaps more so, since Descartes essentially punts on the problem of free will that his mechanical philosophy engendered. Milton never shies from that challenge, for without freedom there is neither virtue nor sin, and religion itself becomes meaningless.

It is for this reason that Milton invokes a heavenly, rather than a classical, muse for his epic poem. He wants to delve into mysteries of the universe that, in his view, a purely secular understanding cannot reach. In the attempt to grapple with such mysteries, human life gains much of its meaning. But, despite his many prose polemics, the Milton of *Paradise Lost* is not a treatise writer. He recognizes his own dependence on allegory and poetic effects. The philosopher Ernst Cassirer drew a distinction between two sharply different ways of trying to make sense of our experience: the mythopoeic and the critical.[6] Peter Gay makes this distinction central to his superb book, *The Enlightenment: An Interpretation*.[7] Descartes embodied the critical mentality that provided a model for so many Enlightenment thinkers. Milton clings to the mythopoeic. He wants to "see and tell / Of things invisible to mortal sight,"[8] a task for which he hopes to find himself, like other blind prophets and sages, particularly qualified. But the invisible must be approached through the visible. As the angel Raphael explains to Adam, "what surmounts the reach / Of human sense I shall delineate so / By lik'ning spiritual to corporal forms / As may express them best."[9] In other words, poetic allegory is inevitable in confronting the deepest mysteries of human life.

But Raphael adds an intriguing question: "what if Earth / Be but the shadow of Heav'n and things therein / Each to other like more than on Earth is thought?"[10] It is a question that is answered only obliquely in the poem, yet the whole premise of Milton's undertaking is that the allegorical language of scripture, which deals with corporeal forms, does express heavenly things best. Milton tries to remain true to that connection throughout his expansion of the scriptural account. Milton wants to channel the voice of God in a sort of Third Testament. He accordingly feels the all-but-overwhelming burden of ensuring that he is writing out of authentic inspiration and constantly seeks assurance that he is up to his self-appointed task. That is why he repeatedly invokes the help of the heavenly muse.

> What in me is dark
> Illumine, what is low raise and support,
> That to the heighth of this great argument
> I may assert Eternal Providence
> And justify the ways of God to men.[11]

It is a tall order. If Milton is to "assert Eternal Providence," he must accept that everything that happens is part of a divine plan. That is what eternal providence means. But, if that is the case, Milton must justify the existence of evil and suffering as part of that divine plan.

The poet and classical scholar A. E. Housman, though a great admirer of Milton, could not resist the quip that "malt does more than Milton can / To justify God's ways to man."[12] Perhaps so. Perhaps insensibility is the only answer to personal and global turmoil. But one could equally contend that the heightened sensitivity of poetry is our finest tool for understanding and appreciating the world in which we live, especially when that poetry seeks to impose a unity and order on experience that makes sense of the whole. Whether Milton succeeds or fails in his attempt, each reader will judge. Yet even Johnson had to acknowledge that "such is the power of his poetry that his call is obeyed without resistance, the reader feels himself in captivity to a higher and a nobler mind, and criticism sinks in admiration."[13]

LIFE

John Milton lived in interesting times. The Thirty Years' War—which raged from his tenth to his fortieth year—left eight million Europeans dead of violence, famine, and plague. England's own civil war—which began when he was thirty-three—led to the deposition and execution of Charles I in 1649. The short-lived commonwealth that Milton championed soon became a "protectorate" under the iron fist of Oliver Cromwell. Yet, within two years of Cromwell's own death, the monarchy was restored under Charles II. Milton was fifty-two. Through the intervention of influential friends and a well-placed royalist brother, Milton largely escaped reprisals against the regicides. But the Restoration devastated his finances, and the Great Fire of London in 1666 completed the job. At the age of fifty-eight, he was blind and virtually penniless.

Milton seemed destined for a far different life when he was born, on December 9, 1608, to an upper-middle-class family, living in the shadow of St. Paul's Cathedral. Milton's father, also named John, was a scrivener, who drew up contracts, notarized documents, and even lent money at interest. He also invested shrewdly in property. His own father had been a Catholic recusant who disinherited his Protestant son. John Sr. was thus, of necessity, a self-made man in an increasingly capitalist society.[14] He became a solid member of the middle class, which was growing rapidly in size and in wealth. He was also an exceptionally talented amateur musician and composer and was on the board of Blackfriars, which served as a winter theater for the King's Men. Shakespeare was a shareholder in Blackfriars, and his late plays *The Winter's Tale* and *The Tempest* were still to be written. The King James Bible, one of the glories of the English language, which Milton would steep himself in and learn virtually by heart, would be published in 1611.

Two of Milton's siblings survived infancy. His older sister, Anne, married a lawyer. His younger brother, Christopher, born seven years later, became a lawyer and was eventually knighted. Milton was home-schooled in Latin beginning at age seven. At the age of eleven or twelve, he went to St. Paul's School, which had been founded by the great humanist scholar John Colet, a friend of Erasmus and Thomas More. The students who attended the school were known as the "pigeons of St. Paul's." There, Milton studied Greek, Latin, and some Hebrew; he was also tutored privately in French and Italian as well as in music. Learning became his overriding passion. As he would later explain:

> My father destined me from childhood to the study of humane letters, and I took to those studies with such ardor that, from the time I was twelve, I hardly ever gave up reading for bed until midnight. This was the first cause of injury to my eyes, which were naturally weak, and I suffered from many headaches. [15]

John Donne became the dean of St. Paul's Cathedral in 1621, and Milton almost certainly heard him preach there. Milton was also captivated by Edmund Spenser's 1590 epic, *The Faerie Queene*, which combined Christian themes with rich poetry and extravagant romance. Even more important, though, was the intimate friendship Milton formed with Charles Diodati. Indulged by his father, and with an almost messianic sense of his own destiny, Milton was ferociously proud and often aloof. But he had a gift for friendship that lasted throughout his life. He also had a deep love of music inherited from his father. Indeed, he viewed music as a form of connection with the divine that "may with sweetness, through mine ear, / Dissolve me into ecstasies, / And bring all Heav'n before mine eyes." [16]

Milton enrolled at Christ's College in Cambridge in February 1625 at the age of sixteen. He was slight and pale, with delicate, even beautiful, features and long, flowing hair. His fellow students—some cruelly yet others with apparent affection—referred to him as the "Lady of Christ's College." Milton did not like his tutor, the highly regarded but rigid and unimaginative William Chappell. Milton quarreled with Chappell and left college for a time. But he soon returned to another, more congenial tutor and settled in, taking his bachelor's degree in 1629 and his master's in 1632. Milton absorbed the Platonic influence then burgeoning at Cambridge in reaction to long years of Aristotelian Scholasticism. The Cambridge Platonists saw Plato as a proto-Christian with a lofty view of the soul and its ability to grasp truth through allegory. That viewpoint is present in Milton's first significant poem, "On the Morning of Christ's Nativity," written when he was just twenty-one. It filters religion through the lens of poetry. Yet Milton also saw his poetic vocation through the lens of religion, as a divine charge driving him "in strictest measure ev'n / To that same lot, however mean or high, / Toward which Time leads me, and the will of Heav'n; / All is, if I have grace to use it so, / As ever in my great Task-Master's eye."[17] It was a heavy burden for such a young man to shoulder.

After Milton completed his master's degree, his teachers and friends expected him to join the church or take a fellowship at Christ's College or, ideally, both. He did neither. Instead, he went to live with his parents in Hammersmith, outside London on the River Thames. He spent the next six years in private study, reading and digesting an astonishing array of books, focusing mostly on Greek and Latin classics but extending into history, music, and mathematics. His parents must have despaired that he would ever have a real job, but they seemed overawed by his genius and sense of vocation.

Milton's reputation grew slowly, nurtured in quiet solitude. He contributed a poem for the Second Folio of Shakespeare's works. In an unsuccessful bid for patronage, he wrote a masque, commonly known as *Comus*, for performance at the castle of an aristocratic family. This series of woodland vignettes, heavily influenced by Shakespeare's *A Midsummer Night's Dream*, was set to music by a noted composer and was highly admired for its exquisite poetry. Too exquisite, perhaps, for later tastes. The modern reader's answer to Comus's question—"Can any mortal mixture of earth's mold / Breathe such divine enchanting ravishment?"[18]—is likely to be "no." Milton also wrote two lovely companion pieces contrasting the life of "heart-easing Mirth"[19] ("L'Allegro") with the life of solemn contemplation ("Il Penseroso"). Despite his efforts to portray the joys and consolations of each, it seems clear that "divinest Melancholy"—which he hopes will lead him to "something like prophetic strain"—is Milton's preferred mode.[20] He was a man with a divine calling, not to be distracted by trifles.

Yet that calling was itself called into question when Milton was not yet twenty-nine. His mother, Sara, died in April 1637. A short time later, a fellow Cambridge student, Edward King, drowned at the age of twenty-five while crossing the Irish Sea to take up an ecclesiastical post. Milton contributed "Lycidas," one of the most famous short poems in the English language, to a collection prepared in King's honor. It is a pastoral elegy with all the standard conventions of that ancient genre, conventions that seem at odds with its stated purpose, which is to ensure that the death of Lycidas (as he refers to King) goes not "unwept."[21] It begins with the narrator-poet lamenting that he is called upon by "bitter constraint, and sad occasion dear,"[22] to compose such a poem before his poetic gift has sufficiently matured.

> Yet once more, O ye laurels, and once more
> Ye myrtles brown, with ivy never sere,
> I come to pluck your berries harsh and crude,
> And with forced fingers rude
> Shatter your leaves before the mellowing year.[23]

More than a century later, when poetic mores had changed, Samuel Johnson would be quite vicious in criticizing "Lycidas" for its lack of genuine grief. "Passion plucks no berries from the myrtle and ivy," Johnson would write, and "runs not after remote allusions."[24] Yet the poem has steadily risen in reputation, and for good reason. All poetry is artificial, but even ancient conventions can take on new life in the hands of a genius. The key point to understand is that "Lycidas" is less about Edward King—though we can assume Milton genuinely mourned his passing—than it is about the inexplicable nature of divine providence. Edward King did everything right; he was a scholar, a poet, and a devout clergyman who, as the ship was sinking, displayed singular courage in comforting his fellow passengers. He was a young man of enormous promise. Yet his life was cut short, without meaning or purpose, and the God to whom he dedicated himself was nowhere in evidence.

Milton seemed genuinely shocked by this event, shocked as only a young man—already stripped raw by the loss of his mother—can be when suddenly confronted with the random death of a friend. Milton considered his poetic talent marked out by God for divine service and was single-minded, even monkish, in seeking the "grace to use it so." Yet his special calling was an illusion and his celibate efforts for naught if chance and circumstance could so readily cut the delicate thread of life.

> Alas! What boots it with uncessant care
> To tend the homely slighted shepherd's trade,
> And strictly meditate the thankless Muse?
> Were it not better done as others use,
> To sport with Amaryllis in the shade,
> Or with the tangles of Neaera's hair?
> Fame is the spur that the clear spirit doth raise
> (That last infirmity of noble mind)
> To scorn delights, and live laborious days;
> But the fair guerdon when we hope to find,
> And think to burst out into sudden blaze,
> Comes the blind Fury with th' abhorred shears,
> And slits the thin-spun life. [25]

These are some of the most beautiful lines in all of English poetry. And they speak directly, despite the remote allusions, to Milton's anguish at the sheer arbitrariness of fate and the inexplicable nature of divine providence.

Milton finds no comfort in established religion. Indeed, he fiercely attacks the established church, which is the primary reason Johnson—a stalwart defender of the Church of England—hated the poem. Milton—who once seemed destined, even in his own mind, to join their ranks—is repelled by the soft lives and rich vestments of the priests, by the increasingly elaborate rituals and high church liturgy of the Anglican service, and by the authoritarian church hierarchy. He rails against churchmen who tyrannize over worship but fail to give their flocks any spiritual nourishment: "The hungry sheep look up, and are not fed."[26] Milton himself is undergoing a spiritual crisis. He knows not where to turn to reestablish a direct connection with God. He knows not how to deal with his own anxieties and doubts about his future. Solitary study, forgoing worldly pleasures, is no guarantor of poetic greatness; it is no guarantor even of living through the day. You can almost hear the young Milton muttering, "What the hell is the point?" He thus resolves on a different set of values and a different sort of life, one that would involve travel and marriage. "Lycidas," in the end, is a poem about self-transformation. "Tomorrow to fresh woods, and pastures new," it concludes.[27] It was the last poem in English that Milton would write for many years.

In the spring of 1638, Milton departed on a fifteen-month grand tour of Europe. He visited Paris and Nice and returned via Switzerland, but Italy was his principal destination. He was much feted there; his reputation as a poet, based mainly on his Latin and Italian poems, was higher in Italy than at home. He reveled in the country's classical past and marked the sad contrast with its fraught, fractured present. Milton mingled with intellectuals wherever he went and saw firsthand the lack of political autonomy and the stifling repression of the Catholic Church. He even met Galileo, under house arrest in Fiesole, grown old and blind, "a prisoner to the Inquisition," Milton would later write, "for thinking in astronomy otherwise than the Franciscan and Dominican licensers thought."[28] He also met in Venice the great Claudio Monteverdi, who composed the earliest operas still in the standard repertoire, including *L'Orfeo* and *The Coronation of Poppea*. Milton brought home with him the scores of numerous works by Monteverdi and other Venetian musicians, much to the delight of his father. He also composed a Latin poem in honor of his friend Charles Diodati, who died while Milton was in Italy. It is yet another pastoral elegy, but its direct expression of grief ought to have satisfied even Johnson. Milton laments the loss of his "sole true friend" and the "unprepared-for day" condemning him to "everlasting pain."[29]

Milton had hoped to visit Greece and Sicily. But civil war was brewing at home, which led him to cut short his journey. Charles I's early efforts to weaken and control Parliament had all failed. He accordingly resisted calling Parliament into session for more than a decade. But Charles needed Parliament in order to raise money. The matter came to a head when the king unwisely sought to impose an episcopal form of government and the Anglican *Book of Common Prayer* on the Presbyterian Church of Scotland. Armed resistance arose, and Charles needed to call Parliament back into session in early 1640 to raise money for his army. The new Parliament promptly passed a law perpetuating itself and denying the king authority to dissolve Parliament. This so-called Long Parliament would last for twenty years, through several armed struggles with the king, his deposition and execution in January 1649, the protectorate of Oliver Cromwell, which began in 1653, and the Restoration of Charles II in 1660.

Milton returned from his grand tour a passionate republican and an advocate for representative government and religious liberty. For the next twenty years, corresponding roughly to the Long Parliament, he devoted

himself largely to the cause of the Puritan Revolution. He was particularly incensed by what he viewed as the creeping Catholicism of the Anglican Church, with its elaborate hierarchy of priests and bishops; its formal,
mandated liturgy; and its penchant for rituals devoid of spiritual content.
He feared, as did many at the time, that Charles I, encouraged by his
Catholic queen, secretly wanted to return England to the Church of
Rome.

Milton became a fierce but masterful polemicist, moving the English
language to new prose heights, as he would later move it to new poetic
heights. The vehemence of his denunciation of prelates and priests is
shocking even today. "Wipe your fat corpulencies out of our light," he
would write, in one of his less elegant prose moments.[30] Milton was a
puritan (small *p*) only in the sense that he wanted to rid the church of all
ornamentation and to allow each individual to encounter the scriptures
unimpeded by dogma or meaningless rituals. He wanted the church to be
a democracy of apostles, which is to say that Milton's ideal church was
really just a holy society in which each member followed his or her
individual conscience. He belonged to no sect. He recognized no heresy.
In defense of spiritual freedom, he strongly objected to any state control
of religious affairs, which put him at odds with many of his Puritan and
Presbyterian allies against Charles I. As we shall see, it is not even clear
that Milton adhered to the Christian doctrine of salvation through Christ.
His focus was on the unmediated love of God and of humankind.

The pamphlets and tracts piled up. But Milton did not neglect his
personal life or his resolve to sound the full range of human experience.
His visited his brother, Christopher, in Reading and then carried on to
Oxford to see Richard Powell, who had borrowed money from Milton's
father but had fallen behind in the payments. Since the payments directly
supported Milton, he went to collect on the debt. He returned, instead,
with a wife, Mary Powell, seventeen to Milton's thirty-three. She was
beautiful, and Milton was immediately smitten. She, in turn, was charmed
by the handsome, witty, musical, and obviously well-off Milton. It must
have seemed an excellent match to Mary—one of nine children—and her
family.

A modest dowry of a thousand pounds was quickly agreed upon. It
might as well have been ten thousand for all of Mary's heavy-drinking
father's ability or intention to pay it. After a month, Milton returned home
to Aldersgate with Mary and three of her siblings. His quiet household

was now a lively and noisy one. But, once the siblings left, it must have been ominously quiet and even depressing for Mary. She lasted only a month before returning to Oxford for what was supposed to be a short family visit. She would not return for three years. Civil war was clearly coming. The Powells were royalists. Milton was decidedly not. The king made his base in Oxford. Parliament was in London. Mary's family claimed that there was no way for her to travel safely from Oxford to London. But there was no indication that she had any desire to do so. Mary's mother, too, had turned decidedly against her radical son-in-law. Milton repeatedly enjoined Mary to return, both by letter and by messenger, but was ignored. Notably, however, he never went to Oxford himself to reclaim his young bride. Instead, he returned to his scholarly, bachelor life, increasingly drawn into the civil war on the side of Parliament and, later, of Oliver Cromwell, who emerged as the key military leader of the opposition.

Out of his personal experience, Milton published several tracts arguing that both men and women should be free to obtain a divorce based on incompatibility of mind and temper and then to remarry. It was another remarkably radical position for his day and was directly contrary to existing canon law, which allowed for dissolution of marriage only on grounds of infidelity or impotence. Milton contended that the principal basis for marriage is companionship rather than procreation. It is the most important and potentially fulfilling personal relationship we will ever have, but if it sours it becomes a nightmare for both parties. The forced continuance of a loveless marriage, he wrote, is "a heinous barbarism both against the honor of marriage, the dignity of man and his soul, the goodness of Christianity, and all the human respects of civility."[31] Remarkably, he seemed to be defending Mary's viewpoint on their separation as well as his own right to pursue another, more suitable mate.

Milton enlivened his household by taking in the two boys of his sister, Anne, for tutoring. Sons of the nobility soon followed, and Milton regularly had six or more pupils. He wrote a treatise, *Of Education*, in 1644 that stressed the importance of humanist learning to a virtuous citizenry. In it, he advocated for a state-supported system of education and a syllabus that included literature, philosophy, mathematics, science, and both ancient and modern languages, as well as a smattering of law, agriculture, and even medicine. The poor nephews! One wonders how well they responded to a workload suited to a Milton or a Descartes. Yet Milton never lost sight of his ultimate objective: "No purpose or respect should sooner move us," he wrote, "than simply the love of God and of mankind."[32] Simple piety and learning were, in his mind, inseparable.

In the same year, Milton also published *Areopagitica*, an attack on prepublication censorship through licensing. There is no more important book in English on the value of a free press. Citing the example of Galileo quoted above, Milton argues that any process of licensing will inevitably suppress the growth of knowledge essential to material improvement and the civil education essential to liberty. Restricting the right to publish and to read whatever one wishes is "the greatest displeasure and indignity to a free and knowing spirit that can be put upon him."[33] No institution has a monopoly on truth or understanding. No hired censor can determine in advance the proper limits of men's thoughts and discoveries. Nor is it necessary, for in any open discussion, truth will eventually win out against error in what later generations would call the marketplace of ideas.

> And though all the winds of doctrine were let loose to play upon the earth, so Truth be in the field, we do injuriously by licensing and prohibiting to misdoubt her strength. Let her and Falsehood grapple; who ever knew Truth put to the worse in a free and open encounter? . . . Truth is strong. . . . She needs no policies, nor stratagems, nor licensings to make her victorious, those are the shifts and the defenses that error uses against her power.[34]

The following year, the royalist cause began to founder. Oxford, which had been a royalist stronghold, fell to Parliament. Mary Powell's family suddenly found it convenient to seek Milton's protection; so, in the summer of 1645 Mary appeared before him without warning and tearfully pleaded for reconciliation. Remarkably, Milton required no convincing. Indeed, he not only took in Mary but soon harbored her parents and five of her siblings as well. He was undoubtedly lonely, and Mary, at twenty-one, was more beautiful than ever; but basic human kindness and Christian charity must also have played a large part in his decision.

Milton and Mary would remain together until her death in 1652. They had four children: Anne was born in July 1646 (barely a year after their reconciliation), Mary in 1648, John in 1651, and Deborah in 1652. Mary died from complications a few days after Deborah's birth. Their son, John, died six weeks later, shortly after his first birthday. The oldest child, Anne, was physically and mentally disabled. Milton himself was almost completely blind, probably of glaucoma, by early 1652 at the age of forty-three. His eyesight had been failing for some time, and it is unlikely he ever had a clear sight of his infant son, much less of Deborah. He would come to write a beautiful sonnet about his blindness that begins, "When I consider how my light is spent, / Ere half my days, in this dark world and wide," and, after extolling the virtues of quiet patience, ends with the exquisite line, "They also serve who only stand and wait."[35]

Yet the younger Milton, in his polemical phase, had rarely been willing to stand and wait. Instead, he sat and wrote, including a stirring defense of the king's deposition and execution, which had been condemned throughout Europe. In it he emphatically rejected the doctrine of the divine right of kings in favor of republican principles. Every ruler holds his authority from the people and must act in their best interests, he argued. When the ruler fails to do so, it is the "right of free-born men" to depose him and "be governed as seems to them best."[36] His work attracted the attention of Cromwell, and Milton was appointed Secretary for Foreign Tongues to the Council of State. In that capacity, Milton became the international apologist for the new regime. It must have been an increasingly uncomfortable role, for the political and religious freedom that Milton championed was not to be. The Puritans and their Presbyterian allies were more repressive in matters of religion than the Anglicans had ever been, and the republic of which Milton dreamed quickly devolved into a new tyranny. Cromwell became Protector in December 1653. By 1657 he was "Lord Protector" and a virtual dictator, claiming a right of succession for his son. Ironically, only after the Restoration did Parliament revive as a representative institution and the Anglican Church eliminate much of its hierarchy and soften its doctrinal mandates. Yet Milton's last political act, in 1660, was to pen a passionate plea to the English people, urging them to retain the republic and not to give away their hard-won freedom. It was courageous but futile. Weary of war, economic dislocation, and a Puritan repression that shuttered the theaters and forbade dancing, England was primed to welcome the return of monarchy.

When Charles II landed at Dover on May 25, 1660, Milton went into hiding. Some say his friends even staged a mock funeral to deceive the king's officers. Milton, having defended the regicide of Charles I, was lucky to escape execution. Those who signed Charles I's death warrant, and who had not fled the country, were put to death in the brutal, archaic fashion then reserved for traitors. The restored regime even dug up the corpses of Cromwell and his intimates and hanged them. Their heads ended up on poles outside Westminster Hall. Many former republicans publicly repented their errors and embraced the new king. Milton simply stayed quiet. But, with the exceptions noted above, Charles II was surprisingly mild in his reprisals. A general act of pardon was passed, and, through the good graces of friends in Parliament and the timely intervention of his royalist brother, Milton was not placed on the list of those persons exempted from the pardon. Despite that, he was arrested and briefly imprisoned in the Tower of London. It must have been both frightening and disorienting to the blind poet. But he was soon released, and the greatest danger seemed to have passed. Indeed, eventually he was even offered a post as a Latin secretary to the king, which he declined, noting privately that he preferred "to live and die an honest man."[37]

Milton remarried in 1656 to twenty-eight-year-old Katherine Woodcock. She died in childbirth, along with their child, just short of her thirtieth birthday. Milton, who of course had never seen her face, wrote a sonnet, "Methought I saw my late espoused saint," which ends with these heartbreaking lines:

> Her face was veiled, yet to my fancied sight
> Love, sweetness, goodness in her person shined
> So clear as in no face with more delight.
> But O as to embrace me she inclined,
> I waked, she fled, and day brought back my night.[38]

Milton had lost two wives and two children. His oldest daughter was disabled. He himself was blind. The bank in which he had kept his substantial savings had failed at the time of the Restoration. And the cause of political, religious, and personal freedom to which he had given twenty years of his life seemed to be in shambles. He should have been embittered yet somehow was not. Visitors—of whom he had many—remarked upon his serenity and ability to seize happiness from simple pleasures.

He began work on *Paradise Lost* in 1658, the same year his second wife and Cromwell died. He would compose verses in his head during the nighttime hours and then dictate them each morning to a scribe. He also had the Hebrew Bible read to him every day for the rest of his life, along with other works in Greek and Latin. He neither belonged to nor attended any church. He rejected the very idea of orthodoxy as antithetical to a free and personal encounter with God.

In 1663, Milton was married a third time, at the age of fifty-four, to twenty-four-year-old Elizabeth Minshull, a cousin of his physician. The marriage was resented by his estranged daughters, who correctly feared that they would lose out in a revised will. Mary, when told of the marriage by Milton's housekeeper, reputedly responded that "that was no news to hear of his wedding but if she could hear of his death that was something."[39] It was undoubtedly a marriage more of convenience than of passion for both parties, yet they seem to have been happy together through the last twelve years of Milton's life.

In 1665, a virulent strain of plague returned to London, chronicled in Samuel Pepys's contemporaneous diary and, later, in Daniel Defoe's fictionalized *A Journal of the Plague Year*. In 1666, the Great Fire of London, also described by Pepys in vivid and dramatic detail, destroyed more than thirteen thousand homes along with numerous churches and businesses, including St. Paul's Cathedral, where many had sought refuge, and the original Milton family home, which was one of Milton's few remaining possessions. His current residence was spared, but he and Elizabeth were close to destitute.

Paradise Lost was finally published in 1667. He followed with several more works: a history of Britain in 1670; *Paradise Regained* and *Samson Agonistes* in 1671; a tract against "popery" in 1673; and a revised and slightly expanded second edition of *Paradise Lost* in 1674, the year he died. The royalties on these books left Milton with a final estate of nine hundred pounds. His daughters challenged the will, which, with ironic intent, left them only the amount still owed by Richard Powell as their mother's dowry (an amount that was, with Powell's death, obviously never to be paid). A final settlement gave two-thirds of the modest estate—about six hundred pounds—to Elizabeth, and one hundred pounds to each of his daughters. Milton died in November 1674, just short of his sixty-sixth birthday. He was buried in St. Giles Cripplegate Church in London. Only in 1737 was a memorial erected in his honor in Poets' Corner at Westminster Abbey.

SATAN

Though *Paradise Lost* invokes the heavenly muse, the poem proper does not start with God. It starts at the point furthest from God, in the depths of the newly created hell into which Satan and his rebel angels have been cast. They were "hurled headlong flaming from th' ethereal sky"[40] and fell through space for nine days and nights before landing in a lake of fire in a region of sorrow and mournful gloom, "where peace / And rest can never dwell [and] hope never comes."[41]

We don't learn the backstory of the rebellion and how the battle raged for three days in heaven until books 5 and 6. The poem starts *in media res* (in the middle of things), with Satan—once the brightest of the archangels—thoroughly defeated and yet magnificently defiant. The poem will move both forward and backward in time and encompass other characters—God, Christ, the archangels Raphael and Michael, Adam and Eve—but, for the first two books, the focus is on Satan, who so thoroughly engages the reader that some critics think the poem never quite gains its balance.

Despite being "racked with deep despair," Satan refuses to submit or even to regret his rebellion.[42] He is the embodiment of courage, determination, and audacity, still brimming with pride that he contended with God "and shook His throne."[43]

> What though the field be lost?
> All is not lost; th' unconquerable will
> And study of revenge, immortal hate
> And courage never to submit or yield—
> And what is else not to be overcome?
> That glory never shall His wrath or might
> Extort from me: to bow and sue for grace
> With suppliant knee and deify His pow'r
> Who from the terror of this arm so late
> Doubted His empire![44]

Pride and ambition were Satan's downfall. He admits that he owed all to God but could not bear "the debt immense of endless gratitude."[45] God created him in all his bright eminence, yet he felt a "sense of injured merit" that he himself, though lifted up so high, was not supreme.[46]

Satan has the creative and imaginative power to impose his own narrative on his fall from grace; it is a counternarrative to combat the word of

God and his angels. Satan condemns the tyranny of heaven and exalts the freedom he and his fellow denizens now enjoy, the freedom to make of the world and themselves what they will. They need not submit or meekly accept what God has decreed for them. They can embrace their fate and, in the process, transform it into something of their own choosing.

> Hail horrors, hail
> Infernal world! And thou, profoundest Hell,
> Receive thy new possessor, one who brings
> A mind not to be changed by place or time!
> The mind is its own place and in itself
> Can make a Heaven of Hell, a Hell of Heaven.
> What matter where, if I be still the same
> And what I should be: all but less than He
> Whom thunder hath made greater? Here at least
> We shall be free.[47]

The heroic aspects of Satan's character are drawn from the epic tradition. Like Achilles kindling his rage into a fire that will consume him and countless Greek heroes; like Odysseus smiting his breast and enjoining his heart to endure; like Aeneas rallying his shipmates' spirits in the midst of a storm; and like Dante's Ulysses urging his men to press beyond the limits of the known world, Satan fuels his malice, resolves to turn suffering into a source of power, inspires his troops to make a heaven of hell, and promises to conquer new, uncreated worlds, and in the process to wreak revenge on God by despoiling man, God's newest creation. Yet Satan turns the epic tradition inside out. He no longer seeks the *kleos* (honor) and *timê* (the traditional marks of public esteem) craved by the Homeric hero. Satan shares the nihilism of Shakespeare's Iago, who festered with his own sense of injured merit. As Satan will later admit, "only in destroying I find ease / To my relentless thoughts."[48] Because God is all-good and omnipotent, Satan believes he must choose between submission and evil.

> None left but by submission and that word
> Disdain forbids me and my dread of shame
> Among the spirits beneath whom I seduced
> With other promises and other vaunts
> Than to submit, boasting I could subdue
> Th' Omnipotent.[49]

The Romantic poets made of Satan a Byronic hero, who they much preferred to Milton's coldly aloof and punitive God. "Nothing can exceed the energy and magnificence of the character of Satan as expressed in *Paradise Lost*," wrote Percy Bysshe Shelley.[50] Samuel Taylor Coleridge added that "around this character [Milton] has thrown a singularity of daring, a grandeur of sufferance, and a ruined splendor, which constitute the very height of poetic sublimity."[51] William Blake said that, in keeping faith with his own genius, Milton could not but exalt the rebel angel, for "he was a true Poet and of the Devil's party without knowing it."[52]

One can indeed trace aspects of Satan's character to Milton's courageous defiance of tyranny and oppression, whether by church or state or even by shopworn moral codes. Milton, too, deliberately seemed to cut himself off from any possibility of forgiveness or reconciliation when he excoriated the English people for allowing the monarchy to return. Disdain and dread of shame forbade his submission. Cromwell also shared traits with Satan. His cry of liberty, like Satan's, turned out to be a bid for domination. Cromwell seduced his followers with promises of political and religious freedom but, in the end, like Satan, sought only his own "honor, dominion, glory and renown."[53]

Yet turning *Paradise Lost* into an exercise in personal biography or political history, however intriguing, is misguided. It is equally misguided to make Satan the hero of the poem, just as it would be to make Iago the hero of Shakespeare's play. Milton does not hide the attractions of the devil's party, but he is not of it. He recognizes and develops Satan's allure, but exposes it as false. Milton makes Satan magnificent to underscore the intensity of the temptation to depart from God and set oneself up as, or in thrall to, a rival deity. In such a rebellion, one finds the illusion of freedom, but it is only an illusion.

In what is justly the most famous line in the poem, Satan declares, "Better to reign in Hell than serve in Heaven!"[54] But Satan does not reign anywhere. His indomitable will and heroic courage are instruments of his own corruption. Satan is the chief protagonist who drives the poem forward and even casts his shadow over the characters of God and Christ. But Satan is "darkness visible,"[55] a black hole of malice, whereas God and Christ increasingly shed their light on all created things. "Myself am Hell," Satan is forced to admit.[56] Pride, ambition, and envy diminish rather than exalt our natures.[57] They are forces that imprison our will: "In the lowest deep a lower deep / Still threat'ning to devour me opens wide."[58] Satan does not represent freedom; he represents submission to forces that gradually but steadily destroy him from within. Virtue is the flourishing of our best nature and hence a true reflection of freedom, whereas vice, like a python, steadily strangles that nature and leaves us hollow and empty, estranged from our very selves. "Love virtue," Milton wrote in *Comus*, "she alone is free."[59] All of *Paradise Lost* is an elaboration and defense of that assertion.

GOD AND FREEDOM

When God finally makes his appearance in book 3, the reader cannot but feel a certain deflation. Unlike Satan, God has neither personality nor charisma. Heaven is governed by reason and obedience; hell by passion and rebellious energy, which are always more interesting. God is, as one critic put it, little more than a collection of abstractions.[60] He is all-knowing. He is all-powerful. He is all-good. But his goodness is harsh and uncompromising—"how awful goodness is," notes Satan[61]—rather than loving and generous. God insists on strict obedience to his commands and will punish any departures. Indeed, goodness is nothing more than acting in accordance with the will of God, which appears to lend support to Satan's claim that God is a tyrant against whom he justly rebelled in the name of personal freedom.

Since God is all-knowing, he anticipates that Satan will be successful in bringing about humankind's fall from grace. Adam and Eve will violate the single injunction that governs their stay in paradise by eating from the tree of the knowledge of good and evil.

> Man will hearken to his glozing lies
> And easily transgress the sole command,
> Sole pledge of his obedience. So will fall
> He and his faithless progeny. Whose fault?
> Whose but his own? Ingrate! He had of Me
> All he could have. I made him just and right,
> Sufficient to have stood though free to fall.[62]

It is worth unpacking this off-putting passage, for the central theological thrust of the poem is compacted within it. It is a hard doctrine, but Milton does not disguise its difficulty any more than he muted the attractions of Satan.

God's first point is that free will is essential to our existence as moral and rational agents.[63] There can be neither virtue nor fault, neither praise nor blame, if we have no choice in what we do and don't do.

> What praise could they receive?
> What pleasure I from such obedience paid
> When will and reason (reason also is choice)
> Useless and vain, of freedom both despoiled,
> Made passive both, had served necessity,
> Not Me?[64]

God has made us, as he made the angels, capable of reasoning and willing, and essential to that capacity is the freedom to choose our actions. Without freedom of choice, men and women would be Cartesian automatons. They would not exist as moral agents.

But allowing humans freedom of reason and will entails the allowance of evil. For if men and women can choose, they can choose evil as well as good. Theologians have long debated how an all-good, all-powerful, and all-knowing God can allow evil to occur. Why doesn't he put a stop to it? How can a just God permit "all our woe"? Because to do otherwise would rob us of our freedom and hence our dignity as moral agents. God ensures our freedom by not intervening, by not preventing us from falling into evil and disobedience. Knowledge of good and evil and moral freedom are two sides of the same coin. With obedience comes the possibility of disobedience. Otherwise, neither concept makes any sense. If reason and will "served necessity," they would be "useless and vain, of freedom both despoiled." That is why God made Adam and Eve, like the angels, "sufficient to have stood though free to fall."

Another question that has plagued theologians is how such freedom is consistent with God's omniscience. God knows all—past, present, and future. He cannot be wrong. So, if he knows in advance that Adam and Eve will succumb to Satan's deceptions, it is necessary that they will do so. They cannot do otherwise.

This is a mystery that even the rebel angels—at least the more philosophical among them—contemplate in hell. In a pointed reference to Dante's limbo, where the virtuous pagans are condemned to an eternity apart from God, and Aristotle is at the center of a group of philosophers seated on a hill apart from the others, Milton writes of the new residents of hell:

> Others apart sat on a hill retired
> In thoughts more elevate and reasoned high
> Of providence, foreknowledge, will and fate,
> Fixed fate, free will, foreknowledge absolute,
> And found no end in wand'ring mazes lost.[65]

It is a deliberately comical moment—one of a surprising number in the poem. The angels who rebelled against God are debating whether they are themselves responsible for their rebellion or whether "fixed fate" and "foreknowledge absolute" bear the blame. To reverse the late Flip Wilson's famous tagline: God (not the Devil) made me do it.

At least since Boethius, theologians have argued that "foreknown" does not mean "foreordained."[66] Our knowledge of the past admits no alteration but does not exclude that it was the product of free choice. The same is true of God's knowledge of the future. God sees all time, forward and backward, from an atemporal present. The entire history of humankind is always before him: "beholding from His prospect high / (Wherein past, present, future He beholds)."[67] But God's knowledge of men's actions does not control those actions.

> If I foreknew
> Foreknowledge had no influence on their fault
> Which had no less proved certain unforeknown.[68]

Adam and Eve have the potential to fall and the potential to stand. Both are within their power. The fall, even if foreknown by God, is not inevitable from their perspective. They had a choice, and God's knowledge of what they would choose did not compel that choice. "Whose fault? Whose but [their] own?"

But there is a more difficult question lurking here that arises from the Cartesian philosophy then sweeping Europe. According to Descartes, all events in the physical world can be explained in terms of mechanics (matter in motion), which can in turn be expressed mathematically. It follows that human action as well is the product of ineluctable mechanical laws. There is no room for the spontaneous interjection of an unconditioned or "free" will. Indeed, there is no room even for God in the unfolding of this mechanical world. At most, God is the clockmaker who wound up the universe and then let it run.

The theological problem of God's foreknowledge is trite in comparison to the philosophical problem of the iron chain of cause and effect in the material universe. Milton seems to allude to this different sort of necessity when he has God say that the fault of Adam and Eve "had no less proved certain unforeknown." That is quite remarkable. God seems to be indicating that the fall of humankind would be "certain" to occur even if he did not know about it in advance. The wheels are already turning to their inevitable conclusion. In any such scenario, will and reason serve neither God nor Satan but causal necessity; they are still "useless and vain, of freedom both despoiled."

We saw that Descartes "solved" this problem by lapsing into incoherence. He posited an entirely separate spiritual realm populated by numerous immortal souls that are free and active agents and can, in some inexplicable way, alter the course of the material world or at least retain the illusion of such action. Milton emphatically rejects Cartesian dualism and provides a far more convincing account of free will as an outgrowth of increasingly refined material forces. Milton was a monist. There is only one underlying substance—"one first matter all."[69] It is a material substance, but it has in its highest forms an increasingly spiritual dimension. Milton believed in what Arthur Lovejoy, in his famous work, would call "the great chain of being."[70]

> One first matter all
> Endued with various forms, various degrees
> Of substance and in things that live of life,
> But more refined, more spiritous and pure
> As nearer to Him placed or nearer tending,
> Each in their several active spheres assigned
> Till body up to spirit work in bounds
> Proportioned to each kind.[71]

For Milton, the spiritual is but a refinement of the material. There is no unbridgeable divide. The body "work[s]" itself "up to spirit . . . in bounds / Proportioned to each kind." That is, there is a hierarchy of being that culminates in God, the source and author of all being. God is the "one first matter all," and everything that exists has value in its relation to God. Differences in degree effectively become differences in kind and, as one ascends that scale, representation becomes more difficult and shades into abstraction and allegory. But we are still the stuff that God is made of, because God has made all things out of his own being.

Johnson suggests that Milton "has unhappily perplexed his poetry with his philosophy."[72] I would say rather that he has freed his poetry from the narrow confines of philosophy. According to Milton, we realize our highest natures in the love of God and our fellow men. That is when we are truly free. We are inherently creatures of reason and will, which makes us self-actualizing. We have a motive force that cannot be reduced merely to mechanical terms. We are organic and alive. We are moral agents. Philosophy cannot explain this; when it tries to do so, it finds no end in wandering mazes lost. Milton's own account of human freedom and virtue is admittedly mythopoeic, but it corresponds to our experience of ourselves as free agents, able to judge and choose between right and wrong. That poetic myth can become our reality if we order our lives in accordance with it, if we continuously nurture a sense of the sacred and of the miraculous in human life and human action. To celebrate God is to celebrate all that exists. We can approach the world with love, kindness, awe, and forgiveness, or with envy, hate, disgust, and anger. The choice is ours and always has been ours.

Despite the many disappointments in his life, Milton still believes in the active reality of goodness, mercy, and justice, and of man's freedom to realize his highest self. Love virtue, she alone is free. Everything else is a form of enslavement and self-corruption; for man, "within himself / The danger lies, yet lies within his power: / Against his will he can receive no harm."[73]

SCENES FROM A MARRIAGE

At its core, *Paradise Lost* is a story of love and marriage and the challenges that beset both in a fallen world. God and Satan, space and time, freedom and necessity, creation and destruction; all these cosmic forces fade into the background. Book 4 narrows its focus to the garden of Eden, and the pastoral setting inspires some of Milton's most beautiful poetry; more beautiful, in my view, than even Dante's description of the earthly paradise in canto 28 of his *Purgatorio*. Milton's Eden is a place where streams and brooks fed by a pure fountain bring forth

> Flow'rs worthy of Paradise which not nice art
> In beds and curious knots, but Nature boon
> Poured forth profuse on hill and dale and plain,
> Both where the morning sun first warmly smote
> The open field and where th' unpierced shade

> Embrowned the noontide bowers.[74]

Plants, trees, and fruits of all varieties feed an array of creatures living in harmony, among them:

> Two of far nobler shape erect and tall,
> Godlike erect with native honor clad
> In naked majesty, seemed lords of all.
> And worthy seemed for in their looks divine
> The image of their glorious Maker shone:
> Truth, wisdom, sanctitude severe and pure,
> Severe, but in true filial freedom placed,
> Whence true authority in men.[75]

Adam and Eve are presented in their native grandeur and innocence. Milton's Eden, unlike Dante's, is a place where sex is one of "nature's works"[76] and a source of profound happiness, not of guilty shame. Milton condemns those hypocrites who defame as impure the rites of connubial love decreed by God.[77] Adam and Eve come tenderly together "in love's embraces met."[78]

They are not full equals. Adam, who was created first, is formed for contemplation and valor; Eve, for softness and "sweet attractive grace."[79] Or so the narrator states. In fact, Eve's superior emotional intelligence is clear from the outset. Her body only "implied / Subjection" when she to Adam

> Yielded with coy submission, modest pride,
> And sweet reluctant amorous delay.[80]

She enjoys their nuptial union as much as he, but she ensures Adam's continued fascination by a coyness that makes of sex something "by her yielded, by him best received."[81] Adam echoes this thought, stressing "the conscience of her worth / That would be wooed and not unsought be won."[82] This wooing and winning, this "sweet reluctant amorous delay," is not quite Keats's Grecian urn, where the lover never catches the beloved. But the effect is the same: "For ever wilt thou love, and she be fair!"[83]

Eve is conscious, and even enamored, of herself from the outset in a way that Adam is not. She recounts to him the moment when she first awoke and found herself on a bed of flowers close to a lake fed by a murmuring stream. She lies upon the bank and, gazing into the water, sees a shape like her own bending over to look upon her. Eve starts back, and so does the watery shape. But she returns and gazes with increasing pleasure and receives "answering looks / Of sympathy and love."[84] Eve, like Narcissus, pines with naive desire for her own reflection, and it takes God to set her straight and lead her to Adam: "To him shalt bear / Multitudes like thyself and thence be called / Mother of human race."[85]

Eve takes a quick look at Adam and finds him tall and fair, "yet methought less fair," she explains, "less winning soft, less amiably mild / Than that smooth wat'ry image."[86] So she promptly turns her back on Adam and moves to return to her own reflection. So much for the future of the human race. Adam calls to her, insisting that they are of the same flesh and bone and soul. As recounted by Eve:

> With that thy gentle hand
> Seized mine, I yielded, and from that time see
> How beauty is excelled by manly grace
> And wisdom which alone is truly fair. [87]

Adam is the instigator, but Eve meets him halfway, "with eyes / Of conjugal attraction unreproved."[88] She discovers that physical love with Adam is far superior to an elusive fascination with her own reflection. But she also recognizes that wisdom is better than either, and in that thought lies the seeds of their fall. Eve does not want simply to enjoy the world; she wants to understand and control it.

The prelapsarian description of their union is beautiful beyond compare. Milton was married three times (four, if you count his separate phases with Mary). He has poured his heart into this account; it is idealized to be sure, but no less moving for that.

Adam says of Eve:

> So much delights me as those graceful acts,
> Those thousand decencies that daily flow
> From all her words and actions mixed with love
> And sweet compliance, which declare unfeigned
> Union of mind or in us both one soul.
> Harmony to behold in wedded pair
> More grateful than harmonious sound to th' ear. [89]

Eve is not lagging in the expression of her own affection. She catalogs the wonders of Eden they enjoy together and attests that none of these "without thee is sweet."[90] And, in my favorite lines of the entire poem, she adds:

> With thee conversing I forget all time,
> All seasons and their change all please alike. [91]

Eve, more than Adam, has become the poet-narrator of her own experience. That is part of the reason she is susceptible to Satan when he
comes to her in a dream. He offers her the chance to expand her narrative
and the consciousness of her worth. Adam and Eve have been granted all
the bounty of paradise, with one exception: they may not eat of the tree of
the knowledge of good and evil. Satan, appearing in the guise of an angel,
calls it the "Tree / Of interdicted Knowledge."[92] Sounding like the Milton
of *Areopagitica*, he rails against the arbitrary prohibition that keeps her in
puerile ignorance. Knowledge is power, and Eve need not remain a mere
helpmate.

> Taste this and be henceforth among the gods
> Thyself a goddess, not to earth confined. [93]

Eve is both troubled and intrigued by the dream, which she relates to
Adam. God sends the angel Raphael to Eden to warn Adam and Eve of
the danger posed by Satan and to remind them both of the awful consequences of transgressing God's sole command.

> In the day thou eat'st, thou diest:
> Death is the penalty imposed. Beware!
> And govern well thy appetite lest Sin
> Surprise thee and her black attendant Death. [94]

Raphael recounts for their benefit the entire history of Satan's rebellion
and fall from grace. He urges them to remember this terrible example and
fear to transgress.[95] He also recounts for them the history of the cosmos
up until the creation of Adam so that they do not feel deprived of earthly
knowledge. But "Heav'n is for thee too high," he cautions, "to know what
passes there. Be lowly wise: / Think only what concerns thee and thy
being."[96]

If anything is calculated to arouse Eve's curiosity, it is precisely an
injunction to "solicit not thy thoughts with matters hid."[97] When she and
Adam prepare to work in the garden the next morning, Eve suggests that
they separate in order to "divide our labors" and accomplish more.[98] But
Adam reminds her of Satan's threat and urges her to stay by his side so
they can face any danger together:

> The wife where danger or dishonor lurks

> Safest and seemliest by her husband stays
> Who guards her or with her the worst endures. [99]

Eve is offended that Adam doubts her firmness and love, which she insists cannot be shaken or seduced. To live in such fear affronts her integrity and treats their happiness as frail. She does not want to be a mere appendage. Adam tries at length to reassure Eve that it is no affront to find strength in mutual dependence. God expressly warned them that they could fall into deception unaware, and together they can keep the strictest watch. It is a lengthy dialogue, but, in the end, Adam's affection beggars his judgment:

> Go, for thy stay, not free, absents thee more.
> Go in thy native innocence, rely
> On what thou hast of virtue, summon all,
> For God towards thee hath done his part: do thine! [100]

It is the fateful turning point in the poem. In his love for Eve, Adam offers her freedom, just as God, out of love, offered freedom to angels and men alike. Eve withdraws her hand from Adam's and departs.

Satan's seduction is all too readily achieved through a combination of flattery and deception. Eve eats of the forbidden fruit in the expectation of acquiring godlike knowledge and wisdom. She thinks her actions are hidden from heaven, so high and remote from things on earth. Her only real dilemma is what to tell Adam. At first, she plans to keep knowledge in her own power to "render me more equal and, perhaps, / A thing not undesirable, sometime / Superior."[101] But then she recollects that if God has seen and she must die, Adam will be "wedded to another Eve," a thought she cannot abide:

> Confirmed then I resolve
> Adam shall share with me in bliss or woe.
> So dear I love him that with him all deaths
> I could endure, without him live no life. [102]

Eve has already so far fallen into sin that, in her twisted reasoning, she will compass Adam's death along with her own and treats that as a sign of how dearly she loves him. Yet Adam is not at all behind in that sentiment. He is horrified at Eve's transgression and knows full well its fatal consequences. She has ruined him as well as herself. And yet:

> How can I live without thee, how forgo
> Thy sweet converse and love so dearly joined

To live again in these wild woods forlorn?
Should God create another Eve and I
Another rib afford, yet loss of thee
Would never from my heart. No! No! I feel
The link of nature draw me, flesh of flesh,
Bone of my bone thou art and from thy state
Mine never shall be parted, bliss or woe. [103]

Odysseus was promised immortality on an island paradise if he remained with the sea goddess Calypso. He chose human love and rocky Ithaca instead and a path of pain and woe. Adam does the same. Unlike Eve, he is not deceived. He knows the consequence of his choice but chooses nonetheless. From a theological perspective, it is of course the wrong choice. He separates himself from God. He will know death, sorrow, and toil. But, from a human perspective, we cannot but admire his devotion and his courage.

EAST OF EDEN

And at the east of the garden of Eden he placed the cherubim, and a sword flaming and turning to guard the way to the tree of life. [104]

After Adam eats the forbidden fruit given him by Eve, their shared exhilaration quickly expends itself in lustful sex, sharpened by guilt and shame. They begin to reproach and blame each other in biting words that can never be withdrawn: "high passions—anger, hate, / Mistrust, suspicion, discord— . . . [shake] sore / Their inward state of mind, calm region once / And full of peace, now tossed and turbulent." [105] Each considers the other most at fault; neither acknowledges responsibility. When confronted by God, after trying to hide their nakedness and sin, they make excuses and continue to accuse each other. All in vain. God pronounces his sentence: they and all their descendants shall know the pain of childbirth, the harshness of the changing seasons, and the reluctance of the land to yield its bounty without endless toil. And they will know death: "For dust thou art and shalt to dust return." [106]

Adam protests that the punishment is out of all proportion to the offense: "Inexplicable / Thy justice seems!" [107] But, in fact, the offense and the punishment are one and the same. In disobeying God, they have become estranged from God. They have lost the unreflective virtue of innocence. Their lives, and the lives of their descendants, will no longer automatically be saturated in God's grace. They must depend upon themselves. They learn to do precisely that, and therein lies their ultimate salvation.

We all know how disagreements can spiral out of control and lead to lasting estrangement. But Eve, reflecting her superior moral intelligence, takes the first step in a remarkable appeal that they set aside anger and recrimination and cling to each other:

> Forsake me not thus, Adam, witness Heaven,
> What love sincere and reverence in my heart
> I bear thee . . .
>
> . . .
>
> Bereave me not
> Whereon I live: thy gentle looks, thy aid,
> Thy counsel, in this uttermost distress
> My only strength and stay![108]

Though both have sinned against God, Eve admits that her fault is greater, for she has sinned "against God and thee."[109] She proposes to importune God to have the entire sentence fall on her as the sole cause of their woe.

Adam's heart relents at Eve's impassioned appeal and the sight of her on her knees before him. He would take all the blame himself if prayers could alter high decrees:

> But rise, let us no more contend, nor blame
> Each other, blamed enough elsewhere, but strive
> In offices of love, how we may light'n
> Each other's burden in our share of woe.[110]

Having passed through the stages of recrimination and reconciliation, they find in their shared loss a new source of strength. Adam and Eve reject the savage self-assertion of Satan in favor of a Stoic philosophy derived from pagan thinkers of the Hellenistic and Roman eras: "the better fortitude / Of patience and heroic martyrdom / Unsung."[111]

The foundational myth of man's fall is not necessarily tied to religion. As C. S. Lewis rather plaintively noted, "in some very important senses [Paradise Lost] is not a religious poem."[112] It is a poetic representation of our natural state. Our grandeur and our misery are inevitably conjoined.

We are free to isolate ourselves morally from one another behind a redoubt of self-interest. But we are also free to lighten one another's burden and to "strive / In offices of love." "Only connect," as E. M. Forster would say. There will be inevitable failures and lapses, but there will also be moments of love sincere—for individuals and for humankind more generally—that illuminate and transform our lives. It is on those moments that the archangel Michael urges Adam and Eve to build. Even though they must leave the garden of Eden, Michael explains, they can each, through acts of love, "possess / A paradise within thee, happier far."[113]

It will not be easy. Michael unveils a future history of man filled with war, famine, pestilence, violence, and oppression—fueled by pride and ambition—that bids to make a hell of earth. But Michael also prophesizes the coming of Christ and his message of peace and love that can bring salvation to men and women who choose to follow that course. Again, though, this message is less doctrinal than symbolic. Christ is the mythopoeic representation of humankind's redemption through suffering and love.

Michael urges Adam and Eve and their descendants to accept and embrace that hope but not to inquire too deeply into the mysteries of religion: "Be lowly wise: / Think only what concerns thee and thy being." "Be lowly wise" seems a rather anti-Enlightenment injunction. But, in fact, it is thoroughly Cartesian. Set aside theological issues, Michael cautions, lest religion remain a battleground "whence heavy persecution shall arise" and exhaust itself "in outward rites and specious forms."[114] For Milton, the only article of faith is to love God and one another. And he justifies that faith, poetically, as the only way to heal our fallen humanity.

Our consciousness is infused with a sense of loss, with a sense that we must somehow work our way, like Odysseus, back to a home from which we have long been absent. *The Odyssey* is one epic of return. *Paradise Lost* offers us a different sort of return as a cure for the alienation and emptiness we try in vain to fill with pride and ambition. Only when we embrace God's grace does the wonder and mystery of life unfold itself, and we can feel at home in the universe.

In our fallen state, God is no longer visible to us. He no longer speaks to us directly. "Yet doubt not," Michael reassures Adam:

> God is as here and will be found alike
> Present and of His presence many a sign
> Still following thee, still compassing thee round

> With goodness and paternal love, His face
> Express, and of His steps the track divine. [115]

For Milton, all of creation is a manifestation of God if we but know how to look, and God's grace is everywhere to be found.

Yet much of creation could just as readily be considered a manifestation of Satan, which brings us back to the question with which Milton started: how to justify God's ways to man; how to embrace "God's providence" in the face of evil and suffering.

The Stoic philosopher Marcus Aurelius offered his readers a stark choice: "Either the world is a mere hotchpotch of random cohesions and dispersions, or else it is a unity of order and providence."[116] In either event, he concluded, the march of history is not within our control. We can become masters only of our good intentions and the firmness of our resolve.[117] Milton goes a step further; he believes that through faith we can transform, if not the world, at least the way the world presents itself to us. Through the love of God and humankind, we can open ourselves to grace and a broader view of divine providence. That providence will not intervene to prevent the death of an Edward King or the restoration of an oppressive monarchy. If we base our happiness on such specific outcomes, we will be of "short joy bereft."[118] But we can instead take the longer view that God's mercy and benevolence will manifest themselves in ways visible to man.[119] And, by so believing, we will make it so.

It is therefore up to us to justify God's ways to man. We can seek connection with God and our fellow men, or we can disdain that connection. If we opt for selfish pride and ambition, the world will look a lot like hell. If we opt for love of God and humankind, it will look a lot like Eden. Milton does not minimize the magnitude or difficulty of the choice. But, thanks to divine grace, we are free to decide.

Adam and Eve depart Eden full of loss and regret, yet also with promise and hope.

> Some natural tears they dropped but wiped them soon.
> The world was all before them, where to choose
> Their place of rest, and Providence their guide.
> They hand in hand with wand'ring steps and slow
> Through Eden took their solitary way. [120]

3

MOLIÈRE

From Farce to Social Comedy

If there are men who have never shown their ridiculous side, it is because it has never been properly looked for.[1]

François de La Rochefoucauld (1613–1680) was a consummate aristo-crat—urbane, witty, and rebellious. He fought and was twice wounded in the unsuccessful series of civil wars against French royal authority known as the Fronde. In his retirement, La Rochefoucauld wrote a collection of maxims that, depending on the reader's perspective, are either bitterly cynical or delightfully clear-eyed. Frankly, they are both, and the reader often feels the uncomfortable shock of recognition. La Rochefoucauld was a favorite of the German philosopher Friedrich Nietzsche, who adopted his style of condensing profound observations about human life, beliefs, and customs into compact and powerful aphorisms on which whole treatises of interpretation could be written.

La Rochefoucauld was a contemporary of the great comic playwright Jean-Baptiste Poquelin, known to us by his stage name, Molière. If ever there was a writer who searched out and revealed the ridiculous side of men and women, it was Molière. Yet, somehow, he never slides into cynicism or bitterness, not even in the so-called black comedies of his maturity—*The School for Wives, Tartuffe, Don Juan,* and *The Misan-thrope.* Molière was the creator of social comedy, in which affectations and pretensions rebound on those who would exempt themselves from common human fallibility. This is not farce—although there are elements

57

of farce in the stage business in each of the plays, no actual masks are worn, and the characters are not just types. Instead, they are forced to confront the vulnerability that connects them with others, whether they ultimately acknowledge it (Arnolphe, Orgon) or not (Don Juan, Alceste). Molière's plays thereby illustrate another of La Rochefoucauld's maxims: "We are so used to disguising ourselves from others that, in the end, we disguise ourselves from ourselves."[2]

The French scholar Jacques Guicharnaud has called Molière "the gravedigger of Descartes."[3] It is an apt remark. Descartes posited an autonomous soul that stands apart from the physical world and is the source of our moral value in an otherwise mechanistic universe. That soul is free and absolute, even though the world in which it acts is an unbroken sequence of causes and effects. Milton similarly thought that man's freedom is to be found in virtue, which is inspired by a love of God and, by extension, one's fellow human beings. We have weight and substance as individuals by the grace of God. For both thinkers, despite their many differences, God is the guarantor of our moral freedom and, hence, of our value as human beings.

But, for Molière, there is no guarantor. Both God and the immortal soul have dropped from sight. We exist in the world with others and do not have absolute value separate and apart from that existence. We determine our value in relation to others, and Molière is focused on exploring those relationships. That is not to say that Molière himself was an atheist or even an agnostic. He might well have had conventional religious beliefs. But, in his plays, religious devotion—at least in its extreme form— is just another human, social phenomenon ripe for satire.

Yet Molière's social comedies are a logical continuation of the line of thought that extends from Descartes through Milton. As we have seen, Descartes knew perfectly well that his mechanistic universe did not need to be underwritten by God. Its truths were discoverable by man using the mathematics of matter in motion. Descartes himself placed brackets around God and dropped him from the equations that described the workings of the world. Something similar happened to the "I" that thinks and therefore guarantees its own existence. That "I" is merely an abstraction, which has no distinguishing characteristics and cannot, intelligibly, break into the chain of material cause and effect. After the "I" plays its part in choosing God over the deceiving demon, the immortal soul with which the "I" is equated is quickly bracketed and plays no further role in Descartes's scientific study of the passions of actual men and women living in the world. For Milton, too, on a plausible reading, God and Satan are but elaborate metaphors warring for the soul of man. What justifies God's ways to man is man's own ability to love and choose virtue over hatred and evil.

Molière takes these views to their logical, secular conclusion. The social and moral order is created by man and in turn shapes what we have become. So Molière offers a purely human look at human society and morals. It is a world, as La Rochefoucauld is quick to point out, in which power is projected and imposed and in which we all play various roles. We are cast adrift from the metaphysical pillars that had long provided man with his sense of innate dignity. We do not have an absolute existence separate and apart from our social selves. Hence, the terrifying *cri de coeur* of Alceste: "Je veux qu'on me distingue." I want people to distinguish me, both in the sense of paying attention to me and in the sense of considering me as someone of value. What Molière's comic heroes crave is society's acknowledgment that they have somehow transcended the social order in which others are mired. They want to demonstrate an *intrinsic* value that sets them apart from the rest of humanity.

Their longing for transcendence could readily lend itself to tragedy, as it does for Molière's two great contemporary playwrights, Pierre Corneille and Jean Racine, whose heroes rely, respectively, on honor and passion to rise above the merely social.[4] Or it could lend itself to sardonic cynicism, as it does in La Rochefoucauld, who sees in virtue only a disguise for self-interest. Or it could even lead to a desperate, if retrograde, leap into religiosity, as it does in Pascal. In Molière, it gives us comedies that probe all the various ways in which we make ourselves inauthentic and ridiculous (Arnolphe, Alceste) or monsters of inhumanity (Orgon, Don Juan) in the quest for distinction. The probing is not gentle. The denouements are not always happy. As one critic notes, there are "no conversions" in Molière.[5] His comic heroes are unreconstructed, which makes them much closer to tragic heroes.

Indeed, Molière deliberately breaks down the hitherto clear demarcation between comedy and tragedy, and shows that even comedy can be cathartic of fear and pity.[6] A younger contemporary of Molière claimed that "la vie est une tragédie pour celui qui sent, et une comédie pour celui qui pense."[7] Life is a tragedy for those who feel and a comedy for those who think. Molière both thinks and feels. But Molière always sees the ridiculous side of heroic poses and grand passions. Molière cannot take men's pretentions seriously enough to rise to the level of tragic grandeur. In *The School for Wives*, he deliberately has Arnolphe adopt the pompous, highly wrought language of one of Corneille's tragic heroes.[8] But Arnolphe is a middle-aged bourgeois, hopelessly in love with and altogether unable to control his young ward. His self-consciously tragic stance inevitably evokes our laughter.

Yet Arnolphe can still be seen as almost touching in a certain light. He, like Molière's other comic protagonists, is never altogether absurd. Arnolphe actually does love his ward and is devastated that his own machinations have made that love impossible; Don Juan is generous and courageous even as he is carried off to a hell in which he doesn't believe; Alceste detests hypocrisy, yet his blunt honesty is exposed as a deeper form of deception. Orgon—who loses his soul and his humanity by turning both over to a fraudulent spiritual adviser—is a tougher sell, but we might be able to find redeeming qualities even in him.

In the end, Molière is a writer of comedies rather than tragedies because his ability to penetrate and expose social disguises exceeds even that of La Rochefoucauld. The social order of his day—which revolved around the all-powerful Sun King, Louis XIV—had become increasingly artificial and conventional over time and was thus a ripe source of satire. Molière saw that we continually disguise ourselves from one another and from ourselves. Like the layers of an onion, the disguises can be peeled back repeatedly. But there is no core. Beneath all the disguises, we are nothing. Or, rather, there is no "beneath." There is always another disguise.

And yet, if that is true, in what sense are these disguises? If we are just the sum total of our social roles, there is no absolute self that lies beneath, hidden and waiting to burst forth. There is no "there" there. The self is just an abstraction from its numerous presentations and, like Descartes's "I," drops out of the equation.

That does not mean, however, that our only choice is between a ridiculous pose and a tragic one. There is a role we can construct for ourselves that shuns both extremes, that of the *honnêtes homme*, a key concept in seventeenth-century France. The virtues of an *honnêtes homme* are modest and unheroic. He or she is decent and honorable; reasonable and tolerant; recognizes our common vulnerability and interdependence; and seeks to connect with others without dominating and deceiving them, or being dominated and deceived in turn. Chrysalde, in *The School for Wives*; Cléante, in *Tartuffe*; Philinte, in *The Misanthrope*; and Don Louis, in *Don Juan*, are largely free from the manias that possess Arnolphe, Orgon, Don Juan, and Alceste in their individual quests for distinction. The *honnête hommes* are not perfect, but they seek to speak the truth as best they can, which, in the context of a social order that thrives on deception, is actually quite heroic. Needless to say, however, they are almost always ineffectual. Obsession does not yield to reason, and the *honnête hommes* can sometimes appear weak and even bland in comparison to the antiheroes in these plays.

Montaigne noted of those seeking to transcend the merely human: "They want to get out of themselves and escape from the man. That is madness: instead of changing into angels, they change into beasts; instead of raising themselves, they lower themselves."[9] Molière would add that, instead of becoming heroic, they become comical. Our only business is living appropriately within the limits of human nature and human society. We can accept our flawed humanity and our need for intimate human connections with as much honesty and humor as we can muster. We can find ourselves and our value in others. La Rochefoucauld dismissed that idea as hopelessly naive. But Molière, while not blind to its difficulties, did not.

LIFE

Jean-Baptiste Poquelin was born on or about January 13, 1622, in Paris. He was christened after his father, but we will refer to him throughout simply as Molière, the name he adopted for the theater and which he made immortal.[10]

Molière's family was prosperous and solidly middle class. His father was an upholsterer and draper to the royal court. His mother, Marie, gave birth to three more children before dying of tuberculosis in 1632, when Molière was ten. The elder Jean-Baptiste mourned his wife but remarried a year later. Two half sisters followed before the second wife also died, leaving Jean-Baptiste to raise six children.

It is not surprising, therefore, that Molière grew close to his maternal grandfather, Louis Cressé, who was also an upholsterer and successful merchant. They shared a love of theater. Molière attended the parish school where he learned the rudiments of Latin. But his afternoon and early evening rambles with his grandfather exposed him to everything from jugglers and acrobats, through low farce to high tragedy. The Italian farces were Molière's favorite. Their stock characters were drawn frequently from the Roman playwright Plautus: military braggarts, clever servants, old misers, incompetent but arrogant doctors, and of course, always, young lovers and the insensitive parents who strive vainly to keep them apart. The farces displayed a broad cross section of society that Molière would make even broader in his own comedies.

Jean-Baptiste wanted Molière to leave school at the age of fourteen to learn the family business. But Molière hated the work and, with the support of his grandfather, was allowed to continue his education at the Jesuit Collège de Clermont. The school placed a heavy emphasis on the Latin language and the classics of Latin literature. The students even put on their own plays in Latin. They also learned mathematics, history, science, and even some Greek.

Molière spent five years at the Jesuit college. He mingled there with the sons of the nobility, though they had separate lodgings and classrooms. He practiced dancing and swordplay, which would come in very handy in his acting career. Thanks to a wealthy friend, he was also invited to join a small group that studied privately with Pierre Gassendi, the noted French scientist and mathematician who was also a proponent of Epicurean philosophy. Molière made time to visit the theaters whenever he could, though now in the company of his fellow students.

Molière earned a law degree in Orléans in 1641, but he practiced only briefly. His father arranged for him a position as royal valet to Louis XIII, which encompassed a variety of duties, including some confidential commissions and court intrigues. But, by 1643, Molière had had enough. He ceded his title of royal valet back to his father; he abandoned the law; and he rejected, once and for all, his future prospects as an upholsterer. Instead, he began acting in amateur theater productions. He became infatuated with the plays of Pierre Corneille (1606–1684), another recovering lawyer and already, at that time, the premier tragic playwright in France. He became even more infatuated with an actress, Madeleine Béjart, who was part of a small family troupe that had toured the provinces and was currently trying to survive in Paris.

As an actor, Molière aspired to tragedy, which was never his forte. He was not handsome, and he had a stutter and a voice that grew irritating when tuned to the pitch of tragic speeches. But he had broad and extremely mobile features and a lively sense of the many ways in which his fellow men made themselves ridiculous. He was born for comedy, not tragedy, though it took him many years and much heartache to accept and embrace that conclusion.

Actors had no social standing, and his respectable father was appalled by Molière's decision. It is said that Jean-Baptiste sent the parish priest to convince Molière to drop his silly ambitions. Yet, after a lengthy discussion about just why Molière loved the theater so much, the priest, too, decided to take up acting.

In June 1643, Molière took the money inherited from his mother and formed an acting company with the Béjart family. That is when he began using the name Molière. They leased an old building, a former tennis court, which they refurbished and named, with great hopes, the Illustre Théâtre. They performed a tragedy, perhaps one by Corneille. No one came except family members and friends who had received free tickets. They tried again and again: established tragedies, ballets, and newly commissioned plays. Nothing helped. The theater became insolvent, despite the acknowledged talent and great beauty of Madeleine Béjart. Molière was jailed for debt. The long-suffering Jean-Baptiste bailed him out, but the theater closed for good in 1645.

Neither Molière nor the Béjarts were prepared to give up on their theatrical dreams. They packed their theater into a cart and took to the road in hopes that the provinces would value their performances more than Paris did. It was a difficult life. They slept where they could and played where they might, using makeshift stages and curtains. Sometimes they were received at private castles; otherwise, they sought licenses for public performances in whichever provincial town they happened to alight. Eventually, they began to enjoy success and were in demand. Molière himself began to write plays, mostly one-act farces in the Italian style, in which he played the comic lead to great acclaim.

Two beautiful young women joined the troupe. Madeleine was relegated to lesser roles both in the plays and in Molière's life, as he took the newcomers in turn as his mistresses. Madeleine ably handled the finances and found romantic consolation elsewhere. They remained close friends and business partners until her death in 1672.

The company briefly enjoyed the support of a wealthy patron, the Prince de Conti, who had been at the Collège de Clermont at the same time as Molière. The troupe returned to Paris in 1658, twelve long years after its ignominious departure. The king's brother, Prince Philippe d'Orléans, replaced Conti as the troupe's principal patron. Conti had found religion and now condemned the theater as godless. But Philippe granted them a pension (which was never paid) and space at the Petit Bourbon, which they shared on alternating nights with an Italian troupe performing standard *commedia dell'arte*, filled with stock characters wearing masks. Molière, who was nothing if not stubborn, continued to produce and perform tragedies, particularly those of Corneille. But they were largely failures. The company enjoyed its greatest success only when it performed comedies, particularly those written by Molière himself. It received increasing patronage from Louis XIV, who was particularly fond of spectacles blending music, ballet, and comedy. The group was eventually dubbed "la Troupe du Roi" and was awarded a pension (which was paid).

Molière's first notable success was a one-act play, *Les Précieuses ridicules*, which translates as *The Precious Ladies Ridiculed* or *The Ridiculously Precious Ladies*. The play, presented in 1659, marked a critical first step in the transition from farce to social comedy. It satirizes two ladies from the provinces who speak in the affected, elaborate language of the most recent novels and who expect any courtship of them to be lengthy and fraught with romantic complications. They accordingly rebuff the two well-off but plain-spoken and simply dressed suitors chosen for them. The suitors are revenged by sending their lackeys—disguised as noblemen in overly ornate outfits and spouting extravagant nonsense—to woo the ladies.

The play drew widespread attention and incited the hostility of certain literary salons whose hostesses felt they were being targeted and ridiculed. This became a common theme. Molière would satirize the exaggerated and artificial behavior of certain sectors of society—jealous husbands, doctors, patients, society women, courtiers, social climbers, and even religious devotees. While those safely outside the groups in question laughed freely, others saw themselves in the fun house mirror he held up to them and were offended. Eventually, Molière managed to offend just about everyone except the king, who was of course—with one notable but subtle exception—beyond social satire, even for Molière.

Molière soon graduated to five-act comedies in verse designed to rival in stature and dramatic merit the tragedies of Corneille and Racine. Indeed, Molière's greatest comedies tell us more about the human condition, in all its vanities, than the somewhat stilted, one-dimensional period pieces of his two great contemporaries. Molière does not reach for the highest notes of tragedy, but his plays are a lot more fun and every bit as cathartic.

In the first of these five-act plays, *The School for Wives* (1662), Arnolphe, an otherwise sensible, intelligent, and prosperous man, is terrified of being cuckolded and thereby subject to ridicule. His solution has been to raise his ward, Agnès, from the age of four to become his ideal of the perfect wife. He has kept her in a convent with just enough education to say her prayers, spin, and sew. He has denied her the company of her contemporaries and left her ignorant of the broader world. Now that he is ready to marry her, he wants her to understand that she is wholly dependent upon his beneficence. She is to have no independent status as a human being; her entire identity is as his docile appendage.

Arnolphe, of course, succeeds only in making himself ridiculous and in guaranteeing his own failure. The innocent, seemingly naive Agnès readily thwarts his plan and asserts her own preference for Horace, the son of Arnolphe's close friend. Horace has made remarkable efforts to visit and woo Agnès in the house where she is kept a virtual prisoner, guarded over by two comically inept and readily bribable servants. The more she demonstrates her independence, the more Arnolphe falls in love with her, which seems never to have been part of his plan, since love entails risk and the possibility of pain. He even renounces his attempt to control her—"You shall have your wish in every way. / . . . Command, and I'll obey you"[11] —but it is too late, for Horace has won her heart. "He made me love him," she explains simply; "why didn't you do the same?"[12]

The School for Wives, like all of Molière's plays, engages in comic exaggeration. Yet Arnolphe is not a stock character. As one critic has noted, "Harlequin speaks to us of theater; Arnolphe speaks to us of man."[13] Arnolphe is an extreme case. He wants Agnès to be solely a reflection of his own needs and desires. But we all attempt more or less to control life and our relationships. Trust in others is risky. It can result in disappointment and humiliation. But we have no choice if we would not live in total isolation. Other people will always surprise us because they are separate from us, with their own needs, thoughts, feelings, and desires. The contingencies of life will not be controlled. In the end, we feel some sympathy with Arnolphe, but not much. Young love, like life, will not be denied.

It is ironic, though, that even as he was playing Arnolphe on the stage, Molière was acting a similar role in his own life. Molière fell hopelessly in love with Armande Béjart, known on the stage as Mademoiselle Menou. She was presented to the world as the younger sister of Madeleine Béjart but was, by common understanding, her illegitimate daughter. Armande was twenty; Molière was forty. A nasty rumor was spread that Armande was Molière's own daughter by his former lover. That is unlikely. Madeleine had many lovers through the years, and Armande appears to have been born before Madeleine became Molière's mistress. Still, it was an awkward arrangement at best. Armande treated Molière with a casualness that bordered on contempt. It was not a happy marriage, and Molière was definitely the cuckold that Arnolphe had feared to become. Was life imitating art or was art imitating life? Regardless, the king consented to be godfather to the couple's first son, Louis, which did much to quiet, if not silence, the mockery. Louis, unfortunately, died within a year. Molière, however, continued to court controversy in his three acknowledged masterpieces.

TARTUFFE

Our virtues are, most often, nothing more than disguised vices. [14]

Molière first read a three-act version of *Tartuffe* to the king in 1664. The king enjoyed it and did not anticipate the shock and condemnation that followed the first performance for the royal court at Versailles. Molière himself could hardly have been surprised. A particularly strict and dour variant of Catholicism was gaining influence in France. We will discuss Jansenism in the chapter on Pascal. But the Catholic revival extended more generally. *Les dévots*, as the revivalists were known, were religious zealots who, like their Puritan counterparts in England, wanted to shutter the theaters and otherwise to suppress both fun and free thought. Molière had already clashed with them more than once, and *Tartuffe*—an attack on religious hypocrisy and religious fanaticism—was his form of revenge.

Bowing to pressure, the king forbade Molière from mounting any public performances. Molière revamped the play and added two acts in 1667. But after a single public performance, the play was again banned. With further revisions, and the waning influence of *les dévots* at the royal court, Molière finally received the king's permission to perform the play in 1669. It may have helped that Molière made the king himself—presented as a wise prince who can see through impostures—the *deus ex machina* who resolves the plot. In the published version, Molière also added a seemingly conciliatory preface, which implied, however, that only those who were themselves religious hypocrites should have any objection to his attempt to distinguish true from false devotion.

Tartuffe was a singular success with the general public and is generally regarded as Molière's greatest play, though my own preference is for *The Misanthrope*. The central character is not the eponymous Tartuffe, however. He does not even appear until act 3. But he is the destructive force that has disrupted the lives of Orgon—a middle-aged, middle-class, and intellectually undistinguished bourgeois—and his family. Orgon has always been pious but sensible and fair to his children and his second wife, Elmire; until, that is, he experiences a midlife crisis. Afraid of losing his natural powers and sinking into insignificance, Orgon chooses to reassert his value and set himself apart from the rest of society through a display of religious zeal. He becomes a *dévot*. The zeal is genuine but extreme. And, disastrously, Orgon chooses Tartuffe as his spiritual guide.

Tartuffe is a thoroughly despicable con man, rather like Chaucer's Pardoner, though lively, manipulative, and verbally adept enough that he also shares traits with the Wife of Bath and Shakespeare's Falstaff.[15] Tartuffe revels in his own hypocrisy. Religion is simply his chosen disguise and humility, his modus operandi. He recognized his mark the instant he saw Orgon at church. Dressed in shabby clothes and presenting a humble manner, Tartuffe made a display of his devotion, weeping and sighing on his knees. Yet he ran to the church door whenever Orgon was leaving in order to offer him holy water. Orgon began to give him gifts, which Tartuffe pretended to resist, and accepted only in order to give half to the poor. Ultimately, Orgon took Tartuffe into his home and installed him as his *directeur de conscience*, somewhat as a novice monk would submit completely to the spiritual direction of the abbot. The importance and power of a spiritual director was a central feature of Jansenism.

Tartuffe becomes Orgon's obsession. When Orgon returns from a journey, his only concern is with Tartuffe, and he continually interrupts an account of his wife's serious illness, interjecting, "Ah. And Tartuffe?"[16] Orgon tries to enhance his own worth by exalting that of Tartuffe. Orgon can praise and honor himself without appearing to do so, by praising and honoring Tartuffe.[17] By making Tartuffe the ultimate authority, and himself merely the instrument of that authority, Orgon can assert tyrannical power over his household. So, too, can Orgon's mother, Madame Pernelle, who joins him in the cult of Tartuffe.

But Orgon and his mother cannot see what is obvious to everyone else: that Tartuffe is a fraud and neither pious nor devout. He may be Tartuffe's dupe, but Orgon is equally culpable in his blindness and his unhealthy religiosity. He has invested all his own value in his relationship with Tartuffe. Tartuffe has tipped Orgon over the edge, from devotion into mania.[18]

Orgon even insists on breaking off the promised engagement of his daughter, Mariane, to a young man she loves so that she may be betrothed instead to Tartuffe. He commands her to state, like a catechism, that she is fond of Tartuffe and would rejoice to be his wife. When Mariane asks why she should say something that is so clearly false, he responds like every fanatic: "Because I am resolved it shall be true."[19]

This fanaticism is both unnatural and inhuman. It is destructive of Orgon's family and his household. When his brother-in-law, Cléante, urges that a true Christian spirit is moderate and humane, Orgon is dismissive. Thanks to Tartuffe, he is a changed man:

> Under his tutelage my soul's been freed
> From earthly loves, and every human tie:
> My mother, children, brother, and wife could die,
> And I'd not feel a single moment's pain.[20]

Cléante is so appalled by this indifference, he can respond only with sarcasm: "Les sentiments humains, mon frère, que voilà!" (Those are fine sentiments for a human being!)[21]

Yet Orgon is all but quoting from the New Testament. In Luke 14:26, Jesus says, "Whoever comes to me and does not hate father and mother, wife and children, brothers and sisters, yes, and even life itself, cannot be my disciple." That injunction is only slightly softened in Matthew 10:37:

"Whoever loves father or mother more than me is not worthy of me; and whoever loves son or daughter more than me is not worthy of me."

We can readily see why *les dévots* hated this play. It was not so much because Tartuffe is an imposter and a *faux dévot*, but because Orgon is a *vrai dévot*, whose extreme and morbid religiosity is exposed as inhuman. Cléante, and by extension Molière, purports to judge the Bible by the standards of an *honnête homme* and finds it wanting. Extremism is bad, even in the purported service of religion. Orgon misuses the authority of scripture to justify outrageous tyranny over his own family.[22] Such is the way of all ideological fanatics. They lose sight of their humanity and ignore the humanity of others. As Montaigne pointed out, they strive to be angels and end up as beasts.

Cléante is the voice of philosophical moderation:

> Ah, Brother, man's a strangely fashioned creature
> Who seldom is content to follow Nature,
> But recklessly pursues his inclination
> Beyond the narrow bounds of moderation,
> And often, by transgressing Reason's laws,
> Perverts a lofty aim or noble cause.[23]

Dorine, the comically plain-spoken servant, is blunter in confronting Orgon's foolish blindness. But neither is effective. Both are simply dismissed and ignored. The same is true for Orgon's hotheaded son, Damis, and his too-pliant daughter, Mariane, who cannot bring herself actively to oppose her father but vows suicide if forced to marry Tartuffe. Only Orgon's second wife, Elmire, succeeds in shocking Orgon out of his abject devotion to Tartuffe. And she does so through cleverness and guile, using disguise to reveal truth, as Molière himself does.

Tartuffe may be willing to marry the daughter, but his real desire is to bed the wife. "Pour être dévot," he explains to Elmire, "je n'en suis pas moins homme" (To be a *dévot*, I don't have to be less human)[24]—a proposition he confirms by justifying his lust in religious terms:

> L'amour qui nous attache aux beautés éternelles
> N'étouffe pas en nous l'amour des temporelles;
> Nos sens facilement peuvent être charmés
> Des ouvrages parfaits que le Ciel a formés.
>
> (The love that attaches us to eternal beauty
> Does not extinguish our love for temporal things;

> Our senses are easily charmed
> By the perfect works heaven has formed.)[25]

He further assures Elmire that the apparent wickedness of his actions is redeemed by the purity of his intentions. That is to say, he can always reconcile his conscience to his desires.[26]

Damis overhears this exchange and immediately confronts his father and Tartuffe with Tartuffe's attempted seduction. But Orgon refuses to believe either Damis or Elmire. Tartuffe turns the situation to his advantage by openly confessing to being a wretched sinner, refusing to defend himself, and even urging Orgon to pardon his son, all the while implying that he, Tartuffe, is the victim of jealous lies. This apparent display of piety and nobility drives Orgon into such a frenzy that he disinherits his family and turns his house and all his property over to Tartuffe. "Be firm, my soul," Orgon chides himself. "No human weakness now."[27] He then tells his daughter that the more she loathes Tartuffe, the better it will be for her soul. "Marry Tartuffe, and mortify your flesh!"[28] Orgon has become genuinely deranged and thoroughly loathsome.

But Tartuffe has overreached. He has boasted to Elmire: "Et je l'ai mis au point de voir tout sans rien croire" (I have brought [Orgon] to the point where he can see everything without believing anything).[29] That gives her an idea. She somehow convinces Orgon to conceal himself under a table while she confronts Tartuffe. Why Orgon agrees is unclear. Perhaps he harbors some doubts of his own, as he will later claim; more likely, he seeks triumphant proof of the integrity of Tartuffe and, hence, of his own superiority. Regardless, in one of the great comic scenes of the theater, Orgon crouches in stupefied paralysis while Tartuffe more and more aggressively and physically imposes himself on Elmire, all the while making disparaging remarks about her useful idiot of a husband.

Orgon is, quite literally, about to see everything without doing anything. Elmire finally coaxes (or, depending on the stage directions, drags) Orgon from his hiding spot, and he confronts Tartuffe. But it is too late. Ordered out of the house, Tartuffe self-righteously points out that it is now, by God's will, his house and that he will not be driven from it by a contemptible conspiracy. It is for Orgon and his family to leave. And that would be the end of the matter but for the timely intervention of the Sun King. His representative, called upon by Tartuffe to evict Orgon, instead arrests Tartuffe, explaining that the king had recognized him as a notorious criminal by another name:

> We serve a Prince to whom all sham is hateful,
> A Prince who sees into our inmost hearts,
> And can't be fooled by any trickster's arts.
> His royal soul, though generous and human,
> Views all things with discernment and acumen;
> His sovereign reason is not lightly swayed,
> And all his judgments are discreetly weighed. [30]

Even by the standards of the Greek playwright Euripides, who made frequent use of a *deus ex machina* to end his plays, it is a shockingly sudden and unexpected denouement. But the play was a comedy and therefore needed a happy ending. And the lengthy paean to the Sun King, who, in his wisdom, sees all and resolves all undoubtedly helped in lifting the interdiction on performance. In a sense, Orgon is France itself, seized and controlled by *les dévots*, who usurped its patrimony and disrupted normal human relationships, before the king finally imposed order and moderation on a country sorely in need of both. During the late civil war, we are told, Orgon served the king and developed a reputation for both wisdom and courage. France is now restored to its senses.

Yet a modern reader cannot but see a certain amount of irony in the treatment of the king's intervention.[31] The extravagant praise seems overblown, as if the king were all-good, all-seeing, and all-powerful, like God himself. Molière underscores this point by giving Tartuffe a short speech—before he knows that the king will turn on him—that echoes Orgon's own remarks about putting God ahead of family.

> My first duty is to serve my King.
> That obligation is so paramount
> That other claims, beside it, do not count;
> And for it I would sacrifice my wife,
> My family, my friend, or my own life. [32]

Molière is evidently, if subtly, drawing a parallel between extreme religiosity and the political worship of a sovereign. One god has been replaced by another. Fanaticism, whether religious, political, or moral, is always suspect. It is a means of asserting power over others that is destructive of family and community. We must make our own judgments based on a healthy and moderate use of human reason. But, as Molière himself shows repeatedly in his plays, the *honnêtes hommes*, however wise, are often ineffective on their own. They need cleverness and even subterfuge to convey their truth and to keep themselves from becoming the victims of others' ideologies. It is a fine line to dance, but Molière is the master.

Perhaps Louis XIV believed his own hype and simply accepted the praise as his natural due. Or perhaps he recognized the mild satire at his own expense and even allowed himself to smile ever so slightly. It would be nice to think so, however unlikely.

DON JUAN

> *No one deserves praise for goodness if he doesn't have the strength to be evil: almost all other goodness is just laziness or weakness of will.*[33]

Molière did not shrink from renewed controversy in his next play. *Don Juan*, first performed in 1665, was a popular success. Yet it was banned after only fifteen performances. If anything, *les dévots* were even more outraged at a play that seemed to celebrate a thoroughly immoral atheist. Don Juan meets a bad end, but he is defiant and unrepentant, and his final downfall is more comical than cathartic.

In some ways, *Don Juan* is a "companion piece" to *Tartuffe*.[34] Orgon, in his extreme credulity, slavishly attaches himself to Tartuffe and upends the duties he owes to others. He becomes a monster and a tyrant in the name of religious devotion. Don Juan is an extreme skeptic. As his valet Sganarelle notes, he doesn't believe in heaven or hell.[35] Yet he is as great a monster as Orgon; indeed, he is worse, because his noble status and enormous talents allow him to trample on those around him with impunity.

Don Juan, like Milton's Satan, is driven by pride and will. He has *la force d'être méchant*, the strength to be evil, and he fears neither earthly nor heavenly sanction. He is a *libertin*, a free thinker. "But one has to believe in something," Sganarelle insists; "what is it that you believe?" "I believe that two and two are four, Sganarelle, and that four and four are eight." "What a fine creed that is! So far as I can see, your religion consists of arithmetic."[36] Don Juan is making deliberate reference to Descartes's new science grounded in mathematics. But, unlike Descartes, Don Juan accepts neither God as a guarantor of that science nor the immortal soul as the foundation of morality. He acknowledges the mathematics of the material world but rejects all religious, moral, and social conventions as empty formalities, as ties that bind only those who are too lazy or too weak to work their will upon the world. Sganarelle accurately summarizes the Don's views: "Nothing matters in this life but getting what one wants."[37] Don Juan was an advocate of the will to power long before Nietzsche.

Blaise Pascal will ask somewhat plaintively just a few years later: "N'aurons-nous donc pas de règle?"[38] Will we, then, have no rule? Is everything to be permitted? Don Juan has already answered that question with an emphatic "yes." He has taken Enlightenment thought to its radical extreme. Small wonder that Sganarelle says, after Don Juan attempts to justify his immorality, "You talk just like a book."[39] Don Juan's libertinage has replaced Orgon's catechism but is every bit as extreme and inhuman. He wants to see himself, and others to see him, as a man free of all cant, including the belief that we have moral obligations to other people. Two plus two equals four. Everything else is pious nonsense.

Without any restraint imposed by religion or morality or even social convention, Don Juan views other people simply as instruments of, or obstacles to, his will. He is capable of no genuine connection. His pleasure lies only in the dominance of seduction. "Once one is the master," he explains, "there's nothing more to say or wish for: the joy of passionate pursuit is over, and all that remains is the boredom of a placid affection."[40] He likens himself to a conquering general "who moves on forever from victory to victory, and will set no limit to his longings."[41] Sganarelle knows his master well: "Your heart is the most restless thing in the world; it likes to slither from one sacred bond to another, and it can't bear to settle in one place."[42] Don Juan does not acknowledge the sacred. Nothing and no one has absolute value, and no one, therefore, is worthy of respect and consideration except insofar as he, too, can impose himself on the world. The most sacred human bond—the intimate connection of man and wife—is employed by Don Juan simply as a tool of his seductions and is discarded without concern or regret.

Other characters, such as Donna Elvira, Don Luis, and Don Carlos, are driven by established codes of conduct. Don Juan ridicules these codes and rightly points out their artificiality and their remoteness from natural human desires and even beliefs. They are merely conventional, not essential to one's being. And they are too often deployed hypocritically. Yet these codes sustain the characters and give them a certain solidity and stability. By rejecting all such codes, Don Juan deprives himself of a similar solidity and stability. If all that matters is getting what one wants, then nothing actually matters. If everything is permitted, then nothing has value, including himself. Don Juan, despite his rigorous logic, attempts to flee from that conclusion. He mocks religion; he mocks honesty; he affronts chastity; he cannot abide intimate relationships between others because he is intimate with no one. Don Juan is a libertine, but not a carefree one. With no internal sense of value, no essential being, he must create and project an image of himself on the world that commands attention. His self-assertion and self-aggrandizement are all directed toward that end.

In many respects, Don Juan mimics the model courtier. He is handsome, daring, courageous, and charismatic. He has intellect and wit. He is a master swordsman. We can admire him in those respects, as many later writers and thinkers did. Even the way Don Juan flouts accepted morals with such utter insouciance has its appeal. He correctly recognizes that the code of nobility and chivalry, suitable to his position, is too often a sham. But he needs to replace it with something that will have the same effect, something that will make him stand out and force others to recognize his unique value. Despite his deliberate show of indifference, Don Juan is obsessed with how others see him, particularly Sganarelle, with whom he maintains a running commentary on all his actions. Don Juan needs an audience to validate his own sense of superiority because he is nothing but his public persona. He defines himself only in a series of encounters. Hollow at the core, his existence is aimless. He floats from one picaresque adventure to another. Like a shark, he must keep moving or die.

Yet Don Juan's exalted sense of self is at odds with the pettiness, even nastiness, of his actual encounters. He sees a young couple in love. Because such shared happiness is impossible for him, Don Juan finds it intolerable and immediately begins plotting to "mar their felicity, and disrupt a union which it pained my heart to behold."[43] Driven by bitter envy, he plans to abduct the bride-to-be while she is out sailing with her fiancé. That plan fails when the boat he has chartered sinks, and he and Sganarelle have to be ignominiously rescued from the sea by two peasants. Unfazed, Don Juan begins to make love to two different peasant girls on shore, promising marriage to each; when they both confront him, he somehow manages to convince each that she is his true love while the other is a delusional stalker. He shows equal wit in so befuddling a creditor that the hapless merchant is rendered incapable of even asking for his money.

These are funny scenes, but they are far from displaying Don Juan as the heroic *libertin* he imagines himself to be. Even amid his own class, the meanness of his actions is clear. He has no religious scruples in luring Donna Elvira from her convent with a sham marriage and professions of undying love. But he quickly tires of her and claims remorse at leading her to violate her sacred vows as the bride of Christ. "I now saw how our marriage was nothing but an adultery in disguise, that it would bring down some dire punishment on our heads, and that I must therefore try to forget you, and let you return to your first commitment."[44] Donna Elvira, unlike the peasant girls, knows he is lying to her and foretells divine punishment, at which he scoffs. Yet, when she tries to purge herself of any earthly passion, Don Juan is again attracted to her: "Her careless dress, her languishing look, her tears stirred up in me a few small embers of a dead fire."[45] He invites her to stay, but she flees back to her convent. She still loves Don Juan and, hence, fears his power over her.

Donna Elvira's brothers are another story. They are driven to avenge the sleight to their sister by what Don Carlos, who would rather be occupied with his own affairs, calls "the tyranny of honor."[46] But they can't agree on just what honor requires. Don Juan intervenes when Don Carlos is set upon by a band of robbers. Don Carlos insists that they must thereby refrain from killing Don Juan for a few days in order to repay him for saving his life. Then they can kill him. The hotheaded Don Alonso insists equally that honor is more precious than life and that it is "utter folly" to defer vindicating their honor "for the sake of a fancied obligation!"[47] The two brothers comically debate the finer points of what honor requires and are even prepared to cross swords over the question. Yet both ignore the reality that Donna Elvira herself might be better off in a convent. Don Juan is a thoroughgoing scoundrel, but the brothers agree on one thing: "[Their] honor demands that she live with [him]."[48]

Don Juan's father, Don Luis, also insists on one thing: that "virtue is our best claim to nobility."[49] He threatens to cut off Don Juan and strip him of his noble rank unless he reforms. Since his status as a nobleman is what allows Don Juan to get away with his many crimes, he resolves to renounce his sinful ways "and embark on an exemplary mode of life."[50] Don Luis is delighted: "Ah, my dear son, how readily a father's love can be restored, and how quickly a few words of repentance can make a son's offenses vanish!"[51] It doesn't seem to matter to Don Luis that Don Juan has no intention of fulfilling this promise any more than the others he has made. His reformation is just "a prudent strategy of deception which I'm forced to adopt," as he explains to Sganarelle.[52] La Rochefoucauld wrote: "Hypocrisy is the homage vice pays to virtue."[53] Going one step further, Don Juan contends that "hypocrisy is now a fashionable vice, and all fashionable vices pass for virtues."[54]

Donna Elvira has returned to the convent, yet her earthly love for Don Juan has not been purged. Don Carlos and Don Alonso are driven by concepts of honor that are artificial and readily manipulated to suit their own ends. Don Luis longs only for the appearance of nobility, which his son can wear like a mask. Surely, Don Juan is justified in finding considerable hypocrisy in these codes and conventions. But he misses altogether the human element that underwrites them.

That failure is clear in his encounter with *le pauvre*, a poor hermit who dedicates his life to prayer and offers to pray for Don Juan. The Don scoffs. *Le pauvre* should pray for a warm coat and not trouble himself about the needs of others. What is the point of praying all day if he lives in utter privation? "It's strange that you should be so shabbily rewarded for all your trouble."[55] To prove his point, Don Juan offers *le pauvre* a gold Louis if he will blaspheme. But he refuses, despite the Don's insistence. Flummoxed by the refusal—by his encounter with a sincerely religious man who would rather starve than take the Lord's name in vain—Don Juan finally gives him the coin regardless, not for the love of God but "for the love of humanity."[56] Don Juan appears to be paying tribute to the one person he has met who is neither hypocritical nor self-interested. But Don Juan doesn't love humanity any more than he loves God. So the gesture is really just another way for him to save face and assert his superiority. *Le pauvre* threatens Don Juan's entire worldview.

Don Juan's fatal encounter with the statue of the Commander is to the same effect. Before Don Juan killed him, the Commander had commissioned a huge, gaudy mausoleum that included a statue of himself dressed as a Roman emperor. It is a monument to his own vanity, and a welcome confirmation of Don Juan's cynicism. Yet Don Juan is attempting to do the same: to create a magnificent self-image to dazzle the world. And his creation is every bit as lifeless and inhuman as the Commander's statue. Thus, when the statue nods its head at Don Juan's irreverent and facetious invitation to dinner, the statue and the Don are meeting on even terms.

Like Orgon, Don Juan's philosophy has "brought him to the point where he can see everything without believing anything." There is more in heaven and earth than is dreamt of in Don Juan's Cartesian mechanical philosophy. "So much for your free-thinkers, who won't believe in anything," Sganarelle mutters.[57] Yet the statue is not a manifestation of divine justice; it is a comic manifestation of poetic justice, of punishment as theatrical necessity. Don Juan's unwillingness and inability to recognize the humanity in others has finally caught up to him. His fatal handshake with the statue is a *reductio ad absurdum* of his relationships with others. "Whatever may happen," he proclaims, "it won't be said of me that I stooped to repentance."[58] He is consumed in flames and swallowed up by a hell of his own making in which he has steadfastly refused to believe. Small wonder that *les dévots* found nothing to their liking in this denouement. Even if radical skepticism meets a harsh end, traditional religion is not thereby affirmed.

Poor Sganarelle finds even less to like in his master's end. In many respects, Sganarelle is a Sancho Panza figure. He prefers snuff to philosophy. He embodies common sense and lowly wisdom. He even spews out a torrent of proverbs in an incoherent but highly comical attempt to convince Don Juan that he must repent his wicked life.[59] And, like Don Quixote, Don Juan feels compelled to explain his actions and his philosophy to Sganarelle. "I take you into my confidence, Sganarelle, because it pleases me that someone should know my true feelings, and the reasons which compel me to act as I do."[60] But the resemblance ends there. Sancho Panza loves Don Quixote in all his touching absurdity. It is said that no man is a hero to his valet, but Don Quixote is an unlikely hero to Sancho. They reaffirm and reinforce the humanity in each other. Don Juan needs to believe that he is likewise a hero to Sganarelle. He uses Sganarelle as a mirror of his own magnificence and expects to dazzle him with his superiority to the common run of mortals. But there is no human connection between the two of them. Don Juan recognizes neither his own nor Sganarelle's humanity. Sganarelle is just a spectator of the mausoleum that Don Juan is constructing for himself. Small wonder, then, that Sganarelle views their relationship in the same self-interested terms as Don Juan. He is concerned not with his master's fate but only with his own loss. "Oh! My back wages! . . . My wages! Who'll pay me my wages?"[61] It is the final deflation of Don Juan's self-deluded attempt to portray himself as a *libertin* hero of the Enlightenment.

Donna Elvira, Don Carlos, and Don Luis are all flawed human beings. But they recognize that, however fraught with uncertainty and contingency, trusting relationships based on mutual interest and desire are essential to happiness and that moral codes and social conventions, however flawed and artificial they might seem, are essential to such relationships. Dogmatism leads to intolerance and fanaticism. But so, too, does nihilistic skepticism. Restrictions on unbridled license are not a manifestation of weakness but of strength. The greater the power, the greater the obligation. As Sganarelle notes, "a great lord who's a wicked man is a frightening thing."[62] Don Juan is no more a hero than Orgon or, as we will see, than Alceste, though Alceste will lay the best claim yet.

THE MISANTHROPE

> *Self-interest speaks many languages and plays many parts, even that of disinterest.*[63]

Just as *Don Juan* can be considered a "companion piece" to *Tartuffe*, *The Misanthrope* has the same upside-down relationship with *Don Juan*. Don Juan trumpets his superiority to others by trampling on social and moral conventions. His vice feeds his vanity. Alceste asserts his superiority by being an absolute stickler for honesty and integrity. His virtue feeds his vanity. Alceste is quite explicit on this point: "Je veux qu'on me distingue."[64] I want to be distinguished. I want others to single me out as a person of singular merit. And, to some extent, he is. Éliante, who loves Alceste in vain, speaks of his "noble, heroic side."[65] Two other women— the coquettish Célimène and the prudish Arsinoé—are each ready to marry him. Oronte seeks his acquaintance and good opinion based on his high reputation. And Philinte, the paradigm of an *honnête homme*, is his most loyal friend.

But, in Molière, virtue carried to its extreme becomes a vice or at least ridiculous. And Alceste repeatedly makes himself ridiculous. He vociferously condemns not just the greater evils of judicial corruption and intimate betrayal, but even the small social lies of convenience and politeness. He must find fault with everyone and everything as a way of advertising his own merit.

All are corrupt; there's nothing to be seen

> In court or town but aggravates my spleen.
> I fall into deep gloom and melancholy
> When I survey the scene of human folly,
> Finding on every hand base flattery,
> Injustice, fraud, self-interest, treachery. . . .
> Ah, it's too much; mankind has grown so base,
> I mean to break with the whole human race. [66]

Alceste is virtuous where Don Juan is vicious. But they share the same underlying malady: each is incapable of forming intimate connections with other people because of his own egotism. Relationships require trust and compromise, and neither Don Juan nor Alceste is willing to make himself vulnerable to others. Alceste insulates himself against disappointment by anticipating and seizing upon the worst in others. Like Don Juan, his true character manifests itself in a series of encounters in which he deliberately refuses to recognize the humanity of other people and, at the same time, prevents others from breaking through his facade and touching him on a human level. He is not a misanthrope because he finds others wanting. Rather, he finds others wanting in order to justify his misanthropy and to nurture his sense of superiority. Alceste cannot be happy unless he is unhappy. It is a profound psychological portrait of our inherent perverseness. And yet, again like Don Juan, Alceste is charismatic precisely because he sets himself apart from others. And we find him moving because, despite himself, he cannot entirely erase his own vulnerability. "Je veux qu'on me distingue" is not just an assertion of merit; it is also the cry of an inner child who is deeply wounded by a world that does not sufficiently acknowledge that merit.

Alceste's opening dialogue with Philinte sets the tone for his other encounters. Alceste is furious with the mild Philinte for "falsify[ing his] heart's affections" by displays of friendship for people to whom he is otherwise indifferent. [67] He condemns as grave crimes all "protestations," "meaningless embraces," "obliging commonplaces," and any form of flattery and unwarranted praise. [68] When Philinte defends such "outward courtesies" as necessary to social life, Alceste will have none of it:

> Ah, no! We should condemn with all our force
> Such false and artificial intercourse.
> Let men behave like men; let them display
> Their inmost hearts in everything they say;
> Let the heart speak, and let our sentiments

Not mask themselves in silly compliments. [69]

Admirable sincerity, we might think. Until, that is, we think about what such ruthless candor would actually mean to social discourse. Alceste is not wrong about the falsity and corruption of polite society. But he is incapable of distinguishing between the trivial and the grave. As Philinte points out, as gently as possible, Alceste has made himself comical with a fury all out of proportion to its cause. He has become a crank, ranting against the manners of the age. Philinte, by contrast, is the voice of moderation:

> This world requires a pliant rectitude;
> Too stern a virtue makes one stiff and rude;
> Good sense views all extremes with detestation,
> And bids us to be noble in moderation.
> . . .
> I take men as they are, or let them be,
> And teach my soul to bear their frailty;
> And whether in court or town, whatever the scene,
> My phlegm's as philosophic as your spleen. [70]

Une vertu traitable is what Philinte advocates, a manageable or pliant virtue, a virtue one can live with. But is moderation in the pursuit of virtue itself a virtue? That is part of what the play asks. Should we compromise our own honesty and integrity in going along to get along, in mildly taking "les hommes comme ils sont"?[71] Is Philinte gently wise or weakly pliant? Is Alceste admirably uncompromising or simply insufferable? The beautiful ambiguity of the play is that each is both at the same time.

Both characters are further revealed in their encounter with Oronte, who has written a breezy sonnet in the modern style to Célimène, thinly disguised as the *Belle Philis*. Philinte deems the sonnet, which alternates between expressions of hope and despair, "exquisite—full of feeling and grace."[72] Alceste, reluctant to criticize the sonnet directly but unwilling to offer any praise, talks of advice he gave to another would-be poet who embarrassed himself with some execrable verses. Oronte repeatedly applies the criticisms to himself, and Alceste just as repeatedly responds, "Je ne dis pas cela; mais . . ." (I don't say that, but . . .), and then piles on even more opprobrium. Oronte grows incensed, Alceste openly insults him, and Philinte must step between them. It is a wonderfully comic scene. Philinte's extravagant praise is insincere. But Alceste is needlessly provocative and, driven in part by his jealous attachment to Célimène, hardly a disinterested critic. Alceste always perceives the self-interest of others but is blind to his own.

Even more interesting are the different reactions of Alceste and Philinte to a pending court case in which Alceste is engaged. His adversary is a scoundrel who nonetheless has significant interest at court. Philinte urges Alceste to lobby the judges and to engage someone with influence to plead his cause. But Alceste will do no such thing. "Must honor bow to guile?" he asks.[73] No. The merits of his position are clear, and he expects "right and justice" to plead for him.[74] Philinte is horrified. But Alceste is adamant. Indeed, he actually hopes to lose his case as further proof of the villainy of his fellow men:

> Oh, I could wish, whatever the cost,
> Just for the beauty of it, that my trial were lost.[75]

The case is indeed lost, and Alceste could not be more pleased at his own misfortune. He will gladly pay the amount lost in the suit because he "gain[s] thereby / The right to storm and rage at human evil."[76]

Most perverse of all, though, is Alceste's love for Célimène, a wickedly funny, beautiful coquette who keeps several men at once paying court to her, in the alternate states of hope and despair noted by Oronte. Célimène is the anti-Alceste. She professes extravagant affection for others in society and then, egged on by her courtiers, skewers them behind their backs with biting wit. She is the embodiment of the courtly dissembling and artificial manners of the age that Alceste despises. And yet, he loves her.

In one sense, of course, Célimène is just another excuse, like his legal case, for Alceste to despise the world. Yet he feels, and we as audience are meant to feel, her charm. She is alive and vibrant; she is funny and smart; she is beautiful and beguiling. Alceste, who lacks the "art of telling pleasant lies,"[77] nonetheless seeks such lies from Célimène: "Pretend, pretend, that you are just and true," he pleads with her, "and I shall make myself believe in you."[78] In a rare moment of vulnerability, Alceste admits that he has entrusted his happiness to her.[79]

The full extent of Célimène's falsity is revealed when some of her correspondence is read aloud. In it, she mocks all of the would-be lovers circling about her like moths to a flame, including Alceste. The other suitors leave in disgust, renouncing Célimène. But Alceste does not. Acknowledging "how strange the human heart is, and how far / From rational we sorry creatures are,"[80] Alceste proposes marriage to Célimène. But he imposes one condition: they must flee from society and live together in isolation, far from town and court. Célimène refuses. She is willing to marry Alceste, but she would die of boredom in a remote hermitage. In her own moment of candor, she admits that she is terrified of solitude: "I fear I lack the force / And depth of soul to take so stern a course."[81]

In the end, Alceste and Célimène are alike. Each constructs a self-image that is dependent on the opinion of others. Alceste asserts his unique superiority by denigrating his fellows for their lack of honesty and integrity. Célimène asserts her unique superiority by attracting a bevy of admirers with her coquetry and wit. Célimène is fully aware of the insincerity of her life but fears any alternative. She craves the attention she gets from flirting with multiple men. That is the measure of her value. She wants lovers to exalt herself in her own eyes and in those of the public, just as Alceste wants admirers of a different sort.

Alceste's cry—"Je veux qu'on me distingue"—is also that of Célimène. Neither can make a genuine commitment to another human being. Alceste has imposed on Célimène the one condition to which he knows she cannot agree. He has entrusted his happiness to one he knows will disappoint him. He can now act the tragic hero he has always considered himself to be:

> Betrayed and wronged in everything,
> I'll flee this bitter world where vice is king,
> And seek some spot unpeopled and apart
> Where I'll be free to have an honest heart.[82]

It is both touching and absurd, both moving and risible. The deep-seated ambiguity of the human psyche and the inherent difficulty of an intimate relationship between two such self-interested people is never resolved, at least not by Alceste and Célimène.

Éliante and Philinte have a presumptively happier ending. Rejected by Alceste, Éliante offers her hand to Philinte, who has long loved her. Theirs is not the "unrewarded, mad, and bitter love" of Alceste.[83] It is milder, quieter, and more pliant. That bodes well for their contentment. They are both fundamentally decent people open to the complexity of human relationships. They try to engage with each other on a human rather than purely conventional level. Each recognizes the other's inherent, not merely social, value. But there is a distinct element of compromise in their relationship. It is more comfortable than passionate. Both are still drawn to the uncompromising Alceste and resolve to reconcile him to humanity, which of course is bound to prove hopeless.

The Misanthrope is neither farce nor tragedy but—like Tartuffe and Don Juan—a new and deeply problematic kind of social comedy, one that calls society itself into question. Alceste's criticisms are over the top (which makes them funny) but not unjustified (which makes them poignant).[84] We are torn between laughing at his posturing and agreeing with his indictment of a world in which casual dishonesty is so commonplace as to be part of the currency of everyday life, in which justice is for sale, and in which love is too often a form of competition and self-aggrandizement—in other words, a society much like our own. Alceste's dreams of a more honest world remain unrealized and likely unrealizable.[85] There is no order of grace of the sort on which Milton grounded his faith and his hope.

"Mon flegme est philosophe autant que votre bile" (My phlegm is as philosophic as your spleen), Philinte insists.[86] Philinte, following Montaigne, preaches the wisdom of moderation and forgiveness. Life is not perfect, he seems to say, but it doesn't have to be tragic. Is that Molière's view as well? Perhaps. Many critics identify Molière with Philinte, Éliante, and the other admirable honnêtes hommes in his plays. He found fuel for comedy in the extremes of human folly, pretention, and self-interest, extremes that make his honnêtes hommes appear to advantage. But we must always remember that Molière also made Tartuffe, Don Juan, Alceste, and Célimène his most compelling characters. Like Shakespeare, his own views and beliefs are elusive. As Raymond Picard notes in his indispensable if brief history of French literature from 1600 to 1800, "man is always more important than concepts for Molière."[87]

Molière died as he lived, in the theater. He collapsed on stage at the conclusion of the fourth performance of The Imaginary Invalid in 1673, a play that, like his earlier Doctor in Spite of Himself, portrayed doctors as mountebanks who use pomp and circumstance and obscure language to disguise their lack of actual knowledge and skill. It is said that no doctor would agree to treat Molière. The parish priests also refused to come to the dying man's bedside. Since he received neither confession nor absolution, Molière was allowed a Christian burial only by intercession of the king. He was interred at night in a section of the parish cemetery reserved for suicides and unbaptized children. A crowd of two hundred people carrying torches—many of them actors and poets—escorted the body. His remains were later transferred, first, to a gaudy mausoleum in the Museum of French Monuments and, later, to a solemn tomb in the Père Lachaise Cemetery. But no one really knew exactly where in the parish graveyard he was buried. So the remains, twice transferred with pomp and circumstance and many solemn words about one of France's greatest sons, may be those of a complete unknown. Molière would have appreciated the joke.

4

PASCAL AND THE HIDDEN GOD

We sail within a vast sphere, ever drifting in uncertainty, driven from end to end. When we think to attach ourselves to any point and to fasten to it, it wavers and leaves us; and if we follow it, it eludes our grasp, slips past us, and vanishes forever. Nothing stays with us. This is our natural condition, and yet most contrary to our inclination; we burn with desire to find solid ground and an ultimate sure foundation whereon to build a tower reaching to the Infinite. But our whole groundwork cracks, and the earth opens to abysses. [1]

In the horizon of the infinite.—*We have left the land and have embarked. We have burned our bridges behind us—indeed, we have gone farther and destroyed the land behind us. Now, little ship, look out! Beside you is the ocean: to be sure, it does not always roar, and at times it lies spread out like silk and gold and reveries of graciousness. But hours will come when you will realize that it is infinite and that there is nothing more awesome than infinity. . . . Woe, when you feel homesick for the land as if it had offered more* freedom—*and there is no longer any "land."* [2]

It would be hard to name two thinkers more disparate than Blaise Pascal and Friedrich Nietzsche. The former was a religious zealot and ecstatic visionary; the latter was a self-proclaimed atheist and free thinker. Yet they shared a vision of the human condition: we drift in uncertainty, far from the solid ground we need to build an intellectual and spiritual home. Nietzsche embraces this condition and even exults in its raw beauty; he shuns all false comforts. Pascal, by contrast, is desperate to find a port in his metaphorical storm; he *needs* to believe in God and the possibility of personal salvation in order to give meaning to life.

There is more than a whiff of hysteria in both reactions. Neither can manage the amused Gallic shrug of Montaigne, who was Pascal's major intellectual antagonist. Pascal and Nietzsche are engaged with their whole beings. Both wager their lives—one in a leap of faith, the other in a rejection of all transcendence.

Pascal—a brilliant, pathbreaking mathematician and physicist—had an ambivalent relationship with his older contemporary, Descartes. In Pascal's view, Descartes drew the boundaries of human knowledge from the inside: we can obtain certain knowledge about the world through the application of mathematics to physical phenomena. But the nature of the "I" that knows these truths, and the nature of the God that guarantees and sustains them, is beyond the powers of reason. Descartes's rather perfunctory attempt to show otherwise only underscored the point.

Pascal accepted the fact that we cannot reason our way to God, not even to the abstract God of philosophy, and certainly not to the anthropomorphized, biblical God of Abraham, Isaac, and Jacob. That requires a direct encounter with the divine, a combination of revelation and inspiration. As Pascal explained, "it is the heart which experiences God, and not the reason. This, then, is faith: God felt by the heart, not by the reason."[3]

Pascal distinguished between the mathematical mind of a Descartes and the intuitive mind of the prophets. He himself possessed both. Pascal made significant discoveries in geometry and physics at a very young age; he invented the first calculating machine and the first public transportation system. He explained the geometry of conic sections and cycloids, and essentially created the discipline of mathematical probability. He also proved the existence of a vacuum, contrary to the physics of both Aristotle and Descartes, and he laid the foundations of the integral calculus. All this in a brief life filled with pain and illness. When he died in 1662, he was only thirty-nine.

In the end, however, Pascal valued the intuitive mind far more than the mathematical one. On November 23, 1654, he had a mystical vision, which he summarized on a single sheet of paper and carried ever after over his heart, sewn into the lining of his coat. For Pascal, religion became a form of affirmation in the face of the meaninglessness, the emptiness, the insignificance of an existence without God. Neither the knowledge of the scholar nor the pleasures of the man of the world will suffice.

Without God we are abandoned to a vast nothingness. We cannot escape the horror of our existence. "The eternal silence of these infinite spaces frightens me," Pascal writes.[4]

Whatever one thinks of Pascal's wager, his unsparing analysis of the human condition has influenced religious and antireligious thinkers ever since, starting with Spinoza and Kant and continuing on through Kierkegaard and Nietzsche to our own day. Some will accept the problem of meaninglessness while shunning Pascal's solution. Others will find new justifications—moral, spiritual, and intellectual—for launching themselves into the arms of a God who is forever hidden from us. Pascal's *Pensées*—his unfinished apology for his faith—is always at the center of their concerns.

LIFE

"Blaise Pascal was, simply, one of the greatest men that have ever lived," writes Morris Bishop in his intellectual biography.[5] Certainly, Pascal's brilliant mind ranged across the full measure of human thought, from mathematics to science, to philosophy, to moral, political, and religious concerns. Enlightenment thinkers were not expected to restrain themselves within specialized disciplines.

Pascal was born on June 19, 1623, in Clermont-Ferrand, a town in south-central France. He had an older sister, Gilberte (born 1620), and a younger sister, Jacqueline (born 1625). Another sister died shortly after birth. Little is known of their mother, Antoinette Begon, other than that she was reputed to be both pious and charitable. She died in 1626, when Pascal was only three years old. A governess was retained for the three young children, but their father, Étienne, was deeply involved in their upbringing and never remarried.

Étienne himself was born in Clermont-Ferrand in 1588. He studied law in Paris. When he returned to his hometown, he became a tax lawyer for the state and rose steadily within the bureaucracy. The family was reasonably well off. But Étienne sold his post in 1630, put his money into government bonds, and moved the family to Paris, where he devoted himself to the education of his children and to the study of science.

Pascal was ill from early childhood. He suffered from headaches, stomachaches, toothaches, and a weakness in his legs so severe as to become crippling at times. He was often depressed. His older sister, Gilberte, doted on and cared for him. But his real affection was reserved for his brilliant and charismatic younger sister, Jacqueline.

Pascal and his sisters were educated at home. They studied languages, mastered grammar, read the classics, and began to explore the natural sciences. Étienne always kept the lessons a little beyond the reach of his children to inspire them to work hard. It was a rich education but a somewhat impoverished life. Pascal and Jacqueline in particular would show the effects of never intermixing at school with children their own age.

Pascal was astonishingly precocious. His father—wishing to develop other skills first—would not allow him to study mathematics until he was sixteen. But perhaps precisely because it was forbidden fruit, Pascal grew fascinated with figures and shapes, even proving one of Euclid's theorems—that the sum of the angles of a triangle is equal to the sum of two right angles—on his own at the age of eight. When his father discovered this work, he was more proud at the display of youthful genius than dismayed that his instructions had been disobeyed. The prohibition on mathematics was quickly dropped.

In a decisive break with Scholasticism, Descartes had firmly established mathematical physics as the road to truth guaranteed by God. Marin Mersenne, the great friend and correspondent of Descartes, gathered a small circle of mathematicians and scientists at his home to debate current issues and discuss new developments. Étienne was a member, as was the great mathematician Pierre de Fermat, with whom Pascal would later develop probability theory. Pascal himself was admitted at the age of thirteen, and no one questioned his claim to a place or the importance of his contributions.

During this period, Cardinal Richelieu ruled France as the chief minister of a weak and indecisive king, Louis XIII. Richelieu was the ultimate Machiavellian, who cared only about the sovereignty of France and the powers of the king, both of which he greatly enhanced during his eighteen-year ministerial career. He even engaged Catholic France on the side of the Protestants and the Dutch in the Thirty Years' War in order to counter the power of Catholic Spain and the Habsburg Empire.

To pay for his wars, Richelieu ordered a dramatic reduction in the interest paid on the government bonds in which most of the Pascal family's wealth was held. Étienne joined an ill-advised protest against the devaluation and then had to flee to Clermont-Ferrand in 1638 to escape Richelieu's wrath.

Fortunately for her father, the thirteen-year-old Jacqueline was as precocious a poet and actress as Pascal was a mathematician. She dazzled society and even Richelieu with her work and her budding beauty. After reciting a poem in Richelieu's presence, she climbed onto his lap and pleaded with him to pardon her father. He did so, and even appointed Étienne as collector of taxes at Rouen—a dubious benefit perhaps, given how hostile and rebellious Rouen was in response to what it viewed as excessive taxation. But Étienne managed to avoid any violence. He moved his family there in 1640, where they became friends with Pierre Corneille, author of *Le Cid* and other tragedies.

The family seems to have been happy during the years in Rouen. Gilberte married her cousin Florin Périer in 1641. Pascal invented a calculating machine to ease his father's burden as a tax collector. It worked, but it was expensive, and hence his dreams of making a fortune with it were never realized. Several of the machines survive, however, and are still in working order. Jacqueline had been struck by smallpox in 1638, the same year she charmed Richelieu, and she bore the scars on her face for the rest of her life. But she contented herself with an increasing absorption in religion. Poetry and the stage were gradually forgotten.

Indeed, the entire family went through a sort of religious conversion when Étienne dislocated a hip in 1646. The two doctors who came to treat him at home were fervent Jansenists. Jansenism was a strict Augustinian sect that believed in man's inherent sinfulness, the necessity of grace, and predestination among the elect or the damned. Jansenists were nominally Catholic, but their doctrines were hard to distinguish from Calvinism, and their condemnation of worldly affairs smacked of the fundamentalist Puritanism then predominant in England. The two medical Jansenists converted father and daughters. Pascal held himself somewhat aloof. He was preoccupied with his calculating machine and with his work in mathematics and physics. He purported to accept Jansenism as an intellectual matter, but his true conversion was yet to come.

Suffering from a variety of ailments, Pascal returned to Paris in 1647, accompanied by Jacqueline. Étienne retired and joined them there in 1648. Gilberte and Florin now lived in Clermont-Ferrand with their growing family. In Paris, Pascal conducted a series of experiments designed to prove the existence of vacuums. Aristotle had pronounced that nature "abhors" a vacuum, which is to say that there is no such thing as empty, unfilled space. It was also a basic tenet of Descartes's physics, as much as he differed from Aristotle on other issues, that matter was continuous and spread throughout space. But when a glass tube filled with mercury was upended in a bowl of mercury, with the closed end pointed upward, a space developed at the top of the tube. Pascal, using a variety of glass tubes and taking measurements at various elevations, was able to demonstrate that the space at the top of the tubes was indeed empty and was not composed of air molecules that somehow managed to penetrate the tube. Air pressure does indeed rush to fill a vacuum (hence Aristotle's maxim), but, if prevented from doing so, a vacuum will persist. Descartes and others were dismissive of the results. Indeed, Descartes, who was twenty-seven years older and world famous, was inclined to condescend toward Pascal, perhaps because he considered the young genius a threat to his own ascendency in mathematics and physics.

By 1643, Richelieu and Louis XIII were both dead. The future Sun King, Louis XIV, was still a child, and the queen mother, Anne of Austria, and Cardinal Mazarin, Richelieu's protégé and successor, ruled France until he came of age. A series of civil wars known as the Fronde—so called from the "slings" that Parisian mobs used to smash the windows of supporters of Cardinal Mazarin—broke out in 1648. The Peace of Westphalia had just ended the devastating Thirty Years' War. But France was still engaged in an expensive war with Spain. First, Parliament led a popular rebellion; later, the nobles led an aristocratic rebellion. Their objectives were somewhat different, but heavy taxation and a desire for constitutional reforms to curb royal power were both implicated. The rebellions failed, and by 1653 both the powers of the king and the position of Mazarin had been solidified.

The Pascal family moved back to Clermont-Ferrand for two years during the Fronde, when Paris was particularly dangerous, but were otherwise unaffected. They were far more disrupted by Jacqueline's increasing piety. Jansenism had its spiritual and physical home at the ancient convent of Port-Royal in Paris. Jacqueline was drawn to it with an irresistible fervor. She wanted to join the Port-Royal convent, but her father insisted that she remain with him. As a compromise, she fashioned her own cloister within the house and rarely ventured outside except to go to mass at Port-Royal and to meet with her spiritual advisor.

When Étienne died in 1651, at the age of sixty-three, Jacqueline re-newed her desire to become a nun. This time it was her brother who opposed. Jacqueline was the sole remaining companion and support for the frequent invalid. Moreover, their combined incomes comfortably sus-tained the household. If Jacqueline joined the convent, her share of the inheritance would go with her. But Jacqueline was insistent and entered the convent as a pauper in 1652. The following year, Pascal relented and signed Jacqueline's portion of the inheritance over to the convent at Port-Royal.

Pascal visited Clermont-Ferrand in a largely unsuccessful effort to recover some monies owed to his father. He may have fallen in love while there or at least contemplated marriage; the evidence is ambiguous and has tantalized biographers ever since. Pascal was entering what he himself called his years "in the world." He became intimate friends with the Duc de Roannez, a young nobleman who had fought bravely for the crown during the late civil wars but who also had serious cultural, moral, and religious interests that he shared with Pascal. Pascal would join Roannez's entourage on trips to the country and excursions to the theater. Despite his chronic ill health, Pascal began to go into society and discov-ered that he enjoyed laughing and conversing with his new friends. He even accompanied two of them, the Chevalier de Méré and Damien Mit-ton, on their frequent gambling outings. They appealed to Pascal to help them better understand the odds. In response, he began to develop the mathematics of chance, a new science of probability, about which he entered into a fruitful correspondence with Fermat.

But Pascal's worldly phase quickly began to pall. He grew depressed and dissatisfied with his life. Late on November 23, 1654, he had what he considered a direct encounter with God, a two-hour vision of the divine presence unmediated by reason. He called it *la nuit de feu*, the night of fire. In the testament he forever carried sewn into his coat, next to his heart, he wrote:

> Fire.
> The God of Abraham, the God of Isaac, the God of Jacob.
> Not of the philosophers and intellectuals.
> Certitude, certitude, feeling, joy, peace.
> The God of Jesus Christ.
> My God and your God.
> Your God will be my God.

Forgetfulness of the world and of everything except God.
One finds oneself only by way of the directions taught in the gospel.
The grandeur of the human soul.
Oh just Father, the world has not known you, but I have known you.
Joy, joy, joy, tears of joy.[6]

The testament continues in the same vein for another dozen or so lines. But the gist is clear. Pascal's life has been transformed by a deeply personal visitation from God. His God is not the abstract God of philosophers and intellectuals. The testament is a direct response to Saint Paul's efforts to Hellenize God and make him appealing to philosophy.[7] It is a repudiation of the tradition, from Aquinas to Descartes, that seeks to delimit God with rational arguments. Pascal, like Saint Augustine and Saint Francis, came to know God with his heart, not with his reason.

Pascal grew ever closer to Port-Royal after this. Jansenism was under siege from the Jesuits and from Cardinal Mazarin, who considered it heretical and extremist. Louis XIV, with the concurrence of the pope, directed his chief minister to stamp out Jansenism and require the residents of Port-Royal to repudiate its key doctrines. Pascal leapt to the defense of Jansenism in a brilliant series of open but anonymous letters. These *Provincial Letters*, as they were known, are more a rhetorical screed against the Jesuits than a considered argument. They frequently resort to irony, sarcasm, and mockery, and have forever after given the term *Jesuitical* its negative connotation of casuistry. The letters were praised by Voltaire in the eighteenth century, both for their rhetorical tricks and because, in his view, the internecine dispute undermined organized religion generally, which was clearly not Pascal's intent.

The letters were eagerly read and discussed. But they did no good. Not even a widely reported miracle involving Pascal's niece, Marguerite Périer—whose eye abscess was cured at Port-Royal by the touch of a sliver of thorn from the crown worn by Jesus during the Crucifixion—could stem the tide. Mazarin continued to hound the Jansenists. A series of formularies repudiating the core tenets of Jansenism were developed to which all priests and nuns were ordered to subscribe. Port-Royal justified compliance with the very sort of rationalizations and intellectual acrobatics that Pascal condemned in the Jesuits. Jacqueline initially refused to sign even the first and mildest of these formularies. But, after being instructed to do so by her spiritual advisor, she wasted away and died in 1661, at the age of thirty-six. Pascal always claimed that she died of a broken heart.

Pascal was invited by Queen Christina to visit Sweden. Given what happened to Descartes, he wisely declined on health grounds. He sent her one of his calculating machines instead. Pascal devoted the years 1658 to 1662, when his various illnesses permitted, to preparing his apology for the Christian religion. It was intended to instill in others the devotion to God that Pascal himself felt at the core of his being. It never attained the form of a treatise, however. All he managed in the time available was a series of notes or thoughts (hence the title *Pensées*), many of which he tied into bundles and labeled, while others were left on scattered scraps of paper. These unfinished notes were first edited and published in 1670. Scholarly debates over their proper organization continue to this day.

Pascal's newfound religious intensity did not lead him to repudiate math and science altogether, but simply to put them in perspective. The deepest truths about the world and human existence cannot be learned by reason or experiment. For that, we need God's grace. Reason and revelation are completely separate forms of knowledge, and the latter is infinitely more important.

Pascal died, likely of stomach cancer, on August 19, 1662. He was thirty-nine. His final words were "May God never abandon me." He is buried near Jean Racine, France's greatest tragic playwright, in the church of Saint-Étienne-du-Mont in Paris.

THE *PENSÉES*

The beauty of the *Pensées* lies in their incompleteness. They present us not with a finished body of thought but with fragmentary insights, like flashes of lightning on an otherwise dark night, flashes that startle and invite contemplation. The individual notes are not designed to follow a logical line of argument, but rather to convince by the immediacy and intensity of the feelings they express.

Pascal travels over and over the same ground, offering different perspectives and different approaches on a single basic proposition: that human life without God is miserable and meaningless. The flip side of that proposition is that only in God can we find happiness and meaning.

Stated this baldly, many modern readers will be put off, which is a prime reason that Pascal is little read today, especially by those who feel comfortable in their acceptance or rejection of religious belief. Pascal is more likely to be read by those who find belief and nonbelief alike to be intellectually and emotionally problematic, just as Pascal himself did.

What I call Pascal's "basic proposition" has four components: first, his analysis of the human condition in a fallen world; second, his exploration of God's grace and the prospect of salvation it offers; third, his famous but widely misunderstood "wager" on the truth of Christianity; and, fourth, his conviction that faith in a higher power allows us to gain this life, not just a future life. All of which is to say that Pascal is trying to convince himself, not just others, of something that is inherently and inevitably uncertain, something that cannot be known but only felt. Pascal's *Pensées* are not a rejection of the Enlightenment faith in reason as an instrument of human progress, but they are a necessary qualification. If war, oppression, and cruelty have not convinced us of that much, then I suppose we have no need of Pascal. Otherwise, we need him as much as ever, whether we wager with or against him.

LA CONDITION HUMAINE

> Let us imagine a number of men in chains, and all condemned to death, where some are killed each day in the sight of the others, and those who remain see their own fate in that of their fellows, and wait their turn, looking at each other sorrowfully and without hope. It is an image of the condition of men. [8]

The chains are, of course, metaphorical, like the chains that keep the prisoners in Plato's cave from recognizing that what they take for reality is merely a series of passing shadows. Only the philosopher, who breaks those chains and struggles up and out of the cave, can see things in their true light, illuminated by the eternal form of the Good. [9]

Pascal accepts the first half of Plato's cave analogy. We live lives of limited illumination. Mathematics and physics may give us a means of understanding and even mastering the world in which we live. But that knowledge is immanent, not transcendent. It lets us make predictions but tells us nothing about why the world exists, what we are doing here, or how we should live.

Unlike Plato, however, Pascal does not believe that philosophy or any other form of rational thought can overcome these limitations. The boundaries of rational thought may be invisible, but they serve as iron constraints regardless. We are condemned to live out our brief lives without any deeper understanding of their purpose or meaning. From the moment we are born, we simply await our turn to die.

It is a decidedly gloomy vision of the human condition that seems far removed from the Enlightenment faith in the progress of reason and science. But, in fact, Pascal largely accepts the Cartesian view of the mechanical world. Reason and experiment can give us extensive knowledge of natural phenomena. The march of science, once begun, is inexorable. But that march takes place within a limited sphere. Science will never tell us what we really need to know. It will not shine light into the darkest corners of our existence.

When it comes to the mathematics of matter in motion, Descartes's demonstrations are compelling. But, as we have seen, his "proofs" of God and the immortality of the soul are perfunctory and unconvincing. More to the point, they are wholly unnecessary to his underlying project. "I cannot forgive Descartes," Pascal writes. "In all his philosophy he would have been quite willing to dispense with God. But he had to make Him give a fillip to set the world in motion; beyond this, he has no further need of God."[10] The same is true of the soul. Descartes posits an "I" that thinks and readily equates that with an immortal soul. But the immortality of the soul, like the existence of a creator God, lies outside the limited sphere of knowledge that Descartes develops. It is merely a postulate, and ultimately superfluous.

Pascal finds that situation intolerable:

> When I see the blindness and the wretchedness of man, when I regard the whole silent universe, and man without light, left to himself, and, as it were, lost in this corner of the universe, without knowing who has put him there, what he has come to do, what will become of him at death, and incapable of all knowledge, I become terrified, like a man who should be carried in his sleep to a dreadful desert island, and should awake without knowing where he is, and without means of escape. And thereupon I wonder how people in a condition so wretched do not fall into despair.[11]

Nothing he found in Descartes alleviated Pascal's despair. To the contrary, Descartes's mechanical universe—with its inexorable laws of cause and effect—merely accentuated Pascal's sense of alienation and of the meaninglessness of human existence. Descartes's mechanical universe is stripped of all enchantment.

Pascal shared his skepticism in the powers of human reason with the great French essayist Michel de Montaigne.[12] Pascal cabined and ultimately dismissed Descartes. But it is fair to say that Pascal was obsessed with Montaigne throughout his life. Montaigne was Pascal's most important predecessor and also his greatest intellectual antagonist.

Pascal is often criticized for direct borrowings from Montaigne. And, indeed, one can cite a number of passages in Pascal drawn directly, but without attribution, from Montaigne.[13] But the *Pensées* are just preliminary notes, jottings, and musings; we cannot hold Pascal to modern standards of attribution. More importantly, the same words in Pascal's hands mean something very different. Pascal has a twist to his thought that turns the purport of Montaigne's own words inside out. T. S. Eliot suggested, in a brilliant and admiring introduction to the *Pensées*, that trying to refute Montaigne with rational arguments would be like trying to dissipate a fog with a hand grenade. It simply wouldn't work because the effect of Montaigne's writings on the reader is far more subtle and (in Eliot's view, following Pascal) far more insidious.

Montaigne, like Pascal, came to doubt that reason can unveil divine intention or anything else beyond the scope of human experience. One might have faith, but knowledge in such matters is beyond our powers. With a simple shrug of his shoulders, therefore, Montaigne set such concerns to one side. He sought wisdom not in abstractions but in experience. As the French scholar Jean Starobinski notes, "Montaigne leaves man at the center of an unknowable universe, confronting an inaccessible divinity about which nothing at all can be asserted."[14] But, for Montaigne, unlike Pascal, this absence of knowledge is a source of liberation, even optimism. With God distant and inaccessible, with knowledge limited to the world of experience, Montaigne has been freed to explore and embrace the richness and variety of that experience without doctrinal constraints. Montaigne sets aside all metaphysical and theological questions as irrelevant to his project of learning how to live. He embraces friendship, fellowship, sex, travel, reading, and even old age as contributions to pleasure and self-knowledge. No wonder he infuriated Pascal!

Pascal and Montaigne are rather like Alceste and Philinte in Molière's *Misanthrope*. Alceste is uncompromising in his condemnation of the failings of humankind. Philinte, the paradigm of an *honnête homme*, is more inclined to understanding and indulgence. It is not that they disagree in their low assessment of men and women; they disagree only in how to react. Montaigne could just as readily as Pascal have written, "If we do not know ourselves to be full of pride, ambition, lust, weakness, misery, and injustice, we are indeed blind."[15] Indeed, Montaigne says as much in many places.[16] But Montaigne would never have added, as Pascal did, "And if, knowing this, we do not desire deliverance, what can we say of a man?"[17] It is a central premise of Montaigne's later essays that we cannot deliver ourselves from ourselves. Zealots "want to get out of themselves and escape from the man," he writes. "That is madness: instead of changing into angels, they change into beasts; instead of raising themselves, they lower themselves."[18] For Montaigne, our only business is living appropriately within the limits of human nature. For Pascal, man's fallen nature is precisely what we must overcome.

Sounding just like the misanthropic Alceste, Pascal catalogs the ways in which we deceive others and ourselves:

> Human life is thus only a perpetual illusion; men deceive and flatter each other. No one speaks of us in our presence as he does of us in our absence. Human society is founded on mutual deceit; few friendships would endure if each knew what his friend said of him in his absence, although he then spoke in sincerity and without passion.
>
> Man is then only disguise, falsehood, and hypocrisy, both in himself and in regard to others. He does not wish any one to tell him the truth; he avoids telling it to others, and all these dispositions, so removed from justice and reason, have a natural root in his heart.[19]

"Well, yes," Montaigne might say. Life is not perfect, but it doesn't have to be tragic. Pascal is appalled at human failings. Montaigne is more indulgent and amused.[20] Philinte is channeling Montaigne when he claims:

> I take men as they are, or let them be,
> And teach my soul to bear their frailty;
> And whether in court or town, whatever the scene,
> My phlegm's as philosophic as your spleen.[21]

"Mon flegme est philosophe autant que votre bile." It is the exact reproach leveled at Pascal by Montaigne's *Essays*, and Pascal has no ready rejoinder. Temperament is not argument; it is the screen through which we see and react to the world. Montaigne is the advocate of what Philinte calls *une vertu traitable*, a manageable or pliant virtue, a virtue one can live with, and Pascal finds that unacceptable.

Even worse is the fact that Montaigne is content to live, as the great literary critic Erich Auerbach puts it, without "fixed points of support."[22] He can bracket and set aside metaphysical and theological questions as if they were of no concern. That is exactly what Pascal could never forgive in Descartes. The Cartesian system needs neither God nor immortal souls. It functions perfectly well on its own. Montaigne's wisdom is the same. He contentedly occupies himself with "transitory and mundane things."[23] Even death for Montaigne is just an event in life: "I want death to find me planting my cabbages, but careless of death, and still more of my unfinished garden."[24]

Montaigne's "transitory and mundane things," Pascal insists, are just distractions from "the natural poverty of our feeble and mortal condition, so miserable that nothing can comfort us when we think of it closely."[25] If we were honest with ourselves, we would acknowledge that the objects for which we strive so earnestly will not make us happy. The uncertainty and fragility of life, and the seeming finality of death, terrified Pascal. He wanted—had a desperate need for—a transcendent order. Rest can only be found in the stability of truth, but truth lies beyond our grasp.

Pascal embraces and even exaggerates Montaigne's account of human frailty. He stresses man's "nothingness, his forlornness, his insufficiency, his dependence, his weakness, his emptiness."[26] Pascal insists that we find ourselves, like Dante, in a dark wood where the true path is lost to us, and we are consumed by "weariness, gloom, sadness, fretfulness, vexation, despair."[27]

Pascal recognizes no worldly solution to this condition. "The Stoics say, 'Retire within yourselves; it is there you will find your rest.' And that is not true. Others say, 'Go out of yourselves; seek happiness in amusement.' And this is not true. . . . Happiness is neither without us nor within us."[28] Pascal must make a leap outside of ordinary human life. He sees no other solution. "We desire truth, and find within ourselves only uncertainty. We seek happiness, and find only misery and death. We cannot but desire truth and happiness, and are incapable of certainty or happiness."[29] Pascal believes that only after we have fully acknowledged our miserable state can we open ourselves to God's grace and a new form of knowledge. We cannot reason our way to God. But we can, with God's help, open our hearts to him. It is by recognizing that our condition is untenable that we begin to sense what we can become. In man's very misery lies the seeds of his salvation. "In a word, man knows that he is wretched. . . . But he is really great because he knows it."[30]

AFTER THE FALL

Pascal admits that the doctrine of original sin appears as "foolishness." And yet, he insists, "this foolishness is wiser than all the wisdom of men."[31] Despite his impeccable Jansenist credentials, Pascal does not read scripture literally. The Old Testament, in particular, "is only figurative."[32] But the story of Adam and Eve and the garden of Eden, like Plato's allegory of the cave, offers Pascal a way to illustrate the dual nature of man: his current darkness and his potential illumination.

Adam and Eve did not literally stand face-to-face with God or walk with him in the garden of Eden or hear his voice. But those anthropomorphic metaphors underscore that God was once felt as a real and vital presence in our lives. He was the creator and sustainer of our existence, and we worshipped him as such. Over time, however, the self and its needs, wants, and pleasures became our preoccupation. We sought power through knowledge. We wanted to control and manipulate the world and others for our own benefit. We ceased to think of the world's "Author and its end."[33] God became at most "a fillip to set the world in motion" and, hence, of no further concern to us. As we narrowed our focus to transitory and mundane things, the world lost its enchantment. We withdrew from God, and God withdrew from us.[34]

This Edenic mood and its loss will be captured beautifully in Wordsworth's "Ode: Intimations of Immortality":

> There was a time when meadow, grove, and stream,
> The earth, and every common sight,
> To me did seem
> Apparelled in celestial light,
> The glory and the freshness of a dream.
> It is not now as it hath been of yore;—
> Turn wheresoe'er I may,
> By night or day.
> The things which I have seen I now can see no more.[35]

The celestial light has gone out. The universe is mute. And yet we still have intimations of our prelapsarian state. We cannot rid ourselves of our Platonic longings. We desire truth and happiness, though we know neither. Those desires and the feelings of emptiness and loss they engender "make us perceive wherefrom we are fallen."[36] We yearn for a home we have never known and yet dimly recollect. We yearn for a reenchanted world.

According to Pascal, such yearnings can only be satisfied by God. "The infinite abyss can only be filled by an infinite and immutable object, that is to say, only by God Himself."[37] Pascal, of course, recognizes that our longings are no guarantee that what we long for exists or even that we can comprehend the nature of this God. Both the beginning and the end of things are "an impenetrable secret."[38] "It is incomprehensible that God should exist, and it is incomprehensible that He should not exist; that the soul should be joined to the body, and that we should have no soul; that the world should be created, and that it should not be created, etc."[39] These fundamental mysteries, these impenetrable secrets, are forever beyond our grasp.

As Descartes's own failure illustrates, we cannot reason our way to God and the soul. In trying, we come up against the limits of rational thought. "The last proceeding of reason is to recognize that there is an infinity of things which are beyond it."[40] The last proceeding of reason, in other words, is to recognize that we can find God only if there is a form of truth that is not accessible through reason. Pascal rejects dogmatism, the claim to know what is beyond man's powers to know. But he also rejects skepticism, the despair that any such truth is possible. "We know truth," he explains, "not only by the reason, but also by the heart."[41] Intuition is knowledge from the heart, and it is by intuition that we know the first principles upon which reason itself depends: "The knowledge of first principles, as space, time, motion, number, is as sure as any of those which we get from reasoning. And reason must trust these intuitions of the heart, and must base them on every argument."[42]

This is not an easy argument even to grasp, much less to accept. But what Pascal is saying is that certain intuitions precede rational thought and are conditions for the exercise of rational thought. We do not derive them from experience or rational argument: we know them like the demonstrations of geometry, which, once understood, are self-evident. They form the structure of thought within which all knowledge is acquired. That is the foundation of Cartesian philosophy.

Pascal suggests that we must view God, creation, and the soul in a similar or analogous light. We cannot derive them from experience or rational argument. But if we accept them, they can illuminate, even if not render fully comprehensible, the beginnings and ends of things. They can explain the dual nature of man. They can lead us toward fulfillment and happiness. Without them we are forever in darkness. But their existence can be neither proved nor disproved; they can only be accepted or rejected. "We have an incapacity of proof, insurmountable by all dogmatism. We have an idea of truth, invincible to all skepticism."[43]

According to Pascal, God is hidden but not invisible. He has given us sufficient signs of his presence if we have but the grace to see them. These signs are perceptible only "to the eyes of the heart, which perceive wisdom!"[44] "It is the heart which experiences God, and not the reason." Religious faith is a matter of choice and of will. It is an emotional commitment rather than a rational proof. Not see, and you shall believe, but rather believe, and you shall see. In his most famous, and often misunderstood, line, Pascal writes: "The heart has its reasons, which reason does not know."[45]

THE WAGER

The question that of course arises is, why should we make that emotional commitment? Why should we believe in a God who is incomprehensible and inherently unknowable? Why should we posit a creation event or declare that we have immortal souls? Why should we engage our hearts in the absence of any certainty?

Because, Pascal responds, life is inherently uncertain. "Nature presents to me nothing which is not matter of doubt and concern."[46] Nothing that truly matters to us is subject to rational demonstration. Love, friendship, the choice of a career, the bearing of children—these are all acts of faith. We have no idea how they will turn out. They may lead to unhappiness and tears. But that doesn't mean we must give way to a passive skepticism. Skepticism is just the flip side of dogmatism, each of which demands absolute certainty and is content with nothing less. But we don't have that certainty except, paradoxically, insofar as we fully commit ourselves to what is inherently uncertain. What we have is love, and love can conquer doubt. What we know is that our lives would be empty without such choices. We therefore launch ourselves into the unknown future with hope. We affirm our lives.

Yes, Montaigne might say, but we at least know the people we love and to whom we commit ourselves. We do not and cannot know God. Pascal neither fully denies nor fully accepts that response.

> If I saw nothing there which revealed a Divinity, I would come to a negative conclusion; if I saw everywhere the signs of a Creator, I would remain peacefully in faith. But, seeing too much to deny and too little to be sure, I am in a state to be pitied; . . . ignorant of what I am or of what I ought to do, I know neither my condition nor my duty.[47]

Yet Pascal is prepared to commit—and constantly to recommit—in this state of chronic uncertainty. Agnosticism is not really an option, any more than staying in bed because you don't know how the day will unfold, tempting as that might sometimes seem. "How many things we do on an uncertainty, sea voyages, battles!" If we must not act on less than a certainty, "then we must do nothing at all, for nothing is certain."[48]

Where religion is concerned, moreover, even a nonchoice is a choice not to believe; it is a rejection of faith, a withholding of love. The existence of God cannot be proved by reason. Nor can his nonexistence. According to reason, you can defend neither proposition. In such circumstances, choosing heads or tails is equally indefensible. "Yes; but you must wager. It is not optional. You are embarked."[49] In a game of chance, where the odds are even, "your reason is no more shocked in choosing one rather than the other, since you must of necessity choose."[50] Applying the doctrine of chance, which measures costs and benefits compared to likely outcomes, the choice should be clear-cut. For what we stake is finite; what we stand to gain is "an infinity of an infinitely happy life."[51] We go to church, we say some prayers, we refrain from gross misconduct. At worst, that time is wasted. At best, we have bought ourselves a ticket to an eternity in paradise.

The terms sound crass and purely utilitarian. We choose God only on spec, only in the hopes of what it will gain for us. There is no real love involved in the transaction. But that mistakes Pascal's real point, which is that belief in God is a moral and emotional choice, almost like choosing a spouse. Certainly, we hope the benefits will outweigh the risks; we hope that we will find happiness together as a couple. But truly to love another human being involves not a cold, rational calculation, but an emotional and moral commitment. The same is true of religion. Choosing God is an engagement of our full being.

We should learn from those who wager all they have, Pascal urges.[52] Cartesian rationalism will not get us there. But Montaigne's skepticism is an abdication. It fails to recognize that we are always "embarked" insofar as we seek any form of happiness. We wager every time we make a choice, and this is the most essential choice of all. Choosing God is an affirmation of life, an affirmation that life has meaning and purpose beyond our narrow, daily concerns. To reject God is to accept the meaninglessness, the emptiness, and the insignificance of our existence. We are limited beings and should choose what will make us whole. "Those who have the living faith in their heart see at once that all existence is none other than the work of the God whom they adore."[53] Those who don't believe will find confirmation for their unbelief—that is, they will find "only obscurity and darkness."[54] We are "embarked" whether we like it or not. We can steer our boats toward a distant, unseen shore or we can let them drift and founder; "there is no time to hesitate, [we] must give all."[55]

It is a remarkably powerful, emotional appeal. It is also ruthlessly honest. Pascal acknowledges that faith is uncertain and must constantly be affirmed. The search for God does not end. Even in finding him we will seek him. We cannot cease to wager.[56] He also acknowledges that he chooses to believe something that is inherently incomprehensible. Paradoxically, in the impenetrable mystery of faith lies much of its attraction. Both hope and uncertainty are essential aspects of the human condition. As T. S. Eliot notes:

> I can think of no Christian writer . . . more to be commended than Pascal to those who doubt, but who have the mind to conceive, and the sensibility to feel, the disorder, the futility, the meaninglessness, the mystery of life and suffering, and who can only find peace through a satisfaction of the whole being.[57]

But why the Christian God? Why does Pascal find in Christianity the best expression of his belief? Is it simply because he was born into that tradition and finds it the most familiar and the most comfortable? That is Montaigne's casual—almost to the point of indifference—approach to religion: we have no knowledge of God and no reason to question existing dogma, so we might as well simply accept the religion in which we were raised. It is so much easier that way. Besides, one religion is as good as another. The doctrinal differences over which men kill one another (the number of sacraments, the instantiation of Christ in the Eucharist, the role of the pope, predestination, etc.) are just so much meaningless nonsense.

Obviously, Pascal did not always feel the same way. He waged a vicious war of words in defense of the doctrinal idiosyncrasies of Jansenism. Yet the Pascal of the *Pensées* is more inclined to view articles of faith as figurative rather than literal. He finds, especially in the New Testament, the best poetic expression of his thoughts about the human condition. Christianity is true, he insists, precisely because it is so paradoxical and thus captures the paradox of our own being: our fall from grace and the possibility of our salvation through Christ. "The Christian religion, then, teaches men these two truths; that there is a God whom men can know, and that there is a corruption in their nature which renders them unworthy of Him."[58] It is the very strangeness of Christianity that appeals to Pascal; it recognizes that man is vile and yet bids him to be like God. This contradiction is reconciled only in Jesus Christ.[59] Only through the example of Christ can we reestablish communion with God.[60] Christ "constitutes the middle course, because in Him we find both God and our misery."[61] Without him, "we know nothing, and see only darkness and confusion in the nature of God, and in our own nature."[62]

GAINING THIS LIFE

If Christ is a middle course, capable of bridging the gap between the corruption of human nature and the splendor of God, then man is not a lost cause. He can become better, and Pascal's wager is not just a wild throw of the dice on a life of infinite happiness after death. It is an approach to life itself. To be sure, Pascal does not believe that man can obtain perfect goodness in this life. Nor does he believe that any of the finite goods of the world (money, power, reputation, even family and friends) can fully satisfy him. But he does seem to believe that man can become marginally better and ameliorate, at least in part, the conditions in which he lives. Even as he was dying, Pascal developed the project, put into practice by his devoted friend Roannez, of a public transportation service, taking poor and working-class passengers from one district to another in Paris. Pascal does not wholly reject the Enlightenment ideal of progress through the use of reason. Pascal's vision for man is not purely ahistorical. That is to say, even if infinite happiness and infinite goodness are not possible in this world, some increase in both happiness and goodness is possible within history.

Pascal, even more than Descartes, is a pivot point to modern philosophy. Plato had proposed to transcend history and to propound eternal truths. That view of philosophy dominated Western thought through Descartes, who accepted the challenge but conspicuously failed to meet it. Pascal exposed the project as impossible of execution. Pascal sees man in the context of history and as unable to escape that context.[63] To be sure, Pascal still clings to his faith in a transcendent God and an afterlife. But he frankly acknowledges the inherent, if still tantalizing, incoherence of both ideas.

The reason that is important is that later thinkers such as Spinoza, Hegel, Marx, and Nietzsche accept much of Pascal's thought. They agree with Pascal that we cannot reason our way to God and the immortal soul. They agree that both ideas are incomprehensible and rationally indefensible. They also agree that human existence is miserable even as they reject the idea that all might be made right after death. Instead, they seek an ideal that gives meaning and purpose to human life without relying on a transcendent God. They believe in a dialectic—a struggle of competing ideas and forces—that will ultimately result in spiritual freedom (Hegel), the classless society (Marx), or the rather extravagant idea of an *Übermensch* (Nietzsche).[64] They accordingly focus all their attention on man as embedded in history. In their view, vital questions concerning the meaning and purpose of life can be answered only within the historical process.

Pascal offers not only an opening for such dialectical views, but a necessary caution as well. Nietzsche, like Hegel and Marx, suggests that the person we are destined to become "lies . . . immeasurably high above [us]."[65] Pascal, too, says that "man infinitely transcends man."[66] But he is talking about man's immortal soul, not his earthly existence. Following Montaigne, Pascal insists that we cannot rise above the basic conditions of that existence. Only incremental, not revolutionary, improvement is possible. As if he foresaw all the tyrannical horrors of communism and fascism, Pascal writes: "Man is neither angel nor brute, and the unfortunate thing is that he who would act the angel acts the brute."[67] Characteristically, Montaigne said it first and said it better: "They want to get out of themselves and escape from the man. That is madness: instead of changing into angels, they change into beasts; instead of raising themselves, they lower themselves."

In a dark moment, Pascal dismisses political philosophy as "laying down rules for a lunatic asylum."[68] But Pascal does not, as Auerbach contends, counsel a passive acceptance of evil and injustice, as if man deserved no better.[69] Rather, Pascal believes that once we acknowledge that God is within our fellow men, just as God was within Christ, we can become better, more Christlike, despite the corruption of human nature. "You will be faithful, honest, humble, grateful, generous, a sincere friend, truthful."[70] You will benefit in this life as well as the next. Nothing is guaranteed. Because human nature is inherently corrupt, human institutions will also be corrupt. There will be no city of God on earth. But accepting that there is a divine spark in others is a wager that will pay off in this world. "I will tell you that you will thereby gain in this life."[71]

Pascal abandons the faith that philosophy can solve all the mysteries of life or fashion a form of government that will rid humankind of greed, injustice, and inequality. But Pascal does not abandon his personal faith in the dignity of thought as within the reach of each and every individual.

> Man is but a reed, the most feeble thing in nature; but he is a thinking reed. The entire universe need not arm itself to crush him. A vapor, a drop of water suffices to kill him. But, if the universe were to crush him, man would still be more noble than that which killed him, because he knows that he dies and the advantage which the universe has over him; the universe knows nothing of this.[72]

Pascal argues that the most philosophic life is "to live simply and quietly."[73] That was the life led by Pascal's truest successor, Benedict de Spinoza, for whom God is wholly immanent, for whom all things are divine, and for whom the very notion of a transcendent God, a God outside time and history, must be set aside. Spinoza was derided as an atheist by his contemporaries. But he was closer to the God-possessed Pascal than any of them realized. Pascal laid down a rule for life that Spinoza embodied more than anyone before or since: "All our dignity consists . . . in thought. By it we must elevate ourselves, and not by space and time which we cannot fill. Let us endeavor, then, to think well; this is the principle of morality."[74]

5

SPINOZA

God without Religion

I believe in the God of Spinoza, who reveals himself in the orderly harmony of the world.

God does not play dice with the universe.

These are two of Albert Einstein's most famous pronouncements. In them, Einstein affirms the regularity and intelligibility of the laws of nature, which Spinoza had equated with the mind of God. Indeed, for Spinoza, as Einstein recognized, God and nature are one and the same. *Deus sive Natura*, God or nature. These are simply different ways of referring to the same underlying substance seen in its different aspects—the first in terms of its intelligible laws; the second in terms of its physical extension.

Descartes had conspicuously failed to provide a satisfactory explanation of the relationship between God and nature. His God was transcendent—that is, wholly removed from the material world. As Pascal noted, Descartes used God simply as a "fillip" to set nature in motion, never to be heard from again. But even that brief, initial connection between an immaterial God and material nature is left unexplained, as is the related connection between mind and body. Somehow the former moves the latter, but just how cannot be understood.

Spinoza sets out to solve both dilemmas. His God is the immanent cause of all things, not the external or transcendent cause. His God simply is substance understood according to the principles of mathematics, causation, and regularity that govern all its manifestations. There are not two substances—God and the world—but only one substance understood in its dual aspects. All explanation is therefore immanent. We must understand the world from within the world. Spinoza's account of God gives free rein to science and demands no exceptions to the laws of nature, since those laws are themselves constituents of what we call God.

So, too, humans are not composed of separate substances—mind and body—that miraculously interact with each other. There is no ineradicable dualism for which we must account. Rather, humans can be described in terms of two vocabularies that are incommensurable with each other—the physical vocabulary of cause and effect, of neurons firing and muscles contracting, and the completely separate vocabulary of human emotions, thoughts, and desires. Neither way of speaking can be reduced to or substituted for the other. Each is autonomous, yet each is perfectly legitimate as a description of human beings, depending on one's purpose and focus.

Spinoza's God is an impersonal God. Pascal, of course, would not accept him as "God" at all, and Spinoza was widely reviled as an atheist during and after his life. That is a mistake. Spinoza believed passionately in both God *and* nature, seen in their different aspects. God is not just a figure of speech, any more than the mind or soul is just a figure of speech; both God and the soul are essential to understanding reality. But Spinoza's God has no anthropomorphic qualities. He (if I may use a pronoun that does have only figurative application here) takes no interest in human affairs; he does not respond to prayers or exhortations; he is neither angered nor pleased by human actions; he neither punishes evil nor rewards good. Indeed, since the soul and the body are simply different ways of referring to the same substance, the soul cannot survive the death of the body. There is accordingly no afterlife in which punishments and rewards can be meted out. All such ways of talking about God are figurative rather than descriptive.

There are two consequences of this view of God and the soul. First, the sacred writings, doctrines, rites, and sacraments of any particular religion—be it Catholic, Protestant, Jewish, or Islamic—are void of any intellectual content or other basis in reality. Rituals can be useful in uniting a community and providing comfort to its members, but the expectation that such ceremonies have any efficacy other than the solidarity of joint worship is a mere superstition. There should be a complete separation of philosophy and theology. Philosophy, broadly understood, seeks truth about the world. Scripture can only be understood figuratively, in moral terms; it is no fit basis for opposing advances in science. Accordingly, Spinoza advocates a radical freedom of thought and expression: "Every man should think what he likes and say what he thinks."[1]

Second, just as God and the soul are immanent rather than transcendent, so, too, the foundations of morality must be found in the structure of reality and our place within it. The study of philosophy reveals that no one person's concerns are privileged over another's. Our private passions lead us to seek our own advantage. But, as our understanding of the world increases, we can attain an intellectual love of God, a love which views the world *sub specie aeternitatis*—in the guise of the intelligible and eternal laws that compose the world. From that perspective, there is no basis for preferring one's own well-being over that of another. Our individual concerns drop away, and we can attain a form of blessedness and selflessness that is the essence of a moral life.

Spinoza is difficult to grasp on a first or even a second reading. His scholastic vocabulary, metaphysical pronouncements, and pretensions to geometric certainty and precision are highly off-putting. They make him seem quite foreign to us, when in fact he is the most modern of philosophers, anticipating the insights of Ludwig Wittgenstein on language, the separation of church and state enshrined in our Constitution, and a morality based not on external rules but on a fuller understanding of humanity and our place in nature.

LIFE

Baruch de Spinoza—known generally by the Latinized version of his name, Benedict—was born on November 24, 1632. Whether in Hebrew or Latin, his given name means "blessed one," an apt but ironic designation in light of his history. His family and friends called him by the Portuguese diminutive Bento.

In 1492—the same year they completed the Reconquista of Spain and financed the expedition of Christopher Columbus—Ferdinand and Isabella ordered all Jews and Muslims living in Spain either to convert to Christianity or to leave the country. Economically, it was a disastrous decision, since Jewish and Muslim merchants were responsible for much of the trade that brought riches to Spain. Politically and morally, it was indefensible. The Moors for centuries had allowed Jews and Christians to live in productive harmony with their Moorish conquerors. There was no reason to believe that such a fruitful coexistence could not continue under a united Spain. Even in terms of promoting religion, it was a mistake. The *conversos* and *moriscos*, as converted Jews and Muslims were known, often practiced their religions in secret, which led to an ever-increasing expansion of the Inquisition and a repression that fell upon the entire country, leaving it an intellectual backwater, largely untouched by the currents of the Enlightenment that would sweep through Europe in the seventeenth century. There were many reasons for Spain's self-inflicted decline as a world power, but religious intolerance—and the wars it engendered—was certainly one of them.

Many Spanish Jews moved to Portugal, where they continued to practice both their religion and their trades. In 1496, Portugal, too, purported to banish Jews and Muslims, but *Marranos*—as they were often known, to distinguish them from true *conversos*, or "new Christians"—enjoyed a certain laxity there and could practice their religions in private without harassment. In 1547, however, Pope Paul III officially established the Inquisition in Portugal. Suspected *Marranos* were once again harried from their homes or worse. Since they were still banned from England and hardly tolerated in France, many Jews settled in what became known as the Dutch Republic, or the United Provinces of the Netherlands, which declared its independence from Spain in 1581. Thus began the Dutch golden age, in which the Netherlands became the greatest maritime and commercial power in the world as well as a hotbed of scientific innovation and artistic genius. It was the home of Rembrandt van Rijn, Johannes Vermeer, and the greatest of all landscape painters, Jacob van Ruisdael. It also offered refuge to the two most important philosophers of the seventeenth century, Descartes and Spinoza.

Bento's father, Michael de Spinoza, was born in Portugal in 1587 and was brought to Amsterdam as a child. He grew up to be a reasonably prosperous importer of sugar, nuts, and dried fruit, as well as a respected member of the growing Jewish community. The Jews of Amsterdam were not restricted to a ghetto. Rembrandt lived around the corner from the Spinozas. But many of the Jews, exiled from their native countries, gathered together in what became the Jewish quarter of the city and continued to speak Portuguese and Spanish with one another. Although the Dutch Republic was officially Calvinist, Jews were allowed to practice their religion largely without hindrance, as long as they did not proselytize or corrupt Christians with their views.

Michael buried three wives and three of his six children. Bento was the product of his second marriage, to Hanna Deborah. His sister Miriam was three years older, and his brother Isaac was somewhere in between. Their mother died when Bento was six.

Bento was sent to a well-regarded Jewish school, where he studied Hebrew, the Bible, and Jewish theology. He was a remarkably precocious student, and his elders expected that he would become a rabbi. But Bento was more excited by the new Cartesian philosophy and the development of science. When his brother Isaac died in 1648, the sixteen-year-old Bento was perfectly willing to end his rabbinical studies and take Isaac's place in the family business. He spoke Portuguese, Spanish, Dutch, and French. He also mastered Latin, the language of science and philosophy, with the help of Franciscus van den Enden, a Dutch physician, scholar, and former Jesuit.

When Michael died in 1654, the family business was already reeling from a general economic downturn and the loss of several shipments seized by pirates and the British Royal Navy. Bento and his younger half brother Gabriel took charge but could do little to salvage the business, or perhaps had little interest in doing so. In either event, the family concern was soon dissolved, and Bento decided to devote himself to "natural philosophy," broadly understood.

Spinoza, as I will refer to him going forward, began to develop his philosophical views along what were then radical lines. He questioned the value of Orthodox Judaism and even the existence of God. He disparaged ceremonial observances as so much superstition. Although he tried to be guarded in how and to whom he expressed his views, enough leaked out to alarm the elders in his congregation. Spinoza was accused of heresy and ordered to repent. When he refused, he was excommunicated at the age of twenty-three in a document whose astonishing harshness is explicable only by the fact that the Jews of Amsterdam had suffered greatly for their religion and therefore clung to it with a passionate intolerance for any deviation. Sadly, they had learned very little from the Spanish-Portuguese Inquisition they had so recently escaped. Baruch, the "blessed one," was well and roundly cursed:

Cursed be he by day, and cursed be he by night; cursed be he when he lieth down, and cursed be he when he riseth up; cursed be he when he goeth out and cursed be he when he cometh in; the Lord will not pardon him; the wrath and fury of the Lord will be kindled against this man, and bring down upon him all the curses which are written in the Book of the Law; and the Lord will destroy his name from under the heavens; and, to his undoing, the Lord will cut him off from all the tribes of Israel, with all the curses of the firmament which are written in the Book of the Law.[2]

Added to these curses was an injunction that exiled him from the Jewish community:

We ordain that no one may communicate with him verbally or in writing, nor show him any favor, nor stay under the same roof with him, nor be within four cubits of him, nor read anything composed or written by him.[3]

Spinoza's response to this furious outburst was remarkably mild, yet he was wholly unintimidated. He thanked the Hebrew congregation for saving him the trouble of separating himself from them and proceeded to make his home among progressive gentiles, even as he abandoned any formal religion. He changed his given Hebrew name, Baruch, to its Latin equivalent, Benedict.

Under that name, Benedict de Spinoza became the first great purely secular thinker. He devoted himself to the natural sciences and supported himself largely by grinding lenses for microscopes and telescopes that were much in demand. In 1660, Spinoza left Amsterdam to live in a small village in the country, near Leyden. Three years later, he moved to Voorburg, near The Hague, and he lived in The Hague from 1670 until his death.

Spinoza had black hair, dark eyes, and a beautiful, if pale, face. His manner, by all accounts, was as soft and gentle as his writing was sharp and forceful. He was neither an ascetic nor a recluse, neither excessively merry nor excessively melancholy, and was unfailingly kind and courteous. He enjoyed wine and his pipe. He received visitors and had a wide correspondence. Sounding quite like Montaigne, he wrote to a friend: "I . . . seek to pass my life, not in sorrow and sighing, but in peace, joy and cheerfulness."[4] He found his greatest joy in the science of nature, especially mathematics and the basic principles of matter and motion that he, following Descartes, considered universally true. He also avidly followed developments in experimental and observational science that were aided by his scientific instruments.

Spinoza wrote an explication of Cartesian philosophy that was published in 1663 and was well received. But he wanted to go beyond Cartesianism and, using similar methods, tackle the problems of God, the soul, and the good life, problems that Descartes first fumbled and then largely avoided. Spinoza explained his motivation in an unfinished *Treatise on the Emendation of the Intellect*:

> After experience had taught me that all the things which regularly occur in ordinary life are vain and futile; seeing that none of the objects of my fears contained in themselves anything either good or bad, except insofar as the mind is affected by them, I resolved at last to find out whether there was anything which would be the true good, which would affect the mind singularly, to the exclusion of all else: whether there was something which, once found and acquired, would give me continuous, supreme, and everlasting happiness.[5]

Spinoza worked quietly on developing his own philosophy, most of which could not be published in his lifetime and certainly not under his own name, for fear that the tolerance of unorthodox views, even in the Dutch Republic, would not stretch so far. The example of his disciple, Adriaan Koerbagh, was enough to deter him. Koerbagh had written works in Dutch arguing that God was the equivalent of nature, the Bible was written by men, and ecclesiastical authority should be abolished. These were all standard doctrines of Spinoza. But, even though Koerbagh published the books anonymously, his printer gave him up, and he was sentenced in 1668 to ten years of hard labor for blasphemy, to be followed by exile. He survived only one.

Spinoza was more circumspect than Koerbagh, or luckier, at any rate. He decided to hold back his magnum opus, the *Ethics*, until he could create a more tolerant climate for its reception. Accordingly, in 1670, he published anonymously in Latin his *Tractatus Theologico-Politicus*. He relied on a close analysis of scripture to argue that the Bible is a historical work of literature with a figurative rather than literal meaning. That is, the Bible teaches us only moral truths, not philosophical and scientific ones, and therefore the former should never restrict the latter. The treatise was an extended argument for total freedom in thought and in writing.

If Spinoza thought his treatise would pave the way for his frank discussion of God, the soul, and the good life, he was sadly mistaken. The work was widely condemned as irreligious, immoral, and dangerous. His authorship, moreover, was an open secret. One reviewer claimed that the book was "forged in Hell by a renegade Jew and the Devil."[6] Spinoza did everything he could to forestall a Dutch translation of the work, assuming correctly that the authorities would have more tolerance for a work written in Latin for scholars than for one directed at a more general audience. His efforts were in vain. In 1674, the Court of Holland banned the book as "sacrilegious and soul-destructive . . . , full of unfounded and dangerous propositions and horrors, to the disadvantage of the true religion and church service."[7] The court left Spinoza alone but proposed serious punishment for anyone who printed, promulgated, or sold the book.

Spinoza was by this time in equal measures famous and infamous throughout Europe. He was invited to take up a professorship in Heidelberg, provided he did not "misuse it in order to disturb the publicly established religion." Spinoza turned the position down, politely but firmly: "I think that I do not know in what boundaries that freedom of philosophizing should be included in order not to make the impression that I have the intention to perturb the publicly-instituted religion."[8] In any event, he wanted to focus on his own research, not on teaching.

He spent the last six years of his life perfecting the *Ethics*, all the while knowing that it was too controversial to be published in his lifetime. On February 21, 1677, Spinoza died of consumption (tuberculosis), a condition undoubtedly aggravated by years of exposure to the dust particles from his work grinding lenses. Per his instructions, his desk, which contained his finished and unfinished manuscripts, was sent to his publisher, Jan Rieuwertsz. At the end of that year, his *Opera Posthuma* was finally published with the aid of friends and admirers. It contained the complete *Tractatus*, the *Ethics*, some of his correspondence, and an unfinished *Political Treatise*, as well as a grammar of the Hebrew language. I have a much-treasured first edition of the *Opera Posthuma*, and no other book in my library excites in me a greater admiration for the audacious power of human thought.

GOD

A basic premise of Western thought through Descartes is the existence of a transcendent God. This God is eternal and all-powerful. He created the world out of nothing through an act of will. He could have created it differently, or at a different time, or not at all. God is not part of the material world he has created. He is immaterial and exists outside time. God created both time and matter when he created the world.

The abstract God of philosophy is a hypothetical first cause and little more. In most religions, however, this transcendent God is portrayed in more colorful and anthropomorphic terms. The God of the Old Testament takes an active interest in his creation and particularly in the men and women who occupy a privileged position in the hierarchy of being. He issues commandments, rewards compliance, and punishes disobedience. He demands ceremonies of worship and appeasement. He will even alter events in the world in response to prayer and sacrifice. Miracles are mere child's play to a God who is omnipotent. Nothing happens except according to his will: if a ship is wrecked, God, in his infinite wisdom, chooses who shall live and who shall die. There is a divine plan that is evident everywhere and in everything and yet remains wholly beyond our comprehension.

This basic premise was already under strain in the hands of Descartes and Pascal. As Pascal pointed out, Descartes's God was needed only as a "fillip" to set the world in motion; he then disappeared from world history to be displaced by the laws of mathematics and motion. Pascal himself bemoaned the fact that God is hidden from us and incomprehensible to us. His faith was a desperate leap into the mystical unknown. It is no coincidence that Pascal believed fervently in the existence of miracles and even suggested that his faith would be impossible without them.

Spinoza rejects outright the premise of a transcendent God—whether the abstract God of philosophy or the anthropomorphic God of religion—as incoherent. There is no creator distinct from the creation. The immaterial God of Descartes—who exists wholly apart from the world—can no more create the material world than Descartes's immaterial mind/soul can act on or be acted on by the material world. There is an unbridgeable gulf between the two. Nor could there be a moment of creation chosen by a God who exists altogether outside time. A transcendent God is not an explanation of existence; it is an admission of despair at even the possibility of such an explanation.

Spinoza starts instead with what we do know: that the world exists and that we exist within the world. All explanation is necessarily immanent. It begins with the world as it exists and tries to understand it. Adopting (and adapting) an Aristotelian concept, Spinoza defines all that exists, in its most generic form, as substance. "By substance I understand what is in itself and is conceived through itself, that is, that whose concept does not require the concept of another thing, from which it must be formed."[9] Substance can be neither created nor destroyed. Substance is *causa sui*, the cause of itself, whose essence simply is its existence. "By cause of itself I understand that whose essence involves existence, *or* that whose nature cannot be conceived except as existing."[10]

Substance, thus conceived, is an abstraction. It is the unknown stuff out of which all things are made. We do not perceive substance directly; we perceive its accidents, the way substance makes up the objects of the world that we can see, hear, touch, smell, and taste. Those accidents can be created or destroyed. But substance endures through all such changes. In this regard, the critical attribute of substance is extension, by which it occupies, encompasses, and composes the material world. Substance in this respect is equivalent to nature.

But we can also perceive substance in a different way: through the intellect. As Descartes demonstrated, nature manifests itself according to certain immutable laws—the mechanics of matter in motion—which can be expressed mathematically. Thus, we can understand nature not just empirically, but also rationally in terms of the clear and distinct ideas that govern it and determine all things. In this regard, the critical attribute of substance is thought, by which the laws of nature are revealed.

Substance, conceived as extension and conceived as thought, is the first cause, the *causa sui*, which has always existed and always will exist, and from it all things unfold according to immutable laws. In other words, substance is what we call God. It is also what we call nature. God and nature are not two separate things; they are the same thing (substance) viewed in its separate attributes, thought and extension. We have two separate ways of speaking about the world—in terms of its physical extension and in terms of its intelligible qualities—each of which is equally valid and neither of which can be reduced to or displaced by the other. It is this dual perspective on substance that overcomes the Cartesian dualism between the material world and an immaterial God. It will also, as we shall see, overcome the Cartesian dualism between matter and mind.

Spinoza's God is an immanent God. He is neither the absentee God of Descartes nor the peek-a-boo God of Pascal. His being unfolds itself to us through the immutable laws that govern nature. God is the immanent cause of all things, just as nature is. "God acts from the laws of his nature alone, and is compelled by no one."[11] God or nature, thought or extension, creator or created, eternal or temporal, reason or experience. All things stem from *Deus sive Natura*, from God or nature.

Spinoza has long been criticized for making a bad argument in favor of the existence of God based on the very concept of God. This is known as the ontological argument, which, put in its crudest form, contends that the concept of God in all his perfection necessitates his existence, because if he did not exist, he would not be perfect. This argument had been commonplace in one form or another since at least the sixth century, when Boethius included a version of it in his *Consolation of Philosophy*.[12] It was developed further by Saint Anselm in the eleventh century and accepted by Descartes in the seventeenth, but was largely demolished a century later by Immanuel Kant, who pointed out that existence is not a predicate.[13] That is, we make no addition to a concept, such as God, when we add that it exists or does not exist.

Spinoza does seem to be offering an ontological argument when he contends that God's essence involves existence.[14] But he is actually making a different and much more subtle point, which starts with the fact of existence. "It pertains to the nature of a substance to exist."[15] If substance did not exist, then nothing would exist. But there is something rather than nothing. Even Descartes, despite his malevolent demon, agreed on that. And that something we can understand either empirically (as extension) or intellectually (as thought). We don't need a transcendent God to guarantee the correspondence between thought and the world, because there is no gap to be overcome. Since God is immanent—and coterminous with what exists, just as nature is—it follows that God and nature coexist. That is the starting point of all explanation and understanding.

A more powerful objection to Spinoza's God is that he is simply a *façon de parler*, a way of speaking that we can choose to adopt or not. Why can't we just talk about nature, even Nature with a capital *N*, and leave God out of it? Spinoza himself seems to admit that all "such phrases are simply a manner of speaking."[16] But Spinoza can justly respond that the intelligible principles that govern all existence, the *causa sui*, to which all things owe their existence, is what we mean by God, and that if we eliminate such references, we will impoverish both our discourse and our understanding.

If there is a single self-creating, self-sufficient, eternally existing, and infinite substance that is the cause of, and reason for, all things, what else are we to call that substance but God? "The universal laws of nature, according to which all things exist and are determined, are only another name for the eternal decrees of God, which always involve eternal truth and necessity."[17] The more we understand those decrees, the more we understand the mind of God: "We have greater and more perfect knowledge of God in proportion to our knowledge of natural phenomena."[18] There is an astonishing confluence between the world of thought and the physical world, which obeys laws we can discern by thought. To quote Einstein again, "the most incomprehensible thing about the universe is that it is comprehensible." According to Spinoza, it is comprehensible because God manifests himself to us in the laws of physics and mathematics that govern the universe. In exploring the harmony of nature, we explore the mind of God.

The beauty of this account of God is that it gives focus to our sense of wonder and awe at the universe. It also gives free rein to science. Science tries to determine the laws of nature so that everything fits together and so that every event within the system has an explanation. But, far from competing with religion, science is itself a form of worship, an attempt to appreciate and understand the mind of God. Its central article of faith is that *Deus sive Natura* is a single, causal system that unfolds according to laws intelligible to man.

Spinoza accepts no final causes in nature. There is no room in his system for either purpose or randomness. Cause and effect proceed inexorably pursuant to the mechanical laws of matter and motion. "In nature there is nothing contingent, but all things have been determined from the necessity of the divine nature to exist and produce an effect in a certain way."[19] As a result, there is no such thing as a miracle, understood as a divine exception to the laws of nature. Everything that happens, happens within nature, and just because we don't know enough to explain an event by the laws of nature does not make it a miracle. Nothing can happen that contravenes nature's universal laws; that would require God to act against or contradict his own nature, which is contrary to reason and therefore "absurd."[20] The power of God is not separate from, but rather manifests itself in, the power of nature. To believe otherwise is "a great obstacle to science."[21]

Spinoza's God is therefore nothing like the God of the Old Testament. He takes no personal interest in us or our world. He does not judge us any more than nature does. He does not issue commands, or hand out rewards and punishments, or listen to our prayers. He is neither good nor bad. Qualities such as mercy, justice, grace, anger, and punishment are all "attributes of human nature, and utterly alien from the nature of the Deity."[22] Stripped of all literary and anthropomorphic connotations, God simply is; he always has been and always will be. "God acts and directs all things simply by the necessity of His nature and perfection, and . . . His decrees and volitions are eternal truths, and always involve necessity."[23] Any talk of God's purposes or desires or emotions or acts of will is purely figurative. So, too, is any reference to scripture as the "Word of God."

The Bible, for Spinoza, is a work of literature, whose value is aesthetic, moral, and historical. It was written and rewritten by a number of human authors over time. Each book must be understood in the context of the time in which it was written, edited, and added to the list of sacred books. The so-called Word of God, Spinoza explains, "is faulty, mutilated, tampered with, and inconsistent," and "we possess it only in fragments."[24] All this is commonplace today. But it was shocking enough at the time to occasion widespread condemnation. Spinoza read the Bible as purely figurative in its treatment of God. The books of the Bible are full of wisdom and of incalculable value in the study of man and as a call to virtue and justice. But the same could be said of Milton's *Paradise Lost*, which is also a work of literature written by a man of great moral and aesthetic sensibility. "Books that teach and tell of the highest things are equally sacred," Spinoza insists, "in whatever language and by whatever nation they were written."[25] The history of the first man and woman, as even Pascal was prepared to admit, is a brilliant and compelling allegory, no more but no less.[26]

Thus, "the Bible leaves reason absolutely free" and "has nothing in common with philosophy [i.e., the search for scientific truth]."[27] The prophets were moral teachers, not teachers of natural philosophy, of which they were largely ignorant. The book of Joshua reports that the sun stood still in its path around the earth to allow more time for the Israelites to vanquish their enemies. "Are we, forsooth," Spinoza asks, "bound to believe that Joshua the soldier was a learned astronomer?" Certainly not. Such "superstition is the bitter enemy of all true knowledge and true morality."[28]

Equally superstitious is belief in the efficacy of prayers, rites, and rituals to earn God's favor. God does not listen to our prayers. He will not work miracles for our benefit, however many animals we sacrifice at his altars. Indeed, he will show neither cognizance nor concern for our well-being or happiness. The personal God to whom we are wont to turn for comfort and reassurance in times of peril and for hope and favor in times of uncertainty does not exist. Devotional rituals, prayers, and sacrifices "are in themselves of no significance."[29] They will not avert evil or aid those "who greedily covet temporal advantages" and seek with prayers and tears to obtain them from God.[30] Nor does God send comets or other signs to foretell future events: "All the portents ever invested with the reverence of misguided religion are mere phantoms of dejected and fearful minds."[31]

The rites, rituals, and ceremonies of the various churches not only have no efficacy with God; they bear no relation to blessedness. They are neither necessary nor sufficient for true piety. A wicked man could be strictly observant, while a good man is wholly ignorant of such devices. The two have nothing to do with each other. A man who "abounds in the fruits of the Spirit, charity, joy, peace, long-suffering, kindness, goodness, faith, gentleness . . . is altogether blessed," regardless of his knowledge of scripture or observance of the rites and ceremonies of organized religion.[32] Interestingly, Spinoza acknowledges that rituals and ceremonies may serve a political function in uniting a community and ensuring obedience in a society where everyone is inclined by nature to seek his or her own interest. But they are utterly meaningless from the perspective of reason, and indeed pernicious, to the extent they are expected to ensnare God's favor.

Spinoza, in short, launches a direct, thorough, and courageous assault on all the anthropomorphic conceptions of God upon which both Judaism and Christianity are formed. Spinoza believes in God but not in religion. Or perhaps it is more accurate to say that Spinoza's only religion is natural science, which reveals God's nature in all its necessity and immanent splendor. Pascal had complained that Descartes's mechanical universe was stripped of all enchantment. Spinoza offers us a new enchantment that sees God everywhere and in everything.

MIND

The unbridgeable gulf between a transcendent God and the material world is paralleled in Descartes by the unbridgeable gulf between individual minds and the material world. This is unsurprising, since, for Descartes, the mind or soul—he ends up using the words interchangeably—is eternal, immaterial, and partakes of the divine. But, as we saw in chapter 1, Descartes can offer no intelligible account of how an immaterial mind is able to act through its associated body or to experience the material world through that body. As soon as one posits two completely separate substances—mind and matter—the interaction between them becomes problematic.

Descartes threw up his hands at this dilemma and tossed out the idea that, perhaps, mind and body interact through the pineal gland, a suggestion that now seems laughable both philosophically and anatomically. Gottfried Leibniz—a towering polymath who made significant contributions to philosophy, science, mechanics, and mathematics, and invented calculus independent of Newton—offered an even more bizarre solution. He dismissed the material world of bodies in space and time as an illusion. Our true and only essence is as "monads," irreducible but immaterial centers of force and thought that merely appear to interact with one another and with the material world. These windowless monads float in sensory-deprived isolation, beguiled by appearances arranged and harmonized for them by God. But the monads also have access through pure thought to the laws and principles (mathematical, logical, and moral) according to which God has ordered the true reality. Remarkably, God, in Leibniz, plays the part of Descartes's deceiving demon, who makes us appear to experience an external world that does not exist. Leibniz, a younger contemporary of Spinoza, adopted this approach because he considered the implications of Spinoza's own solution to the mind/body problem inconsistent with received religion, and therefore dangerous.[33]

Spinoza's solution is not only ingenious but almost certainly correct. Extension and thought are not, as in Descartes, separate and self-contained systems that are incapable of acting on each other. We simply have different modes of description of one and the same thing: a human being. *Deus sive Natura*, God or nature, at the level of the individual becomes, in effect, *Animo sive Corporis*, mind or body. Each mode of description is complete and adequate in itself. "The mind and the body are one and the same thing, which is conceived now under the attribute of thought, now under the attribute of extension."[34] Any apparent dualism is purely a function of confusing one mode of speech with another, of treating mental words and concepts—such as mind, love, perception, thought—as if they were referring to another kind of substance, a substance without extension. The mind is not a different kind of substance, and therefore we have no need to solve the problem of dualism. The "problem" does not exist, because there is only a single human being viewed in terms of his or her different attributes of mind and body.

In this respect, Spinoza is anticipating by three centuries the work of Ludwig Wittgenstein in his *Philosophical Investigations*. Indeed, using almost the exact same words that will become Wittgenstein's rallying cry, Spinoza writes: "Words gain their meaning solely from their usage."[35] In this context, the words *mind* and *soul* gain their meaning from the way we talk about human beings, their thoughts, their aspirations, and their emotions. Again, that does not mean that talk about minds—anymore than talk about God—is just a *façon de parler* that can be readily discarded. We absolutely require the language of thoughts and passions to reflect the complexity and interest of human beings. Imagine how primitive our view of human nature would be—and we ourselves would become—if we did not have a rich vocabulary of human thoughts and emotions. The same is true of animals, for that matter. Spinoza is not compelled to adopt Descartes's all-or-nothing approach to minds. Animals may be simpler than humans but are nonetheless complex and purposive enough for us to attribute to them both thoughts and emotions.

Yet Spinoza contends that, just as there is a total correspondence between the different attributes of God and nature, so, too, "the order of actions and passions of our body is, by nature, at one with the order of actions and passions of the mind."[36] Whether we view human action and passion through the language of ideas or the language of the body, in the end, we are talking about the same thing—a human being—so the two languages, Spinoza concludes, must have an exact correspondence.

> Both the decision of the mind and the appetite and the determination of the body by nature exist together—or rather are one and the same thing, which we call a decision when it is considered under, and explained through, the attribute of thought, and which we call a determination when it is considered under the attribute of extension and deduced from the laws of motion and rest.[37]

Since Descartes demonstrated that "the order and connection of things" is discernable *a priori* in the laws of geometry and cause and effect, the same must be true of "the order and connection of ideas."[38] That is, there must be a discernible geometry of the passions and principles of cause and effect that govern the mind. "I shall consider human actions and appetites," Spinoza writes at the beginning of part 3 of the *Ethics*, "just as if it were a question of lines, planes, and bodies."[39] Hence, the *Ethics* is constructed like a geometry textbook, with definitions, axioms, postulates, and demonstrations.

In providing a geometry of the passions, Spinoza seeks to reduce them to their most basic elements, from which all other passions can be derived. He starts with *conatus*, which he defines as the desire to persist and enhance one's own being. "Each thing," he notes, "as far as it can by its own power, strives to persevere in its being."[40] In some respects, *conatus* anticipates Darwin's survival instinct or struggle for existence. But it also contains elements of self-assertion and an expansion of power. It thus bears a relationship to Freud's libido and Nietzsche's will to power. *Conatus* is man's "very essence."[41] It is the initial quantum of mental energy that powers all thought and all emotion, and attempts to realize its nature through acts that preserve its individual existence and increase its power over the external world.

The external world, however, is largely indifferent to our desires and can be intransigent. It may further our purposes or thwart them. This gives rise to the other two basic elements in Spinoza's system. We experience joy or pleasure (*laetitia*) when our desires are realized and sadness or pain (*tristitia*) when they are thwarted. The self—in the grip of its *conatus*—experiences its own expansion of power of acting and satisfying its desires as joy, and the diminution of that power as sadness.

From these three elements—desire, joy, and sadness—Spinoza derives all other passions and emotions. They are all combinations of desire, joy/pleasure, and sorrow/pain, with varying degrees of knowledge or belief about the external world.[42] Thus, Spinoza writes, "love is nothing but joy with the accompanying idea of an external cause, and hate is nothing but sadness with the accompanying idea of an external cause."[43] Spinoza attempts a similar breakdown of other passions and emotions: wonder, disdain, inclination, aversion, devotion, mockery, hope, fear, confidence, despair, gladness, remorse, pity, indignation, scorn, envy, compassion, humility, pride, repentance, shame. The list can go on indefinitely, but all have the same basic elements—desire, joy, and sadness—all directed at, and either helped or thwarted by, external objects, including especially other people. Spinoza seeks to analyze these emotions with the dispassion of a geometer and to dissolve them into their most basic elements.

There is a long tradition of analyzing and distilling the constituent elements of the human mind, starting with Plato and continuing through Aquinas and Descartes all the way to Freud and beyond. Descartes posited six basic passions: wonder, love, hatred, desire, joy, and sadness.[44] Spinoza cuts that number in half. Like all reductive accounts, it is overly simplistic. Yet we often feel the shock of recognition and insight. What Spinoza is trying to do is reveal to us the conceptual landscape of the human mind, the ways in which our various mental concepts relate to one another and explain our behavior.

What is disconcerting about Spinoza's approach, however, is its strict determinism. He treats the passions of the soul as so many billiard balls set in motion by *conatus* and subject to the same laws of cause and effect that govern the material world. Spinoza refers to the passions and emotions as "affects" and treats them as counterparts to physical affects: "The affects . . . of hate, anger, envy, and the like . . . follow with the same necessity and force of Nature."[45]

This is certainly understandable. As noted, Spinoza thought that the language of mind and the language of physical bodies are just different modes of description of the same thing. If the latter is subject to strict determinism, then the former must be as well, even if the biology of organic things has not come close to such an account—not in Spinoza's day certainly, and not in our day either. Spinoza acknowledges that "no one has yet come to know the structure of the body so accurately that he could explain all its functions."[46] Yet he nonetheless insists that "the mind is determined to will this or that by a cause which is also determined by another, and this again by another, and so to infinity."[47] If the physical world is subject to the laws of cause and effect, it cannot be otherwise with the mind. Mental processes are just physical processes under a different mode of description, and vice versa. A human is a unified whole of body and mind, and this unified whole is subject to the same laws under both descriptions.

Spinoza thus thinks that the language of desires, purposes, and acts of will is prescientific and will ultimately be displaced by a thoroughly precise analysis of physical causes that will reveal human beings as highly complex automatons subject to the inexorable laws of cause and effect. Just as there are no final causes in nature, Spinoza will accept no final causes in a proper scientific account of human actions. It follows that any belief that the mind has absolute power over its own actions is an illusion, and free will, understood as the absence of any causal determination of the will, is impossible. In short, Spinoza views the language of human intentions and will—just as he did the language of traditional religion—as largely figurative.[48]

It is not necessary, however, to accept Spinoza's determinism and scientism to appreciate his basic insights about the mind. One can acknowledge that mind and extension are different modes of description of human beings without concluding that, at some deeper level, they must be exactly coterminous or that the former is but a primitive, prescientific version of the latter. Spinoza did not, in the end, fully appreciate what Wittgenstein would call the autonomy of grammar,[49] and thus thought that scientific descriptions in terms of efficient causes are superior or more fundamental than other forms of discourse. Our language of passion, emotions, purposes, and acts of will is wonderfully rich and evocative. It stands on its own and cannot, without a total loss of sense and nuance, be mapped onto a purely physical vocabulary (whether of bodily movements or brain processes). Of course, one might say the same about our standard, figurative language of God. Spinoza's equation of God with nature can be seen as just another example of the seventeenth century's obsession with science as revealing the true nature of the universe and our place within it, an obsession that will lead to the equally strong counter-reaction of the Romantics.

But questions remain. If all human acts are necessary products of cause and effect, how can we attribute praise or blame to them? How is ethics possible without freedom of will? Is our entire language of morality also to be dismissed as primitive and prescientific? Must everything we value and hold most dear be assimilated to the vocabulary of matter and motion? One might call this last formulation the fundamental dilemma of seventeenth-century scientism.

ETHICS

Spinoza's answer to such questions begins with his theory of knowledge. According to Spinoza, we have three kinds of knowledge, in increasing order of certainty and solidity. We begin with sense experience and the images formed in the mind from our observations of the world. Spinoza calls this "imagination," though empirical philosophers in the English tradition, from John Locke to David Hume, will refer simply to "sense impressions." Following a separate philosophical tradition, from Plato through Montaigne, Spinoza disparages the raw data of the senses as uninformative and unreliable until brought under the active control of reason, which forms what Spinoza calls "common notions," or ideas of the properties common to multiple images. Through these common notions, we develop a vocabulary for, and a way of talking about, the material world. Our growing body of concepts allows us to impose on perceptions a grid that maps the world for us and to develop our understanding of nature and, in particular, the laws of cause and effect. At the level of imagination, everything that happens seems to us random and contingent; it is a blur of images that we passively receive. At the level of reason, we actively formulate the laws that govern nature. We round out our view of the world with a more scientific understanding of nature. We move from inadequate ideas to adequate ones, as we learn to distinguish true from false and recognize that all things are determined.

So far, Spinoza and the British empiricists are on roughly the same track. What distinguishes them from each other—and makes Spinoza a "rationalist," to the extent such labels are useful at all—is the extent to which Spinoza relies on the third level of knowledge, which he calls "intuition." This is the level of pure thought, through which we develop an immediate grasp of necessary truths. We come to understand the self-evident propositions of mathematics, geometry, and metaphysics that govern all things in nature. In effect, we see into the mind of God and the deepest heart of nature. Incomprehensively, as Einstein would put it, *Deus sive Natura* becomes comprehensible to us; or, as Spinoza explains, "the human mind is a part of the infinite intellect of God."[50]

This may all seem a bit mystical. But Spinoza's vision has its origins in Aristotle, as solidly grounded a thinker as ever existed, who also thought that man's highest excellence lies in the exercise of the intellectual functions that separate him from the animals and bring him closest to the divine. Sounding very much like Aristotle, Spinoza writes: "Inasmuch as the intellect is the best part of our being, it is evident that we should make every effort to perfect it as far as possible. . . . For in intellectual perfection the highest good should consist."[51] Aristotle conceives of virtue (*arête*) as human flourishing, as man realizing his highest potential through the exercise of reason, his most distinctive attribute. For Spinoza, too, the greatest good of the mind and its greatest virtue is to know *Deus sive Natura* through theoretical reason.

But Spinoza, of course, recognizes that that is not how most people define good. Driven by *conatus*, we believe that whatever is to our own advantage is good. So we call "good" that which we desire and "evil" that to which we are averse. Our moral judgments are expressions of self-interest rather than statements about the world: "Everyone who is in the state of nature considers only his own advantage, and decides what is good and what is evil from his own temperament, and only insofar as he takes account of his own advantage."[52]

Such an attitude places us in the grip of the external forces that thwart desire and give rise to pain, or that satisfy desire and give rise to pleasure. As we have seen, our passions are the "affects" of these encounters. Our lack of power to moderate and restrain these affects is a form of bondage.[53] We are not our own masters and are unable to know our intrinsic good. Love and hate, desire and aversion pull us away from the rational and intuitive knowledge that makes us distinctly human. Greed, ambition, and lust are all "species of madness."[54] Sounding very much like Pascal, Spinoza writes, in a rare rhetorical flourish: "From what has been said it is clear that we are driven about in many ways by external causes, and that, like waves on the sea, driven by contrary winds, we toss about, not knowing our outcome and fate."[55]

Freedom for Spinoza is freedom from the passions that obscure, and lead us away from, our higher natures. It is the freedom to exercise our reason and to realize our true advantage. To reach that state we must replace a passive acceptance of the passions with an active use of reason. "The mind is more liable to passions the more it has inadequate ideas."[56] Conversely, "an affect which is a passion ceases to be a passion as soon as we form a clear and distinct idea of it."[57] Thus, if we can "separat[e] the affects from the thought of an external cause"[58]—if, that is, we can analyze the geometry of our passions with an increasing degree of objectivity—we can reduce the power of those affects, for "the more an affect is known to us, . . . the more it is in our power, and the less the mind is acted on by it."[59] In this way, the intellect can attain dominion over the affects of the mind caused by the interaction of *conatus* with the external world. "To every action to which we are determined from an affect which is a passion, we can be determined by reason, without that affect."[60]

For Spinoza, freedom consists of action consistent with reason. It does not require an absence of causal determination, which would simply make the action random and incomprehensible. Freedom is, rather, action determined by our highest nature, not by affects of the mind triggered by external causes.[61] In this sense, only God is perfectly free. But man, insofar as he engages his reason and partakes of the mind of God, can achieve a significant measure of freedom.

Ordinarily we say that moral freedom can cut either way: we are free to choose the path of virtue or the path of vice. But, for Spinoza, freedom is asymmetrical. Only virtue is a sign of freedom, because it is action in accordance with our highest natures. Vice is determined by affects triggered by causes outside ourselves.

In order to reach this state of freedom, we must continually replace our confused and inadequate ideas with adequate ideas based on certain knowledge. That is, we must learn to view the world, not just as a series of events in time (*sub specie durationis*), but *sub specie aeternitatis*, in the light of eternal truths that govern all things. Our narrow temporal concerns and the passions that bind us fall away as we approach objective understanding. We cease to strive, and the voice of *conatus*, with its incessant "I want," falls quiet. Essentially, what Spinoza is advocating is, in modern jargon, called mindfulness, our ability to contemplate the world free of the passions and parochial concerns that distort our perceptions.

Spinoza calls this an "intellectual love of God." It is not a personal love, nor can it be, because God has no personal features. Rather, the intellectual love of God is a deep appreciation and sense of awe at what *Deus sive Natura* has wrought. This love makes no demands and seeks no special favors. It is, instead, the foundation of our morality. We love God, and that love extends to all men and women, indeed to all things, which are but manifestations or modes of God. Spinoza, the renegade Jew, as he was frequently called, sees in Jesus the purest exemplar of the moral life. Jesus urged us to love God and to love our neighbor as ourselves. That is precisely what seeing the world *sub specie aeternitatis* entails. We shed our personal sense of self and adopt the disinterested perspective of God. We recognize that we have no privileged place in the universe and have not been granted any dominion over nature. We are all equally part of nature and thereby partake of the divine.

Understanding God and nature is an end in itself because it gives us joy and peace of mind that will not succumb to external fortune. We free ourselves from the emotions that drive our behavior and make us prey to fear and hope alike. "The more we strive to live according to the guidance of reason, the more we strive to depend less on hope, to free ourselves from fear, to conquer fortune as much as we can, and to direct our actions by the certain counsel of reason."[62] We let go of our prephilosophical attachment to the self. We drop our desire for transitory goods coveted by others, goods that have nothing to do with true happiness. The concerns of the self dissolve in the unity of *Deus sive Natura*, and the mind becomes free. As we contemplate the whole of creation, we attain a serenity infused with joy that Spinoza calls blessedness.

In the process, we obtain a form of immortality. Not personal immortality. There is no such thing as a soul that survives the body. There are no eternal rewards or punishments. But we can attain a sort of disinterested immortality. Freed from the "principle of our own advantage," we can identify ourselves with *Deus sive Natura*, which has always existed and always will exist.

Spinoza warns us at the end of his *Ethics* that "all things excellent are as difficult as they are rare."[63] Spinoza is one of the rarest and most difficult of thinkers. And the path he lays out for us is equally so. We may not, in the end, be satisfied equating God with nature. We may not find his solution to the mind/body problem convincing or his "geometry" of the passions enlightening. We may be even more disturbed by his strict determinism and naturalist ethics, which displaces warm human emotions and generous actions with a disinterested contemplation of the universe.

Yet many—and I am among them—find Spinoza's philosophy both compelling and deeply moving. He frees us of the oxymoron of a transcendent but anthropomorphic God, while leaving us to contemplate with wonder and awe the beauty and regularity of the universe. He frees us from an incoherent dualism—and the various unsatisfactory "isms" developed in response, such as behaviorism and central-state material-ism—while leaving us to contemplate the remarkable capacity of life, including nonhuman life, to experience complex emotions and passions. He frees us from deontological ethical theories based on external com-mands of questionable origin, while leaving us with an ethical theory based on the intrinsic value of every man, woman, and child, and their equal entitlement to fulfill their potential as human beings. Perhaps most important of all, Spinoza was a faithful champion of the Enlightenment ideal of progress through free thought and free expression, at a time when that ideal was under great pressure. "Every man should think what he likes and say what he thinks."

6

DEFOE AND SWIFT

Autobiography as Myth

The history of the English novel begins in 1719 with the publication of *Robinson Crusoe*.[1] It continues on a traditional path with the later novels of Defoe, particularly *Moll Flanders* and *Roxana*; follows the epistolary outpourings of Samuel Richardson in *Pamela* and *Clarissa*; and reaches an early maturity in Henry Fielding's *Tom Jones*, published in 1749. Later novelists writing in English—even the greatest ones, such as Jane Austen, Charles Dickens, George Eliot, the Brontë sisters, Joseph Conrad, and Henry James—are sounding variations on themes laid down in the first half of the eighteenth century.

All of these novelists entertain. But they do far more than that. They convey knowledge about human life, feelings, thoughts, and actions. More than any other genre, novels hold up a mirror to ordinary human existence in all its moral and emotional complexity. The novel is the most flexible instrument ever devised for laying bare the human soul and the inherently social nature of the human condition. As such, it is a natural outgrowth of the Enlightenment.

Scientists such as Kepler, Galileo, and Newton abandoned ancient categories of thought that impeded our understanding of the physical world. They built a new science of matter and motion expressed with mathematical precision. Philosophers as disparate as Descartes, Spinoza, and Locke also wanted to start from scratch, using perception and reason (in varying degrees) to reenvision not just the physical world, but also the political, social, and moral structures within which we live.

John Locke, in his 1689 *Essay Concerning Human Understanding*, argued that the human mind is a *tabula rasa*, a blank slate, on which the evidence of our senses makes impressions. Those impressions gradually coalesce to form simple ideas of the objects that give rise to the impressions. From this humble, passive beginning, we develop through reflection our more complex picture of the world. It comes together, quite literally, bit by bit, through experience. The so-called rationalists, with whom Descartes and Spinoza are traditionally grouped, emphasize the innate scaffolding of the mind (mathematics, identity, and the most basic laws of cause and effect), which allows us actively to order and make sense of empirical impressions. But the difference between the two groups of thinkers is really just a matter of emphasis and sequencing: both empiricists and rationalists require a combination of sense impressions and reasoning to provide a foundation for knowledge. They are each like Robinson Crusoe on his island, trying to construct his own version of civilization from the tools at hand, some of which he was able to bring from the ship and others of which he had to make himself.

The English novel in its origins falls decidedly on the Lockean, empiricist end of this spectrum. We know that Defoe had studied Locke, and Defoe tells the story of Robinson Crusoe in a Lockean manner: impression by impression, piling up vivid, concrete details into simple ideas that gradually form an increasingly complex portrait of one man's journey and the emotional, moral, and spiritual resources that sustain him. Descartes and Spinoza had wanted to establish a geometry of the passions, reducing them to their most basic elements. But the traditional novel, from Defoe onward, is not interested in such species classification. It focuses on individual character. In the hands of Defoe and his successors, the novel is a means of psychological, moral, and social understanding and, as such, an instrument of Enlightenment progress—sometimes explicitly, as in Richardson and Dickens, and at other times more subtly, as in Jane Austen and Henry James.

But there is also a countertradition of the novel, beginning with Jonathan Swift, who was seven years younger than Defoe and seven years later with his own masterpiece. *Gulliver's Travels*, published in 1726, is in many respects an answer to and critique of *Robinson Crusoe*. It launches a satiric and ironic movement that is less interested in character than in types, less interested in individual men and women than in Man as a species. This tradition tends to be skeptical of Enlightenment claims to progress. It takes a darker view of man and, as a consequence, tends to hold fast to existing institutions and modes of thought. Whereas *Robinson Crusoe* is an "optimistic" work (a term first coined during the Enlightenment), *Gulliver's Travels* mocks such pretensions, as will Voltaire's *Candide* a few decades later. Other works in this tradition will include Laurence Sterne's *Tristram Shandy*, Lewis Carroll's *Alice in Wonderland*, and the novels and stories of Franz Kafka. Once again, though, these are somewhat arbitrary points on a spectrum rather than a fixed demarcation. Indeed, one might say that both traditions will find their apotheosis almost two centuries later in James Joyce's *Ulysses*.

Daniel Defoe and Jonathan Swift were natural antagonists. One was a dissenter, the other a staunch defender of the Church of England. One was progressive in outlook, the other conservative. One was earnest, the other skeptical. They were both brilliant journalists and launched dueling polemics at each other as if they were artillery shells. They even vied for preferment from the same ministers. Both were disappointed, yet each established his own claim to immortality at the relatively advanced age of fifty-nine.

Neither Robinson Crusoe nor Lemuel Gulliver represents his creator. Crusoe is not Defoe any more than Gulliver is Swift. But the differences in the two characters—in what each experiences and how each reacts to those experiences—reflect the differences between the two writers.

PARALLEL LIVES

Daniel Foe was born in the Cripplegate neighborhood of London in 1660. It was the year of the Restoration, in which Charles II returned from exile in Europe and put an end to the Puritan protectorate established by Oliver Cromwell.

Daniel had two older sisters. Their father, James, was a tallow chandler, which is to say he made candles from animal fats, a prosperous if smoky business. Their mother, Alice, died when Daniel was only eight years old.

The Foes were isolated by the Act of Uniformity in 1662, part of the infamous "Clarendon Code," which prescribed strict adherence to the sacraments, prayers, and doctrines of the official Church of England on pain of exclusion from any public or church office. Remarkably, even extemporaneous prayer from the heart was forbidden; all religious expression was to be channeled through the *Book of Common Prayer*.

As Presbyterians, the Foes instantly became "dissenters," or "nonconformists," a status that would greatly affect Daniel throughout his life. So, too, would the other tumultuous events of his first six years. The Great Plague of 1665—the last full-scale outbreak of bubonic plague in Europe—killed as many as one hundred thousand Londoners, one-quarter of the city's population. It was followed in 1666 by the Great Fire, which devastated vast portions of the city, largely destroying Shakespeare's London. In Daniel's Cripplegate neighborhood, only three houses escaped destruction, one of which belonged to the Foes.

Both plague and fire were memorably chronicled in the diaries of Samuel Pepys. Daniel, too, would later write *A Journal of the Plague Year*, not so much from his own memories of course, but based on thorough research leavened by his vivid imagination. One cannot but think that his eye for compelling and illustrative details—striking in both his journalism and his novels—was shaped by the searing images of his early years. The Great Fire—tragic as it was—created an opportunity for the rebuilding of Shakespeare's London in the neoclassical style of Christopher Wren. So, too, Daniel Foe would fashion a novel style of writing from the sundry ruins of his life.

Daniel attended an academy for dissenters and was intended by his father for the Presbyterian ministry. He received a good education, including modern languages, history, and geography, as well as mathematics and science. But neither Catholics nor dissenters could attend Oxford or Cambridge. And Daniel had no calling for the church. He became a wholesale merchant instead, selling hosiery and other items, including wine and tobacco. He was reasonably prosperous. In 1684, he married Mary Tuffley, who brought him a large dowry and bore seven children, six of whom survived to adulthood. But quiet domestic prosperity seemed not to agree with Daniel's restless and often reckless disposition, qualities he would share with his most famous character.

Charles II died in 1685 without a legitimate heir and was succeeded by his younger brother, who now ruled Scotland as James VII, and England and Ireland as James II. James II was Catholic, and Protestants of all stripes feared a combined papal and French plot to return England and

Scotland to Catholicism. Rebellions broke out in both countries. The one in England was led by James II's illegitimate nephew, the Duke of Monmouth, who claimed to be the rightful heir to the throne. Both rebellions were ultimately crushed, but not before Daniel Foe impetuously joined the Monmouth Rebellion and fought at the decisive and disastrous battle of Sedgemoor.

James II exacted heavy retribution for the failed rebellions, but Daniel somehow managed to avoid punishment, despite writing a pamphlet denouncing James II for his ties to Catholicism and to France and his repression of Presbyterians. Daniel received a formal pardon in 1687, the same year James II issued the Declaration of Indulgence giving religious freedom to both Catholics and dissenters alike. That declaration was strongly opposed by the High Church Anglicans and soon would contribute to James II's downfall in what became known as the Glorious Revolution.

A precipitating factor of that revolution was the birth in 1688 of a son to James II and his Catholic wife. By his first wife, James had a daughter, Mary, who was married to William of Orange of the Dutch Republic. The expectation that Mary and her husband, both Protestants, would rule England on her father's death was a balm of sorts to the Anglicans. But the birth of a son raised the unappealing prospect of a Catholic dynasty. James augmented these concerns by his ill-advised prosecution of seven Anglican bishops for seditious libel in refusing to have the Declaration of Indulgence read in all the churches.

Seizing his opportunity, William of Orange landed in England in November 1688. He met little resistance. James II made a hasty and disastrous retreat to Ireland, hoping the Catholics there would rally to his defense. But William routed them handily at the battle of the Boyne in 1690. He proceeded to subjugate the Catholics in Ireland and settled many Dutch Protestants there, setting the stage for centuries of sectarian strife.

The throne was now firmly in the Protestant hands of William III and Mary II. But religious disagreements were not at an end. There was constant jockeying between High Church Anglicans—who, aside from being ruled by bishops rather than a pope, were hard to tell from Catholics—and the various Protestant dissenters, including Puritans and Presbyterians. The former generally became Tories and tended to support absolute monarchy. The latter were Whigs and favored a constitutional monarchy. Sometimes one party was in the ascendant, sometimes the other, and religious toleration waxed and waned accordingly.

Daniel Foe was more Whig than Tory but firmly aligned with neither party. He was a staunch supporter of William III and served his administration in various positions. His financial life, however, was constantly on the edge. Highly leveraged shipments fell prey to pirates and storms, both of which would figure in the travails of Robinson Crusoe. He borrowed heavily in an attempt to recoup his losses through increasingly risky schemes. He even bought a diving bell with which he hoped to retrieve sunken treasure. By 1692, he was bankrupt and imprisoned for debt. He managed to get released from prison after a few months. But he had lost his wife's entire dowry and his wholesale business, and still owed the modern equivalent of 1.7 million pounds. Some of his creditors would pursue him for the rest of his life, and he grew increasingly secretive and elusive.

To blot the memory of his recent humiliation, Daniel reinvented and ennobled himself as Daniel de Foe, or Defoe, as we now know him. Having failed in business, he turned naturally to journalism and gave advice to others in a wide variety of pieces on politics and practical life. He even wrote a poem in 1700 to honor William III which, despite William's Dutch ancestry, he called "The True-Born Englishman." The poem was extremely popular and jingoistic in the way that Rudyard Kipling would later be. It also took a dim view of religious hypocrisy:

> Wherever God erects a house of prayer,
> The Devil always builds a chapel there:
> And 'twill be found upon examination,
> The latter has the largest congregation. [2]

William III died in 1702 and was succeeded by James's daughter Anne, who showed less tolerance for dissenters. Defoe grew increasingly scathing in his journalism. He had written a piece in 1698 called "An Enquiry into the Occasional Conformity of Dissenters," which attacked dissenters who accommodated themselves to the Church of England. He accused them of playing a "loose game of religion" in order to obtain "public advancement."[3] They take Holy Communion in the Church of England in the morning, he noted, before quietly attending nonconformist services in the afternoon.

Having angered his natural allies among the Whigs, Defoe proceeded to offend the Tories even more. Under Queen Anne, open hostility to dissenters became commonplace, and a bill that demanded more than "occasional conformity" passed the House of Commons and was being debated in the House of Lords. Defoe rushed into print a satiric pamphlet called *The Shortest Way with the Dissenters*. The pamphlet blames dissenters, whom he calls "a race of poisoned spirits,"[4] for a litany of grievous offenses in recent English history, including the English Civil War and the Monmouth Rebellion. It then makes a series of increasingly extreme arguments against any show of tolerance to dissenters and, suggesting that the very survival of the Church of England is in question, ends in a dramatic flourish: "Alas, the Church of England! What with popery on the one hand, and schismatics on the other, how has she been crucified between two thieves! *Now let us crucify the thieves!*"[5]

Defoe's pamphlet succeeded in discrediting the bill. Carried to such an extreme, the various arguments against dissenters were exposed as untenable. But Defoe managed to mimic the manner and matter of the High Church Tories so effectively that many readers thought the pamphlet was genuine. In the ultimate irony, Defoe was charged with conspiring to deny religious toleration to dissenters. He was convicted of seditious libel in 1703 and sentenced to a fine, indefinite imprisonment, and to stand three days in the pillory, a highly hazardous undertaking. But Defoe published a self-deprecating "Hymn to the Pillory" in anticipation of his ordeal, and ended up surrounded by supporters who pelted him with flowers rather than the usual stones and rotten eggs.

Freed from prison with the consent of Queen Anne, Defoe turned pragmatic. He began to serve successive ministries, Whig and Tory alike, with his influential journalism, which he memorably called "writing history by inches."[6] He also served as an advisor and sometime secret agent for Robert Harley, Lord Oxford, Speaker of the House of Commons and, later, secretary of state, who was himself a Whig turned Tory. Defoe gathered intelligence, especially on the ongoing war with France and a potential union with Scotland. He was a strong and effective promoter of the Acts of Union, which eventually joined England and Scotland into a single Great Britain.

Defoe founded an influential periodical journal, *The Review*, which was widely read and much imitated. Politically, *The Review* fell somewhere in between the various Tory and Whig publications. As a moderate, Defoe was detested by both extremes. He championed women's rights, religious tolerance, and social progress. He wrote a longer piece,

The Storm, an account of the Great Storm of 1703, a hurricane that caused widespread damages and killed more than eight thousand people. Weaving together facts and eyewitness accounts in a compelling narrative, *The Storm* was the first book-length work of modern journalism, a predecessor of Sebastian Junger's *The Perfect Storm*:

> The fury of the tempest increased to such a degree, that . . . most people expected the fall of their houses. And yet in this general apprehension, no body durst quit their tottering habitations; for whatever the danger was within doors, 'twas worse without; the bricks, tiles, and stones, from the tops of the houses, flew with such force, and so thick in the streets, that no one thought fit to venture out, tho' their houses were near demolished within. [7]

Defoe was now more prosperous, but he still lived a precarious existence, both financially and politically. He was arrested several more times, either for debt or because his political writings offended one person or another. But he was always bailed out and protected by Harley, until Harley himself suffered a downfall. The underlying cause was the War of the Spanish Succession, in which France battled England and its Austrian and Dutch allies over who was to succeed the childless Charles II, the last Habsburg ruler of Spain, who died in 1700. For eleven years, Britain and its allies were locked in a war with France and the Spanish supporters of Phillip V, a member of the French royal family.

The war threatened to change the balance of power in Europe. Thanks to the military genius of John Churchill, the first Duke of Marlborough and ancestor of Sir Winston Churchill, Britain and its allies won repeated victories against the French, most decisively at the battle of Blenheim in 1704. The French sued for peace but Spain, under Philip V, was intractable, and the war dragged on and grew increasingly unpopular in Britain, especially among merchants and Whigs generally. Under intense pressure, the Tory administration eventually abandoned the allies and came to a separate peace with France in 1711.

The resolution of the war is notable from our perspective because it first pitted the pens of Swift and Defoe directly against each other, though both men were, at the time, ostensibly working for Harley. Swift wrote *The Conduct of the Allies* in 1711, in which he denounced both the Austrian and Dutch allies and the Duke of Marlborough. Defoe responded with *A Defense of the Allies* that exalted Marlborough and condemned the opportunistic abandonment of the Austrians and the Dutch.

Swift proved the savvier polemicist and placed himself on the winning side of this debate. But it did neither man any good in terms of their political careers. Although Harley negotiated the Treaty of Utrecht in 1713, which finally ended the broader war, he was dismissed by Queen Anne shortly before her death in 1714. Anne, the last of the Stuart rulers, was succeeded by her second cousin George, Elector of Hanover and the first British king from the House of Hanover. Some Tories quietly supported replacing George I with Anne's Catholic half brother, James Stuart (commonly known as the Old Pretender). But this "Jacobite Rebellion," though it had some initial success in Scotland, failed miserably in the end, and James returned to his sanctuary in France. The Tories were thoroughly discredited, and Robert Walpole became the first Whig prime minister. Although he was ultimately acquitted of any involvement in the plot, Harley spent two years in the Tower of London.

With Harley's downfall, Defoe largely ceased to be a public figure. He wrote a number of biographies, fake memoirs, and histories. He also penned advice books on family life, child raising, and sex in marriage. And he continued to dodge his creditors. Defoe finally turned to novel writing in 1719 with the colossal success of *Robinson Crusoe*. He wrote a couple of mediocre sequels but solidified his position as the first great English novelist with a series of books written in the five-year period between 1719 and 1724, including *Moll Flanders*, *Roxana*, and *A Journal of the Plague Year*, which made for remarkable reading in 2020, as the coronavirus spread around the world and fundamentally altered the ordinary course of human life. Defoe's fictional narrator reports on the growing anxiety fanned by inadequate government guidance, the self-quarantines (both voluntary and—terrifyingly—involuntary, when houses are padlocked with sick and well alike inside them), the lack of beds and other medical necessities, the hoarding of supplies, and the morbid obsession with the weekly "bills"—that is, the published numbers of those who have died.

Jonathan Swift, too, lost any chance of preferment in England after Harley's imprisonment and reluctantly returned to Dublin. Though born there in 1667, he had never warmed to his native country. Swift was an Englishman and an Anglican by birth and by inclination. At that time, Anglicans made up only 10 percent of the population of Ireland but held most of the land and all the political power. Though Swift would soon become a champion of, and hero to, the Irish people, there was little reason to expect such a transformation in 1714, when Swift treated his return as a sentence of exile and expressed his disgust with the dirty, impoverished, and uneducated Irish people.

Swift's father died before he was born, and he was largely abandoned by his mother. He was raised by a maternal uncle, who seemed to resent the charge. But Swift still received an excellent education. He attended Trinity College, Dublin, and, despite frequent sanctions for skipping chapel services, he graduated in 1686 with a bachelor of arts degree *speciali gratia* (by special grace), which seems to indicate that he barely scraped by.

After pursuing graduate studies for a time, Swift moved to England and worked as a private secretary to Sir William Temple. He felt underappreciated but formed there the most important relationship of his life, with Temple's ward, the nine-year-old Esther Johnson. Swift, who developed a habit of choosing pet names and private endearments for the women who were important to him, called her Stella. They were close friends throughout their lives. Whether there was more to it than that—including a rumored secret marriage—is a question that has bedeviled biographers ever since.

Swift was plagued by Ménière's disease, which causes hearing loss, ringing in the ears, and bouts of vertigo. In 1694, he returned to Ireland and took orders as an Anglican deacon. It was plainly a career choice rather than a calling. He was ordained to the priesthood the following year but languished in a series of undistinguished parish appointments. Lonely and depressed, Swift proposed marriage in 1696 to one Jane Waring, whom Swift called Varina. Unsurprisingly, she turned down the penniless youth, who had neither family connections nor prospects. Swift returned to the service of William Temple and remained there until Temple's death in 1699, when he again returned to Ireland.

Stella and her constant companion, Rebecca Dingley, moved to Dublin at Swift's urging in 1701. Swift received his doctorate from Trinity the following year but still failed to advance within the church. In 1704, he published *A Tale of a Tub*, an allegorical satire about three sons—representing the three main Christian sects: Catholics, Anglicans, and the various Protestant "dissenters"—fighting over their father's testament. The book was published anonymously, but Swift's authorship was an open secret. It made his fame and largely destroyed his career. Though ostensibly a defense of the Anglican religion, the book seems at times to mock all religion. Its many digressions and parodies of "modern authors" overshadow the tale itself; the book is, to be frank, close to unreadable today. But it was wildly popular at the time and so highly regarded that Samuel Johnson, who did not like Swift, insisted that someone else must have written it. It also had two add-ons—*The Battle of the Books*, which describes a literal battle between ancient and modern manuscripts in St. James's Library, with Swift making clear his preference for old learning; and *A Discourse Concerning the Mechanical Operation of the Spirit*, which mocks "enthusiastic preachers" who claim to be possessed of an inward light: "I am resolved immediately," the supposedly unknown author writes, "to weed this error out of mankind, by making it clear, that this mystery, of vending spiritual gifts, is nothing but a *trade*, acquired by as much instruction, and mastered by equal practice and application as others are."[8]

The upshot of these works is a sort of cranky conservatism. Swift thought doctrinal disputes were an absurd presumption and a waste of time, energy, and even life. He believed that everyone in England, Scotland, and Ireland should simply accept the precepts and rituals of the dominant Church of England. He dismissed theological niceties about the Trinity, the transubstantiation of the Eucharist, and discussions about whether God's omnipresence and omniscience were compatible with the existence of evil. Swift cared more about political order and the role of a state-sponsored religion in molding a united citizenry than he did about the exact content of that religion. Interestingly, though, the God envisioned in the third of these works is not far from Spinoza's own deity: distant, unknowable, and indifferent to the affairs of men.

Many applauded the bold cleric. He moved back to London in hopes of preferment and became friends with the leading writers of the day, particularly the poet Alexander Pope. He also formed yet another mysterious bond, this time with Esther Vanhomrigh, whom he called Vanessa. But his most important attachment was with Robert Harley, who found Swift's pen to be every bit as useful as Defoe's in churning out polemical pamphlets. The two writers vied for Harley's attention and favor. It is not clear how often Swift and Defoe might have met. In any event, Swift had no patience for dissenters and Presbyterians, and he spoke slightingly of

Defoe: "The fellow that was pilloried (I have forgot his name) is indeed so grave, sententious, dogmatical a rogue that there is no enduring him."[9]

Swift's highest ambition was to become a bishop in England. Harley would have been happy to oblige. But Queen Anne did not like *A Tale of a Tub*. She found it irreverent, even scandalous, and steadfastly blocked the appointment. The best Harley could do for his protégé was the deanship of St. Patrick's Cathedral in Dublin. Vanessa followed him there. Neither Vanessa nor Stella could have been happy with this arrangement; indeed, Vanessa even dropped Swift from her will shortly before her death in 1723 after he refused to cut ties with Stella. Swift never married that we know. Throughout his life, though, and particularly in his later years, he formed close, flirtatious friendships with numerous women, mostly pretty, young, and aristocratic. Vanessa and Stella were by far his closest confidantes, but Swift was always careful to avoid any occasion for scandal. Stella and Rebecca Dingley often stayed in the deanery, but when Stella herself grew gravely ill in 1728, he had her moved to other lodgings so that it could not be said that she died in his residence. Yet, by all accounts, he deeply mourned the loss, and he even had her buried in St. Patrick's Cathedral.

Gulliver's Travels was published in 1726 to an acclaim as instant and widespread as that which greeted *Robinson Crusoe*. Swift employed that fame in a surprising direction, as a defender of Ireland against English oppression. He had started, in his own self-interest, by defending the Anglican Church in Ireland from a tax imposed on clerical incomes, known as "first fruits." But he soon expanded to broader issues, writing strongly against the exploitation of Ireland's land and its people, and particularly the exorbitant rents charged by absentee English landlords. He went on to protest various protectionist acts designed by Parliament to throttle domestic industry in Ireland by forcing the Irish to export their raw materials, particularly wool, to England and then import the expensive finished goods. Swift unsuccessfully advocated a boycott of British imports. More successfully, he wrote a series of letters, using the pseudonym M. B. Drapier, protesting a debasement of Irish coinage that threatened economic turmoil. These *Drapier's Letters* advocated a form of home rule and independence from the British Parliament that would not be realized for almost two centuries, and even then for only half the country.

Following terrible harvests and brutally cold winters, when tens of thousands of displaced Irish families were starving to death, Swift resorted to satire to highlight the injustice. *A Modest Proposal for Preventing the Children of Poor People from Being a Burthen to Their Parents or Country, and for Making Them Beneficial to the Publick* was published in 1729. In it, Swift describes in agonizing detail the plight of the Irish working poor. He ends with the shocking suggestion that the most effective way to eliminate that poverty is for the poor Irish to sell their children to be eaten by their English overlords. The pamphlet, which caused a sensation, bears comparison with Defoe's *Shortest Way with the Dissenters*, if only to highlight Swift's superior command of sustained irony. No reader could mistake the bitter satire for a serious proposal.

The Irish people treated Swift as their greatest champion. Bonfires and celebrations marked his birthday each year. Unfortunately, not much remained of his productive literary life. Swift began to show symptoms of dementia as early as 1732. He grew depressed and peevish. His poems, always very frank on bodily matters, became even more scatological. [10] One particularly funny poem, "The Lady's Dressing-Room," recounts a lover's secret visit to his mistress's dressing room and his shock at the mess of dirty underclothes; the towels, "Begumm'd, bematter'd, and beslim'd; / With Dirt, and Sweat, and Ear-wax grimed"; the artificial pomades and ointments; the hairs plucked by tweezers from her nose, her eyebrows, and even her chin; and most of all by his realization upon lifting a lid in her cabinet: "Oh! Celia, Celia, Celia, shits!" [11]

Swift was declared unsound of mind and memory in 1742, and a guardian was appointed for his care. He subsequently died in 1745 and was buried in St. Patrick's Cathedral next to his beloved Stella. They were later joined in a single coffin.

Swift's greatest, if unacknowledged rival, Daniel Defoe, preceded him by fourteen years. Defoe was plagued in his final years by bladder stones and an even more painful procedure to remove them. He died on April 24, 1731, and was buried in the same Puritan churchyard as John Bunyan, author of *The Pilgrim's Progress*.

Defoe and Swift were remarkably prolific. They were, and remain, the towering figures of English prose in the first third of the eighteenth century in England. Yet both men ever would be known primarily for the adventures of their two unlikely and unimaginative heroes, Robinson Crusoe and Lemuel Gulliver.

CRUSOE'S EPIC OF RETURN

Aristotle contended that only a god or a beast can live alone. It is ironic, then, that the protagonist of the foundational English novel spends much of his life completely alone. Robinson Crusoe is neither god nor beast. He is not even a particularly remarkable man. He is, as his own father explains, in "the middle state, or what might be called the upper station of *low life*."[12] Virginia Woolf will write, rather disdainfully, of his "solidly matter-of-fact intelligence."[13] And yet Crusoe has a crucial quality that he shares with his epic predecessor, Odysseus. He is *polytropos*, skilled in all ways of contending.[14]

Both Crusoe and Odysseus travel widely and end up marooned on deserted islands. Odysseus enjoys there the company of a goddess and all the comforts she can offer. But he wants human company. He longs to return to his wife, his son, and the land he once governed. Odysseus spends his days on a remote outcrop, groaning and shedding tears as he gazes fixedly out to sea toward far-off Ithaca. The epic of his return has led and will lead him through many hardships and miseries.

Crusoe, too, has a God for company, a Protestant God who sustains and comforts him. And he, too, longs for home. Yet Crusoe spends his days building a home for himself on the island on which providence has landed him. His God is not going to feed, shelter, and clothe him, at least not directly. Everything Crusoe needs is there, either on the wreckage of the ship—providentially sustained on a sandbar—or on the island itself, which has fresh water and considerable game, as well as good soil for growing. So Crusoe sets aside his lamentations and gets to work with persistence and ingenuity. He must transform the raw materials of his environment into what is necessary and useful to him. He responds to the potential tragedy of his situation with quotidian striving.

Crusoe builds a shelter; he constructs fortifications; he makes a chair; he plants a garden; he domesticates the island goats; he learns to bake bread, shape pots, and turn goat's milk into butter and cheese. Much of the novel—and not the least of its interest—is taken up with Crusoe's unceasing efforts to re-create for himself a reasonable facsimile of the British, middle-class existence that he shunned when, ignoring his father's advice, he went to sea. *Robinson Crusoe*, like the *Odyssey*, is an epic of return—the return of one man from a state of nature to a level of civilization and social interaction that we now take for granted. In order to reach that status, he must suffer through "the miseries and hardships, the labor and sufferings of the mechanic part of mankind."[15] That is, he must toil as a common laborer, mastering many trades, in order to regain the state of modest comfort in which he was born. Jean-Jacques Rousseau will claim that this portion of *Robinson Crusoe* "affords a complete treatise on natural education" and is the first book his imaginary student, Émile, will read.[16]

Crusoe may not be a traditional epic hero, but he is a decidedly Lockean one. He awakes on his island to forceful impressions of his potentially hostile environment. He is overwhelmed at first, passive and in despair. Yet gradually he learns to impose order on his experience. Through the application of reason and rational judgment, he writes, "every man may be in time master of every mechanic art. I had never handled a tool in my life, and yet in time by labor, application, and contrivance, I found at last that I wanted nothing but I could have made it."[17] He has some tools. But he must learn to use them and taxes his own ingenuity to recapitulate man's development. Absolutely free and absolutely determined by the needs of his situation, Crusoe must rely on himself to survive. Thomas Hobbes famously called the life of man in a state of nature "solitary, poor, nasty, brutish, and short."[18] Crusoe's life on the island would have been exactly that but for the ideas he has of a better existence and his unceasing labor and ingenuity to make that existence his new reality.

Crusoe's first-person, autobiographical narrative, starting with his contemporaneous journal, plays a similar function. He writes to impose order on experience. In the course of writing, that experience is transmuted into ideas. Crusoe gives meaning to his life by overlaying upon it a literary form. The world and his own self are filtered through his consciousness and his prose. As Montaigne said of his own essays, writing the book both displayed and helped define himself. Crusoe creates his own epic, not to rival the deeds of noble heroes, but to displace and succeed them. It is a middle-class epic, to be sure. But that is the whole point of the novel as it developed over time—to leave no aspect of human life unexplored and unglossed. As Henry James would later explain, "a novelist is one on whom nothing is lost." All of experience is raw material to be shaped and given meaning. The rising middle class following the Glorious Revolution of 1688 formed a receptive audience for a literature directed largely at their circumstances and their concerns. That interest even extended to the doings of the lowest classes, as evidenced by the success of *Moll Flanders*.

Crusoe himself is a limited being. He lacks the range of emotions and depth of thought displayed by James's own characters. As Charles Dickens would later remark, *Robinson Crusoe* is "the only instance of a universally popular book that could make no one laugh and could make no one cry."[19] It is a telling observation. Yet the same could be said of the *Odyssey*. There are moments of high emotion, including the unexpected meeting of Odysseus with his mother in the underworld; the loyalty of the swineherd; Odysseus's reunion with his father; and, perhaps most poignant of all, the recognition by Argos of his long-lost master. There are also vaguely comic, if nonetheless dark, interludes, such as Odysseus tricking the Cyclops; Penelope unraveling the shroud; and Circe's transformation of the crew into swine. In *Robinson Crusoe*, there are counterparts of both sorts—the footprint in the sand and Crusoe's dining in state with his dog, his cat, and his parrot come immediately to mind—but *Robinson Crusoe*, like the *Odyssey*, is neither tragedy nor comedy. It is an adventure story and a spiritual journey rolled into one.

Dickens complained that Robinson Crusoe does not change over the course of the book. He called it a "glaring defect that it exhibits the man who was 30 years on that desert island with no visible effect made on his character by that experience."[20] All novels, including Dickens's own, have the limitations of their qualities. *Robinson Crusoe* is not a psychological study. But Crusoe, like Odysseus, gains a measure of self-knowledge over the course of the work. Odysseus's adventures prepare him for his renewed role as husband, father, and king. So, too, Crusoe's character is strengthened as well as revealed by the ways in which he overcomes adversity.

Many critics have considered Crusoe the embodiment of "economic man" and the "Protestant work ethic," starting with his "inherited" capital—the tools and other goods recovered from the ship—and applying his own human capital to multiply his holdings. Fair enough. Crusoe does find both survival and redemption in work. But there is nothing theoretical, much less ideological, about his motivation. Crusoe is neither Adam Smith nor Karl Marx. He is wholly pragmatic: "Neither did I see any prospect before me, but that of perishing with hunger, or being devoured by wild beasts."[21] The world may seem an unyielding place, but it will yield to persistent toil. Crusoe can create value through his own labor, and the only measure of that value is what is of use to him and will keep him alive and as comfortable as possible. All inessentials are stripped away; well, almost all.

There is a lovely and telling moment when Crusoe is on board the wreck of his ship. He finds there a quantity of gold, which would be worth a great deal in the civilized world but is utterly useless on his deserted island. He expostulates on its uselessness:

> I smiled to myself at the sight of this money. O drug! said I aloud, what art thou good for? Thou art not worth to me, no not the taking off of the ground; one of those knives is worth all this heap; I have no manner of use for thee, e'en remain where thou art, and go to the bottom as a creature whose life is not worth saving. [22]

"However," he adds blandly, "upon second thoughts, I took it away," just as anyone would do. [23] And, indeed, the gold does turn out to be valuable in the end.

Over time, Crusoe develops a sense of "place," precisely what he denied himself, or deliberately avoided, with his penchant for wandering. As he builds a home, he builds a new identity tied to that home. He grounds himself on solid land, or, more literally, solid rock. But he is still alone, and Crusoe's physical isolation is symbolic of the spiritual and moral isolation that he—that all of us—must also overcome. Defoe himself called the book "an allegoric history," [24] and it is surely that in at least two senses.

First, Crusoe must forge a connection with God. This thought is occasioned by the seemingly miraculous growth of stalks of English barley and rice from the otherwise barren ground near his habitation.

> I had hitherto acted upon no religious foundation at all, indeed I had very few notions of religion in my head, or had entertained any sense of anything that had befallen me, otherwise than as a chance, or, as we lightly say, what pleases God; without so much as enquiring into the end of providence in these things, or his order in governing events in the world. [25]

Crusoe is deeply moved by the thought that God is watching over him and performing miracles for his benefit. This initial feeling of thankfulness quickly fades, however, when he recalls that he had shaken out the dusty remains of a bag of chicken feed in that very place before the rains came. No miracle, then; "all this was nothing but what was common."[26] And yet a sense of divine providence has, like the seeds, taken root in his mind and gradually develops into a full-blown religious conversion fed by reading a Bible he recovered from the ship.

With his spirits oppressed, he cries aloud, *"Lord be my help, for I am in great distress."*[27] And God answers him, as he answered Saint Augustine, through a Bible verse chosen at random: "Call on me in the day of trouble, and I will deliver, and thou shalt glorify me."[28] Crusoe becomes convinced that all things come from God and that "nothing can happen in the great circuit of his works, either without his knowledge or appointment."[29] But, Crusoe realizes, "if nothing happens without his knowledge, he knows that I am here, and am in this dreadful condition; and if nothing happens without his appointment, he has appointed all this to befall me."[30] Crusoe assumes that his condition is a punishment for his original sin in disobeying his father and refusing to accept his middle condition. But he reasons that God has preserved him and has allowed him to learn from and overcome his mistakes. From then on, he believes that all that happens is the disposition of providence, which orders "everything for the best."[31]

This religious conversion is far from convincing on a philosophical level. As Marcus Aurelius, the Roman emperor and Stoic sage, pointed out, it ultimately makes no difference whether everything is determined by divine providence or by "the chance interaction of atoms in the void."[32] The two postulates are equally meaningful and equally meaningless. We must act regardless according to our best lights. Spinoza, too, objected strongly to the idea of a God who takes a personal interest in the fate of each person. If God singled out Crusoe alone to survive the shipwreck, that would mean God deliberately condemned the others to die: "What is one man's safety, is another man's destruction," Crusoe notes, and finds it a special cause for thanks that "not one life should be spared but mine."[33] An odd sort of religion, to be sure, and one that Swift would satirize bitterly: "Who, that sees a little paltry mortal, droning, and dreaming, and driveling to a multitude, can think it agreeable to common good sense, that either Heaven or Hell should be put to the trouble of influence or inspection upon what he is about?"[34]

Crusoe, however, is a pragmatist, not a philosopher or a satirist. His conversion is both emotionally convincing and personally necessary. He constructs a God as he constructs a shelter, because he would otherwise perish. Crusoe could easily have gone mad with despair on his isolated island. But he finds peace and serenity in the thought that God is looking out for him: "I will never, never leave thee, nor forsake thee," his God tells him.[35] In the end, Crusoe's religion is not far from Spinoza's own; he sees God's presence everywhere in nature and is thankful for every blessing. Crusoe infuses his world with enchantment because he needs to do so in order to survive. In this, too, he is *polytropos*. His religion is like the talisman of a primitive tribe.

Except that Crusoe has no tribe. He is alone, and even religion will not substitute for human company. This is the second sense in which the book is an "allegoric history" of man's isolation. Crusoe must overcome the solipsism inherent in man's nature. According to Locke—and Descartes and Spinoza before him were no different in this regard—the play of ideas and emotions unfolds in a sort of inner theater of the mind. Everything we experience is filtered through that lens and hence has a self-regarding component. This is a point Defoe makes explicitly in reflecting on the great success of his novel: "Everything revolves in our minds by innumerable circular motions, all centering in our selves. We judge of prosperity, and of affliction, joy and sorrow, poverty, riches, and all the various scenes of life: I say, we judge of them by our selves."[36]

The autobiographical memoir, with its relentless focus on the self and what concerns the self, is an allegory and a literary reflection of man's inherent selfishness. All things Crusoe encounters are described in terms of how they affect and seem to him. The world and his own self are sifted through his consciousness and his prose: "All the reflections which he makes, are to himself; all that is pleasant, he embraces for himself; all that is irksome and grievous, is tasted but by his own palate."[37] Life itself, Defoe concludes, is "but one universal act of solitude."[38] Yet that solitude is ultimately unendurable. Having spent the first half of the novel building fortifications to protect this self, he must now learn to connect with and trust the humanity of others.

When another ship wrecks near his island and all who are on it perish, Crusoe's naked longing for some human connection bursts forth:

> O that there had been but one or two; nay, or but one soul saved out of this ship, to have escaped to me, that I might but have had one companion, one fellow-creature to have spoken to me, and to have conversed with! In all the time of my solitary life, I never felt so earnest,

so strong a desire after the society of my fellow-creatures, or so deep a
regret at the want of it. [39]

Nothing is more difficult, however, than genuine human connection. It
is, in fact, terrifying in its vulnerability and exposure. And it is this
emotion that predominates in that sublime moment when, after two
decades on the island, Crusoe spots a single footprint in the sand and
realizes that some "other" has entered and threatens his self-contained
world. Robert Louis Stevenson called it one of the "supreme moments in
imaginative literature," on a par with Odysseus stringing his great bow or
Achilles issuing his war cry to the terrified Trojans after the death of
Patroclus. [40]

Odysseus and Achilles are prepared to do battle and will slay many
enemies. Crusoe has a similar reaction when he realizes that cannibals are
using *his* island for their bloody feasts. He gathers his rifles, pistols, and
sword and plans to destroy these "savage wretches." [41] Yet, over time, he
questions his own authority to act as "judge and executioner," when the
cannibals have done him no injury and are only following their own
customs, however barbarous. [42] Gradually, Crusoe hits on a different plan,
to try to rescue one of their victims and thereby gain a companion and
deliver himself from what he calls "this death of a life." [43]

And so he does. Yet the relationship he forms is not one of equals. It is
a typical colonial relationship of master and servant. Without even both-
ering to learn the freed captive's actual name, Crusoe simply decrees that
it shall be "Friday" as a constant reminder of the day on which Crusoe
saved his life. Crusoe immediately sets about teaching Friday English and
instructing him "in the knowledge of the true God." [44] Friday is an apt
pupil and readily renounces his pagan, cannibal ways, but shows a native
resistance on some points: "*If God much strong, much might as the Devil,
why God no kill the Devil, so make him no more do wicked?*" [45] Crusoe,
having no answer, pretends not to hear the question, and they settle on a
comfortable Christianity without "niceties in doctrine" and other "disputed points" that are "all perfectly useless." [46]

After this, the narrative accelerates. Other potential victims are rescued, including a Spaniard and Friday's father. An island left untouched
for decades becomes a growing colony of which Crusoe considers himself "absolute lord and lawgiver." [47] Under Locke's theory of property—a
theory highly convenient to British imperialism—the island belongs to

Crusoe, since he cultivated and improved it. Besides, his subjects all owe their lives to him. Only slightly tongue in cheek, Crusoe adds, "It was remarkable too, we had but three subjects, and they were of three different religions. My man *Friday* was a Protestant, his father was a *pagan* and a *cannibal*, and the *Spaniard* was a papist: However, I allowed liberty of conscience throughout my dominions."[48]

Soon, an English ship anchors close to the island. Once again showing the caution and survival instincts of Odysseus, Crusoe lies in wait to observe the doings of the men who have rowed to shore. He soon discovers that mutineers have taken over the ship and plan to murder the captain and his closest mates. Through an Odyssean combination of force and cunning, with echoes of Prospero's enchantments in *The Tempest*, Crusoe thwarts the mutiny and enables the captain to retake the ship. After presenting himself as the governor of the island and leaving the mutineers to decide between hanging and remaining there, they understandably choose the latter. Crusoe leaves them weapons, tools, and instructions on how to survive. Most important, he establishes a social contract and a political system of which he is the rightful, if soon to be absentee, sovereign.

After returning to England, Crusoe eventually marries, "not either to my disadvantage or dissatisfaction"; he has three children; and he becomes a widower—all of which is reported in two sentences.[49] Yet the "wandering life" calls him back, as it did for Odysseus—at least in the reenvisioned versions of Dante and Tennyson. Personal relationships never hold him in the way that commercial ones do. In that, he is the true-born Englishman, for better and for worse. As James Joyce explained:

> He is the true prototype of the British colonist, as Friday . . . is the symbol of the subject races. The whole Anglo-Saxon spirit is in Crusoe: the manly independence; the unconscious cruelty; the persistence; the slow yet efficient intelligence; the sexual apathy; the practical, well-balanced religiousness; the calculating taciturnity. Whoever rereads this simple, moving book in the light of subsequent history cannot help but fall under its prophetic spell.[50]

Under the guise of an autobiographical narrative, Defoe has created a new myth to rival its epic predecessors.

GULLIVER AMONG THE YAHOOS

Lemuel Gulliver is also an Odyssean figure, but more on account of his fantastic adventures than for his skill in contending with them. Crusoe suffers through a realistic shipwreck and describes his day-to-day efforts to survive on the island in vivid and largely convincing detail. Aside from the sheer length of his isolation, his plight could be compared with that of real-life castaways who returned to tell their tales. To be sure, the thirty-year narrative is implausible but, on a day-to-day basis, it constantly reaches for verisimilitude. Indeed, many early readers were convinced it was a factual rather than fictional account.

Odysseus, at least in his own recounting, underwent mythical challenges: his encounter with the Cyclops; Circe turning Odysseus's men into swine; the island of the lotus eaters; Scylla and Charybdis; and the goddess Calypso. One can read these adventures as "allegoric" but not as "history." No one would mistake them for actual events.

Lemuel Gulliver's *Travels into Several Remote Nations of the World* (the actual but rarely used title) is decidedly allegorical as well. It was not intended to be viewed in any other light, despite the infamous Irish bishop who said it "was full of improbable lies, and, for his part, he hardly believed a word of it,"[51] thereby implying that he did take it as a purported travelogue, at least some of which was true. Swift added a letter from the publisher in subsequent editions that duly vouches for the truth of the narrative, but in a way that could not be mistaken for anything but satire: "There is an air of truth apparent through the whole; and indeed, the author was so distinguished for his veracity, that it became a sort of proverb among his neighbors at Redriff, when anyone affirmed a thing, to say, it was as true as if Mr. Gulliver had spoke it."[52]

The work was published anonymously in 1726, though Swift's authorship was an open secret. It enjoyed an immediate popularity comparable to that of *Robinson Crusoe*. But Swift's intentions, unlike Defoe's, are both comical and satirical. The comedy is readily apparent on the face of the story and can charm readers today as much as it did three centuries ago. The satire is more dated but can still be enjoyed on three levels. First, Swift is deliberately mocking the supposed verisimilitude of *Robinson Crusoe* and other such works written in the guise of autobiographical travel memoirs. Second, Swift is exposing the rancid politics of his own day—which is to say, he is settling scores—but in the process is making a broader point about our inherently flawed political institutions. Third, and most interesting, he is setting his back against the entire Enlightenment project of expecting reason fundamentally to change human society and human nature for the better.

The first book begins, like *Robinson Crusoe*, with a description of the hero's modest early life. Gulliver, too, is eager to travel and uses his training as a surgeon to secure his first position. He grows weary of the sea, however, and intends to stay at home with his wife and family. But his economic prospects on shore are repeatedly disappointed, and he sets sail again. The obligatory storm presents itself somewhere in the South Seas, and the ship and its entire crew are lost, except for Gulliver, who "swam as fortune directed me" and managed finally to reach land. Swift's descriptions of the storm, the wreck, and the perilous swim are perfunctory compared with Defoe's. Swift is not striving for realism; his only goal is to get Gulliver ashore, exhausted and then asleep, as compactly as possible. There is a "once upon a time" quality to this beginning that makes Gulliver's subsequent sojourn on the island of Lilliput almost dreamlike.

> As Gregor Samsa awoke one morning from uneasy dreams he found himself transformed in his bed into a gigantic insect. He was lying on his hard, as it were armor-plated, back and when he lifted his head a little he could see his domelike brown belly divided into stiff arched segments on top of which the bed quilt could hardly keep in position and was about to slide off completely. His numerous legs, which were pitifully thin compared to the rest of his bulk, waved helplessly before his eyes.[53]

Thus begins Franz Kafka's novella, *The Metamorphosis*. Gregor Samsa awakes to a world that is the same, but he himself is utterly transformed. Lemuel Gulliver is the same person who went to sleep, but he awakes to a world that is utterly transformed. He finds his arms and legs and even his hair fixed to the ground by numerous thin but strong threads. Even more alarming, small creatures, no more than six inches high, are crawling all over him and even speaking to him in a language he cannot understand.

Much of the uncanny, comic force of Kafka's story lies in Gregor's matter-of-fact reaction, and eventual adjustment, to his transformation. Gulliver, too, after his initial shocks, takes everything at face value, and his minute descriptions and telling anecdotes are intended to give his narrative the same "air of authenticity" as *Robinson Crusoe*.[54] Like any good traveler, Gulliver is curious and receptive to a different culture, including to a race of men and women one-twelfth his size. The comedy and appeal of book 1 lies in his steady adjustment to absurd circumstances. Like Rabelais's Gargantua, Gulliver's stupendous appetite astonishes the Lilliputians, as he downs wheelbarrows full of meat and large casks of drink. The consequences of his appetite are equally prodigious— a copious flow when he makes water, and a large cleanup task by a designated crew for his solid waste. Three hundred tailors are needed to make clothes for him.

One critic notes that "the effect [of the altered scale] is to defamiliarize our everyday experience."[55] One might equally say that the effect is to familiarize the fantastic. The land of the Lilliputians is all too familiar, but on a comically small scale, which casts the same light of triviality on our own doings. The Lilliputians, particularly the politicians, strut and fret their hour upon the stage just like their giant counterparts in England and to no greater effect. They vie for preferment by dancing on a rope two feet long and twelve inches above the ground: "Whoever jumps the highest without falling, succeeds in the office."[56] Even chief ministers must show their skill. "Flimnap, the treasurer, is allowed to cut a caper on the straight rope, at least an inch higher than any other lord in the whole empire."[57] In addition to coveted positions, colored threads are awarded as prizes, akin to the English Orders of the Garter, the Bath, and such like. All the pomp and circumstance simply underscores their—and our own— absurd pretensions. As Sir Walter Scott explained, "nothing could have been more happily imagined to ridicule the pursuits, passions, and intrigues of a court, than supposing them transferred to creatures only six inches high."[58]

It adds only marginally to our enjoyment of the book to know that Swift had Sir Robert Walpole in mind in the figure of Flimnap. The play of Swift's imagination is more important than the specific historical analogues. We could just as delightfully imagine modern U.S. politicians in the various roles. Despite the nation's wealth, the two greatest dangers in Lilliput are political factions at home and potential invasion from abroad. "The animosities between these two parties run so high, that they will neither eat nor drink, nor talk with each other."[59] That certainly sounds familiar enough that a modern reader can fully relate. So, too, with the ambition of the emperor of Lilliput (England) to defeat the nearby island of Blefuscu (France). As a condition of his freedom, Gulliver is induced to fetch the enemy's entire fleet and pull it back across the channel to Lilliput to thwart a planned invasion.

The underlying source of the animosity is that Blefuscuns break their eggs at the traditional big end, whereas the father of the emperor of Lilliput, having once cut one of his fingers on the big end, decreed under grave penalties that all Lilliputians must break their eggs at the smaller end—a somewhat muddled but still quite funny allusion to Henry VIII's break from Rome to enable him to divorce his Catholic wife. Each country declares the other heretics, taking pride in its own culture and showing contempt for its cross-channel counterpart. Gulliver, though he has prevented the invasion of Lilliput, declines to participate in an invasion of conquest against Blefuscu, thereby enraging the emperor. Another grave offense—right out of Rabelais—is that when the royal palace catches fire one night, the only way Gulliver can think of to extinguish the blaze is to urinate on the royal apartments. The empress will never forgive that. Nor will Flimnap, who believes—physical impossibility aside—that Gulliver is carrying on a torrid affair with his wife.

The ministers accordingly plan to kill Gulliver, either by setting fire to his house while he sleeps or by poisoning him. But the emperor, in his mercy, decrees instead that Gulliver shall be blinded and gradually starved. Forewarned of his fate, Gulliver laments, "Of so little weight are the greatest services to princes, when put into the balance with a refusal to gratify their passions."[60] Vowing never again to put his trust in princes and ministers, Gulliver makes his way to Blefuscu, and from there sets sail on a makeshift boat and is picked up by a merchantman who brings him home, where he makes considerable money exhibiting and eventually selling the diminutive cattle he has brought with him.

Gulliver's second voyage is the converse of the first. On the island of Brobdingnag, it is now Gulliver who is tiny in contrast to the enormous bulk of the inhabitants. It is he who is displayed as a public spectacle to gawking crowds. On Lilliput, he could put an entire enemy fleet out of commission. Here, he does courageous battle with rats and with wasps as large as partridges; dodges giant hailstones; is all but smothered by an overly maternal monkey; is tormented by a malicious dwarf, who resents the attention the newcomer receives; and is used as a sort of sex toy by the maids of honor, "wherein," he primly notes, "the reader will excuse me for not being over particular."[61]

"Undoubtedly philosophers are in the right," he explains, "when they tell us, that nothing is great or little otherwise than by comparison."[62] Even his perspective on beauty is forced to change when he is disgusted by the "monstrous breast" of a wet nurse:

> It stood prominent six foot, and could not be less than sixteen in circumference. The nipple was about half the bigness of my head, and the hew both of that and the dug so varified with spots, pimples and freckles, that nothing could appear more nauseous.[63]

Yet Gulliver realizes that English ladies, though they appear beautiful to him, would show the same defects when examined through a magnifying glass.

Once again, Gulliver quickly learns the local language and gains the favor of the royal court. Gulliver expects the people to be savage in light of their size. As he describes their laws and customs, they seem remarkably enlightened to the reader. But not to Gulliver. He considers their learning to be "very defective; consisting only in morality, history, poetry and mathematics. . . . And as to ideas, entities, abstractions and transcendentals, I could never drive the least conception into their heads."[64] Swift's irony—and contempt for much of philosophy—is palpable, and Gulliver is the perfect foil. He notes with shock that their laws are simple and applied with common sense, in the interests of justice and lenity and the speedy determination of civil and criminal causes. No law may be more than twenty-two words long, and "to write a comment upon any law is a capital crime."[65] Gulliver protests in favor of the more elaborate and ponderous customs, ceremonies, and legal institutions in England, upon which the king remarks, "How contemptible a thing was human grandeur, which could be mimicked by such diminutive insects as I."[66]

The comedy is still rich, but the satire darkens considerably in the second book. In his conversations with the king, Gulliver undertakes to explain the history of English politics for the past century, including all the wars, conspiracies, rebellions, religious schisms, and partisan backstabbings. Despite Gulliver's effort to put the best face on all these events, the king finds in them nothing but "avarice, faction, hypocrisy, perfidiousness, cruelty, rage, madness, hatred, envy, lust, malice, [and] ambition."[67] Even institutions that, in their original conception, might have been tolerable appear to have been thoroughly corrupted. The king's judgment is unequivocal: "I cannot but conclude the bulk of your natives, to be the most pernicious race of little odious vermin that nature ever suffered to crawl upon the surface of the earth."[68]

We will pass briefly over Gulliver's third voyage, to Laputa, an island in the sky unmoored to the solid earth. The satire is too labored and grows wearisome for a modern reader. Swift is attacking *the* sacred cow of the Enlightenment: the "new" science of mathematical mechanics touted by Descartes. At least, he is ridiculing highly abstract theories of the universe with little application to practical affairs, a class in which he would unfortunately place Newton, whose *Mathematical Principles of Natural Philosophy*, published in 1687, cast Aristotle aside and laid the foundation for what is now classical physics; though, indeed, Swift accurately predicted that all such "systems"—including Newton's theory of "attraction," which had "exploded" Descartes's vortices—would eventually be displaced in turn.[69] The Laputans are the polar opposite of Robinson Crusoe's pragmatism. "In the common actions and behavior of life," Gulliver notes, "I have not seen a more clumsy, awkward, and unhandy people, nor so slow and perplexed in their conceptions upon all other subjects, except those of mathematics and music."[70] They are the proverbial absentminded scientists and speculative philosophers, so lost in abstract thought that they require a "flapper," who carries a bladder and strikes the mouth of any person who is to speak and the ears of those who are supposed to listen.

Laputans have their counterpart to the Royal Society of London, founded for the advancement of scientific knowledge. This "Academy of Projectors" pursues an array of absurd experiments, touting their great promise for the improvement of humankind. "The only inconvenience," Gulliver explains, is "that none of these projects are yet brought to perfection, and in the meantime the whole country lies miserably waste, the houses in ruins, and the people without food or clothes."[71] Swift, cum Gulliver, makes clear that he is "content to go on in the old forms"[72] and that ancient and Christian learning, developed and refined through the centuries, is preferable to the Enlightenment project, first championed by Descartes, to rethink everything from the ground up on the basis of "clear and distinct ideas" perceived directly by reason.

The final book of *Gulliver's Travels* extends the critique of the Enlightenment from scientism to human nature itself. In the land of the

Houyhnhnms, talking horses reign supreme. They are rational, well-educated, and governed not by laws but by natural benevolence and friendship for one another. They don't even have a term for falsehood other than "the thing which was not,"[73] which no self-respecting Houyhnhnm would ever say. Gulliver describes their society and their customs in utopian terms of breathless admiration.

The subject and decidedly inferior creatures on this island are known as Yahoos. They are Hobbesian in their brutishness. Naked and without language, they move on all fours, with long, sharp claws on both fore and rear legs. Their skin is brown and buff, where not covered by thick, dark hair, and they fight constantly and viciously among themselves. When Gulliver lands on the island, he is surrounded by a group of them and is forced to draw his sword and set his back against a tree to defend himself. Several of them climb the tree and "discharge their excrements upon [his] head."[74] He is rescued only by the arrival of a horse, which causes the Yahoos to flee. "Upon the whole," Gulliver remarks, "I never beheld in all my travels so disagreeable an animal, nor one against which I naturally conceived so strong an antipathy."[75] As one critic notes, the repulsive Yahoos "are flawed, not just physically but also morally, spiritually, and intellectually."[76] Their external filth reflects their internal degradation.

Yet Gulliver, of course, is more Yahoo than Houyhnhnm. The horses are astonished and don't know what to make of Gulliver because he stands upright, is civil and clean, and even demonstrates some marks of rationality. One of the horses, whom Gulliver calls the Master Horse, takes him into his home, teaches him their language, and quizzes him about his background. Gulliver's description of his own society was somewhat tempered in Brobdingnag. Here, it is an untethered catalog of vicious acts and senseless greed. The portrait is savage in its bitterness. Under the influence of the Houyhnhnms, Gulliver sees nothing in so-called civilization but the perversion of reason to justify and indulge our basest passions. We clothe our cupidity and cruelty in the most pious sentiments, particularly when dealing with those in foreign lands we consider uncivilized.

> Ships are sent with the first opportunity, the natives driven out or destroyed, their princes tortured to discover their gold; a free license given to all acts of inhumanity and lust, the earth reeking with the blood of its inhabitants: And this execrable crew of butchers employed

in so pious an expedition, is a modern colony sent to convert and civilize an idolatrous and barbarous people. [77]

Swift's sarcasm reaches its pinnacle when Gulliver explains that, of course, his critique doesn't apply to the British nation, which acts only on motives of wisdom, care, and justice in planting and governing its colonies—Ireland being a case in point.

Gulliver is not allowed to stay in the land of the Houyhnhnms. He is not one of them, and they fear that, with his "rudiments of reason," he might organize a rebellion of the Yahoos. [78] He thus bids farewell to the prospect of a purely rational life. He must accept his kinship to the Yahoos even though he cannot bear them.

Gulliver's misanthropy is shared and acknowledged by his creator. In a 1725 letter to Alexander Pope, Swift wrote:

> I have ever hated all nations, professions, and communities and all my love is towards individuals. For instance, I hate the tribe of lawyers, but I love counselor such a one, judge such a one; for so with physicians (I will not speak of my own trade), soldiers, English, Scotch, French; and the rest, but principally I hate and detest that animal called man, although I heartily love John, Peter, Thomas, and so forth. This is the system upon which I have governed myself many years (but do not tell) and so I shall go on till I have done with them. I have got materials towards a treatise proving the falsity of that definition *animal rationale*; and to show it should be only *rationis capax* [capable of reason]. Upon this great foundation of misanthropy (though not Timon's manner), the whole building of my *Travels* is erected. [79]

Book 4 appears to present a stark dichotomy: the Houyhnhnms are "wholly governed by reason," whereas the Yahoos are "the most unteachable of all brutes." [80] Descartes had argued that God is not a deceiver and that man can therefore by guided solely by his reason, which God has given him. [81] The Houyhnhnms embody the Enlightenment faith—found in Descartes and such disparate successors as Spinoza, Leibniz, and even Locke—that we can use reason to remake the world. We can make a fresh start and reexamine everything from the ground up, placing human life on a firm, even impregnable foundation.

Using horses as the epitome of rationality, however, is meant to be absurd. Swift thought the Enlightenment project was doomed to failure and likely to do more harm than good. Man is not, and never will be, guided by reason alone. The passions will make themselves felt regardless and distort all our arguments and arrangements. Too often, Gulliver learns, we use our "small pittance of reason" only "to aggravate our natural corruptions, and to acquire new ones which nature had not given us."[82] The Master Horse echoes Montaigne, who explained that those who attempt to rise above human nature invariably fall below: "They want to get out of themselves and escape from the man. That is madness: instead of changing into angels, they change into beasts; instead of raising themselves, they lower themselves."[83]

Swift does not disdain reason. But he dislikes and distrusts metaphysics, scientism, sweeping political theories, and anything else that purports to rely strictly on abstract thought. Swift embraces a view of man that harkens back to Saint Augustine, Rabelais, Montaigne, Milton, and Pascal. Man is deeply and inherently flawed, as allegorically reflected in the Christian doctrine of original sin. But this is no counsel of despair. Man is not "wholly governed by reason." But neither is he "unteachable." It is a false dichotomy. Man is *rationis capax*, capable of using reason to control his passions and organize his affairs. Mathematics and logic cannot displace tradition and common sense. Natural religion cannot displace revealed religion. The abstractions of philosophers cannot displace the everyday morality of compassion. Our only business is living appropriately within the limits of human nature. We can find our salvation in the "old forms" and in small acts of kindness and generosity, like the Portuguese sea captain who rescues Gulliver from his makeshift vessel and brings him home.

Robinson Crusoe is in many ways a child of the Enlightenment, using his skills, his natural reason, and his native cunning to build a life for himself. Lemuel Gulliver, at least in books 3 and 4, is an orphan, out of step morally, spiritually, and intellectually with the tenor of his times. Surprisingly, though, Crusoe and Gulliver have more in common than not; they are both flawed characters struggling to establish their place somewhere between the angels and the beasts. Indeed, that might serve as a definition of the modern novel. Where Defoe is earnest, Swift is satirical. But that doesn't mean they are engaged in fundamentally different tasks. As Milton explained, "to know / That which lies before us in daily life / Is the prime wisdom."[84] For Crusoe, "all this was nothing but what was common." For Gulliver, too: "This is all according to the due course of things."[85]

Swift satirizes *Robinson Crusoe* for its supposed verisimilitude as an autobiographical memoir. He makes no similar attempt to provide either realism or consistency for Gulliver, who is naively obtuse in the first two books, skeptical in book 3, and bitterly misanthropic in book 4, according to the needs of the satire. For Swift, all narrative is myth. But myths can illuminate and enrich our daily existence, and the dueling myths of Robinson Crusoe and Lemuel Gulliver do exactly that.

Gulliver ends his memoirs with a vow to "behold my figure often in a glass, and thus if possible habituate myself by time to tolerate the sight of a human creature."[86] Swift's satire is also a glass in which his readers can recognize their flaws. While he may not believe that men can eliminate all folly and vice, Swift believes they can at least better themselves by letting go of their idealism and pride.[87] Defoe, too, uses his narrative as a glass, but one in which readers can recognize their more heroic qualities. While he, too, may not believe that men can eliminate their folly and vice, Defoe believes they can at least better themselves by holding on to their idealism and pride. The modern novel is capacious enough to embrace both perspectives.

7

VOLTAIRE AND THE PHILOSOPHES

Le monde avec lenteur marche vers la sagesse.[1]

François-Marie Arouet, known to us as Voltaire, was born in 1694, in the closing years of the seventeenth century and late in the reign of the Sun King, Louis XIV, who was a believer in the divine right of kings, a scourge of Protestant heretics, and the absolute monarch of France for seventy-two of his nearly seventy-seven years. Voltaire himself would live for more than eighty-three years as Europe's most prominent advocate for religious tolerance, scientific progress, intellectual freedom and, in his later years, legal reform. *Le Siècle de Louis XIV*, as Voltaire titled one of his many historical works, did not give way to the century of Louis XV, a mediocre reactionary. It gave way instead to *le siècle de Voltaire* and, ultimately, to the French Revolution.[2]

Voltaire himself was no revolutionary. He saw little in the way of concrete progress during his long life. Absolute monarchs remained, as did religious persecution, the attempted suppression of controversial ideas, and gross violations of human rights. But Voltaire and the philosophes—the younger French thinkers inspired by his example—changed the way that many people, particularly in the fast-rising middle class, thought about the natural world, about religion, and about freedom and justice. The philosophes advocated for a purely secular science of man and for the free exchange of ideas. In so doing, they set themselves in opposition to the *ancien régime*, which was backed by the repressive power of the Catholic Church. Some of the philosophes were outright atheists. Some, like Voltaire, were deists who believed in a creator God.

But they all dismissed religious disputation as so much nonsense and organized religion as a form of fraud and oppression. *Écrasez l'infâme* ("crush the infamy") was the rallying cry coined by Voltaire.

During his long life, Voltaire wrote tragedies, comedies, opera libretti, epic poetry, occasional verses, and novellas. He was an accomplished historian and all but invented the genre of world history, though always emphasizing culture over war and politics. He authored scientific treatises and innumerable pamphlets, articles, and essays. The Oxford edition of his complete works will number 203 volumes, even without his more than fifteen thousand letters, which are published separately. Voltaire was read avidly throughout Europe, with an influence comparable to that of Desiderius Erasmus on the cusp of the Protestant Reformation.[3] A new book by Voltaire was a pan-European event.

It is often lamented that Voltaire spread his talent too thin. He was neither a great scientist, like Isaac Newton, nor an innovative philosopher, like John Locke. He was not a political theorist like Montesquieu. His plays are not performed today. His poetry is neglected. His histories are rarely read. His innumerable shorter works on political and social issues are of mostly historical interest. Yet Voltaire captured and transformed the spirit of his age. Three of his works stand out in that regard: *Letters Regarding the English Nation*, *Philosophical Dictionary*, and *Candide*. To read those three works is to know Voltaire and to understand his influence.

None of them is systematic. Voltaire rarely strayed far from the individual case. Indeed, he ridiculed systems and theories that keep us from seeing, for better and for worse, the realities of ordinary human life. But these three works convey his energy, his satirical wit, his rapier-like prose, his vast intelligence, and his astonishing range of interests. Voltaire could pack more bite in a single sentence or turn of phrase than other writers could laboriously pour into an entire volume, as when he disparaged the courtiers of Louis XV as "more wig than wit" or dismissed ten centuries of politicians and conquerors as "no more than illustrious villains." Most important, these three works embody the Enlightenment ideals that drove him throughout his life: a love of learning, a healthy skepticism, a respect for pluralism, and an abiding faith that reason and compassion can lead us to an incrementally better world.

EARLY LIFE

Voltaire's father, also named François, was a prosperous lawyer. Voltaire's mother died in 1701, at the age of forty-one, when he was only seven. He carried her picture with him wherever he traveled. He was the last of her three surviving children. His brother, Armand, nine years older, became a rigid Jansenist reactionary. Unsurprisingly, the two did not get along. But Voltaire was strongly attached to his sister, Marguerite-Catherine, who was almost eight years older.

Voltaire received an excellent Jesuit education with the sons of the aristocracy. He was steeped in the Latin classics, especially Virgil, Horace, and Cicero. His father pressured him to study law, but Voltaire quickly abandoned it. He had grander ambitions to become France's leading and most acclaimed poet. "Je n'en veux pas d'autre que celui d'homme de lettres" (I don't want to be anything other than a man of letters), he told his father.[4] Voltaire hoped to match the dramas of Corneille and Racine and the epic poetry of Virgil and thereby attain equal status with the political and social elites of his time.

Voltaire's literary ambitions caused considerable friction with his strong-minded father. François sent his son to Holland to serve as a secretary to the French ambassador. But he was hastily recalled when he developed a passion for an unsuitable young woman. In a vain effort at control, François threatened to have Voltaire deported to America or even thrown into prison. But Voltaire managed the latter feat all on his own. He made fun of the Duke of Orléans, regent for the infant Louis XV, in some unpublished verses and was exiled from Paris for several months in 1716. He returned only to repeat the same indiscretion and ended up in the Bastille for eleven months. In prison, he worked on an epic poem and his first tragedy, while petitioning for his release.

In 1718, the twenty-four-year-old François-Marie Arouet made a dramatic break with his father. Just as Jean-Baptiste Poquelin had changed his name to Molière, François-Marie changed his name to Voltaire, or, more exactly, Arouet de Voltaire, the "de" adding a pretense of nobility. That same year, Voltaire's first tragedy, *Oedipe*, was performed at France's most important theater, the Comédie-Française, once known as the "House of Molière." It was a bold choice of subject for a debut, since Voltaire was implicitly challenging the Greek playwright Sophocles, the Roman playwright Seneca, and the revered Frenchman Pierre Corneille, who had presented his own *Oedipe* in 1659. Voltaire's play was a huge hit, however, and the young author enjoyed both the financial and social success he craved. He also signaled what would be a long-running dispute with clerics, with the much-applauded line "Our priests are not what the foolish people imagine; their wisdom is based solely on our credulity."[5]

The play was written in the neoclassical style of seventeenth-century France, with elegant, declamatory speeches but little or no action. He wrote many follow-up plays, some successful and others not, often departing from classical themes and even introducing exotic, Moorish elements. Voltaire himself sometimes acted in the plays, usually in minor, character roles, as Molière had done. He especially excelled at the comic parts. Collectively, Voltaire's tragedies and comedies earned more for the Comédie-Française than all the plays of Racine and Corneille combined. First and foremost, he was a dramatist, even after the static, neoclassical style he favored went out of fashion.

Voltaire received a pension from the regent, enjoyed the financial success of his plays, and made some astute investments, growing rich in a scheme with a mathematician friend that took advantage of loopholes in the national lottery system. He sought out the company of the aristocracy, staying at their châteaus, relishing their dinners, and even engaging in several affairs. But he also had a seemingly irresistible urge to offend the political and social elite.

Voltaire sought to expand his reputation with *La Henriade*, an epic poem about Henri IV and his resolution of the vicious religious wars between Catholics and Protestants in sixteenth-century France. The Edict of Nantes, issued by Henri in 1598, granted various civil rights to Protestants and the freedom to practice their religion. Louis XIV had vacated the Edict of Nantes in 1685. The persecution of Protestants recommenced and continued into the reign of Louis XV. Many of them moved to Geneva. Praise for Henri IV was implicit criticism of Louis XV and his predecessor. That made publication tricky.

Voltaire also offended on a more personal level. Far from being an *esprit d'escalier*,[6] he never lacked or refrained from a clever retort. On one occasion, he sufficiently offended the Chevalier de Rohan-Chabot that the nobleman sent his lackeys to deliver a beating while he watched from the safety of his carriage. An enraged Voltaire sought to challenge Rohan to a duel. But a commoner could not fight with a noble, and Rohan's family had Voltaire arrested. After six years of rising fortunes, he was back where he started, in the Bastille, and none of his newfound friends would support his side in this dispute.

Voltaire was soon released on the condition that he leave France for a time. He chose to live in London, which had a vibrant French community, including a number of French publishers whom he hoped to interest in his *Henriade*. Voltaire lived in England for two and a half years, from 1726 to 1728, and it changed the trajectory of his life as a writer.

LETTERS REGARDING THE ENGLISH NATION

Voltaire was thirty-two when he went to London. He soon moved in the highest social circles and made friends with England's greatest contemporary writers, including the poet Alexander Pope, the playwright William Congreve, and the satirist Jonathan Swift. Voltaire was delighted with *Gulliver's Travels* and recognized a kindred spirit in Swift's sardonic, irreverent wit.

Voltaire quickly developed a remarkable and nuanced command of the English language, even writing in English an essay on the civil wars and another on epic poetry, which were published together in 1727. He also arranged for publication of a sumptuous edition of his *Henriade*, which was dedicated, with her permission, to the Queen of England. It was an instant and widespread success. When he returned to France in 1728, he was acknowledged, just as he had hoped when he scorned a legal career, as France's leading playwright and poet. A new tragedy, *Brutus*, shone at the Comédie-Française. Other plays and a work of history followed. For five years, Voltaire thrived in Paris, though not without controversy. His essay on French culture, *The Temple of Taste*, purported to rank and critique past and present writers, and was so much resented by living ones that he quickly revised it.

In 1733, Voltaire began an affair with Émilie du Châtelet. She was married, but her husband, a military officer with affairs of his own, had no objection and was even on friendly terms with Voltaire. Émilie was brilliant, highly educated, a dedicated student of science, and emotionally volatile. She had other lovers, as did Voltaire. But their relationship would take a decided turn in 1734, when Voltaire was forced to flee Paris yet again. They left together and sought refuge in the Château de Cirey, in the Champagne region, east of Paris. They lived there together for most of the ensuing fifteen years, from 1734 until her death in 1749.

The cause of the controversy was Voltaire's *Letters Regarding the English Nation*, first published in London in 1733. It was a portrait in twenty-four letters of English institutions and English culture. But this was not a standard travelogue; it was an Enlightenment manifesto, whose overriding theme was freedom: freedom of thought, freedom of religion, and freedom of trade. The praise for England—at times deliberately exaggerated—was rightly seen as an implicit criticism of the rigid and repressive *ancien régime* in France.

Voltaire wrote the book in French but published it first in an English translation. For the French version, he added a twenty-fifth letter confuting Blaise Pascal's *Pensées*. The Pascal add-on did not fit with the English theme, but it fit perfectly with Voltaire's repudiation of religious dogmatism and his advocacy of the empiricist philosophy of John Locke, both of which were anathema to the French establishment. Voltaire realized his danger too late. He tried to delay the French edition—retitled *Lettres philosophiques*—but could not constrain the publisher to whom he had given the manuscript. The book was published, only to be seized, duly condemned by the French parliament, and ceremoniously burned. A *lettre de cachet* was issued for Voltaire's arrest. Forewarned, he and Émilie quickly left Paris.

A casual reader of the *Letters* today might find it difficult to see why it occasioned so much controversy. In context, however, its promotion of pluralism rather than enforced conformity and tolerance rather than persecution was bound to offend. "This is the country of sects," Voltaire writes. "An Englishman, being a free man, goes to Heaven by whatever path he chooses."[7] In France, only one path to heaven was sanctioned.

Voltaire begins, rather surprisingly, with four letters on the Quakers, who were nonconformists, like Defoe, and a distinct if stubborn minority in England. He interviews a simple, plain-spoken Quaker who wears unadorned clothes, keeps his hat on his head, bows to no man, swears no oaths, and speaks "thou" and "thee" to aristocrats and commoners alike. The Quaker dismisses the sacraments as "simply human inventions" nowhere mentioned in the Gospels, and priests as superfluous intermeddlers between the faithful and the Holy Spirit.[8] "I carefully refrained from challenging him," Voltaire explains with feigned condescension; "nothing is gained by confronting an enthusiast: it is not prudent to point out the defects of his mistress to a lover, or the weakness of his arguments to a plaintiff, nor his illogic to a fanatic."[9] Yet the Quaker proves more genuine than the Parisian sophisticate, and his simple faith is more moving than the elaborate ceremonies of the established church. Of course, freedom of religion goes only so far; in England, as in Ireland, no one but a practicing Anglican could hold any official post. "This fact," Voltaire sarcastically notes, "has converted so many nonconformists that today not more than a twentieth part of the population remains outside the dominant Church."[10] He also notes that the Anglican Church jealously retains many Catholic customs, most notably the payment of tithes to the clergy.

Perhaps the most famous passage in the *Letters* deals with the interplay of religious tolerance and free commerce:

> Go into the Royal Exchange in London, a building more respectable than most courts; there you will find deputies from every nation assembled simply to serve mankind. There, the Jew, the Mohammedan, and the Christian negotiate with one another as if they were all of the same religion, and the only heretics are those who declare bankruptcy; there the Presbyterian trusts the Anabaptist, the Anglican accepts the word of the Quaker. Leaving this peaceful and liberal assembly, some go to the synagogue, others go to drink; this one is baptized in a great font in the name of the Father, the Son and the Holy Spirit; that one has his son circumcised while some Hebrew words that he does not understand are mumbled over him; still others go to their church with their hats on their heads to await the inspiration of God, and all are content.
>
> Were there only one religion in England, despotism would be a threat; were there two, they would be at each other's throats; but there are thirty, and they live happily and at peace with one another.[11]

In France, after the expulsion of the Jews, there were only two religions, Catholic and Protestant, and they had been at each other's throat for centuries. That implicit indictment was not lost on the French authorities. Nor was the implication that pluralism and commercial success were conjoined, something Holland and Switzerland quickly learned when they thrived with the help of hardworking and entrepreneurial religious refugees—first Jews, and later Protestants—from Spain and France. In a virtuous cycle, freedom stimulated commerce, which stimulated increased freedom. Nothing is more destructive to commercial success than religious war. "The Romans never knew the dreadful folly of religious wars," Voltaire writes; "this abomination was reserved for those who devoutly preach humility and patience."[12]

Voltaire is equally clear in his preference for commerce over courtiers, despite a pretense of not knowing which is best:

> I, however, do not know which is the more useful to the State: a nobleman in a powdered wig who knows exactly when the king arises and when he retires, and who gives himself airs of greatness while he plays the slave in the antechamber of a minister; or a merchant who enriches his country, who sends orders from his counting house to Surat and Cairo, and contributes to the well-being of the world.[13]

Voltaire even condemns the resistance of the church in France to inoculation against the smallpox. In England, the royal family led the way in promoting inoculation, and many were saved from death or disfigurement. In France, orthodoxy smothered science. "Now, do the French not love life?" Voltaire asks. "Do their wives not care about their beauty? In truth, we are a strange people!"[14]

Scientific and philosophical developments in England occupy a series of six central letters, starting with Francis Bacon, whom Voltaire called the "father" of experimental science, and moving on to John Locke and Isaac Newton. These letters alone would have led to the book's condemnation. After long resistance, France had by now firmly embraced Descartes. Yet Voltaire writes that Newton's *Mathematical Principles of Natural Philosophy* so "destroyed the Cartesian system" that Descartes's works "have in effect become useless."[15] Descartes did well in exposing the errors in Aristotle's physics. He also made huge advances in geometry, comparable to Newton's own. But his desire for system and his faith in innate ideas pushed him into a "swarm [of] errors," including the continuity of matter, vortices, and a strict mind-body dualism.[16]

Voltaire reports these scientific developments with the casualness of a traveler noting quaint new customs in a foreign country:

> A Frenchman arriving in London finds changes in philosophy as in other matters. He left a universe that was filled; he discovers the void; in Paris, they imagine a universe composed of vortices of subtle matter; in London none of this.[17]

Voltaire is at pains to explain to his continental audience the stunning developments in physics, astronomy, and optics made by Newton. He is even the first to report (or invent) the famous anecdote of the apple falling from the tree as the cause of Newton's meditations on the question of gravity. Voltaire considers Newton one of history's greatest men ("whom one might scarcely hope to encounter in the course of ten centuries"[18]), before whom ministers and conquerors fade into insignificance.

When Voltaire deals with John Locke, however, he is more circumspect and treads as lightly as possible. As we have seen, Descartes offered arguments in favor of a beneficent creator and an immaterial soul even though neither played much of a role in his mechanistic natural philosophy. Newton was a devout member of the Church of England. His systematic account of the clockwork universe was every bit as mechanistic and deterministic as that of Descartes, but it, too, left ample room for an active creator God. Indeed, the argument from design was considered by Voltaire and many other philosophes to be the most powerful proof of God's existence.

Locke, however, was dangerous because his empiricist approach to knowledge seemed to leave the soul out of account altogether. He provided an empirical explanation for human reason based on mechanical principles that required neither innate ideas nor an immaterial spirit inexplicably connected to the physical human body.[19] "Having demolished innate ideas and renounced the folly of believing that we are always thinking," Voltaire explains, "Locke demonstrated that all our ideas come to us through the senses."[20] In Voltaire's view, Locke's careful description of the growth of human understanding leads to the possibility that matter itself can think. Indeed, though Voltaire states the point tentatively—"We will never, perhaps, be able to know whether a purely material being can think"[21]—he treats the materialist conclusion as all but inescapable.

Descartes believed that thought is an all-or-nothing proposition; an immaterial mind or soul is either instilled in us by God, or we are simply mechanical automatons. That is how he regarded all animals, as incapable of thought, feeling, or pain. Voltaire rejects that view:

> Animals have the same organs as we, the same feelings, the same perceptions; they have memory, they can put some thoughts together. If God were not able to animate matter and give it feelings, one thing

or the other must be true: either that animals are simply machines, or that they have a true soul.[22]

Of course, neither the "either" nor the "or" in that last sentence is true. Accordingly, what is true is that matter can be animate and have feelings. That is, we don't need to posit an immaterial soul to account for life on earth, whether for plants, animals, or humans, even if (as Voltaire himself thought) we do need a God to account for their design.

It is ironic that Descartes felt compelled to live outside France to avoid persecution for his controversial ideas and that Voltaire was now compelled to leave France for challenging those ideas. But it was an irony that Voltaire himself could appreciate. He notes that Descartes had destroyed the Scholastic system and paid for it with a self-imposed exile, whereas Newton was celebrated in England and was buried with honors befitting a king. Voltaire ends his six letters on natural philosophy with a lovely tribute to his fellow countryman: "I do not think one could properly compare his philosophy with that of Newton; the first is a rough sketch, the second is a masterpiece. But he who put us on the path to truth is perhaps worth as much as is he who later traveled to the end."[23] Newton famously stated some years later that "if I have seen further it is by standing on the shoulders of giants." Unfortunately, Newton never acknowledged that one of those giants was René Descartes. For Voltaire, the lesson to be drawn from the example of Descartes is one of tolerance for new ideas, whose truth will be judged by history.

VOLTAIRE IN EXILE

The Château de Cirey was closer to Switzerland than to Paris. It thus provided an ideal refuge, and both the court and the church were content to leave Voltaire undisturbed there. The house was old, ramshackle, and drafty. Voltaire spent a lot of money making it more comfortable and more elegant. He also expended his own time and energy planting trees and improving the extensive gardens. He even fitted out a small theater so that he and Émilie and their frequent guests could put on theatrical performances, often of Voltaire's latest plays, which continued to appear in Paris even though he could not.

Émilie du Châtelet was a remarkable woman. She shared with Voltaire a passion for Virgil, Horace, and Lucretius, whom they would read aloud together. She spoke Italian and knew English well enough to read Milton and Locke in the original. But her main passion was science. She prepared what is still the definitive translation of Newton's *Principia* from Latin into French with a lengthy explanatory introduction.

Voltaire, too, was strongly interested in science during these years. He wrote a widely read book introducing and explaining Newton's work on physics, optics, and mathematics to the European public. He even ordered scientific equipment from Paris, ostensibly to conduct his own experiments. But Voltaire's gift was for *belles lettres*, not science, and he continued to churn out plays and other popular works, including short tales and works of history. His *Siècle de Louis XIV*, though little read today, exercised a powerful influence on the way history was written, especially on Edward Gibbon, who would publish the first volume of his massive *Decline and Fall of the Roman Empire* in 1776.

Voltaire gradually worked his way back into the good graces of Versailles, largely through the efforts of the king's mistress, Madame de Pompadour. Voltaire wrote the libretti (as Molière had done before him) for two operas to be performed at the royal court. He was appointed historiographer of France in 1745. And, after two earlier attempts were blocked, he was finally elected to the Académie Française in 1746. He even became a gentleman of the king's bedchamber, a largely honorary position.

Voltaire's time as a faithful courtier was short-lived, however. Émilie had a gambling compulsion and often lost large sums of money. After she bet and lost heavily at the queen's tables, Voltaire was overheard suggesting that she had been cheated. The queen was deeply offended, and, once again, Voltaire and Émilie hastily returned to Cirey. If it hadn't been one thing, it would have been another. Voltaire was not born to be a courtier, a lesson he would soon learn again at the court of Frederick the Great of Prussia.

In 1749, Émilie died at the château due to complications from childbirth. Voltaire was devastated by the loss. He had long ceased to love Émilie and was already involved in an affair with his beloved sister's eldest daughter, Marie-Louise Denis. The fifty-year-old Voltaire had offered the twenty-five-year-old widow and orphan his support and protection upon the death of her husband in 1744. But his interest in Madame

Denis quickly became more than avuncular. Their affair, a closely guarded secret, began the following year. The passion was largely on Voltaire's side, not hers. But Voltaire had no intention of leaving Émilie and, indeed, had joyfully anticipated the birth of their child.[24]

Voltaire was sufficiently stunned by Émilie's death that, in 1750, he accepted a long-standing invitation to visit Potsdam and the court of Frederick of Prussia. They had corresponded for some time. Voltaire even helped Frederick, before he ascended the throne, write a book called the *Anti-Machiavel*, and then unwisely quipped that the first thing Machiavelli would advise a new prince to do is to write a book condemning Machiavellianism. In order to accept Frederick's invitation, Voltaire had to resign his various posts in France, where the court looked with disfavor on his decision to attach himself to a rival monarch, even though Voltaire—always willing to play both sides—sought to portray it as intelligence-gathering.

Voltaire hoped to become a close and valued advisor to Frederick. But he soon found himself more in the position of an indentured servant. He got involved in an awkward financial scandal and publicly feuded with another of Frederick's advisors, who happened to be a former lover of Émilie. Voltaire obtained permission to depart Frederick's service in 1753 but was detained and harassed at the border, probably at Frederick's instructions, before finally being allowed to leave.

Unwelcome in Paris due to his association with Frederick, Voltaire was peripatetic for a time, finally moving to Geneva in 1755, where he inevitably riled the authorities with his deist views, his criticisms of Calvinism as overly rigid and puritanical, and his love of producing amateur theatricals at his home. In 1758, Voltaire purchased a large estate at Ferney, just on the French side of the border, and moved there with Madame Denis. Both the house and the gardens required substantial work, and he continued to improve them throughout the rest of his life. He had constant visitors; indeed, a stay at Ferney and a chance to meet Voltaire seemed to be on the grand tour itinerary of every foreign visitor, so much so that Voltaire called himself *l'aubergiste de l'Europe* (the hotelier of Europe).[25] Yet Voltaire found a measure of peace and happiness at Ferney. As he wrote to a friend, "the bulls, the cows, the sheep, the pastures, the buildings, the gardens, all take up my mornings; the afternoons are for study; and after supper, we rehearse the plays which we perform in my little gallery theatre. This way of life makes me want to live."[26] It was here, at Ferney, that he wrote the work for which he is and always will be most known.

CANDIDE

Candide was published in 1759 as the culmination of a series of tales and novellas by Voltaire that have come to be called *contes philosophiques*, though their principal import is the impossibility of reducing the messy complexity of life to philosophical abstractions. *Candide* was published simultaneously in multiple cities throughout Europe in order to thwart both piracy and censorship. In the latter, at least, Voltaire succeeded. Efforts to suppress the book, by church and state alike, were over-whelmed by its popularity. *Candide* was the best-selling book of the entire eighteenth century, outselling *Gulliver's Travels* by a multiple of three. It had a pan-European success comparable to that of *Don Quixote*, with which it bears some affinities.

Everyone knows Candide's parting injunction: "Il faut cultiver notre jardin" (We must cultivate our garden).[27] The words are intended both literally and figuratively. The surviving characters of the tale find a meas-ure of peace and harmony in performing simple daily tasks that contribute to their common welfare and allow them to appreciate the quiet vitality of nature.

After living through the compressed horrors of the Seven Years' War, the Lisbon earthquake, the Spanish Inquisition, and the slaughter of the indigenous peoples of South America, among others, the main characters find themselves on a small plot of land outside Constantinople and seek counsel from a famous dervish. Dr. Pangloss, their Leibnizian philoso-pher, asks the dervish why man was created and what the origin of evil is. "What are you getting into?" answers the dervish. "Is it any of your business?"[28] Woody Allen will borrow the line in *Annie Hall*, when the young Alvy Singer expresses his concern that the universe is expanding. "What is that your business?" his mother retorts. "Brooklyn is not ex-panding!"

Despite the near miracle that they are still alive, each of the principal characters in *Candide* is miserable in his or her own way: Pangloss, because he is not a professor at a distinguished university; Candide, be-cause his longed-for Cunégonde has become ugly and ill-tempered; the old woman, because of her countless ailments; Cacambo, because he is worn out with toil; Martin, because he sees no middle ground between misery and boredom; Paquette, because no one will any longer pay for her faded favors.

The neighboring farmer, who contentedly cultivates twenty acres with his children, explains that the work keeps from them three great evils: boredom, vice, and poverty. And so it proves to be the case for Candide and his friends. Everyone does something useful and begins to feel a sense of purpose. Philosophy is set aside. "Let's work without speculating, said Martin; it's the only way of rendering life bearable."[29]

Voltaire was always suspicious of speculative philosophy, which he ridicules in *Candide* as "metaphysico-theologico-cosmoloonigology."[30] That suspicion turned to disdain when he encountered Leibniz's argument in *Theodicy* that, because God is all-knowing, all-powerful, and all-good, the world he created, out of an infinity of possibilities, must be the best of all the possible worlds. Leibniz did not deny the existence of evil and suffering. Those are inevitable ingredients of any actual world, which will inevitably fall short of the perfection of the Creator himself. But God must have chosen the one world that contains the greatest possible balance of good over evil. Evil and suffering are thus part of a system of greater good. Moreover, since all things are interconnected, no particular instances of evil and suffering could be alleviated without disrupting the overall balance. In short, things cannot get better than they are; any change would only have made them worse.

Voltaire's friend Alexander Pope took Leibniz a step further in his poem "An Essay on Man," suggesting that evil and suffering are simply illusions arising from our partial understanding of the universal good.

> All nature is but art, unknown to thee;
> All chance, direction, which thou canst not see;
> All discord, harmony, not understood;
> All partial evil, universal good:
> And, spite of pride, in erring reason's spite,
> One truth is clear, "Whatever is, is right."[31]

Sweeping metaphysical systems never appealed to Voltaire. They ask too much of human reason and, ungrounded in actual experience, lead, as they did in Descartes, to a "swarm [of] errors." Voltaire much preferred the cautious empirical approach of Locke, reflected in Newton's science, which starts from experience. Dr. Pangloss is absurd because he cannot learn from experience. Not even losing an eye, an ear, and part of his nose to syphilis, witnessing the devastation of the Lisbon earthquake, being hanged by the Inquisition, or being pressed into a galley shakes his faith that everything must be for the best in this best of all possible worlds. "After all I am a philosopher," he explains.[32] For Pangloss, theory precedes and determines reality; all evidence to the contrary is simply ignored.

Voltaire's response to Leibniz and Pope, however, is more emotional than intellectual. The horrors that descend on his characters with such rapidity and such casual malevolence in *Candide* are all real historical events. The Seven Years' War was precipitated by a struggle between Austria and Prussia over the possession of Silesia. It eventually engaged all the major European powers—which had their own sources of grievance with one another—and many minor ones as well. It caused untold suffering, not just in the deaths of soldiers, but in the slaughter of innocent civilians who happened to be in the way and were murdered or raped or left to die of starvation and disease in a devastated land, all for the vanity of princes who wanted a reputation as conquerors. So, too, the Spanish Inquisition and the mass murder of the indigenous tribes of South America in the interests of imperial greed were all too real. Even nature displayed its utter indifference to human suffering in the Lisbon earthquake of 1755, which, along with the ensuing fires and tsunami, killed more than fifty thousand people.

Voltaire wrote a poem, "The Lisbon Earthquake," on the inability of philosophy to explain moral and physical evil. In a preface, he stresses that he is not writing against "the illustrious Pope," whom he has always loved and admired. But he does object to any attempt to explain away or otherwise minimize the wretchedness of humankind. Pope's famous phrase "whatever is, is right," Voltaire insists, "only insults us in our present misery."[33] More importantly, it is a counsel of despair, for it insists upon the inevitability of evil and therefore excludes hope and progress.

The poem was widely read but lacks the impact and interest of *Candide*, which rains disasters on its protagonists with such frequency and intensity that it underscores both the absurdity and the callousness of attributing "whatever is" to divine providence. The miseries suffered by Candide and his friends do not logically refute the proposition that these are "partial evils" counterbalanced by "universal good." But they make any such assertion seem morally bankrupt.

Candide is a battle against what the critic and biographer Richard Holmes has called "the great armies of the European night—fanaticism, intolerance, persecution, injustice, cruelty."[34] To that list we can add squalor, ignorance, poverty, disease, and war. Yet *Candide* is also a comic masterpiece, and the comedy somehow—and here is Voltaire's genius—accentuates the sense of outrage that lies at its core. The vitality and velocity of the narrative, the sharp prose, the wry asides, and the bland reportage of unspeakable horrors all contribute to a stunning contrast between matter and manner equal to that of a philosophical theory that treats evil as a disguised species of good.

Candide, Voltaire tells us, combines gentle manners and "an honest mind with great simplicity of heart."[35] *Candidus*, in Latin, means "white, bright, and shining." Candide is Locke's blank slate ready, in all innocence and eagerness, to be written upon by the world. Like Robinson Crusoe and Lemuel Gulliver, Candide will undertake a fictional journey. But Candide lacks their pragmatic skills in contending with adversity. He stumbles into every disaster of contemporary life, in a parody of literary twists and turns: chance meetings, tempests, shipwrecks, pirates, wars, and even the miraculous reappearance of those thought to be dead. "If this is the best of all possible worlds," he says plaintively, "what are the others like?"[36] Candide is a recidivist victim, sustained only by his own constantly disappointed hope and unfulfilled longing to meet with a measure of kindness and love. Yet somehow, if only occasionally, he does meet with both kindness and love by displaying those qualities himself against all reason and all probability. Samuel Johnson will refer to second marriages as "the triumph of hope over experience." The phrase is even more apt to Candide's naive insistence that things can be better than they are. Happiness may be out of reach, but we can still do useful work and forge human connections that endure over time. All is not for the best, but it can become better through tolerance, kindness, and an attempt to improve the everyday lot of those nearest to us.

Like Proust's Swann and Odette, Candide marries Cunégonde only after he has ceased to love her. And yet Candide, like Swann, still feels the echoes of the love that once obsessed him, and his loyalty to Cunégonde is a tribute to that love. Unlike Gulliver, Candide never becomes a misanthrope. He sheds his delusions without losing his soul. It is in this respect that *Candide* bears affinity to *Don Quixote*. Pangloss, with his arcane philosophy, is the opposite of the earthy Sancho, with his homey bits of wisdom. Yet each serves as a perfect foil and companion in the tragic-comic encounter of romantic ideals and a decidedly unromantic reality.

Responding to Pascal's claim that we must love only God and not his imperfect creatures, Voltaire retorted in the *English Letters*, "We must most tenderly love creatures; we must love our nation, our wife, our father, our children; and it is so necessary to love them that God makes us love them despite ourselves."[37] Man has many flaws; life brings many miseries. But "I dare to take humanity's part against this sublime misanthrope" (J'ose prendre le parti de l'humanité contre ce misanthrope sublime), Voltaire wrote.[38] He is still taking humanity's part in *Candide*.

Another sublime misanthrope, Gustave Flaubert, would famously write, "Madame Bovary, c'est moi," embracing the romantic illusions of his heroine that ended only in bitterness and death. Voltaire could as readily have written, "Candide, c'est moi." Against the great armies of the European night, Voltaire tended his garden and retained his belief that tolerance and kindness are our greatest obligations and the only truly divine commandments.

PHILOSOPHICAL DICTIONARY

One of the major intellectual projects of the Enlightenment was the *Encyclopédie, ou Dictionnaire raisonné des sciences, des arts et des métiers* (*Encyclopedia, or Systematic Dictionary of the Sciences, Arts, and Trades*). Originally conceived simply as a translation of a popular English-language encyclopedia published in 1728, the *Encyclopédie* quickly expanded into a detailed summary of the current state of knowledge and a marker for future progress, in all the various branches of science, the fine arts, the mechanical arts, and *belles lettres*. Original articles were solicited from a wide range of scientists, mathematicians, musicians, physicians, and writers, including Voltaire and Jean-Jacques Rousseau (1712–1778), who later broke decisively and bitterly from his Enlightenment colleagues in favor of a new Romanticism that would come to dominate the late eighteenth and early nineteenth centuries.

The two coeditors of the project were Denis Diderot (1713–1784) and Jean Le Rond d'Alembert (1717–1783). In his *Preliminary Discourse to the Encyclopedia of Diderot*, designed to accompany the first volume, d'Alembert described the underlying assumptions and overriding aspirations of the project. Building on a curious but powerful fusion of Descartes and Locke, d'Alembert proposed a purely secular approach to knowledge, applying reason to experience and accepting nothing on mere authority. He promised a summary of the various branches of knowledge that would reveal "the general principles that form the basis of each science and each art, liberal or mechanical, and the most essential facts that make up the body and substance of each."[39] D'Alembert, that is, sought to uncover the "geometry" of each subject, as well as the more specific knowledge gained in each.[40] He also included a taxonomy of human knowledge that purported to show the interrelationships among all the various disciplines.

Needless to say, d'Alembert's assumption that the scientific/mathematical method proposed by Descartes and perfected by Newton in physics and optics could be applied to uncover "laws" governing widely different subject matters was overly ambitious and hardly a sign of cautious empiricism. But d'Alembert's *Discourse* reflected the almost giddy excitement among the philosophes at the progress already made and still to be made by the application of reason to experience, unhampered by religious, political, and even moral dogmas. And, as Voltaire asserted in his *English Letters*, intellectual and religious freedom also promotes material progress and the creation of wealth, which leads to even more freedom.

Yet the *Encyclopédie*, at least as conceived by d'Alembert, was not as radical as it might first seem. Various articles did reject the possibility of miracles, treat the Bible as simply another book, and refuse to accept religious claims based on revelation rather than reason. Yet certain assumptions appeared to be off-limits:

> It is therefore evident that the purely intellectual concepts of vice and virtue, the principle and the necessity of laws, the spiritual nature of the soul, the existence of God and of our obligations toward him—in a word, the truths for which we have the most immediate and indispensable need—are the fruits of the first reflective ideas that our sensations occasion.[41]

The "fruits of the first reflective ideas," which d'Alembert also calls "these first truths," sound very much like the "innate ideas" of Descartes. Voltaire, as we shall see, would largely accept them, softening his stance from the *English Letters*. But Diderot and others, who were determined to question all received authority and accept only what reason validates, would challenge even first truths, particularly the existence of God and the spiritual nature of the soul.

Originally planned in five volumes, the *Encyclopédie* quickly exploded in scope. Twenty-eight volumes were finally published between 1751 and 1772, including seventeen volumes of articles and eleven volumes of engraved plates containing illustrations and technical diagrams. The first three volumes were published while Voltaire was still in Potsdam. Upon leaving Frederick's employ, he readily agreed to participate going forward and took on a wide variety of articles, consistent with his polymathic interests.

In 1759, however, at the urging of conservative clerics, the parliament condemned the project and revoked a license to print the volumes in France. D'Alembert resigned as editor, but Diderot carried on in secret, soliciting, editing, and writing articles, as well as arranging for the remaining volumes at least to appear to have been published in Switzerland and thus beyond the reach of French authorities.

Voltaire, like d'Alembert, moved on to other projects. It is unlikely that he was concerned about the condemnation. His own works were every bit as provocative as the *Encyclopédie*. But Voltaire was a skeptical thinker, who shied away from any form of systematic thinking, and he may have found the structure and tone of the *Encyclopédie* too definitive and constraining. Voltaire clearly thought he could do a more effective job of promoting Enlightenment thinking in a shorter compass. "A work in twenty folio volumes will never make a revolution," he wrote in a later letter; "it's the little books costing 30 sous which are to be feared."[42] And that is exactly what he produced.

As was his usual habit, Voltaire published the *Philosophical Dictionary* anonymously in 1764. The little "pocket" book was widely condemned by religious and government officials, but was also widely read. Everyone knew Voltaire was the author. But his standard, pro forma denials allowed officials to look the other way. Voltaire at this point was probably too famous, and in any event too close to the Swiss border, for any direct sanctions, though, as we shall see, the indirect attacks were nonetheless vicious.

Although he wanted to keep it short, Voltaire added substantially to the *Philosophical Dictionary* through the years. It is written in a number of different voices, sometimes for comic effect, sometimes to universalize the point being made, and sometimes simply to put the most controversial views in the mouths of largely fictitious interlocutors. Voltaire is not writing philosophy, in the sense of attempting to systematize or otherwise justify our beliefs. There is a skeptical and ironic tone throughout. Voltaire constantly challenges authority and preaches tolerance but is didactic only by indirection. "As for me," he writes, "who have undertaken this little *Dictionary* in order to put questions, I am far from being certain."[43]

Yet there are two articles of faith that Voltaire does announce and that are critical to his overall approach. First, Voltaire makes clear that he is not an atheist. He accepts the argument from design, focusing on the beautiful and lucid mechanics of Newton's clockwork universe as well as the biological complexity of all life forms increasingly revealed by science. Harking back to Aristotle, Voltaire accepts the reality of "final causes" as the only way to explain such intricate designs.[44] He recognizes that there are "difficulties presented by the idea of providence" but embraces it as the only explanation for the effects and appearances he sees.[45]

Second, and relatedly, Voltaire accepts the demands of morality. Virtue comes to us as an obligation from God.[46] It is "not a good, it is a duty: it is a different kind, of a superior order. It has nothing to do with painful or agreeable sensations."[47] Nor does it have anything to do with the consequences of one's actions. Voltaire adopts what has come to be known as a deontological understanding of ethics based solely on right and wrong. These concepts are the first fruits of reflective ideas; that is to say, we understand them intuitively, and they impose upon us a simple, universal moral imperative to treat others with charity; to treat them, that is, as we would have them treat us. That is the basic tenet of Christianity and of other religions as well. "It is obvious to the whole world that a service is better than an injury. . . . It only remains therefore to use our reason to discern the shades of goodness and badness."[48] But any attempt to ground that basic principle with philosophical abstractions is, Voltaire insists, unhelpful. "Christianity teaches only simplicity, forbearance, charity: reduce it to metaphysics and it becomes a source of error."[49]

Voltaire thus identifies himself as a deist but not as a member of any specific religion. He believes in a creator God and in our moral obligations to one another. But the nature and the actions of that God are beyond our human understanding, and nothing but mischief ensues from pretending to know what we do not and cannot know.

> The [deist] is a man firmly convinced of the existence of a supreme being as good as he is powerful, who has created all extended, vegetating, sentient and thinking beings, who perpetuates their species, who punishes crimes without cruelty, and benevolently rewards virtuous behavior.[50]

There are indeed many "difficulties" with this simple profession of faith, and we will discuss those shortly, but let's start with the three conclusions Voltaire draws from his particular brand of deism. First, doctrinaire theology is an abomination. Second, the Bible (like the scriptures of every other religion) is just a book without special status as a divine revelation. Third, organized religion is a scandal and an imposition, *l'infâme* that Voltaire wants us to *écrasez*.

According to Voltaire, "theological religion . . . is the source of all imaginable follies and disorders; it is the mother of fanaticism and civil discord; it is the enemy of mankind."[51] Any religious doctrine that "goes beyond the worship of a supreme being and the submission of the heart to his eternal commands," Voltaire insists, is superstition that breeds sectarianism and intolerance.[52] Each religion inevitably develops theological tenets that separate it from and contradict the teachings of other religions, whether it is the nature of grace, the transubstantiation of the Eucharist, the divinity of Christ, original sin, the Trinity, or anything else decreed by one church council or another. "All councils are undoubtedly infallible," Voltaire sarcastically notes, "for they are composed of men. It is impossible for passions, intrigues, the lust for dispute, hatred, jealousy, prejudice, ignorance ever to reign in these assemblies."[53]

None of the doctrinal fiats that have arbitrarily resulted from the many and varied church councils are provable. For some, belief in transubstantiation is an imbecility; for others, it is a sacred truth.[54] The Trinity is unintelligible and nowhere found in the scriptures, and yet was decreed an unchallengeable dogma of Catholicism.[55] The various religious sects exist precisely because such matters are not proper subjects of knowledge. When the truth is evident, parties and factions do not arise. "There is no sect in geometry," Voltaire notes.[56] "In England nobody says: 'I am a Newtonian,'" because everyone recognizes the truths he taught. "We perhaps still have some Cartesians in France," Voltaire concedes ironically. "This is solely because Descartes's system is a tissue of erroneous and ridiculous fancies."[57]

Voltaire advocates skepticism to promote tolerance: "don't pretend to know what you don't know" is his urgent injunction.[58] Most people are in accord "on the worship of a god and on probity."[59] That is as close as we can come to a "universal religion."[60] Voltaire presents various catechisms: Chinese, Japanese, Indian. But, for a believer, each one reduces to the same thing: "To do good, that is his cult. To submit to god, that is his doctrine."[61] Voltaire even quotes a country priest who has learned the same lesson: "God forbid that I should elaborate on concomitant grace, the efficacious grace we resist, the sufficient grace which does not suffice."[62] Such "futile notions" are of no use to virtue.[63] But charity can replace doctrinal unanimity. "Morality is one, it comes from god. Dogmas differ, they are ours."[64] "After men have disputed for a very long time," the Japanese catechism concludes, "and it has been realized that all these quarrels teach men only to harm one another, they finally decide that mutual toleration is unquestionably best."[65] When, or even whether, that will come remains to be seen.

Voltaire's second point is that we cannot turn to the Bible for divine revelation. It is just a collection of books from various sources and periods, arbitrarily joined together. In his later years, Voltaire spent a great deal of time and energy on biblical exegesis, all with the announced aim of showing that the Bible is not a legitimate source for the theological doctrines adopted by Catholicism and other Christian sects. Here, in the *Philosophical Dictionary*, he makes the argument in more condensed but nonetheless compelling form.

Voltaire considered Jesus a great moral teacher, and he values the Gospels accordingly. But he finds no historical support for the religious myths created in his name. Josephus (37–ca. 100) was the greatest and most thorough historian of the Jewish people. Yet he makes no mention of Jesus and his miracles; or of Herod's massacre of the male children; or of the new star at the birth of Jesus; or of the darkness covering the earth for three hours at his death. These are all embellishments in gospels written long after the death of Jesus and his four eponymous evangelists, in a language they likely did not understand and almost certainly could not read or write. It is well known that many false gospels were initially taken as authentic. We do not know whether the ones that were finally decreed to be canonical were themselves false gospels. Indeed, the distinction is itself an arbitrary one.[66]

Even taking the Gospels at face value, Voltaire notes, Jesus himself never claimed that he was born of a virgin or that he was the son of God. He made no mention of the seven sacraments, and he established no ecclesiastical hierarchies. All these things were decreed by the vote of bishops in councils that occurred long after the death of Jesus. Jesus himself "displayed to mankind only a just man pleasing to god, persecuted by those who envied him, and condemned to death by prejudiced magistrates."[67] Not until the Council of Nicaea, three centuries after the death of Jesus, was his divinity officially declared. "Finally, after many arguments," Voltaire explains, "the holy ghost decided thus in the council, by the mouths of 299 bishops against eighteen," that Jesus was the son of God, begotten by the Father and of one substance with the Father.[68] Jesus the man, morally inspired by God, became himself a god, and fifty years later, at a separate council in Constantinople, the "Holy Ghost" was tentatively added to the Trinity.

The Old Testament doesn't even have the benefit of the simple moral message of the New Testament Gospels. Of Kings and Chronicles, Voltaire writes, "it must be admitted that if the holy spirit wrote this history he did not choose a very edifying subject."[69] The immoral acts of David alone are legion: he lies, steals, commits adultery, betrays erstwhile allies, tortures innocent villagers, and perpetrates mass murder.[70] Solomon is little better and certainly did not write the various books attributed to him. Proverbs is just "a collection of trivial, low, incoherent maxims, made without taste, without selection and without plan."[71] The author of Ecclesiastes is an Epicurean philosopher for whom the only good is to enjoy the fruits of one's labor with the woman one loves; he is "a materialist who is at once sensual and satiated."[72] Song of Songs is an "impious" and "libertine" work with no relation to religion, though still valuable as the only extant Hebrew book of love.[73]

Voltaire also demonstrates, as is commonly accepted today, that Moses could not have written the Pentateuch, generally known as the Five Books of Moses. He has no objection to the story of Adam and Eve as long as it is understood only allegorically; even Jewish scholars considered it as such. Christian ecclesiastics, however, cite it as a historical basis for the doctrine of original sin. That, Voltaire objects, is to accuse God of "the most absurd barbarity, to dare to say that he made all the generations of men in order to torment them by eternal sufferings on the pretext that their first father ate some fruit in a garden."[74]

Voltaire recognizes the historical value and beauty of many of the books of the Bible. He praises the story of Joseph and the story of Job as among "the most precious monuments of antiquity to have come down to us."[75] But any suggestion that the Bible as a whole is the source of divine revelations cannot survive scrutiny.

With neither reason nor revelation to support its doctrines and practices, what is the role of the church? That is Voltaire's third point: *écrasez l'infâme*. Organized religion is a source of oppression and unreason that benefits only its clerical officials and the political status quo. It should be wiped from the face of the earth.

> You have profited from the times of ignorance, of superstition, of folly, to despoil us of our heritage and to trample us underfoot in order to fatten yourselves on the substance of the wretched: tremble lest the day of reason arrive.[76]

Through its system of tithes and pay-to-play sacraments, the church has enriched itself at the expense of those least able to pay. It also has adapted itself to existing forms of political power and thus contributes to their perpetuation. "It is impossible on our wretched globe for men living in society not to be divided into two classes," Voltaire explains, "one of oppressors, the other of the oppressed; and these subdivide into a thousand, and the thousand have further gradations."[77]

The church, which should take the part of the oppressed, has become an instrument of the oppressors. Church and state are joined in an unholy symbiotic relationship. Preachers rail against impurity, lack of observance, and false beliefs. But they are silent in the face of injustice. Worse, the church is directly enlisted in supporting wars of conquest launched by princes and ministers, each of whom has his banners blessed and invokes God's grace before setting off to exterminate his neighbors.[78] "The united vices of all the ages and of all places will never equal the evils produced by a single campaign."[79] Yet "artificial religion encourages all the cruelties done in association, conspiracies, seditions, robbery, ambushes, attacks on towns, pillages, murders."[80] In ancient times, it was thought better to obey God than men. Now, "to follow the laws of the state is to obey god."[81] Christianity, which began as a subversive religion, has become a vital instrument of the state.

"The Catholic religion . . . would be lost if men began to think," Voltaire concludes.[82] The church instills irrational opinions in children before they can exercise their own judgment. But when one is old enough to apply reason to experience, these superstitions can and must be rooted out and cast aside. The ultimate Enlightenment injunction is "Dare to think for yourself."[83]

There are limits, however, to how much thinking even Voltaire will undertake. Certain lines of inquiry—which he dismisses as metaphysical—are simply fruitless and thus best ignored. In this way, he ducks the three main conundrums of the mechanistic universe as envisioned by Descartes and revealed by Newton. First, there is the problem of free will. If all is determined in an endless line of cause and effect, in what sense can one be said to act freely and, hence, to be responsible for one's actions? Second, a clockwork mechanism may have a purpose but does not seem to need a soul. What role, then, does the soul play, and how does it interact with and survive the body? Third, if God is all-knowing, all-powerful, and all-good, how could evil mar his creation? If he could have precluded it but did not, then he is not all-good. If he didn't realize it would arise, then he is not omniscient. If he tried but failed to preclude it, then he is not omnipotent.

On all three questions, Voltaire demurs. "You ask me what will become of free will," he writes. "I don't understand you. I do not know what this free will is that you speak of."[84] We say a man is free if his actions are not controlled. "You are free to act when you have the power to act."[85] That doesn't mean you act without a reason or that your will itself is not determined. "Every effect obviously has its cause, which can be retraced from cause to cause into the abyss of eternity."[86] But a man is free if he can act as he wills.

So, too, with the soul. "We call soul that which animates. We know little more about it, our intelligence being limited."[87] The church teaches that the soul is without extension and survives the body it inhabits. But when does this soul enter the body? At the moment of conception? Some weeks later? If the pregnancy is not carried to term, does the soul retreat and wait for a better opportunity? Where was the soul beforehand? Where does it lodge in the body? Where does it go after death? How does the "I," the identity of the same person, subsist? If a person becomes an imbecile at fifteen and dies an imbecile at seventy, will the soul "pick up the thread of the ideas it had at the age of puberty"?[88]

We can answer none of these questions. "As for me," Voltaire concludes, "I dare have no opinion. I perceive nothing but incomprehensibility in either system, and after having thought about it all my life I'm no further advanced than on the first day. Then it wasn't worth thinking about."[89] We are human beings. We are born, we live, we act, we think, all without knowing whether the soul is mortal or immortal, material or immaterial. Nor do we need to know. "What use would it be to me? Would it make me juster? Would I be a better husband, better father, better master, better citizen?"[90] If not, then leave it alone.

The same applies to the question of why God made the universe as he did and how evil is possible. Voltaire's answer echoes the dervish: it is none of his business. Let the metaphysicians wrestle with such questions, in all their futility. "God is still my master; he's given me the notion of justice; I must follow it. I've no wish to be a philosopher, I want to be a man."[91]

This is the true credo of the philosophes as inspired by Voltaire. They had no wish to be philosophers. Indeed, one scholar justly titled his book on the philosophes *The Anti-Philosophers*.[92] They were public intellectuals. They were men of letters. They were students of science and the arts. They shunned organized religion along with metaphysical systems. But they believed in progress, and they promoted justice, tolerance, and freedom by every means at their disposal.

THE CHAMPION OF JUSTICE

Voltaire in his old age began to deploy his great fame to highlight and protest against individual instances of injustice. Already in *Candide*, he had criticized the 1757 execution of Admiral John Byng, who had tried and failed to relieve a besieged British garrison at the battle of Minorca at the outset of the Seven Years' War. Byng, a friend of Voltaire from his time in London, had acted with both skill and courage. But he was court-martialed and summarily executed all the same. Candide, who sees the firing squad in action, asks the reason for it.

The reason, they told him, is that he didn't kill enough people; he gave battle to a French admiral, and it was found that he didn't get close enough to him. But, said Candide, the French admiral was just as far from the English admiral as the English admiral was from the French admiral. That's perfectly true came the answer; but in this country it is useful from time to time to kill one admiral in order to encourage the others.[93]

The lines show Voltaire's unique ability to compress outrage and wit together in such a way that each enhances the other. "*Pour encourager les autres*" became a well-known catchphrase even among the English.

In subsequent cases, outrage overpowered wit. Voltaire took up the cause of Jean Calas, a Protestant who was convicted in Catholic Toulouse of the murder of his son in 1762. It was alleged, without evidence, that the elderly Calas had killed the boy because he wanted to convert to Catholicism. Most likely, he committed suicide. Yet Calas was savagely tortured and later tied to a wheel, where his limbs were shattered by an iron bar before he was strangled and burned. The rest of his family was in danger of similar treatment before Voltaire got involved, writing over a hundred letters on their behalf and creating enormous public pressure for the release of information about the case. Eventually the king's council ordered the Toulouse parliament to turn over the trial records. After a two-year battle, the Toulouse verdict was annulled, and the prosecutor in the case was removed from his post. Louis XV personally sent financial compensation to the family, though it was hardly recompense for Calas's brutal death.[94]

Other such cases followed, and in each instance, after a prolonged campaign, Voltaire helped the victim obtain, albeit mostly posthumously, a measure of justice. One egregious instance particularly concerned Voltaire, since it seemed to be an indirect attack on him as well. The twenty-year-old Chevalier de La Barre was convicted of desecrating a crucifix, singing impious songs, and failing to remove his hat when a religious procession passed by. At the order of the magistrate, who was apparently jealous of a perceived romantic rival, La Barre was tortured, beheaded, and burned at the stake with a copy of Voltaire's own *Philosophical Dictionary* nailed to his body. Voltaire launched a public campaign against the judicial murder, even as he quietly moved across the border into Switzerland to put himself beyond the reach of French authorities.

Voltaire built upon the facts of the Calas affair to prepare a *Treatise on Tolerance*, in which he attacked the French system of justice and argued that Christianity was unique among religions in its violent persecution of nonbelievers. If it followed the teachings of Jesus, Christianity would be the most tolerant of religions. Yet it has become synonymous with intolerance and oppression. The Roman Stoic Marcus Cato used to end every speech with the phrase *Carthago delenda est* (Carthage must be destroyed). Voltaire now ended every letter with "Écrasez l'infâme."

The elderly man of letters had become a publicly engaged intellectual, launching a French tradition that would proceed through Émile Zola and Jean-Paul Sartre.[95] A man who had long sought acceptance and acclaim from the aristocracy was now a hero of the people in his fight against injustice and oppression.

Voltaire made a triumphant return to Paris in 1778 at the age of eighty-three, after a twenty-eight-year absence. At the border, he declared that he was not carrying any contraband "except myself," a line Oscar Wilde would turn to his own purposes when entering the United States, with the words "I have nothing to declare but my genius."

Voltaire's latest tragedy was performed at the Comédie-Française, and a bust of the author was unveiled and crowned with wreathes in an onstage ceremony. A special session of the Académie Française was held to honor its most distinguished member. The exertion proved too much for the aging writer, and he became gravely ill, but without losing his signature wit. Asked by an importunate clergyman to renounce Satan on his deathbed, he is said to have quipped, "Now, now my good man, this is no time to be making new enemies."

One last macabre scene was to follow. Concerned that he would be denied a religious burial and hence consigned to a mass grave, his family arranged for Voltaire's embalmed body to be propped up in his carriage as if he were still alive and rushed off to the Abbey of Scellières in Champagne, where he was buried before the bishop had time to forbid it.

Voltaire became a posthumous hero of the revolution for his defense of social justice and human rights. Indeed, he seems even to have predicted the stunning events of 1789, when he wrote to the French ambassador in Turin: "Everything that I see sows the seeds of a revolution which will come without fail, but which I shall not have the pleasure to witness."[96] His remains were exhumed, taken in solemn procession to Paris, and reinterred in the Panthéon in 1791. The catafalque that bore his coffin had three inscriptions, one of which read: "Poet, philosopher, historian, he gave a great impetus to the human spirit, and prepared us to be free."[97]

8

SAMUEL JOHNSON ON THE STABILITY OF TRUTH

The irregular combinations of fanciful invention may delight awhile by that novelty of which the common satiety of life sends us all in quest; but the pleasures of sudden wonder are soon exhausted, and the mind can only repose on the stability of truth. [1]

James Boswell's *Life of Johnson* has a legitimate, perhaps overwhelming, claim to be the greatest biography in the English language. [2] The multivolume *Life* is itself a work of literary art. As Boswell explained, he was intent not just on relating the most important events of Johnson's life, but also on "interweaving what he privately wrote, and said, and thought; by which mankind are enabled as it were to see him live, and to 'live o'er each scene' with him, as he actually advanced through the several stages of his life." [3] It was a novel conception of biography, first practiced by Johnson himself, and executed by Boswell to near perfection. To read the biography is to know and love the man, warts and all, for as Johnson himself stressed in defending his criticisms of Shakespeare, "we must confess the faults of our favorite, to gain credit to our praise of his excellencies." [4] Subsequent biographies of Johnson may add specific details and novel interpretations, but even the best of them finds its ballast in retelling anecdotes found in Boswell.

Samuel Johnson packed many lives into his seventy-five years. There was Johnson the Grub Street hack, churning out parliamentary reports and other articles for the *Gentleman's Magazine* to scrape out a precarious existence. There was Johnson the poet, writing adaptations of Juvenal's *Satires* to portray the London of his day, and a neoclassical play, *Irene*, that was hopelessly outdated before it ever reached the stage. There was dictionary Johnson, the great lexicographer who almost single-handedly produced the model of all modern dictionaries, with crisp definitions and chronologically arranged quotations to illustrate each word's evolution. There was Johnson of the *conte philosophique*, weaving an exotic tale of disillusionment that invites comparison with *Gulliver's Travels* and *Candide*. There was Johnson the scholar, preparing a carefully collated edition of the works of Shakespeare. There was Johnson the literary critic, in his *Preface to Shakespeare* and *Lives of the Poets*. Most of all, there was Johnson the talker—perhaps the most famous talker of all time—holding forth at the Turk's Head Tavern and elsewhere. Boswell's *Life* gains much of its bulk from his reconstructed conversations.

Whole volumes can be, and have been, written about each of these aspects of Johnson's lengthy career. He was the finest and most versatile man of letters the English nation has ever known, and the second-most quoted writer in the English language after Shakespeare. But the focus of our study will be on Johnson as a moralist, in his many short essays for the *Rambler* and other periodicals, and as a man who overcame tremendous hardships to affirm his own and others' humanity.

LIFE

Samuel Johnson was born on September 18, 1709, in Lichfield, a small town about sixteen miles north of Birmingham. It was a difficult labor. His mother, Sarah, who was giving birth for the first time at the age of forty, almost died. To spare her health, the infant was sent out to a wet nurse, from whom he developed scrofula, a tubercular infection of his lymph glands that left him scarred, deaf in his left ear, and with severely impaired vision in his right eye.

Sarah took the child to London, pursuant to an ancient superstition, to be "touched" by Queen Anne. The sovereign's laying on of hands did nothing for his disabilities, but Samuel did receive a silver amulet that he wore around his neck for the rest of his life.

He was a fiercely proud child. At the age of three, he attended a local school run by Dame Oliver. One day, no one came to fetch him after school, so he set off for home by himself. Dame Oliver followed behind the nearly blind child, and when Samuel dropped to his hands and knees to cross a gutter that he could not properly see, she rushed forward to help. Humiliated, Samuel sought to drive her away with his tiny fists.[5]

His father, Michael Johnson, was a bookseller, bookbinder, and stationer. He was a big, powerful man, as Samuel himself would become. Michael was elected sheriff and served in other offices in the town. But his wife, who had relations of quality, looked down on her husband's more humble background. They married late—Sarah was thirty-seven and Michael was fifty-two. She was querulous, and he was depressed, another trait his son would inherit. As Samuel himself noted sadly, "my father and mother had not much happiness from each other."[6] They had a second child, Nathaniel, three years after Samuel.

Michael tried unsuccessfully to expand into the manufacture of parchment and fell on hard times financially, which greatly limited Samuel's own opportunities. He entered the Lichfield Grammar School at the age of seven and studied there for the next nine years. The curriculum was heavy on Latin and caning, the latter as an incentive to the former. Samuel was a strong scholar with a remarkable memory. He read constantly and widely, including both classics and romances of chivalry, which he enjoyed throughout his life. He was indifferent to religion during these early years. On Sundays, he would go into the fields to read when he was supposed to be in church.

At the age of sixteen, Samuel was invited to visit nearby Stourbridge by Cornelius Ford, a clergyman and former Cambridge don, who was a cousin on his mother's side. Ford introduced the precocious youth into society, where he shone in conversation, wrote poetry, and continued his extensive reading. He finished his schooling at the Stourbridge Grammar School, acting as a teacher's assistant to defray the fees.

Once back at Lichfield, however, the seventeen-year-old Samuel was at loose ends. For two years he watched other boys, without a fraction of his learning or his intelligence, leave for Oxford and Cambridge. But his chance finally came. His mother received a small legacy that, combined with promises of support from a wealthy school friend in exchange for tutoring, was enough to get him to Pembroke College, Oxford, in the fall of 1728. Dame Oliver brought Samuel gingerbread for the journey and told him he was the best student she ever had, a compliment that delighted him.[7]

Samuel excelled at Oxford, writing Latin poems and English translations, and, most of all, engaging in brilliant, spirited conversations with his tutors and fellow students. One tutor later told Samuel that he had never known a student better prepared for Oxford. His frugality was legendary, as was his pride. His shoes were so well worn that his toes were visible. Yet when another student discreetly placed a new pair outside his door, Samuel threw them away.[8] His mother's legacy was soon exhausted by financial demands at home, and the school friend who had promised to support him left Oxford with no provision for Samuel. After little more than a year, Samuel was himself forced to leave, his future prospects blighted by the lack of a degree. Bitterness and envy were two demons with which he wrestled throughout his life and were the subject of some of his most powerful moral writings.

Again back in Lichfield, the now-adult Johnson fell into a deep and prolonged depression. He did some work in his father's bookshop, but that mostly consisted of reading the books for sale and occasionally, if grudgingly, looking up to speak with a customer. His father had a stall in Uttoxeter on market days. One day Michael was sick, and he asked his son to man the stall. Johnson refused to go out of a combination of inertia and humiliation. Fifty years later, his father long deceased, Johnson did his penance, walking to the market and standing in the rain, without a hat, exposed to the scorn of all who passed, in the very spot where his father's stall had been.

Johnson was big-boned and ungainly. He also suffered a combination of what we now recognize as Tourette syndrome and obsessive-compulsive disorder. Involuntary tics, odd gestures, repetitive motions, and loud exhalations were just some of his off-putting mannerisms, along with such standard compulsions as counting steps, avoiding cracks, and touching each post he passed. Years later, when he lived in London, Johnson was visiting the novelist Samuel Richardson. William Hogarth, painter of the underside of London, came to Richardson's house. Johnson was standing at the window, shaking his head and rolling himself about in a strange and ridiculous manner. Hogarth assumed he was an idiot relative in the care of Richardson. But then Johnson came over and joined in the conversation, displaying an eloquence and power that astonished Hogarth.[9]

His odd mannerisms and lack of an Oxford degree cost Johnson many opportunities to serve as a schoolmaster. Sometimes, moreover, he was too lethargic to even distinguish the hour on the town clock.[10] He feared he would become mad and contemplated suicide. Johnson would often quote the Latin poet Martial: "*Vitam continent una dies*" (One day contains my whole life). He had no sense of progress or hope.

What saved Johnson was his conversation. He made and impressed friends who sought his company. One such was Henry Porter, a Birmingham merchant, and his wife Elizabeth, who declared Johnson, despite his idiosyncrasies, "the most sensible man that I ever saw in my life."[11]

After her husband died, Elizabeth and Samuel became one of the most famous odd couples in literary history. They married in 1735. He was twenty-six, with limited prospects. Tetty (as Johnson affectionately called her) was a well-off, attractive widow of forty-six with three children. Despite ensuing difficulties, Johnson always insisted "it was a love marriage on both sides."[12] He was attentive, affectionate, and fiercely loyal. Johnson was always cognizant of Tetty's sacrifice in marrying him. Shunned by family and friends alike, she gave up nearly everything for a second start with Johnson, and he bore the burden of that guilt.

In later years, Tetty drank too much and took laudanum (a liquid form of opium). David Garrick, the famous Shakespearean actor, described her as "very fat, with a bosom of more than ordinary protuberance, with swelled cheeks, of a florid red, produced by thick painting, and increased by the liberal use of cordials."[13] The British historian Thomas Macaulay was even crueler, referring to Tetty as "a short, fat, coarse woman, painted half an inch thick, dressed in gaudy colors, and fond of exhibiting provincial airs and graces."[14] Both seem to have been exaggerating for comic or malicious effect. Regardless, as Boswell tactfully explained, Johnson never lost "the impressions which her beauty, real or imaginary, had originally made upon his fancy."[15]

With her consent, Johnson used Tetty's dowry to establish a school of his own. Only a few students enrolled. One was Garrick, who would become a lifelong friend, though the friendship was strongly tinged with rivalry. According to Garrick, the students would peer through the keyhole when Johnson and Tetty were tumbling together in bed, and Garrick would later mimic the scene. The school ultimately failed. Much of Tetty's capital was gone. Johnson longed to be a lawyer, but, without a degree, all professions were closed to him. So, in March 1737, he traveled to London with Garrick and only the proverbial "twopence halfpenny" (meaning next to nothing) and an unfinished tragedy in his pocket. Johnson would seek his fortune as a writer; Garrick would gain his as an actor. Tetty remained in Lichfield for the time being, the first of many separations that became longer through the years.

Johnson settled in Grub Street, now legendary as the abode of penniless writers, would-be poets, and low-end publishers. On occasion, he couldn't even afford the cheapest lodging and would wander the streets all night with the rakish poet Richard Savage, whose "life" Johnson wrote in 1744. Soon, though, Johnson found steady if not particularly remunerative employment with Edward Cave, publisher of the *Gentleman's Magazine*, a popular periodical with articles on a huge range of subjects, from poetry to commerce to politics. One of Johnson's specialties became a series of accounts of speeches in Parliament. It was unlawful at the time to report directly on the doings of Parliament, so Cave adopted the transparent pretense of reporting on Gulliver's fictional Senate of Lilliput.[16] Johnson would be told the general topic of discussion, the names of the speakers, and the basic positions they adopted. He would then draft the sort of speeches he would have given in the circumstances. The speeches were long regarded as genuine and, indeed, sometimes made the reputations of their putative speakers and found their way into anthologies. Late in life, Johnson regretted the imposture and tried in vain to set the record straight.

Johnson went back to Lichfield for a time to finish his tragedy, and he soon returned to London with Tetty to lodgings that were extremely poor but still more than he could readily afford. Tetty hated the crowded, airless misery of the city. Johnson continued his hack journalism but also published a poem, "London," in 1738, when he was just shy of thirty. It was an imitation of Juvenal's third satire and was praised by as major a figure as Alexander Pope. It did little, however, to improve Johnson's financial position, as one of its couplets makes clear:

> This mournful truth is everywhere confessed,
> Slow rises worth, by poverty depressed.[17]

Johnson once remarked that "a decent provision for the poor is the true test of civilization."[18] Even in his deepest poverty, he would place a penny in the pockets of children sleeping in the street so that when they awoke they could have a modest breakfast and, with that small gesture of kindness, find the world a slightly less bleak place.

One anecdote from this period bears repeating. Johnson was engaged to prepare a catalog of books for sale from a collection newly purchased by one Thomas Osborne. Osborne upbraided Johnson for delays and, dismissing his legitimate excuses, called him a liar. Johnson knocked Osborne down with a particularly large folio volume, put his foot on him, and threatened to kick him down the stairs if he rose.[19] The chastened bookseller quibbled no more. Unlike in his early encounter with Dame Oliver, Johnson was now a full-grown man with large fists. No one physically challenged Johnson, even while pacing the dangerous streets of London at night. He often carried a heavy walking stick, though his disheveled and threadbare clothes made him appear hardly worth robbing.

While Johnson struggled to gain purchase as a writer, David Garrick enjoyed more immediate success. He was quickly regarded as the premier actor of his age. When he became manager of the Drury Lane Theatre, he staged Johnson's tragedy, *Irene*, in 1749. Garrick suggested a number of changes to make the play more appealing to modern theater audiences. Johnson was heard to complain that this "fellow wants me to make Mahomet run mad, that he may have an opportunity of tossing his hands and kicking his heels."[20] He did agree to a few alterations, Boswell notes, "but still there were not enough."[21] Despite some wonderful speeches, even Boswell had to admit that the play was "deficient in pathos."[22] Moreover, Garrick's attempt to infuse some action into the drama resulted in an opening night fiasco. Irene was to be strangled on stage, but cries of "Murder!" filled the house, and she had to be carried off alive to be strangled in the wings. The play was not a success, but Garrick kept it running nine nights, which resulted in some welcome income for Johnson. Many years later, when visiting a country house, someone chose to read the play aloud to the company. After a time, Johnson left the room, explaining disconsolately, "I thought it had been better."[23]

The same year *Irene* was finally produced, Johnson published his finest and longest poem, "The Vanity of Human Wishes," based on Juvenal's tenth satire. As the title suggests, the poem is about man's penchant to chase after phantom goods and to suffer constant disappointments:

> Remark each anxious toil, each eager strife,
> And watch the busy scenes of crowded life;
> Then say how hope and fear, desire and hate,

O'erspread with snares the clouded maze of fate,
Where wavering man, betrayed by venturous pride,
To tread the dreary paths without a guide,
As treacherous phantoms in the mist delude,
Shuns fancied ills, or chases airy good;
How rarely reason guides the stubborn choice,
Rules the bold hand, or prompts the suppliant voice.[24]

The poem is not easy to read—it is Latinate in its compression. Garrick, with typical hyperbole, said it was "as hard as Greek."[25] In it, however, Johnson established the themes that would dominate his writing for the next decade.

In 1750, Johnson began a twice-weekly periodical called the *Rambler*. Over the next two years, from the first issue on March 20, 1750, to the last on March 14, 1752, Johnson wrote 208 essays. They occupy three volumes in the Yale edition of his works and constitute an invaluable body of moral thought, focused not on philosophical abstractions but on the felt realities and challenges of daily life. In these essays, he develops and expands on the ways in which "hope and fear, desire and hate," and, most of all, "venturous pride" can cloud our judgment and cause us to chase "treacherous phantoms." Yet he always holds out the possibility that reason can "guid[e] the stubborn choice" and "rul[e] the bold hand."

Tetty, after reading the first few issues, told her husband, "I thought very well of you before; but I did not imagine you could have written anything equal to this."[26] After Johnson finished with the *Rambler*, he continued to contribute essays to the *Adventurer*, and later started a new weekly periodical, the *Idler*, which ran from 1758 until 1760. Johnson rounded off his moral writings with a philosophical tale called *Rasselas*.

It was a remarkably productive decade for Johnson, for he was also preparing his famous *Dictionary of the English Language*, which he had started at the behest of a consortium of booksellers in 1746. In a mere nine years, he completed what had taken large teams of scholars in Italy and France multiple decades. Johnson set up a workshop in a house at 17 Gough Square, now a Johnson museum. He raced through acres of English books of literature, science, philosophy, and industry, marking passages to be transcribed by six assistants on strips of paper and arranged under the relevant words he had underlined. He then ordered the quotes chronologically and addressed issues of orthography, pronunciation, and etymology. In his preface, Johnson explained that writing the definitions was the hardest part, trying to find just the right synonym or paraphrase and to capture "the exuberance of signification which many words have obtained."[27]

The *Dictionary* contained 40,000 words and 114,000 illustrative quotations from every conceivable field, forming, as Johnson explained, "a kind of intellectual history."[28] He defined *lexicographer* in the *Dictionary* as "a harmless drudge." But he was never that. He was one man trying to bring order to "the boundless chaos of a living speech."[29]

In anticipation of publication, Johnson was granted the degree of master of arts from Oxford, an honor he had long wanted. But that triumph and even the greater one of the *Dictionary* were both bittersweet. His beloved Tetty had died in 1752, at the age of sixty-three. Johnson was not yet forty-three, but he never remarried. He once explained that, "by taking a second wife, [one] pays the highest compliment to the first, by showing that she made him so happy as a married man, that he wishes to be so a second time."[30] His more famous pronouncement, however, was that remarriage constitutes the "triumph of hope over experience."[31] Regardless, Tetty's death cast its pall over the preface, where Johnson notes, "I have protracted my work till most of those whom I wished to please have sunk into the grave, and success and miscarriage are empty sounds: I therefore dismiss it with frigid tranquility, having little to fear or hope from censure or from praise."[32]

Johnson's original prospectus for the *Dictionary* had been dedicated to Lord Chesterfield, who consented to be a patron for the project but then showed no further interest and offered no material support. Johnson was even arrested for debt in 1753 and had to borrow money from Samuel Richardson. Yet Chesterfield, in 1755, published two letters announcing the completion of the *Dictionary* as if he had some hand in it. Johnson was furious. He had already in the *Dictionary* defined *patron* as "a wretch who supports with insolence, and is paid with flattery." Now he sent Lord Chesterfield one of the most famous letters in English literary history, excerpted here:

> I have been pushing on my work through difficulties of which it is useless to complain, and have brought it at last to the verge of publication without one act of assistance, one word of encouragement, or one smile of favor. Such treatment I did not expect, for I never had a patron before. . . . Is not a patron, my Lord, one who looks with unconcern on a man struggling for life in the water, and, when he has reached

ground, encumbers him with help? The notice which you have been pleased to take of my labors, had it been early, had been kind; but it has been delayed till I am indifferent and cannot enjoy it, till I am solitary and cannot impart it, till I am known and do not want it. I hope it is no very cynical asperity not to confess obligations where no benefit has been received, or to be unwilling that the public should consider me as owing that to a patron, which Providence has enabled me to do for myself.[33]

To his credit, Lord Chesterfield took this declaration of authorial independence in good spirit, showing the letter to others and praising the style and force of the writing.

Despite his astounding output—both in quantity and in quality—Johnson still struggled financially. His own needs were modest, but he was also supporting an odd assortment of characters bequeathed to him by others: aging servants, an aspiring blind poet, a freed slave from Jamaica, and an impecunious doctor without degree who treated London's poorest.

Johnson took on another massive project in 1756, a complete edition of Shakespeare to be finished in eighteen months, with notes and commentary. He worked by fits and starts, however, and it would not be finished until 1765. His mother died in 1759, at the age of ninety. The following year, Johnson, now in his fifties, fell into another depression comparable to that in his twenties. This bout, too, would last five long years.

There were, however, a few brighter moments. In 1762, he was awarded a royal pension by George III of three hundred pounds a year. It did not make him rich, but it finally eliminated the near-constant financial anxiety. Johnson met the king himself a few years later. He had been invited to use the library at the Queen's House. George III asked to be informed when Johnson was there and quietly came to him in the library. They talked on a variety of subjects. The king asked Johnson what he was writing, and Johnson demurred, saying he thought he had already done his part as a writer. "I should have thought so too," replied the king, "if you had not written so well."[34] Johnson, a confirmed monarchist, was mightily pleased with the compliment and would often repeat it in company. The king then urged him to write a literary biography of the country, which Johnson would in fact soon undertake. As reported by Boswell, "Johnson talked to his Majesty with profound respect, but still in his firm manly manner, with a sonorous voice, and never in that subdued tone which is commonly used at the levee and in the drawing-room."[35]

In 1763, Johnson first met Boswell, who was twenty-two to Johnson's fifty-three. Boswell had been angling for an introduction to Johnson, but they finally overlapped by chance in a bookseller's shop. Johnson was both charmed and a bit irritated by the eager awe of the younger man, but the former feeling gradually, and then decisively, prevailed. Boswell was the eldest son of a Scottish laird, who had pushed him into the study of law. Boswell himself was more inclined to politics, literature, and illicit sex. But Boswell had an uncanny gift for capturing Johnson's conversation, and Johnson valued Boswell for his ingenuous affability. "I have heard you mentioned as a man whom everybody likes," Johnson said to Boswell. "I think life has little more to give."[36]

The following year, the painter Joshua Reynolds, in an effort to cheer his friend, proposed to Johnson that they start a club to meet once a week at the Turk's Head Tavern for food, drink, and conversation. As Leo Damrosch writes in his charming book *The Club*:

> The members [eventually] included Samuel Johnson, James Boswell, Edmund Burke, Edward Gibbon, and Adam Smith—arguably the greatest British critic, biographer, political philosopher, historian, and economist of all time. Others were equally famous at the time: the painter Joshua Reynolds; the playwrights Richard Brinsley Sheridan and Oliver Goldsmith; and David Garrick, the greatest actor of the century.[37]

It would be hard to imagine a more distinguished company. Needless to say, invitations to join the club, which required a unanimous vote, were highly sought after. Johnson loved the give and take of conversation, which he treated as a blood sport. As Boswell explained, Johnson was always "talking for victory, and determined to be master of the field."[38] He offended at times but was equally determined in his apologies. "Johnson, to be sure, has a roughness in his manner," Goldsmith noted, "but no man alive has a more tender heart. He has nothing of the bear but his skin."[39]

Johnson's edition of Shakespeare was finally published in 1765, which lifted a heavy load of guilt, since he had collected subscriptions for it many years before. His textual criticism and notes have been outdated by modern methods of philology, although he had excellent instincts in correcting corrupted editions of the plays. But his *Preface to Shakespeare* is still among the finest things ever written on the Stratford playwright.

The year 1765 was also the occasion of Johnson's fortuitous meeting with Henry and Hester Thrale. Henry was a wealthy brewer. Johnson was friends mostly with the husband at first, but Hester was a remarkable person in her own right and ultimately played the more critical role in nurturing Johnson back to health and something close to happiness. She knew Latin, Greek, French, Italian, and Spanish. She wrote poetry and, later, a memoir of Johnson. The couple essentially adopted Johnson. He lived at their house for extended periods, traveled with them to Wales and France, and was a regular at their many dinners and other social events. When Henry was dying in 1781, Johnson sat by his bedside and "looked for the last time upon the face that for fifteen years had never been turned upon me but with respect and benignity."[40] With him, Johnson added, "were buried many of my hopes and pleasures."[41] Three years later, Hester shocked her family, her friends, and Johnson by marrying Gabriel Mario Piozzi, an Italian music teacher who taught singing to her eldest daughter. Johnson wrote her a letter of reproach but later repented and sent a touching note of farewell:

> I wish that God may grant you every blessing, that you may be happy in this world for its short continuance, and eternally happy in a better state. And whatever I can contribute to your happiness, I am very ready to repay for that kindness which soothed twenty years of a life radically wretched.[42]

Johnson's years with the Thrales were not particularly productive in terms of writing, though he wrote many prefaces and letters to promote the works of friends, and sometimes lent his invisible hand to the works themselves, including for a hapless clergyman about to be hanged for forgery. When questioned about the authenticity of a powerful address published by the convict, Johnson remarked, "Depend upon it, Sir, when any man knows he is to be hanged in a fortnight, it concentrates his mind wonderfully."[43]

In 1773, Johnson took a trip with Boswell to the Highlands and Western Isles of Scotland. When they stopped at Boswell's house in Edinburgh, Johnson first met Boswell's wife, who proved less than enamored with the hold Johnson had on her husband. Showing some wit of her own (and unconsciously echoing Goldsmith), she remarked, "I have seen many a bear led by a man; but I never before saw a man led by a bear."[44] Two other anecdotes from the trip warrant mention, since they show Johnson in high spirits. One evening, a young and pretty woman playfully sat on Johnson's knee and, encouraged by the company, put her hands around his neck and kissed him. "Do it again," said Johnson, "and let us see who will tire first."[45] On another stop, Johnson was explaining to a group about an extraordinary animal in Australia known as a kangaroo and decided an imitation was in order. "He stood erect, put out his hands like feelers, and, gathering up the tails of his huge brown coat so as to resemble the pouch of the animal, made two or three vigorous bounds across the room!"[46]

This trip produced two books—one by Johnson, a fairly straightforward account of the land and its people; the other by Boswell, in the form of a journal, focused on the character and conversation of Samuel Johnson.[47] Some years ago, on a trip to the same locations, I brought along Johnson's book. I should have brought Boswell's!

Johnson, however, had one great work—some would say his greatest—still to come. In 1777, at the age of sixty-eight, he undertook to write brief lives and prefaces for a series of editions of British poets from the past century. Unsurprisingly, the work grew exponentially in Johnson's hands. Some of the "lives" were short, but others—Milton, Dryden, Savage, and Pope—were more than a hundred pages long. The first twenty-two were published in 1779. Another thirty were completed in 1781. They constitute the most brilliant body of sustained literary criticism ever produced in English, combining in-depth biographies with aesthetic and moral analysis of the works. Boswell called *Lives of the Poets* "the richest, most beautiful, and indeed most perfect, production of Johnson's pen."[48] Initially published with the volumes of poetry, *Lives* soon had an existence of its own. It occupies three full volumes in the Yale edition of Johnson.

Johnson suffered a paralytic stroke in 1783. Concerned that his mind was affected, he composed in his head a prayer in Latin verse. "The lines were not very good," he acknowledged, "but I knew them not to be very good."[49] Johnson recovered, but continued to deteriorate physically. He nonetheless met with friends, found topics of common interest, and spoke in polished paragraphs. Johnson refused to follow the practice of the sick, whose "first talk . . . is commonly of themselves."[50] "I will be conquered," he explained. "I will not capitulate."[51] Samuel Johnson died on December 13, 1784, at the age of seventy-five.

JOHNSON AS MORALIST

W. Jackson Bate, in his seminal study, *The Achievement of Samuel Johnson*, grouped Johnson's moral thought under three sweeping headings: "the hunger of imagination," "the treachery of the human heart," and "the stability of truth." I would interpose between the last two "a disposition to be pleased." What Johnson calls the "hunger of imagination"—our restless quest for changed circumstances and new objects of desire—finds repose only in a deeper understanding of human nature. This same symmetry, on a smaller scale, is found in Johnson's contrast between the many ways in which the heart betrays itself through vanity and self-interest and the gentle joys of pleasing and being pleased. Our discussion thus will be structured somewhat like an *ABBA* rhyme scheme, in which the second of each pair complements and corrects the first, while the outer pair brackets the whole.

The Hunger of Imagination

John Locke argued that the mind is a passive recipient of sense impressions. It is a *tabula rasa* on which the world writes. Johnson strongly disagrees with Locke. The mind is not passive, he insists; it is constantly shaping and coloring our experience. Objects do not have an objective value or interest. They are given value and interest by the activity of our minds.

Desire is fundamental to our nature. We need food, shelter, and clothing; we need physical protection—all the things Robinson Crusoe first provided for himself. But "the wants of nature are soon supplied, the fear of their return is easily precluded."[52] As even Crusoe found, we need something more for which to live. We need a focus for our physical and mental energies; we need an outlet for our passions and emotions. Our minds cannot rest quiescent. To desire is to be alive, and we feed our desire by imagining the happiness that future attainments will bring. We are thus driven by "that hunger of imagination which preys incessantly upon life, and must be always appeased by some employment. Those who have already all that they can enjoy, must enlarge their desires."[53] In other words, "from having wishes only in consequence of our wants, we begin to feel wants in consequence of our wishes."[54]

It is commonly accepted that objects give rise to desire. But the incidental objects of desire are not themselves the essence of desire. Desire is undifferentiated. It is an inarticulate but powerful "I want," sounding at the core of our being. Such wanting has no end; our desires have no limits. We seize on some object or end, but "the capacity of the imagination" is much larger than any actual enjoyment.[55] The objects of our desire never fully satisfy our desires. "We desire, we pursue, we obtain, we are satiated; we desire something else, and begin a new pursuit."[56] There are no permanent sources of satisfaction, though we may fool ourselves into believing otherwise. "The mind of man is never satisfied with the objects immediately before it, but is always breaking away from the present moment, and losing itself in schemes of future felicity."[57] As one of the characters in *Rasselas* notes, the pyramids are "a monument of the insufficiency of human enjoyments."[58]

The present moment is constantly slipping away from us. It "leaves us as soon as it arrives, ceases to be present before its presence is well perceived."[59] We know it only by the effects it leaves behind or the promises it makes for the future. "So few of the hours of life are filled up with objects adequate to the mind of man . . . that we are forced to have recourse every moment to the past and future for supplemental satisfactions, and relieve the vacuities of our being, by recollection of former passages, or anticipation of events to come."[60] We are happy or miserable only in retrospect or in anticipation. Even if we obtained all that we thought we wanted, it would not be enough. No object or circumstance has the "power to fill the attention, and suspend all perception of the course of time."[61] Yet the elusive search for permanent sources of satisfaction is fundamental to our natures.

We accordingly delude ourselves that happiness only requires a change of circumstance. If we are single, we long for a mate; if poor, for wealth; if obscure, for fame; if weak, for power. If we live in the city, we dream of a rural retreat. We may publicly dismiss what we cannot obtain, and yet long for it regardless. As Johnson candidly admits, "when I was running about this town a very poor fellow, I was a great arguer for the advantages of poverty; but I was, at the same time, very sorry to be poor."[62] Johnson was sympathetic to the desire for riches, fame, and power, but showed little patience when the wealthy purported to long for rustic simplicity or the famous and powerful for an obscure retirement. Hester Thrale praised the line from David Garrick's pastoral poem "Come, Come, My Good Shepherds": "They smile with the simple, and feed with the poor."[63] Johnson would have none of such hypocrisy from his extremely wealthy friend: "Poor David! Smile with the simple! What folly is that! And who would feed with the poor that can help it? No, no; let me smile with the wise, and feed with the rich."[64]

Johnson, ever the pragmatist, acknowledges that wealth is better than poverty and recognition more pleasing than obscurity. But neither is an end in itself; neither extinguishes desire but merely leads to more esoteric desires. "Of riches, as of everything else, the hope is more than the enjoyment. . . . No sooner do we sit down to enjoy our acquisitions, than we find them insufficient to fill up the vacuities of life."[65]

Change in itself is nothing, for our next wish is always to change again. Even scholars who long for the completion of their long-labored projects—the *Dictionary* and the edition of Shakespeare being cases in point—find that the satisfaction falls short. "There would . . . be few enterprises of great labor or hazard undertaken, if we had not the power of magnifying the advantages which we persuade ourselves to expect from them."[66] Our expectations always exceed the reality. Yet such expectations are the driving force of our lives. "The natural flights of the human mind are not from pleasure to pleasure, but from hope to hope."[67]

Johnson's description of the human condition is both profound and sympathetic. The hunger of imagination can be put to good use or bad. But it cannot be escaped while life persists. We live by contrasts: "day and night, labor and rest, hurry and retirement, endear each other."[68] We no sooner complete one pursuit than we begin another. Recognizing that reality, and living with it, is the key to a richer life, a life not engaged simply in "disburden[ing] the day"[69] or filling up the vacuities of our being. For "he, who has so little knowledge of human nature, as to seek happiness by changing anything, but his own dispositions, will waste his life in fruitless efforts, and multiply the griefs which he purposes to remove."[70]

The Treachery of the Human Heart

In one well-known essay, *Adventurer* no. 84, Johnson describes a coach ride taken by various strangers, each trying to impress the others with his or her haughty demeanor and arrogant reserve. When they finally fall to talking, one speaks of his substantial stock investments, another of the many servants she is used to at home, while a third peppers his conversation with references to lords and dukes. In fact, the first is a clerk to a broker, the second keeps a cook shop, and the third is a nobleman's valet. Their pretense brings them no material benefits. None of them believes the others or even expects to be believed by them. Yet "all assume that character of which they are most desirous."[71]

Playing such a part lets them indulge their fancies and imagine themselves as, literally, more imposing than they really are. All of us—in big ways or in small—try to impose on others the image we want to have of ourselves. Our self-esteem is a function of the esteem we appear to inspire in others. If we can project a favorable image—however briefly, however falsely—it somehow validates the self-esteem we so strongly desire. When we tell our stories, therefore, we inevitably augment and embellish. Nor are pretense and self-deception limited to any particular class. Indeed, embellishment is even more likely among those who aspire to learning and sophistication. Thus, "the ambition of superior sensibility and superior eloquence disposes the lovers of arts to receive rapture at one time, and communicate it at another; and each labors first to impose upon himself, and then to propagate the imposture."[72]

The vanity of the coach riders seems harmless; it even incites pathos. But it prevents them from connecting with one another in any meaningful respect. Each rides in a cocoon of his or her making. That is where the "treachery of the human heart" comes in. The hunger of imagination is channeled in ways that prevent the active sympathy with, and understanding of, others that is essential to our own happiness.[73] We cannot have genuine and satisfying human relations without honesty with ourselves and others. In his own practice, Boswell reports, Johnson stressed the importance of "strict and scrupulous veracity" and "was known to be so rigidly attentive to it, that even in his common conversation the slightest circumstances was mentioned with exact precision."[74]

Johnson offers a frank and unstinting portrayal of the many ways in which we try to conceal our unimportance from ourselves.[75] Some are trivial and largely self-correcting. Johnson describes a newly published author who visits the coffeehouses, eager to learn what others are saying about his book, prepared to accept praise with humility and criticism with condescending forbearance. But, of course, no one talks of his book. No one even seems aware of its publication. He makes the common mistake of thinking that the world is much more interested in his doings than it actually is. "He that considers how little he dwells upon the condition of others, will learn how little the attention of others is attracted by himself."[76]

Other by-products of vanity are more serious. "The vanity of being known to be trusted with a secret," Johnson notes, "is generally one of the chief motives to disclose it."[77] We would rather display our want of probity in order to show off our influence than to "glide through life with no other pleasure than the private consciousness of fidelity."[78] So, too, with small lies of convenience and the seemingly infinite forms of selfish behavior.

We tend to minimize such faults in ourselves as "casual failures, and single lapses," rather than "habitual corruptions, or settled practices,"[79] though we do the opposite with the faults of others. We thus ignore "the gradual growth of our own wickedness, endeared by interest, and palliated by all the artifices of self-deceit."[80] A lack of self-knowledge lies at the bottom of all human misconduct.[81] Seduced by vanity and interest, we give way to ambition, avarice, and, worst of all, envy, which wishes harm to others without benefit to oneself. At least a man's pursuit of self-interest, Johnson notes, "requires . . . discernment to mark his advantage, courage to seize, and activity to pursue it."[82] But "to spread suspicion, to invent calumnies, to propagate scandal, requires neither labor nor courage."[83]

Although none of us is "exempt from the enticements of hope, the solicitations of affection, the importunities of appetite, or the depressions of fear,"[84] some vices deserve less censure than others. Rashness is generally preferable to cowardice; profligacy to avarice; bluntness to cunning; presumption to despondency.[85] It is easier to take away superfluities than to supply defects. Overconfidence is readily dented; timidity is "more obstinate and fatal."[86] We should accordingly show our greatest diligence against the vices from which we have the greatest danger. But that requires brutal honesty with ourselves, and we shrink from such self-knowledge as from a "disagreeable acquaintance."[87]

Literature, however, can play a key role in deepening our understanding of human nature. Here, Johnson's interests as critic and moralist coalesce. It is the job of the poet "to copy nature and instruct life."[88] Shakespeare was the supreme "poet of nature, the poet that holds up to his readers a faithful mirror of manners and of life."[89] His characters are examples of "common humanity" who act and speak "by the influence of those general passions and principles by which all minds are agitated and the whole system of life is continued in motion."[90] Literature can thus increase our knowledge of the human heart and of ourselves, and Johnson judges the poets about whom he writes accordingly.[91] So much is uncontroversial. But Johnson would go further and evaluate works of literature on whether their morality is sound as well as whether their representations are just. He thus regrets that Shakespeare is "so much more careful to please than to instruct that he seems to write without any moral purpose."[92] Modern criticism would not accept that "it is always a writer's duty to make the world better."[93] And yet there is something to be said for Johnson's metric. Works of literature almost always take a moral point of view; evaluating the soundness of that viewpoint is an essential part of reading. It is the duty of criticism, Johnson explains, "to hold out the light of reason, whatever it may discover; and to promulgate the determinations of truth, whatever she shall dictate."[94]

Johnson self-deprecatingly notes that "a man writes much better than he lives."[95] Anyone can master maxims of prudence and principles of virtue for biweekly publication. We consider ourselves zealous in virtue's cause when "no particular passion turns us aside from rectitude."[96] But "there is nothing which we estimate so fallaciously as the force of our own resolutions."[97] Snares and traps are everywhere. "Truth and virtue are . . . frequently defeated by pride, obstinacy, or folly."[98] Inordinate desires are the enemy not only of happiness but of virtue. We grow obsessed with wealth, power, and fame in proportion as they are denied to us.[99] Poverty begets greed; indifference begets bitterness; the success of others gives rise to resentment. Knowledge of the world tends to make men cunning rather than good.[100] How then, in a world "full of fraud and corruption, malevolence and rapine,"[101] is a man to master his own soul? How do we keep vanity, interest, and self-deception from distorting our desires and preventing us from living a full and rich life in sympathy with others? How do we attain "the dignity of a human being"?[102] We must start, Johnson insists, with our own dispositions.

A Disposition To Be Pleased

In one particularly delightful passage, Boswell reports that Johnson, who was then near seventy, was returning from church when he was approached by Oliver Edwards, a former classmate at Oxford. In the midst of a lively conversation, Edwards said to him, "You are a philosopher, Dr. Johnson. I have tried too in my time to be a philosopher; but, I don't know how, cheerfulness was always breaking in."[103]

The idea that philosophy is inherently gloomy and severe, with no room for good cheer, is one the older Johnson would have resisted. In "The Vanity of Human Wishes," he had asked:

> Must helpless man, in ignorance sedate,
> Roll darkling down the torrent of his fate?[104]

There, his only answer was that happiness is indeed out of man's reach, though "celestial wisdom" can at least make bearable the ills of the world.[105] In his *Rambler* essays, however, Johnson wrote himself into a significant change in outlook. Not only did cheerfulness repeatedly break through, but it became, in his eyes, something of a moral obligation as well as a key to human felicity.

Johnson was not naively optimistic. External evils are real. We cannot, with the "exalted enthusiasm" of the Stoic sage, dismiss them as of no account. But "the calamities of life, like the necessities of nature, are calls to labor and exercise of diligence."[106] We can bear them with decency and propriety.[107] "The cure for the greatest part of human miseries is not radical, but palliative."[108] If we shun "the mournful privileges of irresistible misery,"[109] we can preserve a great measure of peace of mind without heightening the pain or prolonging its effects. The Stoic's "boast of absolute independence is ridiculous and vain, yet a mean flexibility to every impulse, and a patient submission to the tyranny of casual troubles, is below the dignity of th[e] mind."[110]

Most passions direct us to their own cure "by inciting and quickening the attainment of their objects."[111] For sorrow, however, there is no remedy but time and employment. Sorrow is fixed upon the past; "it requires what it cannot hope, that the laws of the universe should be repealed; that the dead should return, or the past should be recalled."[112] When Edwards asked him if he had ever been married, Johnson responded, "I have known what it was to have a wife and (in a solemn tender faltering tone) I have known what it was to lose a wife.—It had almost broke my heart."[113]

It is possible to gird oneself for the major blows of life and to soften their effects over time. But human felicity is more pedestrian. It depends largely on our unguarded responses to everyday events. Johnson stresses the importance of "little incidents, cursory conversation, slight business, and casual amusements"; they "make the draught of life sweet or bitter by imperceptible instillations."[114] With respect to such quotidian affairs, it is not time or employment but disposition that counts. Life will never unfold exactly according to our wishes and desires. Accordingly, "too close an attention to minute exactness, or a too rigorous habit of examining everything by the standard of perfection, vitiates the temper rather than improves the understanding, and teaches the mind to discern faults with unhappy penetration."[115] An unwillingness to be pleased is proof of neither understanding nor high standards; it is a "symptom of some deeper malady."[116]

Yet through constant vigilance we can disburden ourselves of petty irritations. "No disease of the mind can more fatally disable it from benevolence, the chief duty of social beings, than ill humor or peevishness; . . . it wears out happiness by slow corrosion, and small injuries incessantly repeated."[117] We will never find happiness proportionate to the expectations that incite our desires. Yet neither are the evils of life as formidable in reality as our imaginations depict them.[118] As Johnson advised Boswell, "be . . . well when you are not ill, and pleased when you are not angry."[119] In other words, don't seek out reasons for discontent, but "contentedly yield to the course of things."[120]

Some, like Johnson's college friend Oliver Edwards, are blessed with "a constant and perennial softness of manner, easiness of approach, and suavity of disposition."[121] Others must develop "a habit of being pleased,"[122] as they would any other good habit.

Johnson suggests we begin every day with the reflection that we are born to die.[123] Contemplating our own deaths may seem a paradoxical path to cheerfulness. But, according to Johnson, it encourages us to enjoy the blessings of life rather than to let them "glide away in preparations to enjoy them."[124] "The disturbers of our happiness, in this world," Johnson notes, "are our desires, our griefs, and our fears, and to all these, the consideration of mortality is a certain and adequate remedy."[125]

We can come to expect more of ourselves and demand less of others. "A man grows better-humored . . . [when] he learns to think himself of no consequence and little things of little importance; and so he becomes more patient, and better pleased."[126] That, in turn, will spark pleasure in others, for "the most certain way to give any man pleasure, is to persuade him that you receive pleasure from him."[127] Cheerfulness begets cheerfulness in a virtuous circle; "the greater part of mankind are gay or serious by infection, and follow without resistance the attraction of example."[128] We cannot counterfeit or manufacture such cheer. "Nothing is more hopeless than a scheme of merriment."[129] But we can be alive to its possibility and seize its opportunities. "Our brightest blazes of gladness are commonly kindled by unexpected sparks."[130]

With no wife or children, Johnson's greatest joy was in conversation and the company of others. "Life has no pleasure higher or nobler than that of friendship," he insisted.[131] Friends will "not only be firm in the day of distress, but gay in the hour of jollity; not only useful in exigencies, but pleasing in familiar life; their presence should give cheerfulness as well as courage, and dispel alike the gloom of fear and of melancholy."[132] His warmhearted paean to friendship warrants comparison with the more famous treatments by Aristotle, Cicero, and Montaigne:

> Let us return the caresses of our friends, and endeavor by mutual endearments to heighten that tenderness which is the balm of life. Let us be quick to repent of injuries while repentance may not be barren of anguish, and let us open our eyes to every rival excellence, and pay early and willingly those honors which justice will compel us to pay at last.[133]

The Stability of Truth

A disposition to be pleased is not a disposition to be complacent. Nor is Johnson encouraging us to view the world through rose-colored glasses. He frankly admits that there is in human life "more to be endured than enjoyed."[134] But we can still achieve a measure of happiness if we educate our desires in the light of experience.

Life is messy, as Johnson is the first to admit. It is not reducible to theory, system, or tidy prescriptions. In that sense, Johnson is not a "philosopher." He firmly rejects the philosophical view—standard in the age of Newton's clockwork universe—that the strict succession of cause and effect makes free will impossible. "All theory is against the freedom of the will," he notes, but "all experience for it."[135] He is equally dismissive of Bishop Berkeley's argument that matter does not exist, but only our sense impressions. When Boswell suggests that it is impossible to refute that doctrine, Johnson will have none of it. "I never shall forget the alacrity with which Johnson answered, striking his foot with mighty force against a large stone, till he rebounded from it—'I refute it *thus*.'"[136] Obviously, Johnson is not meeting either Berkeley or the determinists on their own terms with a philosophical counterargument. Rather, Johnson dismisses theories that defy common sense and everyday experience.

He is pragmatic about human life, from whose cyclical mixture of joys and sorrows no one is exempt. He writes with almost biblical cadence:

> It is well enough known to be according to the usual process of nature, that men should sicken and recover, that some designs should succeed and others miscarry, that friends should be separated and meet again, that some should be made angry by endeavors to please them, and some be pleased when no care has been used to gain their approbation; that men and women should at first come together by chance, like each other so well as to commence acquaintance, improve acquaintance into fondness, increase or extinguish fondness by marriage, and have children of different degrees of intellects and virtue, some of whom die before their parents, and others survive them.[137]

The wise and the ignorant, the exalted and the low, spend much of their lives in the same manner.

> Men, however distinguished by external accidents or intrinsic qualities, have all the same wants, the same pains, and, as far as the senses are consulted, the same pleasures. . . . We are all naked till we are dressed, and hungry till we are fed; and the general's triumph, and sage's disputation, end, like the humble labors of the smith or plowman, in a dinner or in sleep.[138]

We cannot exempt ourselves from our common humanity. Our goal must be not to extinguish our desires but to regulate them. As noted, Johnson has no objection to "the accumulation of honest gain" or "the ambition of just honors."[139] As a free agent, man is able to make such moral and personal choices. But "to prize everything according to its real use, ought to be the aim of a rational being."[140] Again, realizing that goal requires unsparing honesty.

Like the travelers in the stagecoach, "every man in the journey of life . . . disguises himself in counterfeited merit, and hears those praises with complacency which his conscience reproaches him for accepting."[141] Our motives are never completely pure, but we can train our minds to rely on true perceptions and a genuine understanding of ourselves and the world in which we live. "Truth, such as is necessary to the regulation of life, is always found where it is honestly sought."[142]

A proper "management of the mind" can be acquired only gradually.[143] It is an active process that combines thoughtful meditation with an "accurate observation of the living world."[144] Reason, schooled alike by learning and experience, must keep constant guard over the imagination.[145] We can tame "fancied ills" and "airy goods" alike if we weigh our experience to discover what is wanting and what will enhance rather than impoverish life and our relations with others. Reconciling our inner life with the truth about the external world is not an all-or-nothing process but a gradual education of desire by experience. Bate aptly calls it "the incorporation of knowledge into feeling."[146]

Wealth, acclaim, and pleasure may contribute to a full and rich life, but they are not ends in themselves. They are not guarantors of happiness. The future is uncertain. The present moment is fleeting. Ultimately, our greatest happiness is "to be able to look back on a life usefully and virtuously employed, to trace our own progress in existence, by such tokens as excite neither shame nor sorrow."[147] We must live so that our memories will be well stocked against time and regret.

Only a few things contribute to such happiness, and therefore only a few things are to be ardently desired.[148] These include the company of family and friends, along with "the gentle pleasures of sympathy," the "warmth of benevolence," and the "honest joys which nature annexes to the power of pleasing."[149] Johnson would also add the "calm delight" of contemplation and, interestingly, vigorous physical activity.

"How much happiness is gained," he writes, "and how much misery escaped by frequent and violent agitation of the body."[150] Johnson, as a young man of limited prospects in Lichfield, would often walk to Birmingham and back, a distance of over thirty miles, to master his distorted imagination and stimulate his spirits. He walked all over nighttime London even into his late years, carrying his heavy walking stick. He would challenge friends to footraces and roll down a hill for the sheer joy of doing so.

> The dance of spirits, the bound of vigor, readiness of enterprise, and defiance of fatigue, are reserved for him that braces his nerves, and hardens his fibers, that keeps his limbs pliant with motion, and by frequent exposure fortifies his frame against the common accidents of cold and heat. [151]

Most important for Johnson, however, was sustained intellectual work. Despite the many deprecations of his own indolence, Johnson could look back on his *Dictionary*, his edition of Shakespeare, and his *Lives of the Poets* with a feeling of accomplishment. We all need a broader sense of purpose, of goals set and milestones achieved. If the object is worthy, such labor is its own reward, as he repeatedly and eloquently insists:

> Life affords no higher pleasure, than that of surmounting difficulties, passing from one step of success to another, forming new wishes and seeing them gratified. He that labors in any great or laudable undertaking, has his fatigues first supported by hope, and afterwards rewarded by joy; he is always moving to a certain end, and when he has attained it, an end more distant invites him to a new pursuit. [152]

We of course magnify the advantages we expect from such projects. The reality will inevitably fall short. Diligence may meet with misfortune; the wisest schemes may be broken by unexpected accidents; constant perseverance may toil without visible recompense. But, in fact, the process itself is the recompense. Happiness is a by-product of the endeavor.

> To strive with difficulties, and to conquer them, is the highest human felicity; the next, is to strive, and deserve to conquer: but he whose life has passed without a contest, and who can boast neither success nor merit, can survey himself only as a useless filler of existence; and if he is content with his own character, must owe his satisfaction to insensibility. [153]

No moralist other than Aristotle and Montaigne has offered us such a balanced and realistic prescription for human flourishing. Despite the inevitability of sorrow, loss, and failure, Johnson's message is ultimately optimistic. "It is necessary to hope, tho' hope should always be deluded, for hope itself is happiness, and its frustrations, however frequent, are yet less dreadful than its extinction."[154]

9

DAVID HUME AND THE END OF PHILOSOPHY

If we take in our hand any volume—of divinity or school metaphysics, for instance—let us ask, Does it contain any abstract reasoning concerning quantity or number? No. Does it contain any experimental reasoning concerning matter of fact and existence? No. Commit it then to the flames, for it can contain nothing but sophistry and illusion. [1]

In his *Dialogues Concerning Natural Religion*,[2] David Hume makes passing reference to an old joke among philosophers. A disciple goes to an Indian guru and asks, "On what does the earth rest?" The guru responds, "A giant turtle." The disciple goes off and thinks about this for some time and returns. "On what does the turtle rest?" "Another turtle" is the answer. This exchange is repeated several times before the exasperated guru finally answers, "It's turtles all the way down."

To the extent the joke is funny—and, admittedly, it takes a certain slant to find it so—that is largely due to Hume, who is generally acknowledged as the greatest philosopher to write in English. Philosophy as practiced before Hume had been largely a search for giant turtles on which language, science, and morality were to rest secure. For Plato, the turtle was the Form of the Good, which illuminates the entire metaphysical substructure of the world. For Descartes, it was the "I" of consciousness and the clear and distinct ideas that inform that consciousness. For Kant, responding to Hume, it will be the unknown and unknowable "thing in itself," which somehow transmutes itself into God, freedom, and immortality. Despite their undeniable interest, all these attempts to find a noncontingent, ahistorical grounding for our actions and beliefs are ultimately little better than the guru's "giant turtle." They are variations—metaphysical, epistemological, and theological—on a single premise: that we can use abstract reasoning to uncover the foundations of human knowledge and experience.

David Hume set out from a young age to destroy that premise. He attacked the innate ideas—self, substance, and causation—that Descartes made the basis of his mechanical universe. He sought to demonstrate that morality is grounded in neither reason nor religion. He dismissed what were then the standard arguments for the existence of God, and condemned the "monkish virtues" that were the product of a morbid religious enthusiasm. Needless to say, Hume was a controversial figure, and he was repeatedly denied an academic appointment because of his heretical views.

For Hume, there are only two sorts of legitimate propositions: abstract propositions of mathematics and logic, and contingent propositions concerning matters of fact. Only the former can be known with certainty and without regard to experience. The latter are not objects of knowledge but only of belief based on habit and experience. Hume was sometimes dismissed as a radical empiricist and a skeptic who rejected things that we all know to be true: that the chair in which I am sitting exists independent of me and will continue to exist even when I am out of the room and cannot see it; that the succession of physical events is necessarily determined by cause and effect; that we distinguish right from wrong by thought alone; that there is a rational order in the universe created by God and accessible to reason.

Hume did not question the validity of our commonsense beliefs. Nor did he disparage the mechanical science of Newton or suggest that moral principles were somehow illusory. Quite the contrary. Hume advocated the autonomy of science, including social sciences such as psychology, economics, political science, and even morality. He rejected only the claim that they depend for their first principles on reason or revelation. That is, he rejected the assumption made by so many philosophers that such matters *require* a giant turtle to give them a foundation. In so doing, he gave birth to an entirely different approach to philosophy that would culminate in the twentieth-century writings of Ludwig Wittgenstein, a man who, ironically, found reading Hume unbearable.

LIFE

David Hume was born in 1711, four years after Scotland became part of Great Britain and ceased to exist as a separate country. His family was reasonably prosperous. Their estate at Ninewells, in Berwickshire, south of Edinburgh, was large enough for his father to be considered a country laird. David, as the second son, would inherit neither the title nor the estate.

David's father died of tuberculosis when David was only two. His mother, Katherine, never remarried and raised both boys and a daughter with the help of private tutors. David was only ten when he left for the University of Edinburgh with his twelve-year-old brother, John. Even in that era, matriculating at such a young age was unusual.

David studied classics, mathematics, and natural philosophy. He also got a heavy dose of religion of the austere Scottish Presbyterian, Calvinist variety that believed in predestination, viewed man as inherently sinful, and pretty much outlawed fun. Even a casual stroll on a Sunday was forbidden.

David spent four years at Edinburgh, finishing his university studies before most youths even began theirs. As a younger son, David needed a profession. Both his father and his grandfather (on his mother's side) had been lawyers. Accordingly, David briefly tried law but soon dismissed it as "a laborious occupation, requiring the drudgery of a whole life."[3] He later claimed to have developed "an insurmountable aversion to everything but the pursuits of philosophy and general learning."[4] Like Voltaire, Hume did not want to be anything other than a man of letters.

Fortunately, he had a small annuity, and his mother had no objection to him staying at home and following his passion. Free of all constraints, Hume embarked on a lengthy period of independent study, during which he read every important work of philosophy, science, literature, and history he could put his hands on, whether in English, Latin, or French. He even taught himself Italian.

After four years of intense and constant study, however, Hume suffered a breakdown in 1729 at the age of eighteen. As he described his condition in a letter to a London physician: "All my ardor seemed in a moment to be extinguished, and I could no longer raise my mind to that pitch, which formerly gave me such excessive pleasure."[5] Suffering from anxiety and depression, he was unable to concentrate.

Hume accordingly eased off from his studies and focused on eating healthy food, taking exercise, and relaxing in company. It took him several years to recover his mental and physical health, as well as his enthusiasm for philosophy. He even worked briefly as a merchant's clerk in Bristol.

Seeking a change in scene and the isolation he needed to bring his first work to completion, Hume moved to La Flèche, in France, in May 1735. La Flèche is where Descartes had attended college from 1606 to 1614. The choice of location seems appropriate, since Hume sought as radical a change in philosophy as Descartes had effected a century earlier. He stayed in La Flèche until August 1737, by which time he had completed a draft of the first two books of his planned *Treatise of Human Nature*. Hume was twenty-six, and, with a philosophical masterpiece in hand, went to London in search of a publisher. It took longer than he expected. The first two books, *Of the Understanding* and *Of the Passions*, were not published until 1739. A third, *Of Morals*, followed in 1740.

Hume's *Treatise* launched the intellectual project that would largely occupy him for the rest of his life: to understand human nature as revealed in experience. He had no interest in metaphysical foundations or transcendent conclusions. Hume wanted an empirical science of man. He wanted to approach human nature solely by way of experience, without reliance on any of Descartes's innate ideas. Descartes had argued that God was necessary to ensure that a malicious demon was not deceiving us as to the reliability of our senses. Hume rejected the idea that any such guarantee was either necessary or possible. He also rejected the suggestion that the mechanical laws of matter and motion proposed by Descartes and perfected by Newton were anything other than contingent statements based on empirical observation. Humans may have no option but to believe in the regularity of external events; but that belief is always subject to refutation by further experience. Hume did not, of course, reject Newton. He rejected only the idea that Newton's mechanics somehow enjoyed a special philosophical immunity from doubt.

Though brilliantly written in parts, Hume's *Treatise* was dense; it was new; and it was radical in its attempt to overthrow the entire Cartesian system. Even receptive readers didn't know quite what to make of his extreme empiricism, which seemed to question all our claims to knowledge. Hume later lamented that his *Treatise* "fell dead-born from the press, without reaching such distinction, as even to excite a murmur among the zealots."[6] He was exaggerating for effect, but certainly the work made little headway. Ironically, his ideas were more warmly received in France, the home of Descartes, than in England.

Hume concluded that the manner was more problematic than the matter. Indeed, he never swerved far from the central ideas of the *Treatise*. But he decided to make those ideas more accessible. Accordingly, he abandoned his plan to add two more books, on politics and the arts. Instead, he published a set of *Essays, Moral and Political*, in 1741, which were very popular and gave him the literary reputation he coveted.

Hume continued to live at Ninewells with his mother, brother, and sister. Several attempts to secure academic appointments were blocked by objections to his skepticism and perceived atheism. Hume's mother died in 1745, the same year that Bonnie Prince Charlie—the eldest son of James Francis Edward Stuart, grandson of James II and VII, and the Stuart claimant to the throne of Great Britain—landed in Scotland and tried to gain support for his father's claims among the Highlanders. Despite some early successes on which the prince failed to capitalize, the Stuart's pretensions ended in a total defeat at Culloden in April 1746. Bonnie Prince Charlie went into hiding and, disguised as a woman, ultimately escaped from Scotland and returned to exile in France. Despite the sense of nostalgia and romance he has since evoked, the defeat of Bonnie Prince Charlie was undoubtedly a boon for Scotland. Trade with Britain and its empire was growing rapidly, leading to a significant increase in the numbers and prosperity of the middle class. Glasgow in particular dominated the tobacco trade with America. Education was also spreading among the middle class. Scotland, with a smaller population, had five universities compared to only two in Britain. The Scottish Enlightenment, of which Hume and Adam Smith were the most significant figures, was well under way. David Hume, however, was not welcome at any of those five universities.

Hume instead spent 1745 as tutor to the Marquis of Annandale, a young nobleman with mental health problems. In 1746, he went to France for the first of several stints on the continent as secretary to General James St. Clair. All the while, Hume worked on more accessible treatments of his ideas. *An Inquiry Concerning Human Understanding*, which reworked the first book of his *Treatise*, was published in 1748. *An Inquiry Concerning the Principles of Morals* followed in 1751. He also continued to write essays on morals, politics, economics, and literature that were published between 1741 and 1752.

From 1749 to 1751, Hume again lived with his brother, John, and sister, Katherine, at Ninewells. John married in 1751, likely precipitating Hume's and Katherine's departure to Edinburgh, where Hume became the focal point of a lively group of intellectuals and formed a close and lasting friendship with Adam Smith. Smith would hold the Chair of Moral Philosophy at the University of Glasgow from 1752 to 1764. Both his *Theory of Moral Sentiments* (1759) and even his more famous *Wealth of Nations* (1776) were heavily influenced by Hume's *Inquiry Concerning the Principles of Morals* and by Hume's political and economic essays.

Hume, who never married, stressed that "friendship is the chief joy of human life."[7] He had a gift for it. "I was," he noted in his brief autobiography, "a man of mild dispositions, of command of temper, of an open, social, and cheerful humor, capable of attachment, but little susceptible of enmity, and of great moderation in all my passions. Even my love of literary fame, my ruling passion, never soured my temper, notwithstanding my frequent disappointments."[8] Hume considered a disposition "to see the favorable than unfavorable side of things" to be "a turn of mind which it is more happy to possess, than to be born to an estate of ten thousand a year."[9] Hume, in short, had precisely "the disposition to be pleased" that Samuel Johnson, too, considered so valuable.

In 1752, Hume was appointed librarian at Edinburgh's Faculty of Advocates, which gave him, in addition to a small income, access to the books he needed and ample time to produce a *History of England* in six volumes, which he wrote between 1754 and 1762. It remained the standard history of England until 1848, when Thomas Babington Macaulay published the first two volumes of his own *History of England*.

After the Treaty of Paris ended the Seven Years' War in 1763, Hume was appointed private secretary to the British ambassador to France, Lord Hertford, and later became the *chargé d'affaires*. Hume was much celebrated in France, both for his Enlightenment ideas and for his winning personality. *Le Bon David*, they called him.

Hume was less fortunate, however, in his friendship with Jean-Jacques Rousseau, who would reject Enlightenment thinking in favor of a new Romanticism. Rousseau attracted great attention with his genius and his startling ideas, but he was prickly to the point of paranoia. When a warrant was issued for Rousseau's arrest in 1766, after the publication of his

Émile, Hume graciously offered him sanctuary in England. Rousseau was at first extravagant in his praise of Hume, but soon began to imagine slights and efforts to control him. Hume had been warned by another Enlightenment philosopher, the Baron d'Holbach, that Hume would be "painfully undeceived" in his good opinion of Rousseau. "I tell you frankly that you are warming a viper in your bosom."[10] Rousseau and Hume broke in a very public quarrel that was provoked by Rousseau but did credit to neither man. It may have been the only time in his life when pique got the better of Hume's amiable disposition.

In 1767, Hume was recalled to London as undersecretary of state for the Northern Department. But he finally retired to Edinburgh in 1769. With pensions from his various secretarial appointments, and the popularity of the *Essays* and the *History of England*, Hume was a rich man. He built a house in the new section of town joined to the old part of Edinburgh by a narrow path across a bog. One day, when traversing the path, the overweight Hume fell into the bog and could not get out on his own. A passing fishwife recognized him as the "wicked unbeliever" David Hume, and made him repeat the Lord's Prayer before helping to extract him. Hume delighted in retelling the story. Despite his unbelief, he was a beloved figure. The residents called the street where he lived St. David's Street, a name it retains to this day.

Hume did very little new writing in his remaining years. He revised his various works for a collected edition, and he continued to tinker with his *Dialogues Concerning Natural Religion*, which would only be published three years after his death and even then provoked considerable controversy. In his lifetime, Hume was best known for his *Essays* and his *History of England*, both of which—though still in print—are largely, if unjustly, neglected today. But it was his work on human understanding, morality, and religion that changed the course of philosophy.

CAUSE AND EFFECT

From Plato through Descartes, philosophers have sought to use abstract reasoning to answer such disparate questions as "What is the essential nature of the external world?"; "Is there a God?"; and "What are our moral obligations?" Rational thought was the gold standard that was supposed to govern what we believe and how we act. Plato likened reason to the driver of a chariot with two horses, representing passion and appetite, which must always be held in check by the driver.

It is not much of an exaggeration to say that Hume's central mission as a philosopher was to unseat reason from that privileged position. He wanted to expose how little abstract thought can accomplish on its own and, thus, to obtain a better understanding of actual human knowledge and behavior.

Let's start with the first question: What is the essential nature of the external world? Plato argued that there was an eternal, immutable realm of Forms or Ideas of which the physical world known to us was but a flickering shadow. Descartes more modestly sought to use reason to establish a firm foundation for the basic laws of matter and motion that could be known to us prior to experience.

Hume, by contrast, draws a fundamental distinction between "Relations of Ideas" and "Matters of Fact." The former include propositions of mathematics and logic, which are "discoverable by the mere operation of thought, without dependence on what is anywhere existent in the universe."[11] The latter include every proposition we might make about what does and does not exist. Such matters of fact are inherently contingent; that is, they could be otherwise. "The contrary of every matter of fact is still possible, because it can never imply a contradiction."[12] An analysis of the relations of ideas will not resolve any questions of fact. That requires observation and experience.

Hume pushes this line even further by noting, following John Locke, that observation and experience themselves depend, ultimately, on our sense impressions. Bishop Berkeley pointed out the paradox of this position: we have no way of knowing for certain that our perceptions accurately reflect reality, because our perceptions are the only reality we know. As Hume explains, it is impossible to determine "whether the perceptions of the senses be produced by external objects resembling them."[13] Indeed, we cannot even know, in any demonstrably certain way, that there is an external world independent of our perceptions of it. Berkeley did not need Descartes's malicious demon to throw everything we thought we knew about the world into question.

Hume accepted Berkeley's analysis, but only to an extent. Hume did not in fact doubt or even think it reasonable to doubt that the desk at which I am currently sitting continues to exist when no one is looking at it and that the desk, as an object independent of my impressions, resembles those impressions. Hume simply stressed that we could not prove it to be the case, because all proof concerning the world depends on impressions, and it would be circular to argue that my impressions (or those of others) somehow prove that the desk has an existence independent of, and resembles, those impressions. "The mind has never anything present to it but the perceptions, and cannot possibly reach any experience of their connection with objects. The supposition of such a connection is, therefore, without any foundation in reasoning."[14]

Berkeley's arguments, Hume notes, "admit of no answer and produce no conviction."[15] The second half of this sentence is as important as the first. We may not be able to prove that objects exist independently of our perceptions of them, but we of course believe that they do so and necessarily act on that belief. "Thus I refute Berkeley," said Johnson, while kicking a rock. Hume says pretty much the same, though with more explanation. We refute Berkeley every moment of the day by our actions. We don't need a "foundation in reasoning" for our commonsense beliefs about physical objects or for the science that refines and extends those beliefs.

The same holds for the relationship between cause and effect. "All reasonings concerning matter of fact seem to be founded on the relation of cause and effect."[16] Science is a search for correlations that allow us to predict events based on causes. We see two events conjoined; Hume gives the example of a moving billiard ball colliding with and setting into motion a stationary one. From that result we infer not only that the former movement is the cause of the latter, but that the same effect—given the same speed and angle of impact—will continue to follow from the same cause. That is why we can line up a shot when playing pool, and our ancestors could bring down a moving animal with the cast of a spear.

The very terms *cause* and *effect* seem to assume each other. The cause looks forward to the effect, and the effect looks back to the cause. But the actual connection between any given cause and its effect is nonetheless contingent. It is a matter of fact, not a relation between ideas. The effect is not logically contained in the cause; like all matters of fact, it could be otherwise. Knowledge of a causal relationship comes entirely from experience, not through reason.[17] "We are determined by custom alone to expect the one from the appearance of the other."[18]

The regularity of cause and effect is what allows us to function in the world. We form expectations and react to events based on experience.

This process of inductive reasoning, "which we possess in common with beasts, and on which the whole conduct of life depends, is nothing but a species of instinct . . . that acts in us unknown to ourselves."[19] There is no guarantee that the future will continue to behave like the past. It is not inconceivable that a causal relationship that held in the past will not do so in the future. Inductive reasoning deals in probabilities, not certain knowledge, and hence is always open to revision based on further experience. We can see a thousand white swans and conclude that all swans are white, only to be confronted by a black one.

But Hume is not just saying that rare events can refute our inductive reasoning. More radically, Hume insists that inductive reasoning itself cannot be proved to be valid. It would be circular to rely on the regularity of experience to prove the regularity of experience. Just because inductive reasoning has worked for us in the past doesn't mean that it is necessarily correct. Science teaches us to "control and regulate future events by their causes."[20] There is nothing wrong with talking about the *laws* of nature and inductive *proofs* that a given cause will have a given effect where the regularities are clearly established, so long as we recognize that we are not talking about the deductive, certain proofs of mathematics and logic. We are talking about things that could conceivably be otherwise and may, in the end, turn out to be otherwise. However solid Newton's laws of matter and motion within the fixed structure of space and time may seem, an Einstein can come along and radically change our viewpoint; and a Heisenberg can challenge our very conception of cause and effect.

If we can't prove that inductive reasoning is a valid scientific method, how can we rely on it? Because it works. Its validity is shown not by a proof but by its predictive power. "It is not, therefore, reason which is the guide of life, but custom. That alone determines the mind in all instances to suppose the future conformable to the past. However easy this step may seem, reason would never, to all eternity, be able to make it."[21] "We are determined by custom alone to suppose the future conformable to the past."[22]

There are two implications of Hume's approach. First, we can't deploy innate ideas or so-called fundamental laws of nature as a straitjacket that limits scientific inquiry. We have to be open to the possibility that our theories and explanations, however well established, are wrong. Even Newton's laws of motion are just scientific hypotheses, not innate ideas or deductive certainties. Hume was thus remarkably forward-thinking on the nature of scientific inquiry. His radical empiricism is a caution against any form of dogmatism that blinds us to actual experience. It is a plea to keep science free from metaphysics.

Second, Hume does away with the search for giant turtles once and for all. Our ordinary commonsense beliefs, like our sophisticated scientific theories, don't need a theoretical foundation to validate them. All justifications are themselves based on experience. What matters is what works. "We can give no reason for our most general and most refined principles, beside our experience of their reality."[23] But that is all we need. As Wittgenstein would later write, "If I have exhausted the justifications I have reached bedrock, and my spade is turned. Then I am inclined to say: 'This is simply what I do.'"[24] We use inductive reasoning not because we can prove its validity but because it works. We treat nature as uniform and regular because we couldn't survive otherwise. The past establishes a rule for the future. We cannot doubt that, in practice, that will continue to hold true. But we cannot demonstrate that the future must look like the past.

It is worth stressing, however, that Hume is a passionate believer in the scientific method and the progress of knowledge. His treatment of miracles is a case in point. He rejects miracles, based solely on experience. "Though experience be our only guide in reasoning concerning matters of fact," he writes, "it must be acknowledged that this guide is not altogether infallible, but in some cases is apt to lead us into errors."[25] We accordingly proportion our belief to the evidence. Where experience is a strong indicator of a given event, belief is correspondingly strong; indeed, it can be so strong as to be regarded as "a full proof of the future existence of that event."[26] In other instances, such as where the event occurs only two-thirds of the time, we proceed with more caution. Hume gives the example of an expectation that any given day in June will have better weather than a given day in December. That is probable, but no guarantee is possible. You just have to wait and see.

A miracle, by definition, is "a violation of the laws of nature; and as a firm and unalterable experience has established these laws, the proof against a miracle, from the very nature of the fact, is as entire as any argument from experience can possibly be imagined."[27] It wouldn't be a miracle unless contrary to uniform experience. A wet and cold day in June would hardly qualify. That means the testimony in favor of the miracle would have to be so strong that "its falsehood would be more miraculous than the fact which it endeavors to establish."[28] No purported miracle in history has had that sort of evidentiary support. Judging from experience, it is far more probable that the witness or witnesses who testify to a miracle are deceived or deceiving, particularly when one considers the natural human eagerness to embrace and incite surprise and wonder, and the fact that reports of miracles are chiefly made among ignorant and primitive people.

Descartes had argued against miracles on the grounds that God was not a deceiver and had established a mechanical universe that admits no exception and whose fundamental laws are guaranteed. Hume's rejection of miracles is very different; in keeping with his whole philosophy, it is empirical rather than dogmatic; it is secular rather than religious; it is scientific rather than metaphysical. Everything in Hume is based on human nature and experience, and he will carry that through in his discussion of ethics.

NEITHER GOD NOR REASON

Having cleared the ground of metaphysics, Hume sought to establish a new science of human nature to match the accounts of the physical world and the human body developed by Isaac Newton and William Harvey, respectively. Hume wanted to bring their same scientific rigor and methods to bear on human understanding, feelings, behavior, and relationships. Like Descartes, Hume rejects any resort to final causes. Unlike Descartes, however, his new science invokes neither God nor innate ideas as its foundation. Man's nature has evolved over time, shaped by numerous forces, and is to be explained historically and psychologically based solely on inductive reasoning applied to experience. Hume extends such explanations to economics and politics. Though he had numerous predecessors, stretching back to Aristotle, it would not be too great an exaggeration to call Hume the father of the social sciences. Even religion itself, as we shall see, is to be approached as a human phenomenon to be explained in purely secular and historical terms. For Hume, human nature is the center of every inquiry. We must "hearken to no arguments but those which are derived from experience."[29]

This focus on human nature is nowhere more striking than in Hume's treatment of ethics. He considered his *Inquiry Concerning the Principles of Morals* to be, "of all my writings, historical, philosophical, or literary, incomparably the best."[30] Certainly, it was seen by his contemporaries as a shocking change in the traditional treatment of moral questions, although it was prefigured in Spinoza, who argued for a morality based not on external rules but on a fuller understanding of humanity and our place in nature.

For the typical pious Scotsman of the eighteenth century, right and wrong were determined by revelation. God himself, in the sacred writings of the church, and in particular the example and teaching of Jesus Christ, told us how we are to live our lives. Piety was whatever the Bible, the church fathers, and Calvin said it was.

More than two thousand years earlier, Socrates had already considered and rejected such an approach to ethics when he asked Euthyphro a disarmingly simple question: Do the gods love piety because it is pious or is it pious because the gods love it? Through a series of further questions, Socrates forces Euthyphro to admit, contrary to his initial impulse, that the gods love piety because it is pious; it is not pious because the gods love it. Describing an incidental affect or quality of piety—that it is loved by the gods—does nothing to advance our understanding of the essential nature of piety.[31]

In this simple exchange, Socrates established philosophy as an independent discipline, with its own methodology and subject matter. It is the job of philosophy, through careful, precise analysis, to determine what is pious, what is just, what is courageous, and temperate—to determine, in short, what is virtue and the good life for man. No appeal to outside authority can satisfy us. Man, through the application of *logos* (reason: what can be understood and expressed in speech), must work out these matters for himself. The nature of human virtue, he concludes, is a human problem to be determined by human reason.[32]

Hume agreed with only half of this statement. He thought the nature of human virtue was a human problem to be understood in human terms. But he had no faith in human reason as an arbiter of morality. Indeed, he thought that reason, so understood, had only a limited and decidedly secondary role in morals, for two related reasons.

First, reason deals with what is, not what ought to be. We express our moral judgments in terms of duties and obligations: "We ought to keep our promises"; "We should do unto others as we would have them do unto us"; "We must be loyal to our country." *Ought*, *should*, and *must* are modal verbs, each expressing, in the context of these sentences, a moral injunction. Hume's point is that we don't arrive at such moral principles through a chain of argument and deduction. Reason judges either of matters of fact or relations between ideas. Moral principles are neither. As Hume famously put it: you cannot get an "ought" from an "is." That is, you cannot reason from factual, nonmoral observations about the world to moral conclusions. Reason cannot bridge the gap between a description of facts and circumstances and a moral obligation.

> For as this *ought*, or *ought not*, expresses some new relation or affirmation, 'tis necessary that it should be observed and explained; and at the same time that a reason should be given, for what seems altogether inconceivable, how this new relation can be a deduction from others, which are entirely different from it. [33]

Put differently, you cannot deduce a modal term such as *ought* from other propositions that contain no such term. It is "altogether inconceivable" to make that leap. Once we know all the factual circumstances, the role of reason is at an end. "The approbation or blame which then ensues cannot be the work of the judgment but of the heart; and it is not a speculative proposition or affirmation, but an active feeling or sentiment." [34] Reason can tell me that there is a human being lying in front of me who is injured and in need of assistance. But something more is required to instill in me a sense that I have a moral obligation to help that person.

This gap between "is" and "ought" is related to the second point, which Hume again puts provocatively: "Reason is, and ought only to be, the slave of the passions, and can never pretend to any other office than to serve and obey them." [35] Reason is solely instrumental. It may help us to achieve our desires. But reason alone does not tell us what to desire or value. Reason is inert. Our motives for action reside elsewhere.

That is not to say that reason is unimportant. It can determine a proper course of action—such as how best to help the injured person—but passion has to provide the impulse to that action. Although reason can "instruct us in the pernicious or useful tendency of qualities and actions, it is not alone sufficient to produce any moral blame or approbation." For that we need a sentiment "to give a preference to the useful above the perni-cious tendencies."[36]

Passion, then, sets the goal, and reason works out the means. Even an outlandish preference does not contain a false belief, and is therefore not demonstrably unreasonable. "'Tis not contrary to reason to prefer the destruction of the whole world to the scratching of my finger. 'Tis not contrary to reason for me to choose my total ruin, to prevent the least uneasiness of . . . [a] person wholly unknown to me."[37] It is, however, contrary to human nature to adopt either extreme.

Neither God's commandments nor the exercise of reason can tell us what we ought to do. Once again, Hume rejects the *a priori* options. There is no transcendental source for morality. His stance seems skepti-cal, but, in fact, it is deeply and solidly grounded in human nature. Our morality does not need foundations. It arises naturally from the senti-ments and affections of humankind. We approve of actions and characters insofar as they promote the good of society and its members. Hume turns the Socratic query upside down: an action is not good because the gods love it; it is good because human beings love it. Our morality is a reflec-tion of our own humanity and the society we have formed. It neither has nor needs any outside warrant.

Two objections to Hume's approach to morals immediately present themselves. First, his account seems reductionist. That is, when we talk about a moral action or character trait, we are talking about the moral quality of the action or trait in question, not our own reactions to it or even its perceived public utility. As Voltaire put it: Virtue is "not a good, it is a duty: it is a different kind, of a superior order. It has nothing to do with painful or agreeable sensations."[38] We may well approve of generos-ity, but to call an action or person generous is not the equivalent of saying "I approve." That was exactly what Socrates pointed out to Euthyphro: mistaking an incidental affect of generosity—that we approve of it—for the actual characteristic of generosity.

But this mistake is not one Hume is making. Hume notes that our moral vocabulary is grounded in and inspired by human sentiments, but it is not reducible to expressions of those sentiments. Using modal verbs, our moral discourse purports to describe duties and obligations. "The end of all moral speculations is to teach us our duty, and, by proper represen-tations of the deformity of vice and beauty of virtue, beget correspondent habits, and engage us to avoid the one, and embrace the other."[39] This is a critical part of our education. In learning the vocabulary of morality, we learn how to make nice moral distinctions. "The epithets, *sociable, good-natured, humane, merciful, grateful, friendly, generous, beneficent*, or their equivalents, are known in all languages, and universally express the highest merit which human nature is capable of attaining."[40]

The modal grammar of morality is autonomous. It is not reducible to facts about human sentiments of benevolence and sympathy. But such sentiments are critical to our ability to undertake this education. Our language reflects our values. "Extinguish all the warm feelings and pre-possessions in favor of virtue, and all disgust or aversion to vice; render men totally indifferent toward these distinctions; and morality is no long-er a practical study, nor has any tendency to regulate our lives and ac-tions."[41] It would be like trying to teach a blind person the vocabulary of color. Unless moral distinctions are "founded on the original constitution of the mind, the words *honorable* and *shameful, lovely* and *odious, noble* and *despicable* had never had place in any language, nor could politi-cians, had they invented these terms, ever have been able to render them intelligible or make them convey any idea to the audience."[42]

What Hume proposed was to undertake an Aristotelian analysis of our moral vocabulary as a means of reaching our full human potential as moral beings.

> We shall analyze that complication of mental qualities which form what, in common life, we call "personal merit"; we shall consider every attribute of the mind which renders a man an object either of esteem and affection or of hatred and contempt; every habit or senti-ment or faculty which, if ascribed to any person, implies either praise or blame and may enter into any panegyric or satire of his character and manners.[43]

Hume never fully finished this task; not in any systematic way. But it has been carried through brilliantly by P. M. S. Hacker in his tetralogy on human nature, particularly in the last two volumes, *The Passions* and *The Moral Powers*.[44] With great subtlety and a stunning array of examples from English and European literature, Hacker carefully explores such concepts as pride, guilt, envy, virtue, vice, anger, love, friendship, and happiness. He fleshes out our conceptual scheme of passion and morality, and in the process gives us profound insights into human nature, of a sort long promised by philosophers from Socrates to Hume.

The second objection to Hume's treatment of morals derives from Thomas Hobbes and, to a lesser extent, John Locke. Their approach truly is reductionist. Neither believes in the possibility of altruism or benevolence. Hobbes in particular adopts a highly negative view of human nature as innately selfish and depraved, incapable of generosity or self-sacrifice. All our actions are simply reflections of self-interest. On such a view, which Hume emphatically rejects, "all benevolence is mere hypocrisy, friendship a cheat, public spirit a farce, fidelity a snare to procure trust and confidence."[45] "We must renounce the theory," Hume insists, "which accounts for every moral sentiment by the principle of self-love."[46]

Hume contends that certain benevolent feelings, such as tenderness to offspring, love, and friendship, cannot be denied. We feel affection for others and wish to promote their good as well as our own. Hume is not naive. He recognizes that selfishness is pervasive. But certain positive feelings toward others are also part of our natural makeup, and our moral language and judgments depend upon those sentiments. "It is sufficient for our present purpose, if it be allowed, what surely, without the greatest absurdity, cannot be disputed, that there is some benevolence, however small, infused into our bosom; some spark of friendship for humankind; some particle of the dove kneaded into our frame, along with the elements of the wolf and serpent."[47] Hobbes and Locke, though they viewed humankind as irretrievably selfish, themselves led irreproachable lives.[48] Hume, too, was liberally endowed with the character traits that Johnson considered so important to human felicity: a disposition to be pleased and a great capacity for friendship.

Hobbes thought that an authoritarian government was necessary to control and suppress our inexorable self-interest. Men and women must give up all freedom to the protection of the state.

> During the time men live without a common power to keep them all in awe, they are in that condition which is called war; and such a war as is of every man against every man. . . . To this war of every man against every man, this also is consequent; that nothing can be unjust. The notions of right and wrong, justice and injustice, have there no place. Where there is no common power, there is no law; where no law, no injustice. Force and fraud are in war the two cardinal virtues.[49]

Perhaps no more pessimistic assessment of human relations has been penned since Machiavelli, if then. Hobbes thought that there could be no constraint on human self-interest other than harsh laws to prevent a "war of all against all." But Hume insisted that man has evolved with society and has internalized genuine social virtues such as compassion, generosity, and honesty. To be sure, these virtues are often honored in the breach; Machiavelli made that a matter of policy. Selfishness and altruism do battle in our own breasts as well as in the makeup of society. But, for Hume, human nature fulfills itself best in a social and political setting that balances freedom and restraint.

Although he was too early to put his argument in evolutionary terms, Hume offers an organic and historical account of moral sentiments that is "essentially a Darwinian view."[50] Altruism is a trait that began first within family and tribal units, and gradually spread to a broader society. We developed altruism out of self-interest because it made for stronger, safer, and more secure groups. But that etiology does not vitiate altruism, which is now more or less ingrained.

Far from supporting an authoritarian regime, therefore, Hume advocates a limited role for government in which both personal and commercial relationships can flourish. The primary purpose of government is to protect persons and property and to establish a rule of law within which individuals can simultaneously pursue their own good and the public good. Again, Hume is far from naive. He recognizes that the desire for property is driven by self-interest. "This avidity alone, of acquiring goods and possessions for ourselves and our nearest friends, is insatiable, perpetual, universal, and directly destructive of society."[51] But allowing commerce to flourish will increase freedom and morality, as well as wealth. The very impersonality of commercial relations allows scope for human freedom and independence by people who are no longer dependent on a tribal chieftain or feudal overlord or absolute monarch to maintain order. People can fashion their own lives within a governmental structure that guarantees their property and their safety from both external and internal threats. In the process, Hume contends, they will internalize the values of that society by respecting the person and property of others and by honoring contracts and other promises. Trust, honesty, and integrity are valued in commercial relations and thereby fostered. In such a secure structure, without a war of all against all, sociability and benevolence will also increase. In short, public utility can be the basis of a morality that extends beyond mere notions of utility and promotes virtue and justice based on social institutions that benefit us all.

It is a noble vision even if it seems, to many today, to be a tarnished one. This classical liberalism was at the core of what we call the Scottish Enlightenment, which so influenced the American Founding Fathers. A number of the key ideas in Adam Smith's *Wealth of Nations*—free trade; the division of labor; the importance of capital; the invisible hand that allows self-interest to operate within the rules of a commercial structure—are also to be found, in capsule form, in Hume, which is to take nothing away from Smith's massive achievement. Hume even anticipated the two most salient criticisms of capitalism, one assailing too much freedom and the other, too much authority.[52]

First, Hume recognized that a commercial society would invariably have winners and losers. Inherent advantages of mind and body, of circumstance, and of sheer luck (good and bad) will have substantial consequences for each individual's success or lack of success in such a system. But government, he believed, cannot erase those advantages or their consequences. It could not, therefore, equalize possessions without tyranny and the abolition of human freedom. Hume was also a pragmatist, however, and one must not attribute to him a rigid "either/or" that pits commercial freedom against the very social virtues that Hume thought so important. Although Hume thought that material affluence goes hand in hand with limited government, he stressed that "the good of mankind is the only object of all these laws and regulations."[53] He did not, therefore, foreclose the possibility that, "for the peace and interest of society," our sense of justice could evolve further in the direction of equality while still valuing commercial freedom.[54]

Second, Hume recognized that individuals would pay a price in personal autonomy for the division of labor and specialization that replaced the broader array of skills and activities that was once common. He considered the price worth paying to relieve the poverty of the worst off and to raise the standard of living generally. The Romantics, led by Rousseau, came to consider that price too high. They saw conflict between the individual and his society as inevitable and even desirable. Hume himself, had he witnessed the full effects of the Industrial Revolution, might have asked more urgently whether capitalism was a form of freedom or, for many, a new type of serfdom. But Hume was convinced that men must sacrifice some untrammeled individual freedom in order to "reap the fruits of mutual protection and assistance."[55]

Hume accordingly focused on both the overall material well-being of society as a benefit to all its members and the freedom of individuals, within that society, to find their own road to happiness. In a series of four essays—perhaps his most famous—Hume analyzes various classical theories of human happiness: Epicurean, Stoic, Platonic, and Skeptical. Unsurprisingly, Hume favors the Skeptical and questions the value of the whole enterprise of happiness by rule.

The Epicurean stresses the pleasures of friendship, conversation, and sex. The Stoic exhorts men to vigorous action and strenuous virtue in order to exalt the powers of the human mind over the vagaries of fortune. The Platonist shuns the "ignorant applause of men" in favor of contemplating the mind of God as reflected in the order and beauty of nature.[56]

For the Skeptic, however, there is no one path to happiness and virtue. Experience shows us a "vast variety of inclinations and pursuits among our species"; even within a single life, many changes are to be found.[57] "Of all the fruitless attempts of art," Hume notes, "no one is so ridiculous, as that which the severe philosophers have undertaken, the producing of an artificial happiness, and making us be pleased by rules of reason, and by reflection."[58]

Philosophy has no particular claim to practical wisdom, just as it had none to theoretical wisdom. Whatever wisdom is to be found must be drawn from experience. "While we are reasoning concerning life, life is gone; and death, though perhaps they receive him differently, yet treats alike the fool and the philosopher."[59]

THE DEATH OF A PHILOSOPHER

Though it may simply reflect his love of irony, Hume reputably said that he never thought to question the existence of God until he read and found wanting the proofs of God's existence fashioned by British philosophers John Locke and Samuel Clarke. In keeping with his general skepticism of the powers of reason, Hume may have been an agnostic rather than an out-and-out atheist. Certainly, he was careful to keep his views ambiguous—and in some cases unpublished during his lifetime—to avoid potential prosecution. But it is clear that he was no believer in the divinity of

Christ or the authority of scripture. Nor did he believe in a life after death in which the good are rewarded and the wicked are subjected to everlasting torment.

As already discussed, Hume found no need for a providential order or a religious basis for morality. Indeed, he considered religion morally corrupting. According to James Boswell, who was both fascinated and repelled, Hume said that, when he "heard a man was religious, he concluded he was a rascal, though he had known some instances of very good men being religious."[60] Hume was undoubtedly tweaking the pious Boswell, who was himself rather a rascal. But there is no question that Hume valued reading, conversation, love, and friendship over any form of religious devotion.

In *The Natural History of Religion*, published in his forties, Hume approached religion, as he approached every subject, for what it could tell us about human nature. He viewed religion anthropologically, as a human phenomenon with a "natural history." It was a purely secular and psychological study, anticipating Freud. Hume assumed that polytheism—a belief in many gods—came first in time and that monotheism was a later development. That premise has since been called into question. But Hume's more important focus was on the origins of religious belief, which he traced to two sources: superstition and enthusiasm.

Superstitious religion arises from the weakness, fear, and ignorance of primitive man, who everywhere saw "invisible, unknown powers."[61] Superstitious religion seeks to placate these hostile forces with "frivolous observances" and "absurd" mysteries,[62] and enlists priests to mediate with the divine. Enthusiastic religion, by contrast, is born of "hope, pride, presumption, a warm imagination, together with ignorance."[63] It shows a "propensity to adulation."[64] It shuns ecclesiastics, as well as "forms, ceremonies, and traditions," relying instead on rapture, transports, and divine inspiration.[65] These "opposite principles"—fear and adulation—have always rested uneasily together. "Our natural terrors present the notion of a devilish and malicious deity: Our propensity to adulation leads us to acknowledge an excellent and divine."[66] But ignorance is their common thread. Man both fears and worships the unknown.

Hume condemns both superstition and enthusiasm as "the corruptions of true religion."[67] In typical fashion, however, he does not explain what "true religion" is left after superstition and enthusiasm are subtracted, leaving the reader to suspect that it is the null set. Hume even argues that one cannot "draw any certain inference in favor of a man's morals, from the fervor or strictness of his religious exercises, even though he himself believe them sincere."[68] Indeed, he claims that typical religious "virtues" are anything but public goods; they have adverse effects on both the individual and society. "Celibacy, fasting, penance, mortification, self-denial, humility, silence, solitude, and the whole train of monkish virtues . . . serve to no manner of purpose; neither advance a man's fortune in the world, nor render him a more valuable member of society; neither qualify him for the entertainment of company, nor increase his power of self-enjoyment."[69] All they do is "stupefy the understanding and harden the heart, obscure the fancy and sour the temper."[70] The religious principles that have prevailed in the world, Hume concludes, are nothing but "sick men's dreams."[71]

Strong stuff; and this is from his published writings! Hume does press on to explore whether there is a nobler form of religion, a "true religion" in which we may obtain knowledge of a "supreme Creator" through the exercise of human reason upon the visible works of nature.[72] But exactly how he answers that question is still a matter of dispute.

The *Dialogues Concerning Natural Religion* was written around the same time as the *Natural History of Religion*, but did not appear until three years after Hume's death. His usual publisher, William Strahan, refused to publish the book, and even his dear friend Adam Smith declined Hume's request to see to its publication. The work survived thanks to Hume's nephew, who felt duty-bound to honor his uncle's "extreme solicitude" that the *Dialogues* be published.[73]

The book is written in dialogue form both to facilitate the interplay and testing of ideas and also to maintain a certain ambiguity about the author's own views. The reader is compelled to draw his or her own hard-won conclusions. As the title indicates, the *Dialogues* concerns "natural," not revealed, religion. Revealed religion is found in various sacred works, such as the Hebrew Bible, the New Testament, and the Koran. Some Christians contend that the divinity of Christ is proved by the miracles recorded in the New Testament and the fulfillment of earlier prophecies from the Old Testament. Hume had already debunked such arguments in his earlier treatment of miracles.

In the *Dialogues*, Hume turns to the question of whether it is possible to obtain knowledge of God through reason rather than an unquestioning faith in revelation. All three speakers purport to accept the existence of

God. Their disagreement is about what we can know, and prove, about God's nature. But, of course, no such clean separation is possible. If we know nothing about God's nature, the assertion that God exists is empty of content. That in fact proves to be the case and is the major, if somewhat disguised, thrust of the *Dialogues*.

Hume considers two types of argument, though the line between them is decidedly blurry. First are *a priori* arguments that are true in any possible world and hence do not depend on the particulars of experience. Second are *a posteriori* arguments that draw their conclusions from our experience of this world. Of the three principal participants in the *Dialogues*, Demea offers the first type of argument and Cleanthes the second. Philo, an inveterate skeptic, attacks both, enlisting Cleanthes against Demea and Demea against Cleanthes.

Demea's main *a priori* argument, often called the "cosmological" argument for God's existence, is that nothing can exist without a creator or first cause that is responsible for that existence. This "first cause" we naturally call God. Even if we posit that there is an infinite series of causes and effects, something outside that causal chain must still be responsible for its existence. "We must, therefore, have recourse to a necessarily existent being who carries the *reason* of his existence in himself; and who cannot be supposed not to exist without an express contradiction."[74] God is a necessary being because, without God, nothing else could exist. "Finite, weak, and blind creatures," Demea continues, "we ought to humble ourselves in his august presence, and, conscious of our frailties, adore in silence his infinite perfections which eye hath not seen, ear hath not heard, neither hath it entered into the heart of man to conceive them."[75]

Cleanthes disparages this argument as "mystical," because it tells us nothing whatsoever about the nature of God. God is simply a stand-in for the unknown origins of the universe, a point we saw first in Spinoza. A transcendent God is not an explanation of existence; it is an admission of despair at even the possibility of such an explanation. We worship in total ignorance.

More fundamentally, Demea's argument rests on a simple error of logic. We can formulate an abstract concept of God as a creator or first cause, but the concept alone cannot tell us whether such a being exists. "Nothing is demonstrable [*a priori*] unless the contrary implies a contradiction," explains Cleanthes. "Nothing that is distinctly conceivable implies a contradiction. Whatever we conceive as existent, we can also conceive as non-existent."[76] In other words, we can form a concept of God as the first cause and creator of all that exists. But whether such a God exists is not something deducible from the concept itself. It is not a logical contradiction to say that God—conceived as a first cause or creator—does not exist. The notion of a "necessary being"—a being whose existence is inextricable from its essence—is incoherent. Only experience will allow us to determine whether something exists or not.

Cleanthes thus attempts to come up with an argument for God's existence based on experience. He contends that the inherent order of the universe reflects divine providence. If we see an intricate mechanism such as a clock, we instantly assume that an intelligent being made that clock. The solar system, as Newton showed, is like a giant clock, the parts of which all fit together to form an intricate and intelligible whole. Similarly, plants and animals are perfectly designed for their environments. Just look at the perfection of the eye, Cleanthes urges. We cannot accept the materialist, Epicurean view that everything we know has developed through the chance interaction of atoms in the void. The careful and orderly design of the many complex mechanisms and organisms that make up the universe demands an explanation, and that explanation can only lie in the all-powerful, all-knowing, and beneficent creator we call God. As Philo characterizes this argument from design, before attacking it, there must be a creator because "a purpose, an intention, a design strikes everywhere the most careless, the most stupid thinker."[77]

Between them, Demea and Philo offer many objections to the argument from design. Four in particular warrant mention. First, while Cleanthes accuses Demea of mysticism, Demea counters with the charge of "anthropomorphism," the attribution to God of human characteristics such as intelligence and goodness. Cleanthes wants to infer these qualities from the world that God created. But such inferences require likeness. Thanks to Boyle, we know about the circulation of blood in humans. Whenever we see a human, we can justly infer that his or her blood circulates in the same manner. But extending that inference to a frog, Philo notes, would be a weaker conclusion, at least without empirical verification. The more dissimilar two things are, the weaker the inference that they share particular characteristics. How much weaker, then, when we jump from finite physical entities to an infinite, immaterial creator? Positing God's "similarity to human mind and intelligence"[78] ignores the unbridgeable gulf between the finite and the infinite, between mere human knowledge and divine omniscience, between feeble human power and divine omnipotence. We don't even know what it means to attribute such qualities by analogy to the divine.

Second, even if anthropomorphism were acceptable, we could not infer divine goodness. Men everywhere seem to be engaged in Hobbes's war of all against all.

> Oppression, injustice, contempt, contumely, violence, sedition, war, calumny, treachery, fraud; by these they mutually torment each other: And they would soon dissolve that society which they had formed, were it not for the dread of still greater ills, which must attend their separation.[79]

At best, the world is a mixture of good and evil. What, then, can we infer about God? "Is he willing to prevent evil, but not able? Then is he impotent. Is he able, but not willing? Then is he malevolent. Is he both able and willing? Whence then is evil?"[80] Philo contends that "nothing can shake the solidity of this reasoning, so short, so clear, so decisive; except we assert, that these subjects exceed all human capacity, and that our common measures of truth and falsehood are not applicable to them."[81] Thus, even if we accept God as the first or original cause, we can't infer anything about his moral nature from our experience of the world. Positing such a cause tells us nothing about how to live our lives.

Third, Philo asks what we gain "in tracing the universe of objects into a similar universe of ideas."[82] Cleanthes argues that a divine intelligence is necessary to explain what order exists in the physical world. But why is it not equally sensible, Philo asks, to conclude that the parts of the material world fall into order, of themselves, and by their own nature? "Can the one opinion be intelligible, while the other is not so?"[83] Here, Philo invokes the aforementioned Indian philosopher. "If the material world rests upon a similar ideal world, this ideal world must rest upon some other; and so on, without end. *It were better, therefore, never to look beyond the present material world*."[84] Since an infinite regress is incomprehensible, we should stop with what we know. We should stop at the material world.

Finally, Philo points out, we have in science a legitimate alternative to the "religious system" of explanation.[85] The material world does not invite an immaterial explanation. "The whole presents nothing but the idea of a blind nature, impregnated by a great vivifying principle, and pouring forth from her lap, without discernment or parental care, her maimed abortive children!"[86] In a remarkable set of passages anticipating scientific developments still well in the future, Hume-cum-Philo criticizes Cleanthes for presuming to place limits on what science may teach us. To pursue his argument from design, Cleanthes must resort to the Aristotelian terminology of final causes, decisively rejected by Descartes and Newton. Cleanthes contends that both the inanimate objects and the living things that surround us are not the product of natural forces of cause and effect but must be understood in terms of their teleology, the purpose for which they were fashioned by God. This is a repudiation of the basic premise of empirical science. Physics and biology will tell us whatever we can learn about the nature and origins of our world and the creatures that inhabit it, not the sort of speculation in which Cleanthes engages.

Hume even seems to offer something like the "big bang" hypothesis of the twentieth century.[87] "Suppose," he writes, "that matter were thrown into any position, by a blind, unguided force."[88] The initial result would be chaos. But if "the actuating force, whatever it be, still continues in matter," and gives it "a perpetual restlessness" over many ages, a "seeming stability in the forms" may eventually evolve.[89] In current terms, even in the midst of overall entropic progression, pockets of low-level entropy will develop, resulting in stars, planets, and even life.

> May we not hope for such a position, or rather be assured of it, from the eternal revolutions of unguided matter, and may not this account for all the appearing wisdom and contrivance, which is in the universe?[90]

Hume also suggests that the complexity of the various life forms is explicable by a form of natural selection: "I would fain know how an animal could subsist, unless its parts were so adjusted."[91]

We obviously cannot give Hume credit either for modern physics or for evolutionary biology. But we can give him credit for insisting that we keep faith with science and scientific explanations of natural phenomena in terms of material causes rather than throwing up our hands and leaping to an entirely different form of explanation in terms of divine intentions of which we can know nothing whatsoever. As science becomes more sophisticated and is able to explain more, we have no need to accept the premise that the material world must be explained in terms of a prior, immaterial order.

Hume never embraced atheism. He never denied the empirical possibility of a divine creator. The idea of God is not a contradiction in terms, and hence cannot be excluded *a priori*. Nor did Hume deny that many of us have a natural impulse or longing to believe in a supreme creator who has imparted order and meaning to the universe. Such a belief cannot be refuted by reason any more than it can be established by reason. As Pascal insisted, the heart can have reasons that reason does not know. Hume's point is, rather, that once religion is purged of superstition and enthusiasm, of mysticism and anthropomorphism, there is little or nothing left of it.

So, too, there is little or nothing left of us when we die, Hume argued in an essay, "Of the Immortality of the Soul," which was also printed only after his death.[92] In keeping with his life's work on ethics as a reflection of human nature and human needs, Hume rejects any suggestion that a belief in life after death, with rewards and punishments, is necessary to morals. Indeed, he argues, any system of eternal punishment for temporary offenses cannot itself be morally justified. "Heaven and hell suppose two distinct species of men, the good and the bad. But the greatest part of mankind float between vice and virtue."[93]

Reason cannot tell us whether something exists or doesn't exist. Only experience can do that. But our experience is limited to the present life and provides no warrant for believing in a future one. Even if it makes sense to speak of an immaterial soul attached to and controlling a material body—a paradox that Descartes never resolved—"no form can continue, when transferred to a condition of life very different from the original one, in which it was placed."[94] We decline both mentally and physically with age. In experience, everything changes and dissolves. How, then, can we assume that one single form, the soul, is immortal and indissoluble and continues to exist in wholly different conditions? Vladimir Nabokov called human life "a brief crack of light between two eternities of darkness."[95] That may be true for the collective as well as the individual.

David Hume died in 1776. He faced death with equanimity and even cheerfulness, reflecting that "a man of sixty-five, by dying, cuts off only a few years of infirmities."[96] His death sparked considerable controversy because so many believed that, faced with the terror of annihilation, he would repent and embrace religion in the end. Boswell even made a special trip to his bedside in hopes of witnessing and even provoking such a recantation. But it never came. Adam Smith, who was with Hume in his final days, noted in a letter to Hume's publisher, that he "submitted with the utmost cheerfulness, and the most perfect complacency and resignation"; he spent his time reading and conversing with friends, "free from anxiety, impatience, or low spirits."[97]

Hume, who had been reading his favorite Greek satirist, Lucian, even joked with Smith about possible excuses he might make to Charon, the ferryman of the dead, in order to obtain a little delay, such as correcting his works for a new edition. "Have a little patience, good Charon," he might further urge, "I have been endeavoring to open the eyes of the public. If I live a few years longer, I may have the satisfaction of seeing the downfall of some of the prevailing systems of superstition."[98] What Hume actually said, Smith later admitted, was, "Till I have the pleasure of seeing the churches shut up, and the clergy sent about their business."[99] But Smith's letter was controversial enough, and he softened that final remark. Smith ended his letter with praise of Hume echoing what Plato said of Socrates:

> Upon the whole, I have always considered him, both in his lifetime and since his death, as approaching as nearly to the idea of a perfectly wise and virtuous man, as perhaps the nature of human frailty will permit.[100]

David Hume may not have had an immortal soul, but he justifiably enjoys a species of immortality in his writings. Hume has a fair claim to be the first modern philosopher. One could even argue that he is the first post-philosophy philosopher. Physics, biology, psychology, morality, the arts, and politics are all now purely empirical and secular subjects. Philosophy, with its claims to a special form of nonempirical insight, has slowly disappeared, like the Cheshire Cat, leaving only its knowing grin behind.

10

KANT AND THE CLAIMS OF REASON

I openly confess, the suggestion of David Hume was the very thing, which many years ago first interrupted my dogmatic slumber, and gave my investigations in the field of speculative philosophy quite a new direction.[1]

Immanuel Kant lived in a Newtonian universe of rigid, mechanical causation in space and time. Yet he also believed in the ability of humans to act freely in accordance with the precepts of a binding moral law. He based his belief in God on that moral freedom. Kant thus found himself with a need to limit the realm of the natural sciences (the realm of knowledge) in order to make room for faith. At the same time, he was hostile to organized religion insofar as it was dogmatic and sought to impede the free exercise of reason and the development of the natural sciences. Thus, while he set limits on knowledge to make room for faith, he also, with equal if not greater vigor, set limits on faith to make room for knowledge.

In many respects, Kant was the antithesis of Hume. Where Hume rejected all innate ideas, Kant argued that there are conditions necessary to experience, and hence we can know those conditions with certainty prior to and apart from experience, including a self that has the experience, an external world that is experienced, and the strict succession of events governed by cause and effect. Where Hume argued that morality arises naturally from the sentiments and affections of humankind, Kant argued that morality has a formal nature known to reason from which our categorical duties as humans necessarily follow. Where Hume rejected all arguments for the existence of God and immortality, Kant contended that

God and immortality were necessary postulates to make sense of our moral duty.

Yet the overlaps between the two thinkers are as important and interesting as the differences. Both rejected traditional metaphysics. Both revered science based on empirical investigation. Both believed that human freedom was compatible with the mechanical operation of cause and effect. Both rejected a morality based on divine command. Both found the traditional arguments for the existence of God totally wanting. And both rejected the rites, prayers, and rituals of traditional religion as so much superstition.

But Kant wanted to salvage philosophy from Hume's skeptical assault on reason. He sought to reconcile the strict empiricism of Locke, Berkeley, and Hume with the rationalism of Descartes, Spinoza, and Leibniz. Kant himself said that *Critique of Pure Reason* was an attempt to affect a Copernican revolution in thought. By this he meant that traditional metaphysics treated the mind as merely a stationary mirror of reality, which revolved around it; whereas he treated the mind as an active, moving force. But the analogy is misleading. Copernicus replaced a worldview in which the earth was the center of the universe with one in which the earth was but a speck of dust whirling around a random star in a random corner of a random galaxy. Kant, by contrast, restored man to the center of his universe by focusing on the shaping power of his own mind in creating that universe as it is known to him. He believed the structure of that universe is shaped by the categories of our understanding, which offer necessary truths about the world in space and time, and provide a solid foundation for the natural sciences. At the same time, Kant traced the boundaries of human reason, from the inside, so to speak, in such a way as to leave open at least the possibility of a realm outside those boundaries, a realm in which God, freedom, and immortality—while not objects of knowledge—could remain as objects of belief.

LIFE

Immanuel Kant is, or ought to be, the patron saint of all late bloomers. Had he died in early 1781, just short of his fifty-seventh birthday (an age that already exceeded the average life span of his contemporaries), he would have been, at best, a short footnote in the history of philosophy.

Instead, he published his hastily composed but much considered master-work, *Critique of Pure Reason*, later that year, and produced book after book that revolutionized philosophy over the remaining twenty-three years of his life.

Kant was born on April 22, 1724, in Königsberg, the capital of East Prussia and a small but not insignificant trading center on the Baltic Sea. (The town no longer exists, having been largely destroyed during World War II and replaced with the Russian naval base of Kaliningrad.) Although his mind traveled over the entire span of human knowledge, he never strayed far from the town of his birth.

Kant was the fourth of nine children to survive childhood. His father was a harness maker. Both parents were devout Pietists (a movement within Lutheranism that stressed each individual's direct relationship with God and was hostile to any attempt to intellectualize faith). He received a heavily religious education, in the clutches, as he himself put it, of "pietist fanatics," before starting at the University of Königsberg at the age of sixteen.

Unable to obtain an academic position upon graduation, he worked for years as a private tutor. At the age of thirty-one, he was finally appointed a "private docent," a position that gave him no salary but allowed him to give public lectures for which he could charge a fee. Fortunately, his lectures—on a range of subjects including mathematics, physics, and geography, as well as philosophy—were extremely popular, with students arriving as much as an hour early to secure a seat. He also began to make a name for himself with his writings. After turning down several offers from other cities, he became a university professor of logic and meta-physics in 1770, at the age of forty-six.

Kant was small (five feet, two inches) and slight, with a narrow and sunken chest, but attractive features. Although he was extremely sensitive to changes in his environment and could not bear vigorous physical exer-cise, he was, as he explained, "healthy in a weak way." He was also extremely sociable. Elegant in dress and manner, he dined in society on a regular basis, played cards, and went to the theater. He was so fond of good wine that he reportedly had problems on occasion finding his way back to his modest lodgings after an evening out. He was much sought after by Königsberg society for his wit and brilliant conversation.

Kant's behavior, however, underwent a dramatic change in his forties. He felt the need to regularize his conduct and began to live according to carefully considered "maxims," rational principles to govern his behavior. From this time dates the story that the wives and burghers of Königsberg could set their clocks by the regularity of his daily, solitary walk. Kant's maxims gradually squeezed out much of his social life, and he focused more and more on developing his thoughts. He went through a quiet period of almost ten years, during which he wrote very little, leading up to *Critique of Pure Reason*.

RATIONALISM AND EMPIRICISM

Kant's writings are among the most fascinating in all of philosophy, but they are not for the faint of heart. His thinking is always intricate, his prose is often labored, and his basic doctrines seem at crucial points absurd. But the same might be said of Einstein and, as we will see, there are some interesting parallels between the two thinkers, despite their completely different approaches to understanding the underlying nature of reality. Carefully considered and understood in context, Kant's work is deeply compelling and, in one form or another, has shaped our modern consciousness.

As he explains in the preface to the first edition of *Critique of Pure Reason*, "the chief question [for the philosopher] is always simply this: what and how much can the understanding and reason know apart from all experience?"[2] Kant, in his capacity as a philosopher, is not interested in what we can learn *from* experience. That is the realm of the scientist. Kant wants to know what we can know "*a priori*"—that is, apart from and prior to experience.

That may seem an odd question. We are deeply steeped in the British empiricist tradition touted by Hume in which all knowledge derives from experience. But Kant believes that experience itself—to be intelligible to us—has a necessary form and structure and that the philosopher, by exploring that form and structure, can thereby chart the boundaries of *possible* experience. In the process, the philosopher gains certain knowledge; knowledge that must be universally true of all experience because it is a condition of experience. In this way, the philosopher can simultaneously refute the claims of the Skeptics—who refuse to acknowledge even the possibility of objective knowledge—and the metaphysicians, who would go beyond the boundaries of possible knowledge.

Kant's mature philosophy was formed in immediate reaction to two other thinkers, both extreme representatives of their respective traditions. The first, Gottfried Leibniz (1646–1716), was a proponent of rationalism. Leibniz believed that we can ascertain necessary truths about reality through the exercise of reason alone. Correspondingly, he denigrated the world of commonsense experience as one of mere appearance. Reality is known only through the direct perception of certain innate ideas that are part of our birthright as rational beings. Leibniz argued that space and time have no objective reality; they are merely relations between what we perceive as physical objects and events. We have knowledge of reality independent of space and time, and hence independent of the material world, because we have knowledge of our own core being, the "I" that thinks and reasons. For Leibniz, this reality consists of "monads," irreducibly simple, eternal centers of force and thought arranged and harmonized by God. Even though we humans appear to interact in the world of mere appearance, the monads themselves do not interact. They float in isolation, beguiled by appearances, but with access through reason to a parallel, more genuine reality. It is the philosopher's job to adopt the perspective of God and to understand the laws and principles (mathematical, logical, and moral) according to which he has ordered reality.

The second philosopher against whom Kant reacted was David Hume, whom Kant presents as the opposite extreme from Leibniz. For Hume, in Kant's version, there is no such thing as objective knowledge. All beliefs come from sense experience and hence are dependent on the subjective perceptions of the observer. Necessity is to be found only in the relations of ideas, not in the world. In this sense, all knowledge is *a posteriori* (after experience) rather than *a priori* (prior to experience). These views led Hume to a radical skepticism. The physical world is only a construct of individual sense impressions. We have no knowledge that objects exist independent of our observations of them. Nor do we have knowledge that the law of cause and effect—which is only a by-product of the association of ideas—will hold true in future experience. Even the "I," which is the possessor of all my thoughts and experiences, is only a construct. We have no direct knowledge of an immaterial self that persists through time. As we saw, Hume's views are more subtle and compelling than Kant portrays them. The same is true of Leibniz. But they both serve as useful foils in explaining Kant's own position.

Kant is leery of the claims of Leibniz. But it is Hume whom he says has awakened him from a "dogmatic slumber." Kant considers it a scandal that philosophy is unable even to acknowledge the claims to genuine knowledge provided by Newtonian physics. In the spirit of Descartes, Kant accordingly wants to provide a solid foundation for such knowledge and to refute Hume's skeptical arguments. At the same time, he wants to banish the flights of pure fancy indulged in by Leibniz and other rationalists. Put differently, Kant wants to embrace the best of each tradition and, in the process, to put empiricism on a solid rationalist foundation.

EMPIRICAL REALISM

Kant's solution to the dilemma posed by Hume and Leibniz lies in his recognition that neither experience nor reason alone provides knowledge. Both are needed and both make a critical contribution. "Without sensibility," he explains, "no object would be given to us, without understanding no object would be thought."[3] In the first point, he agrees with Hume that experience is critical to give content to our concepts. But the second point is much more subtle: what Kant suggests is that there is no such thing as unfiltered experience. Experience is intelligible to us only because our understanding acts on it and orders it by way of concepts.

Here, we need to introduce some Kantian terminology. Kant is very much focused on mental faculties. The key ones are sensibility and understanding. Sensibility operates on what Kant calls intuitions (what Hume calls sense impressions). Understanding operates on concepts (what Hume calls ideas). Both are necessary, Kant tells us, for any sort of knowledge. "Thoughts without content are empty, intuitions without concepts are blind."[4] Concepts must be tied to intuitions if they are to have any genuine content. But intuitions must be brought under concepts if they are to be intelligible. The organization of intuitions into concepts is not a result of experience, as Hume thinks, but a necessary precondition of experience.

This is not to say that we don't make empirical judgments based, as Hume believes, on abstractions from sense impressions. But Kant believes that all such judgments have certain formal characteristics that correspond to the categories of our understanding. We impose these characteristics upon experience in making it an object of possible knowledge.

Because the characteristics are the necessary conditions of knowledge, we can know them *a priori*. Those characteristics, however, have a subjective rather than objective source. They are essential to our experience not because they inhere in the objects of our understanding, but because they are inseparable from our understanding itself. If experience *has to be* a certain way for it to be intelligible to us, then those critical features of experience are something that we impose upon it, rather than derive from it. "We can know *a priori* of things only what we ourselves put into them."[5] There is a necessary order and structure to experience, but only because our understanding plays an active role in shaping that experience so as to make it intelligible to us.

So what are these necessary features of experience? Kant argues that, for experience to be intelligible, for it to be an object of possible knowledge, there must be an "I" that has the experience and an "it" that is experienced. More specifically, experience requires an "I" persisting through time, and it requires objects external to our consciousness that exist in space and time and that follow regular rules of causation and reciprocal interaction. This seems like a big jump, so let's take it one step at a time.

We'll start with space and time. Leibniz views space and time as simply abstractions from relations between objects and events, with no independent reality. For Kant, space and time are not abstractions *from* our perceptions; they are the necessary *forms* of all our perceptions. We can imagine space empty of objects, but we cannot imagine the nonexistence of space. Similarly, we can imagine time empty of events, but we cannot imagine any perception or experience that would not take place in time. In this, Kant is closer to Newton, who views space and time as absolutes: space is a limitless, empty box in which the universe is placed; time is a cosmic clock ticking uniformly from and for all eternity. But Kant adds a dramatic twist to Newton. Newton's view, Kant thinks, involves the absurdity of two eternal and infinite self-subsistent nonentities which are there without anything real being there, merely to receive everything real into themselves. Things exist in space. Events occur in time. Space cannot itself be a thing nor time an event. Kant accordingly concludes that space and time are neither objects of perception nor empirical concepts derived from experience. They are necessary conditions of objects and events as they appear to us. They are necessary features of our own sensibility.

This will seem bizarre, and it is, but modern physics is in some ways closer to Kant than to either Newton or Leibniz on this question. Much of the reason that Kant feels that time and space are features of our own sensibility (pure forms of perception rather than either objects perceived or relations between objects perceived) is that, without time and space, experience itself would be impossible because we would not be able to form a conception of objects distinct from our experience of them, which means we would not be able to form a conception of a self persisting through time that has these experiences. This is an intricate and absolutely brilliant point that still has philosophers marveling to this day.

Hume takes the intelligibility of sense impressions (intuitions) for granted. He assumes we can construct ideas of objects, on the one hand, and the self, on the other, from that raw, unfiltered data. But what Kant shows, and shows convincingly, is that Hume has it backward. The unity of consciousness *"precedes* all experience, and . . . makes experience itself possible."[6] My experience consists of the flow through time of my intuitions and thoughts (which together Kant refers to as representations). But they must all be "my" representations to allow me to impose an order upon them that makes them intelligible. "It must be possible for the 'I think' to accompany all my representations. . . . All the manifold of intuition has, therefore, a necessary relation to the 'I think' in the same subject in which this manifold is found."[7] Kant calls this, rather obscurely, the "unity of pure apperception," but the idea is quite simple: there must be a subject persisting through time that has all these representations. I don't develop the idea of that subject by combining various representations. Rather, the subject makes any such combination possible, by persisting through time and unifying the various representations. "We are conscious *a priori* of the complete identity of the self in respect of all representations which can ever belong to our knowledge, as being a necessary condition of the possibility of all representations."[8]

But, and here is the critical step, to support this concept of "self" it is also necessary to have the concept of something independent of the self. I have no perception of the "I" that has these experiences. How, then, am I able to think this "I" that cannot be intuited? Kant's insight is that the self can be understood and comprehended only in contrast to the external objects of experience. Experience must allow for a distinction between what is experienced and my experience of it. My experience must be understood as only one path through an objective world that exists independent of my experience. I must have experience of *something* distinct from myself, and persisting through time, about which I can make objective judgments. This is necessary if the degree of self-consciousness (these are all *my* representations) required for consciousness (the bringing of intuitions under concepts) is possible.

Since impressions (upon which Hume constructs all knowledge) are unintelligible standing alone, they must be brought under concepts that are public and shared and, as such, objects of potential knowledge. Hume thinks that subjective intuition alone gives content to our concepts and hence that those concepts are themselves subjective. But, for Kant, objective concepts are a precondition of any sort of intelligible experience. As Kant explains, "inner experience is itself possible only mediately, and only through outer experience."[9] Hume's "appearances might, indeed, constitute intuition without thought, but not knowledge; and consequently would be for us as good as nothing."[10]

Thus, no intelligible experience is possible without such an objective ordering of objects in space and time. Continuity in consciousness—which is necessary to bring intuitions under concepts—presupposes continuity in the objects of perception. It follows, Kant thinks, that Hume is talking nonsense when he suggests that we have no knowledge of the existence of an external world separate from our intuitions. In fact, our intuitions are themselves intelligible only in the context of our knowledge of an external world. We have certain knowledge of the persistence of objects in space and through time because such knowledge is a precondition of intelligible experience. Moreover, Kant thinks, because space and time are necessary as the pure forms of perception, we can have necessary knowledge of certain axioms about space and time. We know that time is one-dimensional, that it flows in one direction (the arrow of time), and we know that different moments in time are successive, not simultaneous. We also know, thanks to Euclid, the geometry of space. Like all rationalist philosophers since Plato, Kant places critical reliance on geometry as a paradigm of *a priori* knowledge. But, for Kant, the *a priori* geometry of space is explicable only as a necessary feature of our own sensibility that we impose upon experience.

Kant also believes that the external world must obey certain physical laws to be an object of knowledge and that we can therefore know those laws *a priori* as well. Specifically, substance must persist through time with its "quantum in nature . . . neither increased nor diminished,"[11] and it must be subject to the laws of cause and effect and reciprocal interaction. Again, this is a big jump. But Kant's central argument seems sound. To develop the concept of an external world, the framework of space and time must provide a matrix for identifying objects as persisting through time. We need a stable backdrop against which change through time can be determined. That means that when objects change, they must do so according to laws that we can comprehend. We will not be able to reidentify and relocate objects through time if substance simply disappears, if events happen without causes, and if objects do not stand in relation to— and react with—one another in space. We require an abiding, law-governed, and unified world existing in space and time as the object of our experience if we are to have any intelligible experience at all. We require, in short, Newton's billiard-ball universe, in which, if you know the position and velocity of all particles in space at time A, you could predict with certainty their positions at any time B.

We will discuss some of the problems with this specifically Newtonian vision in our post-Einsteinian universe. But it is worth taking a moment first to marvel at Kant's accomplishment. He answers Hume's skepticism in convincing fashion and puts in its place an "empirical realism" that validates our standard conceptions of an external world persisting in space and time. By refocusing philosophy on the conditions of possible knowledge, he shows how certain *a priori* claims can be established and, in the process, change man from a mere spectator into an active participant in the process of imposing a conceptual order on the world. He provides an apparently solid foundation for the physical sciences. Yet, at the same time, he charts the outer bounds of such knowledge. And, in so doing, he lays the foundation for a devastating critique of speculative metaphysics, to which we will turn in the next section.

THE ILLUSIONS OF METAPHYSICS

The flip side of Kant's empirical realism is what he calls transcendental idealism. The choice of terms is unfortunate because it seems as if Kant is proposing an affirmative metaphysical doctrine. But the thrust of his transcendental idealism is supposed to be purely negative and cautionary. Beyond their empirical reach, our concepts have no meaningful application. We can know the conditions, and hence the limits, of possible experience, but we can never transcend those limits. That is, we cannot take our *a priori* concepts, abstract them from experience, and purport to form judgments about some ultimate, underlying reality. "The pure concepts of understanding can never admit of transcendental but always only of empirical employment."[12]

It follows, Kant thinks, that we can have no knowledge of things as they are in themselves. We know objects as they appear to us, as they are shaped by the combined forces of our sensibility and understanding. Those objects are empirically real. They are not just constructs out of our sense perceptions, because their objective reality is necessary to a determination of our own existence through time. In that sense, standard idealism is refuted. But we can still know them only as objects of possible experience. They must be given to us in perception. In that sense they are "transcendentally ideal." We have no idea what they are in themselves, apart from our experience of them. Indeed, the whole notion of an "object" has only empirical content and hence no legitimate application outside of experience. Thus, the contrasting notion of things-in-themselves, or "noumena," as Kant sometimes calls them, is a purely negative one. A noumenon is "not the concept of an object" but a "problem unavoidably bound up with the limitation of our sensibility."[13] This problem tells us that we have reached the limits of possible knowledge and ventured into a realm of pure speculation.

Such ventures are inevitable and even admirable, but nonetheless doomed to failure. "Human reason," Kant explains, "has this peculiar fate that . . . it is burdened by questions which . . . it is not able to ignore, but which, as transcending all its powers, it is also not able to answer."[14] We feel that we can break free of everyday experience and apply our reason to the reality that underlies experience. But pure reason, untethered from experience, unconditioned by intuition, leads only to fallacy and illusion.

> The light dove, cleaving the air in her free flight, and feeling its resistance, might imagine that its flight would be still easier in empty space. It was thus that Plato left the world of the senses, as setting too narrow limits to the understanding, and ventured out beyond it on the wings of the ideas, in the empty space of the pure understanding. He did not observe that with all his efforts he made no advance—meeting no resistance that might, as it were, serve as a support upon which he could take a stand, to which he could apply his powers, and so set his understanding in motion.[15]

Kant develops a typology of metaphysical illusions in a section called the "Transcendental Dialectic." The term *dialectic* is a direct reference to Plato, who contends that the true nature of the forms can be understood through a process of conceptual analysis abstracted from experience. Kant takes the *a priori* concepts derived from his analysis of possible experience and shows how, when applied beyond possible experience, they necessarily lead us astray. His true target in this section, however, is not Plato but Leibniz.

Accordingly, Kant begins with the Leibnizian notion of a monad, conceived of as a thinking substance that is absolutely simple in nature, that persists through time, and that would continue to exist even in the absence of a material world. You will recall that Kant considers the "unity of pure apperception" to be critical to any concept of experience. "I think" must be capable of accompanying all my representations. But this "I" that thinks is a purely formal concept, a requirement that a temporally extended series of experiences have sufficient unity and connectedness to constitute a single, subjective path through an objective world. The unity of apperception is not the perception of unity. The "I" is not itself a possible object of intuition.

Thus, the logical simplicity of my thought of my self does nothing to guarantee that this self is a simple substance (or indeed any kind of substance). The reason the thought is simple is that it is utterly abstract. It is given no content by means of intuition. It is merely the thought of that which thinks my thoughts. Similarly, the fact that this "I" is always the subject does not mean that the "I" is a persistent something. Nor is there any basis for concluding that this "I" would continue to exist in the absence of material things (including my own body). At the same time, there is no basis for concluding the opposite: that the "I" is not a simple substance, that it does not persist through time, and that it could not exist in the absence of material things. Kant rejects both dualism and materialism. Neither has any legitimate claim to knowledge. Both theories try to go beyond the legitimate application of our concepts to experience and hence, from the standpoint of reason, are purely speculative.

Kant draws a similar boundary for cosmological speculation. Here, he develops a series of "antinomies" in which he shows that, once we go beyond the limits of Newtonian physics, both a proposition and its apparent contradiction can lay an equal claim to validity, which is to say that neither is an object of knowledge. Kant focuses primarily on the world in space and time. He presents us with pairs of propositions such as: The world has a beginning in time; the world has no beginning in time. The world is limited with regard to space; the world has no limits in space. Everything in space and time is composed of irreducible simples; everything in space and time is subject to infinite dissection.

Kant develops "proofs" for each of these propositions that consist largely in showing that the alternative is incoherent. For example: The world cannot have a limit in time because then it is always legitimate to ask what happened before that beginning; yet the world cannot be unlimited in time because it would then have no beginning leading to the present moment. The proofs themselves are far from convincing, but that is really part of the powerful point that Kant is making. Beyond the limits of possible experience *in* space and time, our standard concepts begin to break down, and it is difficult to make coherent and persuasive claims to knowledge. We are engaged largely in speculation. The proper role for the philosopher, then, is to keep away from both positions (finite and infinite). That is not to say that scientists cannot continue to expand our knowledge of space and time and the ultimate constituents of matter (though Kant himself is thoroughly embedded in Newtonian physics as a complete blueprint for possible scientific knowledge). But insofar as they make progress, scientists do so by giving experiential content to the expanding application of our concepts. Most philosophers, by contrast, attempt to divorce our concepts from the experience that gives them meaning and to apply them outside the bounds of sense. Only illusion can result from such a practice.

Kant's third category in the typology of metaphysical illusion deals with the standard proofs for the existence of God. He exposes those proofs as thoroughly inadequate. God is not an object of theoretical knowledge, and yet Kant finds ample, alternative grounds for faith that depend precisely on the limitations of our knowledge. Before we turn to Kant's leap of faith, however, it is worth exploring a bit further how the platform from which Kant takes that leap—his peculiar combination of empirical realism and transcendental realism—survives in a post-Newtonian universe.

KANT AFTER EINSTEIN

Most thinkers of Kant's day believed that Isaac Newton had solved all the basic problems of physics. Details remained to be filled in, but the central laws of the universe had been revealed and were subject to mathematical formulation. All events are strictly determined within the absolute grid of space and time. The planets follow a fixed course in the heavens based on the effects of gravity. The smallest elements of matter obey similar laws in their interactions. The universe is, in effect, a huge, three-dimensional billiard table, and if we know the position, size, and velocity of every particle at a given point in time, we can calculate the exact position of all those particles both back in time and into the future. Things get a bit fuzzy at the margins (the exact nature of the basic constituents of matter; how gravity is able to act on objects at a distance; what it means for space and time to be infinite, empty receptacles), but the essential principles are in place and are not going to change.

Kant finds these principles both exhilarating and debilitating—exhilarating, because their very simplicity and elegance renders the universe comprehensible to man; debilitating, because the mechanistic nature of this universe leaves no room for human freedom or divine intervention. Kant's solution, as already noted, is to distinguish the sphere of science from the sphere of religion and morality. He does so by arguing that some of Newton's most fundamental principles—strict causation; the Euclidean grid of space; the mathematical sequence of time; the conservation of matter—do not apply to things as they are in themselves, but rather are imposed on the world of experience by the action of our sensibility and understanding.

Despite the implausibility of this position, we have seen that Kant has some compelling arguments in its favor. But what happens to those arguments in a world of quarks, general relativity, alternative geometries, quantum mechanics, and string theory? Should Kant simply be dismissed as a quaint artifact of solely historical interest? No. Kant actually adapts to modern science in very interesting ways.

Take general relativity. Einstein showed, contra Newton, that space and time are not absolutes. They depend on the viewer's frame of reference, and measurements of time can be radically different for different observers, even though space-time—in which time is conceived as a fourth dimension inextricably connected with the three dimensions of space—is invariable from every frame of reference. If anything, general relativity seems to fit more closely with the Kantian view that space and time are forms of our sensibility that we impose upon experience. In general relativity, space and time do not have existences independent of each other. They are not empty containers for objects and events, but form a fabric of space-time with its own shaping force imposed upon the objects of perception.

Alternative geometries can also be accommodated by Kant. Kant thinks Euclidean geometry is the *a priori* geometry of space. But non-Euclidean geometries, in which lines with a common perpendicular can converge or run away from one another, had not yet been discovered. The elliptic geometry of general relativity (in which space-time is bent by the gravitational force of matter) can still fit, albeit less comfortably, within Kant's model of *a priori* knowledge.

But Kant seems wholly out of place in the subatomic world of quantum mechanics, in which the laws of causation (which Kant thinks are an *a priori* feature of experiential reality) break down altogether. Einstein himself launched quantum mechanics with his discovery that light simultaneously behaves like particles and waves. This insight led in turn to the realization that the behavior of subatomic "particles" is not strictly deterministic. Quantum reality obeys statistical laws, but not laws of rigid cause and effect. Werner Heisenberg's "uncertainty principle" established that it is not possible to measure both the position and the velocity of a particle at the same time, since the very act of measuring one changes the other. But this "uncertainty" is not just a limitation on our ability to know both position and velocity; it is a fundamental feature of quantum reality, in which it makes no sense to talk about a particle having an actual position until it is measured.

Einstein rejected the implications of quantum mechanics, infamously opining that "God does not play dice with the universe."[16] He accordingly spent the last decades of his life searching for a "unified theory" that would reconcile general relativity (which works on vast scales), classical mechanics (which works very well on our everyday, human scale), and quantum mechanics (which works on a very small scale) in a single overarching system of equations that did not depend on probability and chance. He did not succeed, and in fact Einstein (the rebel par excellence who did more than anyone else to break with classical physics and usher in the modern age) was increasingly viewed by the Young Turks as a reactionary conservative.

But Einstein may turn out to be right after all, and so, in a curious way, may Kant. Certainly, the modern proponents of superstring theory believe that it is possible to unify all the known natural forces in a single set of equations by replacing point-like particles with one-dimensional, extended objects known as strings. In the process, however, they have to posit (because, otherwise, their equations don't work) at least nine dimensions of space and one of time. Moreover, space turns out not to be empty after all, but is itself teeming with quantum irregularity (think of it as random wrinkles), which led to the formation of the stars, planets, and galaxies. The arrow of time turns out to be simply a function of gradually increasing entropy, as the universe steadily degenerates from the highly ordered state at its inception. And in string theory, both space and time turn out not to be continuous, but rather to have a discontinuous, atomic structure.

More fundamentally, as Brian Greene, a leading string theorist, explains, string theory works on a scale at which the usual concepts of space and time may simply not apply. Space and time may only be "approximate, collective conceptions."[17] The unified space-time of experience may be an "illusion" that "emerges from the collective behavior of strings."[18] This sounds very much like Kant's assertion that space and time are mere appearances that we impose upon experience. They are not fundamental features of reality, even though they have an "all-embracing positio[n] in experiential reality."[19] As Greene puts it, space and time are "silent, ever-present markers delineating the outermost boundaries of human experience."[20]

It is tempting, then, to view string theory as consistent with Kant's fundamental distinction between appearances (as shaped by our sensibility and understanding) and things-in-themselves (an underlying, unknowable reality). But that would be a mistake. String theory certainly runs counter to our everyday experience, as does quantum mechanics and even general relativity. But insofar as those theories are legitimate (and the legitimacy of string theory is still very much in dispute), they have an experimental and hence experiential content that keeps them on the "appearances" side of Kant's great divide. String theory doesn't uncover what Kant called "things-in-themselves" any more than classical mechanics did.

So when Brian Greene notes that "the overarching lesson that has emerged from scientific inquiry over the last century is that human experience is often a misleading guide to the true nature of reality,"[21] he is not making a Kantian point about phenomena and noumena. He is making a scientific point, which is that our intuitive sense of space and time and even of causation turns out not to be very accurate when investigating very small or very large events. That is a point that Kant could embrace, though not without significant adjustments to his *a priori* categories. Kant himself, as a fervent admirer of the Enlightenment, would never purport to impose limits on scientific inquiry. He simply supposes that there are fixed boundaries to possible human knowledge created by our own sensibility and understanding. What modern science indicates is that those boundaries may be much more fluid than he imagines. But Kant's essential point remains: through our concepts and the form of our judgments, we impose a certain order on the world, and when we push those concepts beyond their application in experience, they begin to break down. Not even string theory can give a coherent explanation of a time before time or of a condition before the universe was born.

Kant believed that moral and religious discourse is fundamentally different from our everyday talk about objects and events in space and time. Even if all scientific questions could be answered, the question of the meaning and purpose of life would remain. Kant, accordingly, asks "What ought I to do?" and "What may I hope?" and he finds their answers to be intimately related.[22]

GOD, FREEDOM, AND IMMORTALITY

In a strictly Newtonian universe, there is little room for God (except, perhaps, as the original winder of the cosmic clock) and no room at all for personal freedom. All actions and events are strictly determined in space and time. Kant, however, by limiting the sphere in which scientific knowledge has sway, by showing that we ourselves impose these mechanistic categories on experience, creates an opening for belief.

This recognition of the limits of pure reason, Kant thinks, has "the inestimable benefit that all objections to morality and religion will be for ever silenced, and this in Socratic fashion, namely, by the clearest proof of the ignorance of the objectors."[23] But, although a proof of ignorance may silence objectors, it is hardly an auspicious beginning for believers. Kant tries to provide such a beginning in his distinction between pure and practical reason.

Pure reason may deduce *a priori* judgments about experience; but when it attempts to extend those judgments beyond all possible experience, it reaches a dead end. That includes judgments about God, conceived of as a perfect being and the author of all that exists. In the "Transcendental Dialectic," Kant catalogs and methodically dismantles the traditional arguments for the existence of God, which he says are of three, and only three, types. We already saw most of these arguments rejected by Hume, but they are more fully and systematically refuted by Kant.

Ontological arguments contend that God must exist because the very concept of God is that of a perfect being, and God could not be perfect unless he existed. What Kant shows is that existence adds nothing to the concept of an object. A concept is defined by its predicates, but existence is not itself a predicate. We make no addition to the concept of an object when we further declare that the object exists. The concept is complete, and an object fitting that concept either exists or does not; just as existence does not change the concept, so, too, nonexistence does not reduce its supposed perfection. Put another way, there is no contradiction in denying the existence of a perfect being. "If its existence is rejected, we reject the thing itself with all its predicates; and no question of contradiction can then arise."[24] We must go outside the concept to ascribe existence to the object. "When . . . I think a being as the supreme reality, without any defect, the question still remains whether it exists or not."[25] Thus, the mere concept of God is no guarantee of the existence of God.

Cosmological arguments claim that there must be a noncontingent ground upon which all contingent being depends. If anything contingent exists, there must be a being whose existence is necessary. The same argument can be put in terms of causation: insofar as there are causal connections in the world, there must be a first cause that started the sequence. Something must have set the cosmic clock in motion. Kant's response to this line of argument parallels his response to the antinomies, discussed above. Concepts such as necessity and causality have meaning and criteria only for their application in the sensible world. The cosmological argument attempts to employ these concepts beyond the bounds of their legitimacy. "The concept of necessity is only to be found in our reason, as a formal condition of thought; it does not allow of being hypostatized as a material condition of existence."[26] Since we can have no experience of the unconditioned, we have no justification for concluding that a contingent series terminates in something that is absolutely necessary.

Arguments from design, or what Kant calls physical-theological proofs, attempt to argue by analogy to human artifacts that the intricate perfection of the universe could not possibly have arisen simply by accident but requires a divine clockmaker.

> This world presents to us so immeasurable a stage of variety, order, purposiveness, and beauty, as displayed alike in its infinite extent and in the unlimited divisibility of its parts, that even with such knowledge as our weak understanding can acquire of it, we are brought face to face with so many marvels immeasurably great, that all speech loses its force, all numbers their power to measure, our thoughts themselves all definiteness, and that our judgment of the whole resolves itself into an amazement which is speechless, and only the more eloquent on that account.[27]

Notwithstanding the emotional appeal of the argument, which Kant says "always deserves to be mentioned with respect," Kant finds it inadequate as a proof.[28] We cannot break outside "the solid ground of nature and experience."[29] We must instead rely on scientific explanations within the realm of experience to account for the order and diversity of nature. Everything in experience is conditioned; thus, nothing gives us knowledge of the unconditioned. Knowledge concerning the ultimate design of nature and the things-in-themselves that underlie our experience is denied to us.

In short, none of the traditional arguments for the existence of God can compel assent. So far, Kant is in tune with Hume. But Kant finds the argument from design a powerful inducement to belief because it satisfies his sense of wonder at the universe. An even more powerful inducement is to be found in the "moral law within." Here, Kant focuses not on "what exists" but on "what ought to exist" as the guarantee of the highest possible good. Once we understand the moral law, Kant thinks, we must postulate "a moral being, as the original source of creation," and the highest fulfillment of that law.[30] It is fruitless to employ reason in theology in any purely speculative manner. So Kant proposes a theology based not on ideas but on ideals, ideals which have "practical power (as regulative principles), and form the basis of the possible perfection of certain actions."[31]

Kant begins with the question of how morality is even possible in a world of strict cause and effect. If all my actions are determined, then I have no freedom of choice. In that case, no moral judgment could attach to my actions because I could not do otherwise. Yet, Kant thinks, we all have direct knowledge of our own freedom to act in accordance with the moral law. "Ought," he famously remarks, "implies can." Moral laws are necessarily laws of freedom, laws that we can choose to follow in accordance with our sense of duty. Insofar as we believe in the moral law, therefore, we believe in the possibility of freedom. "We do not understand [this freedom], but we know it as the condition of the moral law which we do know."[32]

The central focus of Kant's ethical theory, therefore, is on the good will—that is, the will that acts in accordance with the moral law and for the sake of the moral law alone. "To have moral worth an action must be done from duty."[33] There can be no admixture of the personal. Compassion, affection, a desire to help—none of these feelings are relevant to the morality of the action. Nor is the consequence of one's action: whether it actually helps anyone or adds to the sum total of the world's happiness. The only thing that matters is the good will, by which Kant means that the action is done solely out of a desire to conform to one's moral obligation. This is a very austere ethics; and it is diametrically opposed to Hume's morality based on human inclination. We must be "beneficent not from inclination but from duty."[34] We must not only conform our actions to the moral law, but we must act solely "for the sake of the law."[35]

This very austerity is critical to Kant's notion of moral freedom. By the "moral law," Kant means a law that is binding on all rational beings solely as rational beings. The morality of an action cannot depend on the unique perspective of the actor: his wants, desires, needs. It depends, rather, on the objective point of view of a free, moral agent who transcends his personal circumstances and acts solely according to the mandate of reason. "Only a rational being has the capacity of acting according to the conception of laws, i.e., according to principles."[36]

But how can reason alone determine the proper course of action? Here, Kant's genius and originality are again on full display. Kant believes we can determine the formal (*a priori*) conditions of morality that are binding on all rational beings, in much the same way that we were able to determine the formal (*a priori*) conditions of experience. But whereas the latter resulted in *a priori* judgments as to the conditions for any possible experience, the former results in *a priori* imperatives that any moral action must satisfy.

Kant draws a fundamental distinction between hypothetical and categorical imperatives. A hypothetical imperative has an "if/then" quality: if I want to have friends, I should be kind and loyal. The action is good to some purpose in promoting my happiness. Hypothetical imperatives are practical maxims, guides to the good life. A categorical imperative, by contrast, is absolute: I must act in accordance with the moral law regardless of my own wants and desires. "The categorical imperative would be one which presented an action as of itself objectively necessary, without regard to any other end."[37]

Kant formulates the categorical imperative in various ways. The most famous is that you must "act only according to that maxim by which you can at the same time will that it should become a universal law."[38] In other words, you must be able to say of any given action that every moral being in comparable circumstances should act in the same way. If you lie to evade an inconvenient obligation, then you must accept that others should lie in similar circumstances. If, by contrast, you recognize that evading obligations by lying should not be a universal law—since our trust in one another would break down—then you recognize that you should not do so either. You cannot make a personal exception: by taking any given action, you in effect bring it under a maxim that commands the action for all persons in similar circumstances.

This imperative is only a "formal" condition for any valid moral law, and yet it has tremendous practical force. Indeed, it comes very close to the Christian precept to treat others as you would have them treat you. A related formulation offered by Kant is that you must "act so that you treat humanity, whether in your own person or in that of another, always as an end and never as a means only."[39] In other words, every individual has an intrinsic worth and value that precludes simply using that person for your own ends. The key to morality is to recognize the inherent moral worth of others as rational beings and to treat them as equal in value to oneself. "Every rational being exists as an end in himself and not merely as a means to be arbitrarily used by this or that will."[40]

I will not discuss Kant's ethical theory in any detail here, though I will note that philosophers are still strongly influenced by his account of the formal conditions that any ethics must satisfy. The more important point for our purpose is that, by making the moral law a command binding on all rational beings, Kant can divorce moral action from all the normal determinants of behavior (desires, needs, ambitions). Accordingly, our apprehension of the moral law is itself an indication of our possible freedom. Here, Kant comes very close to Spinoza. "Independence from the determining causes of the world of sense (an independence which reason must always ascribe to itself) is freedom."[41] Only when our actions are determined by the moral law—by the dictates of practical reason rather than the dictates of self-interest—do we escape the tyranny of the laws of nature. "A free will and a will under moral laws are identical."[42] Or, as Spinoza put it, "to every action to which we are determined from an affect which is a passion, we can be determined by reason, without that affect."[43]

This idea—that freedom lies not in doing what you want to do but in doing what is absolutely required—is paradoxical in at least two respects. First, as Hume noted, we generally conceive of freedom as an absence of external constraints. We are free precisely when we are able to realize our own desires, not when we are commanded to set aside those desires. Kant, again like Spinoza, redefines freedom as an ability to transcend our parochial concerns and choose to act solely from a sense of duty. But that leads to the second and more fundamental paradox. Kant must acknowledge that the possibility of escaping the tyranny of the laws of nature, that is, of acting outside the chain of Newtonian causation, is not strictly intelligible to us.[44] Freedom, as conceived here, is a transcendent idea. And Kant spent most of his great work explaining why the application of concepts beyond the empirical world leads only to metaphysical illusion.

This is Kant's great leap beyond the bounds of sense. The dictates of practical reason (what we ought to do) lead us to recognize a transcendental freedom that we experience but cannot fully comprehend. Speculative reason can never resolve this paradox; practical reason can, but only in action according to the moral law. Through our apprehension of the moral law, we *know* the possibility of freedom. We must accordingly view ourselves from two different standpoints: as belonging to the world of the senses subject to the laws of nature; and as belonging to a world of freedom subject to moral laws founded on practical reason.

Through our freedom, then, through our ability to act in accordance with the moral law, we have a window into the "thing-in-itself" that underlies the world. I exist not only as a being in the world bound by the laws of nature but also as an autonomous will bound by the moral law, the law of practical reason. I am simultaneously determined and free. I am one thing conceived in contrasting ways. The precise conclusion that we could not reach using pure reason alone (that the "I think" which can accompany all my representations is a "thinking substance" that somehow stands outside the constraints of space and time) is the conclusion that practical reason demands. That "self" is a member of a moral realm to which the categories of the understanding do not apply.

So what exactly does that mean, and how does it relate to the existence of God? It would be easy enough to recast Kant's insight in Humean terms. We could simply note that scientific discourse in terms of cause and effect and moral discourse in terms of reasons for action are each autonomous, independent of each other, and of equal validity. There is no contradiction between simultaneously discussing a given event in scientific terms (including the firing of neurons in the brain) and in moral terms (including action against self-interest in accordance with one's duty). Neither form of discourse has priority over the other; each has its own grammar and its own criteria for its application.

In this instance, however, such recasting would miss the fundamental point. Hume wants to demystify our ordinary language of moral obligation. Kant wants us to focus on the veritable miracle of a moral law that is binding on all rational beings and that demands that we transcend our individual self-interest. Such a law can exist—it can have a legitimate claim on us—only if it takes us outside the world of surface appearances in space and time. We each feel the claim of this moral law, Kant believes. It is a fundamental fact of our existence. Through this moral law, therefore, we are connected to a transcendental realm, even if we cannot comprehend it with reason alone.

Kant grounds his belief in God and immortality upon this connection. Speculative reason could not prove either the existence of God or the immortality of the soul. But neither could it disprove them. Hence, we are free to believe, as even Hume admits. For Kant, our apprehension of the moral law gives us the reason to believe. Indeed, it makes such belief "morally necessary"[45] because our concept of the highest good can be realized only if God exists and the soul is immortal. If the highest good cannot be realized, "then the moral law which commands that it be furthered must be fantastic, directed to empty imaginary ends, and consequently inherently false."[46] Yet we know, to a moral certainty, that the moral law is valid and binding upon us.

Kant here lapses into two rather unconvincing subarguments. First, the ideal of the moral law is that of a pure will that acts solely from duty in accordance with the dictates of practical reason. It is morally required that we strive for this state of holiness, but it is impossible to realize such perfection in the empirical world. Accordingly, we must postulate immortality to allow for the "endless progress"[47] of the soul and the ultimate realization of the highest good. Second, the good will acts solely from duty, not from a desire for happiness, and there is no guarantee in the empirical world that morality will bear any relationship to happiness. Yet there is "a natural and necessary connection between the consciousness of morality and the expectation of proportionate happiness as its consequence."[48] Accordingly, we must postulate "a cause adequate to this effect"[49]—that is, a supreme, all-powerful, and beneficent creator.

As I said, neither of these arguments, baldly stated, seems very compelling. But the central thrust of Kant's moral theology is compelling indeed. In a sense, God underwrites our freedom as moral agents. In a deeper sense, morality underwrites our belief in God. We must believe we are free in order to act in accordance with the moral law. The possibility of such freedom is not fully comprehensible, but the reality of that freedom is known to us directly and through it our existence as autonomous moral agents standing outside the realm of mere appearances. We have a window on ultimate reality conceived of as a realm in which the moral law holds sway, however imperfectly realized it may be on this earth. This, in turn, leads to a belief in a moral being as the author of the world and in the possibility of a Kingdom of Ends in which morality reaches its perfection. So conceived, God is the guarantor of the highest possible good and bids us to live a life that transcends our private, merely selfish concerns. God is an object of both veneration and hope, and our highest aspiration is to live in "harmony with this will."[50]

RELIGION WITHIN THE LIMITS OF REASON ALONE

For Kant, we do not derive our morality from our belief in God; rather, it is our direct encounter with the moral law that leads to our belief in God. It follows, Kant thinks, that our only religious duty is "good life-conduct" and that "anything which the human being supposes that he can do to become well-pleasing to God is mere religious delusion and counterfeit service of God."[51] In his book *Religion within the Limits of Reason Alone*, Kant accordingly rejects the hierarchy of the established church, the traditional rituals of worship, the superstitious belief in miracles and the efficacy of prayer, the primacy of Christianity, and the divinity of the Bible. Once again, Kant is on the same page with Spinoza and Hume.

This book—like Spinoza's *Ethics* and Hume's *Dialogues Concerning Natural Religion*—shows Kant's courage in following the path of reason as he conceived it. After it was published, Kant was forbidden to write further on religious topics by Frederick Wilhelm II and did not do so again until the death of that monarch. Kant was fortunate not to have been stripped of his academic position and his pension; his widespread fame protected him from that fate, but he certainly tempted it with an attack on the "sorcery" and "fetishism" of standard religious worship that would seem more appropriate to a Voltaire than to the quiet scholar of Königsberg.

The thrust of Kant's argument is that religion, properly understood, can require no duties other than the duties of morality that we owe to our fellow man. He is accordingly dismissive of all doctrine that is not focused on promoting the moral law. A doctrine such as the Trinity, he explains, "has no practical relevance at all."[52] It is thoroughly unintelligible to us, and whether there are said to be three or ten persons in God can make no difference to our rules of conduct. The same is true for any scriptural teachings that we can know only by "revealed faith." Such faith "is not in itself *meritorious*, and lack of such faith, and even doubt opposed to it, in itself involves no *guilt*. The only thing that matters in religion is *deeds*."[53] Thus, the Bible (or the Koran or any other avowedly religious text) can be considered a vehicle of religion only insofar as it promotes the moral precepts of reason by propagating them publicly and strengthening them within men's souls.

Kant strongly objects to the hierarchy of priests, with their focus on church rituals and doctrinal revelations. Instead of helping the members of the church realize their moral obligations, they become "the exclusive chosen interpreters of a holy Scripture."[54] As a result, rules of faith and observances, rather than principles of morality, make up the essence of the church. Kant calls this "fetish-service," an attempt to win divine favor through the equivalent of bribery and flattery. It is a delusion to think that through religious acts of cult—such as the profession of statutory articles of faith or the observance of ecclesiastical practices—we can achieve anything in the way of justification before God. Such actions are morally indifferent; they can be performed by the wickedest human being just as well as by the best. Attempts to conjure up God's support through formulas of invocation, through professions of a servile faith, through ecclesiastical observances, and the like is a kind of "sorcery" that "borders very closely on paganism."[55]

Kant also wholly rejects the influence of spiritual beings or divine forces or miracles as inimical to scientific inquiry and the free exercise of reason. To want to perceive heavenly influences in daily life is a kind of "madness" and "a self-deception detrimental to religion."[56] He accordingly rejects prayer as well, whether conceived as "an inner ritual service of God" or as "the declaring of a wish" to God.[57] It is "an absurd and at the same time impudent delusion to have a try at whether, through the insistent intrusiveness of our prayer, God might not be diverted from the plan of his wisdom (to our present advantage)."[58]

What Kant advocates is a pure and natural religion—the one sought in vain by Hume—governed by one *universal* rule: do your duty from no other incentive except the unmediated appreciation of duty itself. In other words, love God (the embodiment of all duties) above all else. Kant contends that this universal religion of reason is the supreme and indispensable condition of each and every religious faith. "In what really deserves to be called religion, there can be no division into sects (for since religion is one, universal and necessary, it cannot vary)."[59] The one and true religion contains nothing but moral laws that are unconditionally binding on each of us.

Kant does not reject churches and sects altogether. They can serve a useful function in promoting and propagating the good and in awakening and sustaining our attention to the true service of God. Nor does he wish to disparage the uses and ordinances of one sect as contrasted with another. But he distinguishes sharply between the statutory teachings that compose *ecclesiastical* faith and the moral teachings that compose pure *religious* faith. The former are all "accidentality and arbitrariness."[60] The latter are universal and necessary. A division into sects can never occur in matters of pure religious belief. It is always to be found where ecclesiastical faith is mistakenly treated as essential rather than merely contingent.

In Kant's view, a pure religious faith is within the grasp of every human being. The concept of God arises naturally from reflection upon the sacred nature of morality. Kant echoes Plato's *Meno*—in which the slave boy was shown to have the truths of geometry innately accessible to him—when he argues that "this faith can be elicited from every human being, upon questioning, in its entirety, without any of it having ever been taught to him."[61]

What, then, does it mean for Kant to believe in God? Everything and nothing. Nothing, because such belief arises from our moral duties; it does not give rise to those duties or alter them in any respect. Everything, because then hope can arise that we will someday be rewarded for adhering to those duties. Nothing, because the commands of practical reason would be exactly the same even if God did not exist. Everything, because immortality and the Kingdom of Ends are thereby guaranteed. Nothing, because God is not an active force in the world; we can have no intuition of God (and could not trust it as other than a delusion if we did). Everything, because life and the empirical world are thereby given a purpose.

This last point became particularly important to Kant in his later years. He grew increasingly dissatisfied with Newton's mechanical view of the universe. In his *Critique of Judgement*, written when he was sixty-six, Kant is inclined to view the world in teleological terms—that is, in terms of purposes and goals. He famously remarks that there could never be a Newton to explain a single blade of grass.[62] Life is not reducible to the blind interaction of mechanical forces. Organisms are self-generating and self-organizing. The whole is not explained by the parts; rather, the parts are explained in terms of their function within the whole. Kant suggests that it is helpful to view all of nature *as if* it were itself an organism in which each individual object and creature plays a role in the overall design, somewhat the way the parts of a single animal (heart, lungs, legs) play a role and have a function in the life of that animal. Viewing nature in teleological terms, Kant argues, is a useful "regulative idea," because it assumes purposiveness and order. Ever the careful empiricist, Kant does not suggest that we have any theoretical basis for concluding that all of nature is like an organism in this sense. Nor does he suggest that God actively intervenes in the world of our experience in any direct manner. But he argues that we should nonetheless presuppose something intelligible in our scientific inquiries that allows us to comprehend nature and bring it under laws.

Kant thus circles back to the argument from design, which he has always found compelling if not theoretically conclusive. In the process, he goes some way toward bridging his own divide between appearances and things-in-themselves. For if all of nature is seen as the product of a divine understanding, the distinction between the natural and the divine begins to disappear, as in Spinoza. So, too, does the paradox of an empirically determined being acting freely in accordance with the moral law.

In this regard, Kant once again anticipates Einstein. Like Kant, Einstein places morality at the center of all human endeavors. "Our inner balance and even our existence depend on it. Only morality in our actions can give beauty and dignity to life."[63] Like Kant, Einstein also traces the natural progression from scientific ideas to religious ones. He is dismissive of the idea of "a personal God" actively intervening in human affairs or influencing the course of events in response to prayers and ritual observances. Yet he feels that, behind all the discernible laws and connections of nature, "there remains something subtle, intangible and inexplicable," something "whose beauty and sublimity reaches us only indirectly."[64] Einstein feels "veneration for this force beyond anything that we can comprehend" and "utter humility toward the unattainable secrets of the harmony of the cosmos."[65] This, he declares, "is my religion."[66] It is Kant's religion as well.

Immanuel Kant died on February 12, 1804. Inscribed on his tombstone, which can still be seen, adjacent to the reconstructed cathedral in Kaliningrad, are words that summarize the great preoccupations of his life and work: "Two things fill the mind with ever new and increasing admiration and awe, the oftener and more steadily we reflect on them: the starry heavens above me and the moral law within me."[67]

ACKNOWLEDGMENTS

I have not tried to document every source for the ideas in this book. But my extensive debt to generations of Enlightenment scholars and translators will be obvious to those in the field. I have tried to list the books and articles on which I most relied, as well as those from which general readers would most benefit, in "Suggestions for Further Reading." I also cite there, and in the notes, the many excellent translations from which the quotations in the text are derived.

Darrin Leverette once again worked through the entire manuscript, checking the citations, the facts, and the prose, and saving me from numerous errors. His intelligence, attention to detail, ability to track down obscure sources, and sensitivity to the nuances of language have been indispensable. So, too, was the work of Susan Cohen, who carefully and thoughtfully read each chapter. My longtime assistant, Marilyn Williams, kept me and the entire project on schedule and put the manuscript in its final form. I would also like to thank Veronica Jurgena for her meticulous editing, which improved the prose and sharpened the ideas.

I have dedicated this book to my wife, Dr. Lucy Pugh, as I did in the first book that I wrote. The year 2020 was difficult in many respects. But she, along with our children—Baird, Cole, and Camille—brought joy on a daily basis.

NOTES

INTRODUCTION

1. Peter Gay, *The Enlightenment: The Science of Freedom* (1969; repr., New York: W.W. Norton, 1977), 11–12.

2. Samuel Johnson, *The History of Rasselas, Prince of Abyssinia*, in *Selected Poetry and Prose*, ed. Frank Brady and W. K. Wimsatt (Berkeley: University of California Press, 1977), 93.

3. Immanuel Kant, "An Answer to the Question: What Is Enlightenment?" in *Practical Philosophy*, ed. and trans. Mary J. Gregor (Cambridge: Cambridge University Press, 1996), 17.

4. Ibid., 18.

5. See Steven Pinker, *Enlightenment Now: The Case for Reason, Science, Humanism, and Progress* (New York: Penguin Books, 2019).

6. Quoted in John Gribbin, *The Scientists: A History of Science Told Through the Lives of Its Greatest Inventors* (New York: Random House, 2003), 164.

7. Francis Bacon, *The New Organon*, ed. Lisa Jardine and Michael Silverthorne (Cambridge: Cambridge University Press, 2000), 2.52, 219–20.

8. René Descartes, *Discourse on the Method*, in *Selected Philosophical Writings*, trans. John Cottingham, Robert Stoothoff, and Dugald Murdoch (Cambridge: Cambridge University Press, 1988), 47.

9. Alexander Pope, "An Essay on Man," epistle 2, ll. 1–2, in *The Major Works*, ed. Pat Rogers (Oxford: Oxford University Press, 2006), 281.

10. Voltaire, *Les Lois de Minos: Tragédie en cinq actes* (n.p.: Ligaran, 2015), 3.5; my translation.

11. Montesquieu, *The Spirit of the Laws*, ed. and trans. Anne M. Cohler, Basia C. Miller, and Harold S. Stone (Cambridge: Cambridge University Press, 1989), 19.4, 310.

12. James Boswell, *The Life of Samuel Johnson* (New York: Heritage, 1963), 3:200.

13. Quoted in Dennis C. Rasmussen, *The Infidel and the Professor* (Princeton, NJ: Princeton University Press, 2017), 183.

14. David Hume, "Of Interest," in *Essays: Moral, Political, and Literary*, ed. Eugene F. Miller, rev. ed. (Carmel, IN: Liberty Fund, 1987), 300.

15. Quoted in Gay, *Enlightenment*, 50.

16. Adam Smith, *The Wealth of Nations*, ed. Edwin Cannan (New York: Modern Library, 2000), 4.5, 581.

17. David Hume, *An Inquiry Concerning the Principles of Morals*, ed. Charles W. Hendel (Indianapolis, IN: Bobbs-Merrill, 1957), 92.

18. Peter Pesic, *Polyphonic Minds: Music of the Hemispheres* (Cambridge, MA: MIT Press, 2017), 179.

19. Thomas Hobbes, *Leviathan* (Indianapolis, IN: Bobbs-Merrill, 1958), 107.

I. DESCARTES AND THE MECHANICAL UNIVERSE

1. Stephen Gaukroger, *Descartes: An Intellectual Biography* (New York: Oxford University Press, 1997), 4.

2. See Jonathan I. Israel, *Radical Enlightenment: Philosophy and the Making of Modernity 1650–1750* (New York: Oxford University Press, 2001), 11.

3. Gaukroger, *Descartes*, 23.

4. René Descartes, *Discourse on the Method*, in *Selected Philosophical Writings*, trans. John Cottingham, Robert Stoothoff, and Dugald Murdoch (Cambridge: Cambridge University Press, 1988), 22.

5. Ibid.

6. Ibid.

7. Ibid.

8. Ibid., 24.

9. Ibid.

10. Ibid., 22.

11. Ibid., 23.

12. Ibid.

13. Ibid., 24.

14. René Descartes, *Rules for the Direction of our Native Intelligence*, Rule 1, in *Selected Philosophical Writings*, 1.

15. Josh. 10:12–13 (King James Version).

16. Desmond M. Clarke, *Descartes: A Biography* (Cambridge: Cambridge University Press, 2012), 3.

17. Quoted in Gaukroger, *Descartes*, 290–91.

18. Descartes, *Discourse*, in *Selected Philosophical Writings*, 47.

19. René Descartes, *Meditations on First Philosophy*, in *Selected Philosophical Writings*, 76.

20. Descartes, *Discourse*, in *Selected Philosophical Writings*, 29 (emphasis added).

21. Ibid., 36.

22. Descartes, *Meditations*, in *Selected Philosophical Writings*, 77.

23. Marcel Proust, *Swann's Way: In Search of Lost Time*, trans. C. K. Scott Moncrieff and Terence Kilmartin, rev. D. J. Enright, vol. 1 (New York: Modern Library, 2003), 1.

24. Descartes, *Meditations*, in *Selected Philosophical Writings*, 79.

25. Ibid., 80.

26. Descartes, *Discourse*, in *Selected Philosophical Writings*, 36.

27. Ibid.

28. Ibid., 37.

29. Descartes, *Meditations*, in *Selected Philosophical Writings*, 99.

30. Descartes, *Discourse*, in *Selected Philosophical Writings*, 40.

31. See Walter Isaacson, *Einstein: His Life and Universe* (New York: Simon & Schuster, 2007), 462.

32. Descartes, *Meditations*, in *Selected Philosophical Writings*, 107.

33. Ibid., 97.

34. Quoted in Hanoch Ben-Yami, *Descartes' Philosophical Revolution: A Reassessment* (New York: Palgrave Macmillan, 2015), 164. See Gaukroger, *Descartes*, 362.

35. Descartes, *Discourse*, in *Selected Philosophical Writings*, 40.

36. Descartes, *Meditations*, in *Selected Philosophical Writings*, 84.

37. Ibid., 86.

38. Ibid., 92.

39. Bernard Williams, *Descartes: The Project of Pure Enquiry* (Harmondsworth, UK: Penguin Books, 1978), 237.

40. Ben-Yami, *Descartes' Philosophical Revolution*, 13.

41. Descartes, *Meditations*, in *Selected Philosophical Writings*, 110.

42. Quoted in Ben-Yami, *Descartes' Philosophical Revolution*, 25.

43. Gaukroger, *Descartes*, 242.

44. Ibid., 227.

45. Quoted in Ben-Yami, *Descartes' Philosophical Revolution*, 174.

46. Gaukroger, *Descartes*, 255.

47. See Gilbert Ryle, *The Concept of Mind* (New York: Barnes & Noble Books, 1969), 15–16.

48. See Ben-Yami, *Descartes' Philosophical Revolution*, 86–87.

49. René Descartes, *Treatise on Man*, in *The Philosophical Writings of Descartes*, trans. John Cottingham, Robert Stoothoff, and Dugald Murdoch, vol. 1 (Cambridge: Cambridge University Press, 1985), 99.

50. René Descartes, *The Passions of the Soul*, in *Selected Philosophical Writings*, 220–22.

51. Ben-Yami, *Descartes' Philosophical Revolution*, 107.

52. Descartes, *Discourse*, in *Selected Philosophical Writings*, 44.

53. Ben-Yami, *Descartes' Philosophical Revolution*, 87.

54. Descartes, *Meditations*, in *Selected Philosophical Writings*, 82 (footnote omitted).

55. Ibid.

56. Ibid., 81.

57. Descartes, *Discourse*, in *Selected Philosophical Writings*, 36.

58. Ibid.

59. Descartes, *Meditations*, in *Selected Philosophical Writings*, 83.

60. Williams, *Descartes*, 284.

61. Descartes, *Discourse*, in *Selected Philosophical Writings*, 45.

62. The pineal gland is a small gland shaped like a pinecone in the back of the brain. According to modern science, it secretes melatonin and modulates sleep patterns. Almost all vertebrates have a pineal gland, so it is not unique to humans.

63. Descartes, *Meditations*, in *Selected Philosophical Writings*, 116 (footnote omitted).

64. Ibid., 115 (footnote omitted).

65. Descartes, *Discourse*, in *Selected Philosophical Writings*, 36.

66. Homer, *The Odyssey*, trans. Robert Fagles (New York: Viking Penguin, 1996), 11.247–53.

67. Descartes, *Passions of the Soul*, in *Selected Philosophical Writings*, 233.

2. JOHN MILTON AND THE PARADISE WITHIN

1. John Milton, *Paradise Lost*, ed. Gordon Teskey (New York: W. W. Norton, 2005), 1.1–6.

2. *Beowulf*, written in Old English, and Chaucer's *Troilus and Criseyde*, in Middle English, are the only serious contenders. See Michael K. Kellogg, *The Wisdom of the Middle Ages* (Amherst, NY: Prometheus Books, 2016), chaps. 4, 10. Edmund Spenser's *The Faerie Queene* is an episodic romance that lacks the

unity Aristotle rightly considered essential to epic poetry. For all their virtues, which are indeed great, none of the three is as ambitious as, or carries the authoritative weight of, *Paradise Lost*. The same holds for Shakespeare's two narrative poems, *Venus and Adonis* and *The Rape of Lucrece*. They are minor epics, rightly dwarfed by the plays and sonnets.

3. Excerpt from *Lives of the English Poets*, by Samuel Johnson, in Milton, *Paradise Lost*, 386.

4. Ibid.

5. Excerpt from "Lecture 4," by Samuel Taylor Coleridge, in Milton, *Paradise Lost*, 391.

6. Ernst Cassirer, *An Essay on Man: An Introduction to a Philosophy of Human Culture* (New Haven, CT: Yale University Press, 1962), 75.

7. Peter Gay, *The Enlightenment: An Interpretation* (1966; repr., New York: W. W. Norton, 1977), 89.

8. Milton, *Paradise Lost*, 3.54–55.

9. Ibid., 5.571–74.

10. Ibid., 5.574–76.

11. Ibid., 1.22–26.

12. Excerpt from "Terence, This Is Stupid Stuff," by A. E. Housman, in Milton, *Paradise Lost*, 399.

13. Johnson, *Lives of the English Poets*, in Milton, *Paradise Lost*, 387.

14. Neil Forsyth, *John Milton: A Biography* (Oxford: Lion, 2008), 16.

15. Quoted in Douglas Bush, *John Milton: A Sketch of His Life and Writings* (New York: Collier Books, 1967), 21.

16. John Milton, "Il Penseroso," ll.164–66, in *Milton's Selected Poetry and Prose*, ed. Jason P. Rosenblatt (New York: W. W. Norton, 2011), 33.

17. John Milton, "Sonnet VII," ll.10–14, in Rosenblatt, *Selected Poetry and Prose*, 80.

18. John Milton, *A Masque Presented at Ludlow Castle*, ll.244–45, in Rosenblatt, *Selected Poetry and Prose*, 46.

19. John Milton, "L'Allegro," l.13, in Rosenblatt, *Selected Poetry and Prose*, 25.

20. Milton, "Il Penseroso," ll.12, 174, in Rosenblatt, *Selected Poetry and Prose*, 29, 34.

21. John Milton, "Lycidas," l.13, in Rosenblatt, *Selected Poetry and Prose*, 69.

22. Ibid., l.6.

23. Ibid., ll.1–5.

24. Excerpt from *Lives of the English Poets*, by Samuel Johnson, in *Classic Writings on Poetry*, ed. William Harmon (New York: Columbia University Press, 2005), 246.

25. Milton, "Lycidas," ll.64–76, in Rosenblatt, *Selected Poetry and Prose*, 71.

26. Ibid., l.125, 73.

27. Ibid., l.193, 75.

28. John Milton, *Areopagitica*, in Rosenblatt, *Selected Poetry and Prose*, 363.

29. John Milton, "Damon's Epitaph," ll.108–11, in Rosenblatt, *Selected Poetry and Prose*, 220.

30. Quoted in Forsyth, *John Milton*, 72.

31. John Milton, *The Doctrine and Discipline of Divorce*, in Rosenblatt, *Selected Poetry and Prose*, 245.

32. John Milton, *Of Education*, in Rosenblatt, *Selected Poetry and Prose*, 321.

33. Milton, *Areopagitica*, in Rosenblatt, *Selected Poetry and Prose*, 359.

34. Ibid., 375–76.

35. John Milton, "Sonnet XIX," ll.1–2, 14, in Rosenblatt, *Selected Poetry and Prose*, 87–88.

36. John Milton, *The Tenure of Kings and Magistrates*, in Rosenblatt, *Selected Poetry and Prose*, 393.

37. Bush, *John Milton*, 132.

38. John Milton, "Sonnet XXIII," ll.10–14, in Rosenblatt, *Selected Poetry and Prose*, 90.

39. Quoted in A. N. Wilson, *The Life of John Milton* (Oxford: Oxford University Press, 1984), 220.

40. Milton, *Paradise Lost*, 1.45.

41. Ibid., 1.65–66.

42. Ibid., 1.126.

43. Ibid., 1.105.

44. Ibid., 1.105–14.

45. Ibid., 4.52.

46. Ibid., 1.98.

47. Ibid., 1.250–59.

48. Ibid., 9.129–30.

49. Ibid., 4.81–86.

50. Excerpt from "A Defence of Poetry," by Percy Bysshe Shelley, in Milton, *Paradise Lost*, 394.

51. Samuel Taylor Coleridge, "Unassigned Lecture Notes," in Milton, *Paradise Lost*, 391.

52. Excerpt from *The Marriage of Heaven and Hell*, by William Blake, in Milton, *Paradise Lost*, 389.

53. Milton, *Paradise Lost*, 6.422.

54. Ibid., 1.263.

55. Ibid., 1.63.

56. Ibid., 4.75.

57. Stanley Fish, preface to *Surprised by Sin: The Reader in "Paradise Lost,"* 2nd ed. (Cambridge, MA: Harvard University Press, 1998), xxix.

58. Milton, *Paradise Lost*, 4.76–77.

59. Milton, *Masque*, l.1019, in Rosenblatt, *Selected Poetry and Prose*, 68.

60. Excerpt from "The Problem of Satan," by Balachandra Rajan, in Milton, *Paradise Lost*, 412.

61. Milton, *Paradise Lost*, 4.847.

62. Ibid., 3.93–99.

63. See ibid., 3.99–111.

64. Ibid., 3.106–11.

65. Ibid., 2.557–61.

66. See Kellogg, *Wisdom of the Middle Ages*, 107–10.

67. Milton, *Paradise Lost*, 3.77–78.

68. Ibid., 3.117–19.

69. Ibid., 5.472.

70. See Arthur O. Lovejoy, *The Great Chain of Being: A Study of the History of an Idea* (Cambridge, MA: Harvard University Press, 1936), 164.

71. Milton, *Paradise Lost*, 5.472–79.

72. Samuel Johnson, *Lives of the English Poets*, in *Selected Poetry and Prose*, ed. Frank Brady and W. K. Wimsatt (Berkeley: University of California Press, 1977), 439.

73. Milton, *Paradise Lost*, 9.348–50.

74. Ibid., 4.241–46.

75. Ibid., 4.288–95.

76. Ibid., 4.314.

77. Ibid., 4.741–47.

78. Ibid., 4.322.

79. Ibid., 4.298.

80. Ibid., 4.307–11.

81. Ibid., 4.309.

82. Ibid., 8.502–3.

83. John Keats, "Ode on a Grecian Urn," l.20, https://www.poetryfoundation.org/poems/44477/ode-on-a-grecian-urn.

84. Milton, *Paradise Lost*, 4.464–65.

85. Ibid., 4.473–75.

86. Ibid., 4.478–80.

87. Ibid., 4.488–91.

88. Ibid., 4.492–93.

89. Ibid., 8.600–606.

90. Ibid., 4.656.

91. Ibid., 4.639–40.

92. Ibid., 5.51–52.

93. Ibid., 5.77–78.

94. Ibid., 7.544–47.

95. Ibid., 6.909–12.

96. Ibid., 8.172–74.

97. Ibid., 8.167.

98. Ibid., 9.214.

99. Ibid., 9.267–69.

100. Ibid., 9.372–75.

101. Ibid., 9.823–25.

102. Ibid., 9.828, 9.830–33.

103. Ibid., 9.908–16.

104. Gen. 3:24 (New Revised Standard Version).

105. Milton, *Paradise Lost*, 9.1123–26.

106. Ibid., 10.208.

107. Ibid., 10.754–55.

108. Ibid., 10.914–21.

109. Ibid., 10.931.

110. Ibid., 10.958–61.

111. Ibid., 9.31–33.

112. C. S. Lewis, *A Preface to "Paradise Lost"* (London: Oxford University Press, 1961), 132. Compare A. S. P. Woodhouse, *The Heavenly Muse: A Preface to Milton* (Toronto: University of Toronto Press, 1972), 178 ("When full allowance is made for Milton's heresies, *Paradise Lost* remains unequivocally a Christian poem.").

113. Milton, *Paradise Lost*, 12.586–87.

114. Ibid., 12.531–34.

115. Ibid., 11.349–54.

116. Marcus Aurelius, *Meditations*, trans. A. S. L. Farquharson (New York: Alfred A. Knopf, 1992), 6.10.

117. See Fish, preface to *Surprised by Sin*, lv.

118. Milton, *Paradise Lost*, 11.628; see Fish, preface to *Surprised by Sin*, lii–liii.

119. Helen Vendler, excerpt from introduction to *"Paradise Lost": A Poem in Twelve Books*, ed. John T. Shawcross (San Francisco: Arion, 2002), in Milton, *Paradise Lost*, 525.

120. Milton, *Paradise Lost*, 12.645–49.

3. MOLIÈRE

1. François de La Rochefoucauld, *Maximes* (Paris: Garnier-Flammarion, 1977), 311. This and subsequent quotations from La Rochefoucauld's *Maximes* are my own translations.

2. La Rochefoucauld, *Maximes*, 119.

3. Jacques Guicharnaud, ed., introduction to *Molière: A Collection of Critical Essays* (Englewood Cliffs, NJ: Prentice-Hall, 1964), 8–9.

4. See Martin Turnell, *The Classical Moment: Studies of Corneille, Molière and Racine* (1948; repr., Westport, CT: Greenwood, 1975), 45–48.

5. Robert J. Nelson, "The Unreconstructed Heroes of Molière," in Guicharnaud, *Critical Essays*, 111.

6. See J. D. Hubert, *Molière and the Comedy of Intellect* (Berkeley: University of California Press, 1973), 74 ("Molière, . . . far from denying the existence of tragedy, has succeeded in deforming, transforming, and transvaluating it into comedy and sometimes into farce without impairing its emotional impact.").

7. The maxim is commonly attributed to the seventeenth-century French essayist Jean de La Bruyère. Just as often, it is attributed to the eighteenth-century politician and author Horace Walpole, who wrote: "The world is a comedy to those that think; a tragedy to those that feel."

8. See W. D. Howarth, *Molière: A Playwright and His Audience* (Cambridge: Cambridge University Press, 1982), 140–41.

9. Donald M. Frame, trans., *The Complete Essays of Montaigne* (Stanford, CA: Stanford University Press, 1965), 3.13, 856.

10. Details from Molière's life are drawn from a number of sources, including Mikhail Bulgakov, *The Life of Monsieur de Molière*, trans. Mirra Ginsburg (New York: New Directions, 1986), and Howarth, *Molière*.

11. Molière, *The School for Wives*, in *Four Comedies*, trans. Richard Wilbur (New York: Harcourt Brace Jovanovich, 1982), 137–38.

12. Ibid., 134.

13. Guicharnaud, introduction to *Critical Essays*, 5.

14. La Rochefoucauld, *Maximes*, epigraph, 45.

15. Michael K. Kellogg, *The Wisdom of the Middle Ages* (Amherst, NY: Prometheus Books, 2016), 298–300 (Wife of Bath), 302–3 (Pardoner); Michael K. Kellogg, *The Wisdom of the Renaissance* (Amherst, NY: Prometheus Books, 2019), 308–9 (Falstaff).

16. Molière, *Tartuffe*, in Wilbur, *Four Comedies*, 327.

17. See Lionel Gossman, *Men and Masks: A Study of Molière* (Baltimore: Johns Hopkins Press, 1969), 102–4.

18. Turnell, *Classical Moment*, 66.

19. Molière, *Tartuffe*, in Wilbur, *Four Comedies*, 346.

20. Ibid., 331.

21. Molière, *Le Tartuffe*, in *Oeuvres Complètes II* (Paris: Garnier-Flammarion, 1965), 1.5.280. For the most part, I quote in text from the admirable verse translation of Richard Wilbur. In a few places, however, I offer my own, more literal translations undistorted by the demands of rhyme and meter. When doing so, I cite directly to line numbers in the French edition.

22. Howarth, *Molière*, 203.

23. Molière, *Tartuffe*, in Wilbur, *Four Comedies*, 333.

24. Molière, *Le Tartuffe*, in *Oeuvres Complètes II*, 3.3.966.

25. Ibid., 3.3.933–36.

26. See ibid., 4.5.1488–92.

27. Molière, *Tartuffe*, in Wilbur, *Four Comedies*, 421.

28. Ibid.

29. Molière, *Le Tartuffe*, in *Oeuvres Complètes II*, 4.5.1526.

30. Molière, *Tartuffe*, in Wilbur, *Four Comedies*, 467.

31. See P. Muñoz Simonds, "Molière's Satiric Use of the *Deus Ex Machina* in *Tartuffe*," in *"Tartuffe": A Verse Translation, Backgrounds and Sources, Criticism*, ed. Constance Congdon and Virginia Scott, trans. Constance Congdon (New York: W. W. Norton, 2009), 168; Gossman, *Men and Masks*, 144.

32. Molière, *Tartuffe*, in Wilbur, *Four Comedies*, 465–66.

33. La Rochefoucauld, *Maximes*, 237.

34. Turnell, *Classical Moment*, 78.

35. Molière, *Don Juan*, trans. Richard Wilbur (San Diego: Harcourt, 2001), 9.

36. Ibid., 72–73.

37. Ibid., 20.

38. *Pascal's "Pensées,"* trans. W. F. Trotter (New York: E. P. Dutton, 1958), no. 260, 76 (English translation).

39. Molière, *Don Juan*, 15.

40. Ibid.

41. Ibid.

42. Ibid., 13.

43. Ibid., 19.

44. Ibid., 25.

45. Ibid., 123.

46. Ibid., 80.

47. Ibid., 87.

48. Ibid., 139.

49. Ibid., 115.

50. Ibid., 134.

51. Ibid., 132.

52. Ibid., 134.

53. La Rochefoucauld, *Maximes*, 218.

54. Molière, *Don Juan*, 135.

55. Ibid., 77.

56. Ibid., 78.

57. Ibid., 95.

58. Ibid., 144.

59. Ibid., 136–37.

60. Ibid., 134.

61. Ibid., 146.

62. Ibid., 10.

63. La Rochefoucauld, *Maximes*, 39.

64. Molière, *Le Misanthrope*, in *Oeuvres Complètes III* (Paris: Garnier-Flammarion, 1965), 1.1.63.

65. Molière, *The Misanthrope*, in Wilbur, *Four Comedies*, 252.

66. Ibid., 168.

67. Ibid., 164.

68. Ibid., 166.

69. Ibid., 166–67.

70. Ibid., 171.

71. Molière, *Le Misanthrope*, in *Oeuvres Complètes III*, 1.1.149, 1.1.163.

72. Moliere, *The Misanthrope*, in Wilbur, *Four Comedies*, 184.

73. Ibid., 174.

74. Ibid., 172.

75. Ibid., 174.

76. Ibid., 280.

77. Ibid., 189.

78. Ibid., 265.

79. Ibid., 266.

80. Ibid., 297.

81. Ibid., 298.

82. Ibid., 300.

83. Ibid., 265.

84. See Wilbur, introduction to *The Misanthrope*, in *Four Comedies*, 155–56.

85. Hubert, *Molière and the Comedy of Intellect*, 144.

86. Molière, *Le Misanthrope*, in *Oeuvres Complètes III*, 1.1.166.

87. Raymond Picard, *Two Centuries of French Literature*, trans. John Cairncross (New York: McGraw-Hill, 1970), 92.

4. PASCAL AND THE HIDDEN GOD

1. *Pascal's "Pensées,"* trans. W. F. Trotter (New York: E. P. Dutton, 1958), no. 72, 19–20.

2. Friedrich Nietzsche, *The Gay Science*, trans. Walter Kaufmann (New York: Vintage Books, 1974), 180–81 (sec. 124).

3. *Pascal's "Pensées,"* no. 278, 78.

4. Ibid., no. 206, 61.

5. Morris Bishop, *Pascal: The Life of Genius* (Baltimore: Williams & Wilkins, 1936), 1.

6. Marvin R. O'Connell, *Blaise Pascal: Reasons of the Heart* (Grand Rapids, MI: Wm. B. Eerdmans, 1997), 96.

7. See Michael K. Kellogg, *The Wisdom of the Middle Ages* (Amherst, NY: Prometheus Books, 2016), 52.

8. *Pascal's "Pensées,"* no. 199, 60.

9. See Michael K. Kellogg, *Three Questions We Never Stop Asking* (Amherst, NY: Prometheus Books, 2010), 49–52.

10. *Pascal's "Pensées,"* no. 77, 23.

11. Ibid., no. 692, 198.

12. See Michael K. Kellogg, *The Wisdom of the Renaissance* (Amherst, NY: Prometheus Books, 2019), chap. 7.

13. See, for example, Sarah Bakewell, *How to Live, or, A Life of Montaigne* (New York: Other Press, 2010), 144–45.

14. Jean Starobinski, *Montaigne in Motion*, trans. Arthur Goldhammer (Chicago: University of Chicago Press, 1985), 95.

15. *Pascal's "Pensées,"* no. 450, 126.

16. See, for example, *The Complete Essays of Montaigne*, trans. Donald M. Frame (Stanford, CA: Stanford University Press, 1965), 2.1, 242; 3.2, 620; 3.9, 766.

17. *Pascal's "Pensées,"* no. 450, 126.

18. *Complete Essays of Montaigne*, 3.13, 856.

19. *Pascal's "Pensées,"* no. 100, 32–33.

20. See Bakewell, *How to Live*, 145.

21. Molière, *The Misanthrope*, in *Four Comedies*, trans. Richard Wilbur (New York: Harcourt Brace Jovanovich, 1982), 171.

22. Erich Auerbach, *Mimesis: The Representation of Reality in Western Literature*, trans. Willard R. Trask (Princeton, NJ: Princeton University Press, 1968), 311.

23. *Complete Essays of Montaigne*, 3.9, 728.

24. Ibid., 1.20, 62.

25. *Pascal's "Pensées,"* no. 139, 39.

26. Ibid., no. 131, 38.

27. Ibid.

28. Ibid., no. 465, 130.

29. Ibid., no. 437, 123.

30. Ibid., no. 416, 110.

31. Ibid., no. 445, 124.

32. Ibid., no. 658, 185.

33. Ibid., no. 146, 45.

34. Ibid., no. 77, 23; no. 242, 71–72.

35. William Wordsworth, "Ode: Intimations of Immortality from Recollections of Early Childhood," https://www.poetryfoundation.org/poems/45536/ode-intimations-of-immortality-from-recollections-of-early-childhood.

36. *Pascal's "Pensées,"* no. 437, 123.

37. Ibid., no. 425, 113.

38. Ibid., no. 72, 17.

39. Ibid., no. 230, 64–65.

40. Ibid., no. 267, 77.

41. Ibid., no. 282, 79.

42. Ibid.

43. Ibid., no. 395, 106.

44. Ibid., no. 792, 234.

45. Ibid., no. 277, 78.

46. Ibid., no. 229, 64.

47. Ibid.

48. Ibid., no. 234, 69.

49. Ibid., no. 233, 66.

50. Ibid., 67.

51. Ibid.

52. Ibid., 68.

53. Ibid., no. 242, 71.

54. Ibid.

55. Ibid., no. 233, 67.

56. Excerpt from *The Hidden God: A Study of the Tragic Vision in the "Pensées" of Pascal and the Tragedies of Racine*, by Lucien Goldmann, in *Blaise Pascal*, ed. Harold Bloom (New York: Chelsea House, 1989), 65.

57. T. S. Eliot, introduction to *Pascal's "Pensées,"* xix.

58. *Pascal's "Pensées,"* no. 555, 153.

59. Ibid., no. 683, 193.

60. Ibid., no. 242, 71.

61. Ibid., no. 526, 143.

62. Ibid., no. 547, 147.

63. Excerpt from *Pascal and Theology*, by Jan Miel, in Bloom, *Blaise Pascal*, 115.

64. See ibid., 122; Goldmann, *Hidden God*, in Bloom, *Blaise Pascal*, 71–72.

65. Friedrich Nietzsche, *Schopenhauer as Educator*, in *Untimely Meditations*, ed. Daniel Breazeale, trans. R. J. Hollingdale (Cambridge: Cambridge University Press, 1997), 129.

66. *Pascal's "Pensées,"* no. 434, 121.

67. Ibid., no. 358, 99.

68. Ibid., no. 331, 93.

69. Excerpt from *Scenes from the Drama of European Literature*, by Erich Auerbach, in Bloom, *Blaise Pascal*, 32 (according to Pascal, "our world is evil, but it is just that this should be so").

70. *Pascal's "Pensées,"* no. 233, 68.

71. Ibid.

72. Ibid., no. 347, 97.

73. Ibid., no. 331, 93.

74. Ibid., no. 347, 97.

5. SPINOZA

1. Benedict de Spinoza, *Theologico-Political Treatise*, in *Works of Spinoza*, trans. R. H. M. Elwes, vol. 1 (New York: Dover, 1955), 265.

2. Quoted in Roger Scruton, *Spinoza* (Oxford: Oxford University Press, 1986), 8–9.

3. Ibid.

4. Quoted in Steven Nadler, *Spinoza: A Life* (Cambridge: Cambridge University Press, 2001), 216.

5. Quoted in Matthew Stewart, *The Courtier and the Heretic: Leibniz, Spinoza, and the Fate of God in the Modern World* (New York: W. W. Norton, 2006), 55.

6. Scruton, *Spinoza*, 12.

7. W. N. A. Klever, "Spinoza's Life and Works," in *The Cambridge Companion to Spinoza*, ed. Don Garrett (Cambridge: Cambridge University Press, 1996), 45.

8. Ibid., 42.

9. Benedict de Spinoza, *Ethics*, ed. and trans. Edwin Curley (New York: Penguin Books, 1996), 1.D3, 1. For an explanation of the letters used in the citations to the *Ethics*, see ibid., xix.

10. Ibid., 1.D1, 1.

11. Ibid., 1.P17, 13.

12. See Michael K. Kellogg, *The Wisdom of the Middles Ages* (Amherst, NY: Prometheus Books, 2016), 103–4.

13. See chapter 10 in this book.

14. Spinoza, *Ethics*, 1.P11, 7.

15. Ibid., 1.P7, 4.

16. Spinoza, *Theologico-Political Treatise*, in *Works of Spinoza*, 191.

17. Ibid., 44.

18. Ibid., 59.

19. Spinoza, *Ethics*, 1.P29, 20.

20. Spinoza, *Theologico-Political Treatise*, in *Works of Spinoza*, 92.

21. Spinoza, *Ethics*, 1.P33.S2, 23.

22. Spinoza, *Theologico-Political Treatise*, in *Works of Spinoza*, 64.

23. Ibid., 65.

24. Ibid., 165.

25. Spinoza, *Theologico-Political Treatise*, quoted in Steven Nadler, *A Book Forged in Hell: Spinoza's Scandalous Treatise and the Birth of the Secular Age* (Princeton, NJ: Princeton University Press, 2011), 142.

26. Spinoza, *Theologico-Political Treatise*, in *Works of Spinoza*, 66.

27. Ibid., 9.

28. Ibid., 27, 33.

29. Nadler, *Book Forged in Hell*, 156.

30. Spinoza, *Theologico-Political Treatise*, in *Works of Spinoza*, 4.

31. Ibid.

32. Ibid., 80.

33. For a lively account of the relationship between Leibniz and Spinoza and their sharply contrasting views, see Stewart, *Courtier and the Heretic*.

34. Spinoza, *Ethics*, 3.P2.S, 71.

35. Spinoza, *Theologico-Political Treatise*, in *Works of Spinoza*, 167. Compare Ludwig Wittgenstein, *Philosophical Investigations*, trans. G. E. M. Anscombe, 3rd ed. (New York: Macmillan, 1973), sec. 43 ("For a large class of cases—though not for all—in which we employ the word 'meaning' it can be defined thus: the meaning of a word is its use in the language.").

36. Spinoza, *Ethics*, 3.P2.S, 71.

37. Ibid., 73.

38. Ibid., 2.P7, 35.

39. Ibid., preface to part 3, 69.

40. Ibid., 3.P6, 75.

41. Ibid., 3.P59.S, 104.

42. Ibid., 3.P59.D, 102.

43. Ibid., 3.P13.S, 78.

44. René Descartes, *The Passions of the Soul*, in *"The Passions of the Soul" and Other Late Philosophical Writings*, trans. Michael Moriarty (New York: Oxford University Press, 2015), 223 (2.69).

45. Spinoza, *Ethics*, preface to part 3, 69.

46. Ibid., 3.P2.S, 72.

47. Ibid., 2.P48, 62.

48. See ibid., 2.P48.S, 62; preface to part 3, 68–69; 3.P2.S, 72–73.

49. Michael K. Kellogg, *Three Questions We Never Stop Asking* (Amherst, NY: Prometheus Books, 2010), 77–91.

50. Spinoza, *Ethics*, 2.P11.C, 39.

51. Spinoza, *Theologico-Political Treatise*, in *Works of Spinoza*, 59.

52. Spinoza, *Ethics*, 4.P37.S2, 136.

53. Ibid., preface to part 4, 113.

54. Ibid., 4.P44.S, 140.

55. Ibid., 3.P59.S, 103.

56. Ibid., 3.P1.C, 71.

57. Ibid., 5.P3, 163.

58. Ibid., 5.P20.S, 170.

59. Ibid., 5.P3.C, 163.

60. Ibid., 4.P59, 147.

61. See Don Garrett, "Spinoza's Ethical Theory," in *Cambridge Companion to Spinoza*, 299.

62. Spinoza, *Ethics*, 4.P47.S, 141–42.

63. Ibid., 5.P42.S, 181.

6. DEFOE AND SWIFT

1. Some would give this claim to John Bunyan's *Pilgrim's Progress*.

2. Daniel Defoe, "The True-Born Englishman," pt. 1, reprinted at http://www.gutenberg.org/files/30159/30159-h/30159-h.htm.

3. Quoted in Richard West, *Daniel Defoe: The Life and Strange, Surprising Adventures* (New York: Carroll & Graf, 2000), 70–71.

4. Quoted in William P. Trent, *Daniel Defoe: How to Know Him* (Indianapolis, IN: Bobbs-Merrill, 1916), 56.

5. Quoted in John Charles Olmsted, ed., *A Victorian Art of Fiction: Essays on the Novel in British Periodicals 1851–1869* (1979; repr., New York: Routledge, 2016), 629.

6. Quoted in West, *Daniel Defoe*, 116.

7. Daniel Defoe, *The Storm*, ed. Richard Hamblyn (London: Penguin Books, 2005), chap. 3. Throughout this chapter, spelling and capitalization has been modernized in the quotations.

8. Jonathan Swift, *A Discourse Concerning the Mechanical Operation of the Spirit*, in *The Essential Writings of Jonathan Swift*, ed. Claude Rawson and Ian Higgins (New York: W. W. Norton, 2009), 119–20.

9. Quoted in Leo Damrosch, *Jonathan Swift: His Life and His World* (New Haven, CT: Yale University Press, 2013), 175.

10. Swift's explicit, some would say pornographic, focus on bodily functions was shared by his later countryman James Joyce. See Camille Kellogg, "Stifled with Filth: The Inescapable Body in *Gulliver's Travels* and *Ulysses*" (BA thesis, Middlebury College, 2017).

11. Jonathan Swift, "The Lady's Dressing-Room," l. 118, in Rawson and Higgins, *Essential Writings*, 606.

12. Daniel Defoe, *Robinson Crusoe*, ed. Michael Shinagel (New York: W. W. Norton, 1994).

13. Excerpt from *The Second Common Reader*, by Virginia Woolf, in Defoe, *Robinson Crusoe*, 286.

14. Homer, *The Odyssey*, trans. Robert Fitzgerald (New York: Farrar, Straus and Giroux, 1998), 1.2.

15. Defoe, *Robinson Crusoe*, 5.

16. Excerpt from *Emilius and Sophia: or, A New System of Education*, by Jean-Jacques Rousseau, in Defoe, *Robinson Crusoe*, 262.

17. Defoe, *Robinson Crusoe*, 51.

18. Quoted in Jennifer J. Popiel, introduction to *Leviathan*, by Thomas Hobbes (New York: Barnes & Noble Books, 2004), xi.

19. Excerpt from *The Life of Charles Dickens*, by John Forster, in Defoe, *Robinson Crusoe*, 274.

20. Ibid.

21. Defoe, *Robinson Crusoe*, 36.

22. Ibid., 43.

23. Ibid.

24. Excerpt from *Serious Reflections During the Life and Surprising Adventures of Robinson Crusoe*, by Daniel Defoe, in Defoe, *Robinson Crusoe*, 242.

25. Defoe, *Robinson Crusoe*, 58.

26. Ibid.

27. Ibid., 67.

28. Ibid., 69.

29. Ibid., 68.

30. Ibid.

31. Ibid., 80.

32. Marcus Aurelius, *Meditations*, trans. A. S. L. Farquharson (New York: Alfred A. Knopf, 1992), 6.10.

33. Defoe, *Robinson Crusoe*, 135.

34. Swift, *Mechanical Operation of the Spirit*, in Rawson and Higgins, *Essential Writings*, 119.

35. Defoe, *Robinson Crusoe*, 83.

36. Excerpt from Defoe, *Serious Reflections*, in Defoe, *Robinson Crusoe*, 244.

37. Ibid.

38. Ibid.

39. Defoe, *Robinson Crusoe*, 136.

40. Quoted in West, *Daniel Defoe*, ix.

41. Defoe, *Robinson Crusoe*, 121–22.

42. Ibid., 124.

43. Ibid., 144.

44. Ibid., 156.

45. Ibid., 158.

46. Ibid., 160.

47. Ibid., 174.

48. Ibid.

49. Ibid., 219.

50. Excerpt from "Daniel Defoe," by James Joyce, in Defoe, *Robinson Crusoe*, 323.

51. A. W. Ward and A. R. Waller, eds., *The Cambridge History of English Literature*, vol. 9 (Cambridge: Cambridge University Press, 1952), 103.

52. Jonathan Swift, *Gulliver's Travels*, ed. Albert J. Rivero (New York: W. W. Norton, 2002), 5.

53. Franz Kafka, *The Metamorphosis*, in *Collected Stories*, ed. Gabriel Josipovici (New York: Alfred A. Knopf, 1993), 75.

54. Sir Walter Scott, excerpt from introduction to *Gulliver's Travels*, in Swift, *Gulliver's Travels*, 312–13.

55. Damrosch, *Jonathan Swift*, 363.

56. Swift, *Gulliver's Travels*, 31.

57. Ibid., 32.

58. Scott, excerpt from introduction to *Gulliver's Travels*, in Swift, *Gulliver's Travels*, 314.

59. Swift, *Gulliver's Travels*, 40.

60. Ibid., 44.

61. Ibid., 99.

62. Ibid., 72–73.

63. Ibid., 76–77.

64. Ibid., 113.

65. Ibid., 114.

66. Ibid., 89.

67. Ibid., 110.

68. Ibid., 111.

69. Ibid., 168.

70. Ibid., 137.

71. Ibid., 150.

72. Ibid.

73. Ibid., 199.

74. Ibid., 190.

75. Ibid., 189–90.

76. Kellogg, "Stifled with Filth," 5.

77. Swift, *Gulliver's Travels*, 248.

78. Ibid., 235.

79. Swift to Alexander Pope, September 29, 1725, in Rawson and Higgins, *Essential Writings*, 676.

80. Swift, *Gulliver's Travels*, 199, 230.

81. T. O. Wedel, "On the Philosophical Background of *Gulliver's Travels*," in *Twentieth Century Interpretations of "Gulliver's Travels,"* ed. Frank Brady (Englewood Cliffs, NJ: Prentice-Hall, 1968), 33.

82. Swift, *Gulliver's Travels*, 218.

83. *The Complete Essays of Montaigne*, trans. Donald M. Frame (Stanford, CA: Stanford University Press, 1965), 3.13, 856.

84. John Milton, *Paradise Lost*, ed. Gordon Teskey (New York: W. W. Norton, 2005), 8.192–94.

85. Swift, *Gulliver's Travels*, 250.

86. Ibid., 249.

87. See Kellogg, "Stifled with Filth," 15.

7. VOLTAIRE AND THE PHILOSOPHES

1. "The world moves slowly toward wisdom." Voltaire, *Les Lois de Minos: Tragédie en cinq actes* (n.p.: Ligaran, 2015), 3.5.

2. Will and Ariel Durant accordingly titled their three successive volumes on this period *The Age of Louis XIV*, *The Age of Voltaire*, and *Rousseau and Revolution*.

3. See Michael K. Kellogg, *The Wisdom of the Renaissance* (Amherst, NY: Prometheus Books, 2019), chap. 2.

4. Quoted in Geoffrey Turnovsky, "The Making of a Name: A Life of Voltaire," in *The Cambridge Companion to Voltaire*, ed. Nicholas Cronk (Cambridge: Cambridge University Press, 2009), 17.

5. Quoted in Ian Davidson, *Voltaire: A Life* (New York: Pegasus Books, 2010), 14.

6. This phrase, which means "staircase wit," refers to someone who thinks of a perfect turn of phrase only after he has left the salon or other gathering where he hoped to shine.

7. Voltaire, *Philosophical Letters: Or, Letters Regarding the English Nation*, ed. John Leigh, trans. Prudence L. Steiner (Indianapolis, IN: Hackett, 2007), letter 5, 15.

8. Ibid., letter 1, 3; letter 2, 5.

9. Ibid., letter 1, 2–3.

10. Ibid., letter 5, 15.

11. Ibid., letter 6, 20.

12. Ibid., letter 8, 23.

13. Ibid., letter 10, 32.

14. Ibid., letter 11, 35.

15. Ibid., letter 14, 47, 49.

16. Ibid., 50.

17. Ibid., 47.

18. Ibid., letter 12, 37.

19. Ibid., letter 13, 42.

20. Ibid., 43.

21. Ibid.

22. Ibid., 44.

23. Ibid., letter 14, 50.

24. Émilie's daughter died before her second birthday. Whether she was also Voltaire's daughter has long been debated.

25. Davidson, *Voltaire*, 395.

26. Ibid., 303.

27. Voltaire, *Candide*, ed. Nicholas Cronk, trans. Robert M. Adams, 3rd ed. (New York: W. W. Norton, 2016), 81.

28. Ibid., 79.

29. Ibid., 81.

30. Ibid., 4.

31. Alexander Pope, "An Essay on Man," epistle 1, ll.289–94, in *The Major Works*, ed. Pat Rogers (Oxford: Oxford University Press, 2006), 280.

32. Voltaire, *Candide*, 76.

33. Voltaire, preface to "The Lisbon Earthquake," in *The Portable Voltaire*, ed. Ben Ray Redman, trans. Tobias Smollett (New York: Penguin Books, 1977), 558.

34. Excerpt from *Sidetracks: Explorations of a Romantic Biographer*, by Richard Holmes, in Voltaire, *Candide*, 91.

35. Voltaire, *Candide*, 3.

36. Ibid., 15.

37. Voltaire, *Philosophical Letters*, letter 25, 107.

38. Ibid., 101.

39. Jean Le Rond d'Alembert, *Preliminary Discourse to the Encyclopedia of Diderot*, trans. Richard N. Schwab (Chicago: University of Chicago Press, 1995), 4.

40. Ibid., 46–48.

41. Ibid., 14.

42. Quoted in Davidson, *Voltaire*, 306.

43. Voltaire, *Philosophical Dictionary*, ed. and trans. Theodore Besterman (London: Penguin Books, 2004), 107.

44. Ibid., 57.

45. Ibid., 386.

46. Ibid., 98.

47. Ibid., 68.

48. Ibid., 272.

49. Voltaire, *Philosophical Letters*, letter 25, 102.

50. Voltaire, *Philosophical Dictionary*, 386.

51. Ibid., 359.

52. Ibid., 382.

53. Ibid., 149.

54. Ibid., 397.

55. Ibid., 41.

56. Ibid., 374.

57. Ibid.

58. Ibid., 80.

59. Ibid., 375.

60. Ibid.

61. Ibid., 386.

62. Ibid., 96.

63. Ibid., 181.

64. Ibid., 273.

65. Ibid., 99.

66. See generally ibid., 115–41 ("Christianity"), 194–96 ("Gospel").

67. Ibid., 118.

68. Ibid., 138.

69. Ibid., 236.

70. Ibid., 168–71.

71. Ibid., 367.

72. Ibid., 369.

73. Ibid., 370–73.

74. Ibid., 331.

75. Ibid., 259, 261.

76. Ibid., 16.

77. Ibid., 182.

78. Ibid., 233.

79. Ibid., 234.

80. Ibid., 233.

81. Ibid., 356.

82. Ibid., 279.

83. Ibid., 281.

84. Ibid., 175.

85. Ibid., 278.

86. Ibid., 111.

87. Ibid., 21.

88. Ibid., 23–24.

89. Ibid., 237.

90. Ibid., 177.

91. Ibid.

92. R. J. White, *The Anti-Philosophers: A Study of the Philosophes in Eighteenth-Century France* (New York: St. Martin's, 1970).

93. Voltaire, *Candide*, 60.

94. For a detailed discussion of the Calas affair, see Davidson, *Voltaire*, 316–31.

95. When Sartre was charged with civil disobedience during the student strikes in 1968, Charles de Gaulle intervened and dismissed the charges with the words "One does not arrest Voltaire."

96. Quoted in Davidson, *Voltaire*, 333.

97. Ibid., 461.

8. SAMUEL JOHNSON ON THE STABILITY OF TRUTH

1. Samuel Johnson, preface to *The Plays of William Shakespeare*, in *Selected Poetry and Prose*, ed. Frank Brady and W. K. Wimsatt (Berkeley: University of California Press, 1977), 301.

2. Other claimants among literary biographies include Leon Edel's five-volume *Henry James*, Richard Ellmann's *James Joyce*, and Johnson's own collective, *Lives of the Poets*.

3. James Boswell, *The Life of Samuel Johnson* (New York: Heritage, 1963), 1:4.

4. Ibid., 1:355.

5. Ibid., 1:12.

6. W. Jackson Bate, *Samuel Johnson* (New York: Harcourt Brace, 1979), 14.

7. Boswell, *Life of Johnson*, 1:15.

8. Ibid., 1:38.

9. Ibid., 1:92.

10. Ibid., 1:30.

11. Ibid., 1:52.

12. Ibid., 1:54.

13. Ibid., 1:56.

14. Thomas Macaulay, *Samuel Johnson*, in *Complete Works* (New York: Houghton Mifflin, 1900), 59.

15. Boswell, *Life of Johnson*, 1:160.

16. Ibid., 1:69.

17. Samuel Johnson, "London," ll.176–77, in *Selected Poetry and Prose*, 52.

18. Boswell, *Life of Johnson*, 1:452.

19. Ibid., 1:98.

20. Ibid., 1:129.

21. Ibid.

22. Ibid., 1:131.

23. Ibid., 3:130.

24. Samuel Johnson, "The Vanity of Human Wishes," ll.3–12, in *Selected Poetry and Prose*, 57.

25. Boswell, *Life of Johnson*, 1:127.

26. Ibid., 1:140.

27. Samuel Johnson, preface to *Dictionary of the English Language*, in *Selected Poetry and Prose*, 287.

28. Ibid., 290.

29. Ibid., 282.

30. Boswell, *Life of Johnson*, 1:412.

31. Ibid., 1:450.

32. Johnson, preface to *Dictionary*, in *Selected Poetry and Prose*, 298.

33. Johnson to Lord Chesterfield, London, February 7, 1755, in *Selected Poetry and Prose*, 33.

34. Boswell, *Life of Johnson*, 1:383–85.

35. Ibid., 1:387.

36. Ibid., 3:61.

37. Leo Damrosch, *The Club: Johnson, Boswell, and the Friends Who Shaped an Age* (New Haven, CT: Yale University Press, 2019), 1.

38. Boswell, *Life of Johnson*, 1:426.

39. Ibid., 1:405.

40. Ibid., 3:193.

41. Quoted in Peter Martin, *Samuel Johnson: A Biography* (Cambridge, MA: Harvard University Press, 2008), 494.

42. Johnson to Hester Thrale, London, July 8, 1784, in *Selected Poetry and Prose*, 45.

43. Boswell, *Life of Johnson*, 2:393.

44. Ibid., 2:96n2.

45. James Boswell, *Journal of a Tour to the Hebrides* (New York: Literary Guild, 1936), 226.

46. Ibid., 98n6.

47. See Samuel Johnson, *A Journey to the Western Islands of Scotland*, and James Boswell, *Journal of a Tour to the Hebrides*, ed. Peter Levi (Harmondsworth, UK: Penguin Books, 1984).

48. Boswell, *Life of Johnson*, 2:344.

49. Ibid., 3:306.

50. W. Jackson Bate, *The Achievement of Samuel Johnson* (Chicago: University of Chicago Press, 1978), 60.

51. Boswell, *Life of Johnson*, 3:426.

52. Samuel Johnson, *Rambler*, no. 49, in *Selected Essays from the "Rambler," "Adventurer," and "Idler,"* ed. W. Jackson Bate (New Haven, CT: Yale University Press, 1968), 104–5.

53. Samuel Johnson, *The History of Rasselas, Prince of Abyssinia*, in *Selected Poetry and Prose*, 123.

54. Johnson, *Rambler*, no. 49, in *Selected Essays*, 105.

55. Samuel Johnson, *Rambler*, no. 104, in *The Yale Edition of the Works of Samuel Johnson*, ed. W. Jackson Bate and Albrecht B. Strauss, vol. 4 (New Haven, CT: Yale University Press, 1969), 191.

56. Johnson, *Rambler*, no. 6, in *Selected Essays*, 20.

57. Johnson, *Rambler*, no. 2, in *Selected Essays*, 3.

58. Johnson, *Rasselas*, in *Selected Poetry and Prose*, 123.

59. Johnson, *Rambler*, no. 41, in *Selected Essays*, 89.

60. Ibid., 87.

61. Samuel Johnson, *Idler*, no. 44, in *Selected Essays*, 305.

62. Boswell, *Life of Johnson*, 1:312.

63. David Garrick, "Come, Come, My Good Shepherds," l. 16, https://www.bartleby.com/333/28.html.

64. Bate, *Samuel Johnson*, 301.

65. Samuel Johnson, *Idler*, no. 73, in *The Yale Edition of the Works of Samuel Johnson*, ed. John M. Bullitt, W. Jackson Bate, and L. F. Powell, vol. 2 (New Haven, CT: Yale University Press, 1969), 228.

66. Johnson, *Rambler*, no. 2, in *Selected Essays*, 5.

67. Ibid., 4.

68. Johnson, *Rambler*, no. 6, in *Selected Essays*, 20.

69. Bate, *Achievement of Johnson*, 98.

70. Johnson, *Rambler*, no. 6, in *Selected Essays*, 21.

71. Samuel Johnson, *Adventurer*, no. 84, in *Selected Essays*, 240.

72. Johnson, *Idler*, no. 50, in *Selected Essays*, 315.

73. See Bate, *Achievement of Johnson*, 95.

74. Boswell, *Life of Johnson*, 2:229.

75. Johnson, *Rambler*, no. 146, in *Selected Essays*, 189.

76. Johnson, *Rambler*, no. 159, in *Selected Essays*, 202.

77. Johnson, *Rambler*, no. 13, in *Selected Essays*, 33.

78. Ibid., 34.

79. Johnson, *Rambler*, no. 28, in *Selected Essays*, 65.

80. Johnson, *Rambler*, no. 8, in *Selected Essays*, 24.

81. Johnson, *Rambler*, no. 24, in *Selected Essays*, 57.

82. Johnson, *Rambler*, no. 183, in *Selected Essays*, 214.

83. Ibid.

84. Johnson, *Rambler*, no. 14, in *Selected Essays*, 39.

85. Johnson, *Rambler*, no. 25, in *Selected Essays*, 58–59.

86. Ibid., 60.

87. Johnson, *Idler*, no. 27, in *Selected Essays*, 284.

88. Johnson, preface to *Plays of Shakespeare*, in *Selected Poetry and Prose*, 314.

89. Ibid., 301.

90. Ibid.

91. Ibid., 304.

92. Ibid., 307.

93. Ibid.

94. Johnson, *Rambler*, no. 93, in *Selected Essays*, 161.

95. Johnson, *Rambler*, no. 14, in *Selected Essays*, 39.

96. Johnson, *Rambler*, no. 76, in *Selected Essays*, 135.

97. Johnson, *Idler*, no. 27, in *Selected Essays*, 285.

98. Johnson, *Rambler*, no. 87, in *Selected Essays*, 149.

99. Johnson, *Rambler*, no. 183, in *Selected Essays*, 213.

100. Johnson, *Rambler*, no. 4, in *Selected Essays*, 13.

101. Johnson, *Adventurer*, no. 137, in *Selected Essays*, 274.

102. Johnson, *Rambler*, no. 183, in *Selected Essays*, 217.

103. Boswell, *Life of Johnson*, 3:17.

104. Johnson, "Vanity of Human Wishes," ll.345–46, in *Selected Poetry and Prose*, 67.

105. Ibid., ll.367–68, 67.

106. Johnson, *Rambler*, no. 32, in *Selected Essays*, 84.

107. Ibid., 83.

108. Ibid., 82.

109. Ibid., 85.

110. Johnson, *Rambler*, no. 6, in *Selected Essays*, 16.

111. Johnson, *Rambler*, no. 47, in *Selected Essays*, 98.

112. Ibid., 99.

113. Boswell, *Life of Johnson*, 3:17.

114. Johnson, *Rambler*, no. 72, in *Selected Essays*, 123–24.

115. Johnson, *Rambler*, no. 74, in *Selected Poetry and Prose*, 188.

116. Ibid., 186.

117. Ibid., 185.

118. Johnson, *Rambler*, no. 29, in *Selected Essays*, 73.

119. Boswell, *Life of Johnson*, 3:431.

120. Johnson, *Idler*, no. 51, in *Selected Essays*, 319.

121. Johnson, *Rambler*, no. 72, in *Selected Essays*, 124.

122. Ibid.

123. Johnson, *Rambler*, no. 17, in *Selected Essays*, 51.

124. Johnson, *Rambler*, no. 2, in *Selected Essays*, 4.

125. Johnson, *Rambler*, no. 17, in *Selected Essays*, 51.

126. Boswell, *Tour to the Hebrides*, 169.

127. Johnson, *Rambler*, no. 72, in *Selected Essays*, 125.

128. Johnson, *Rambler*, no. 188, in *Selected Essays*, 220.

129. Johnson, *Idler*, no. 58, in *Selected Essays*, 323.

130. Ibid.

131. Johnson, *Idler*, no. 23, in *Selected Essays*, 281.

132. Johnson, *Rambler*, no. 64, in *Selected Essays*, 116.

133. Johnson, *Rambler*, no. 54, in *Selected Poetry and Prose*, 181.

134. Boswell, *Life of Johnson*, 1:448.

135. Ibid., 3:7.

136. Ibid., 1:334.

137. Johnson, *Idler*, no. 50, in *Selected Essays*, 314.

138. Johnson, *Idler*, no. 51, in *Selected Essays*, 318.

139. Johnson, *Adventurer*, no. 119, in *Selected Essays*, 264.

140. Ibid., 267.

141. Johnson, *Adventurer*, no. 84, in *Selected Essays*, 244.

142. Johnson, *Rasselas*, in *Selected Poetry and Prose*, 91–92.
143. Boswell, *Life of Johnson*, 2:233.
144. Johnson, *Rambler*, no. 4, in *Selected Essays*, 10.
145. Johnson, *Rambler*, no. 8, in *Selected Essays*, 24.
146. Bate, *Achievement of Johnson*, 142.
147. Johnson, *Rambler*, no. 41, in *Selected Essays*, 90–91.
148. Johnson, *Adventurer*, no. 119, in *Selected Essays*, 267.
149. Johnson, *Rambler*, no. 47, in *Selected Essays*, 101.
150. Johnson, *Rambler*, no. 85, in *Selected Essays*, 143.
151. Ibid., 144.
152. Johnson, *Adventurer*, no. 111, in *Selected Essays*, 260.
153. Ibid.
154. Johnson, *Idler*, no. 58, in *Selected Essays*, 325.

9. DAVID HUME AND THE END OF PHILOSOPHY

1. David Hume, *An Inquiry Concerning Human Understanding*, ed. Charles W. Hendel (Indianapolis, IN: Bobbs-Merrill, 1955), 173.
2. David Hume, *Dialogues Concerning Natural Religion*, ed. Martin Bell (London: Penguin Books, 1990), 72.
3. David Hume, "Of Eloquence," in *Essays: Moral, Political, and Literary*, ed. Eugene F. Miller, rev. ed. (Carmel, IN: Liberty Fund, 1987), 102.
4. David Hume, *My Own Life*, in Dennis C. Rasmussen, *The Infidel and the Professor* (Princeton, NJ: Princeton University Press, 2017), 240.
5. "Hume to Unnamed Physician, 1734," in *The Cambridge Companion to Hume*, ed. David Fate Norton (New York: Cambridge University Press, 1993), 346.
6. Hume, *My Own Life*, in Rasmussen, *Infidel and the Professor*, 240.
7. Hume, *Inquiry Concerning Human Understanding*, 149.
8. Hume, *My Own Life*, in Rasmussen, *Infidel and the Professor*, 245.
9. Ibid., 242.
10. Quoted in Rasmussen, *Infidel and the Professor*, 138.
11. Hume, *Inquiry Concerning Human Understanding*, 40.
12. Ibid.
13. Ibid., 161.
14. Ibid., 162.
15. Ibid., 163n2.
16. Ibid., 41.
17. Ibid., 42.
18. Ibid., 57.

19. Ibid., 115–16.

20. Ibid., 87.

21. David Hume, "An Abstract of a Treatise of Human Nature," in *Inquiry Concerning Human Understanding*, 189.

22. Ibid.

23. David Hume, introduction to *A Treatise of Human Nature*, ed. L. A. Selby-Bigge (Oxford: Clarendon, 1888), xxii.

24. Ludwig Wittgenstein, *Philosophical Investigations*, trans. G. E. M. Anscombe, 3rd ed. (New York: Macmillan, 1973), sec. 217.

25. Hume, *Inquiry Concerning Human Understanding*, 118.

26. Ibid.

27. Ibid., 122.

28. Ibid., 123.

29. David Hume, *An Inquiry Concerning the Principles of Morals*, ed. Charles W. Hendel (Indianapolis, IN: Bobbs-Merrill, 1957), 8.

30. Hume, *My Own Life*, in Rasmussen, *Infidel and the Professor*, 242.

31. Plato, *Euthyphro*, 9e, trans. G. M. A. Grube, in *Complete Works*, ed. John M. Cooper (1997; repr., Norwalk, CT: Easton, 2001).

32. See Michael K. Kellogg, *The Greek Search for Wisdom* (Amherst, NY: Prometheus Books, 2012), 239.

33. Hume, *Treatise of Human Nature*, 469.

34. Hume, *Inquiry Concerning Principles of Morals*, 108.

35. Hume, *Treatise of Human Nature*, 415.

36. Hume, *Inquiry Concerning Principles of Morals*, 105.

37. Hume, *Treatise of Human Nature*, 416.

38. Voltaire, *Philosophical Dictionary*, ed. and trans. Theodore Besterman (London: Penguin Books, 2004), 68.

39. Hume, *Inquiry Concerning Principles of Morals*, 5.

40. Ibid., 9.

41. Ibid., 6.

42. Ibid., 42; see Hume, *Treatise of Human Nature*, 500.

43. Hume, *Inquiry Concerning Principles of Morals*, 7.

44. P. M. S. Hacker, *The Passions: A Study of Human Nature* (Hoboken, NJ: Wiley Blackwell, 2018); P. M. S. Hacker, *The Moral Powers: A Study of Human Nature* (Hoboken, NJ: Wiley Blackwell, 2021).

45. Hume, *Inquiry Concerning Principles of Morals*, 113.

46. Ibid., 47.

47. Ibid., 92.

48. Ibid., 114.

49. Thomas Hobbes, *Leviathan*, ed. A. P. Martinich and Brian Battiste, rev. ed. (Toronto: Broadview, 2011), 125, 127.

50. Terence Penelhum, "Hume's Moral Psychology," in *Cambridge Companion to Hume*, 124.

51. Hume, *Treatise of Human Nature*, 491–92.

52. See Arthur Herman, *How the Scots Invented the Modern World* (New York: Broadway Books, 2001), 200–206.

53. Hume, *Inquiry Concerning Principles of Morals*, 23.

54. Ibid.

55. Ibid., 43.

56. David Hume, "The Platonist," in *Essays*, 157.

57. David Hume, "The Sceptic," in *Essays*, 160.

58. David Hume, "The Epicurean," in *Essays*, 139. It is unfortunate that Hume did not include an essay on Aristotle. Had he done so, he would have found it far more in keeping with his own morality of public virtue. See Michael K. Kellogg, *Three Questions We Never Stop Asking* (Amherst, NY: Prometheus Books, 2010), chap. 5.

59. Hume, "The Sceptic," in *Essays*, 180.

60. Quoted in introduction to *Dialogues*, 1.

61. David Hume, *The Natural History of Religion*, ed. H. E. Root (Stanford, CA: Stanford University Press, 1957), 65.

62. Ibid., 70.

63. David Hume, "Of Superstition and Enthusiasm," in *Essays*, 74.

64. Hume, *Natural History of Religion*, 66.

65. Hume, "Superstition and Enthusiasm," in *Essays*, 74–75.

66. Hume, *Natural History of Religion*, 66.

67. Hume, "Superstition and Enthusiasm," in *Essays*, 73.

68. Hume, *Natural History of Religion*, 72.

69. Hume, *Inquiry Concerning Principles of Morals*, 91.

70. Ibid., 91.

71. Hume, *Natural History of Religion*, 75.

72. Ibid.

73. See Rasmussen, *Infidel and the Professor*, 192–94.

74. Hume, *Dialogues*, 99.

75. Ibid., 51.

76. Ibid., 99.

77. Ibid., 125.

78. Ibid., 53.

79. Ibid., 105–6.

80. Ibid., 108–9.

81. Ibid., 112.

82. Ibid., 73.

83. Ibid.

84. Ibid., 72 (emphasis added).

85. Ibid., 97.

86. Ibid., 121.

87. Ibid., 94–95; see J. C. A. Gaskin, "Hume on Religion," in *Cambridge Companion to Hume*, 328.

88. Hume, *Dialogues*, 94.

89. Ibid., 94–95.

90. Ibid., 95.

91. Ibid.

92. David Hume, "Of the Immortality of the Soul," in *Essays*, 590–98.

93. Ibid., 594.

94. Ibid., 596.

95. Brian Greene, *Until the End of Time: Mind, Matter, and Our Search for Meaning in an Evolving Universe* (New York: Alfred A. Knopf, 2020), 13 (quoting *Speak, Memory: An Autobiography Revisited*).

96. Hume, *My Own Life*, in Rasmussen, *Infidel and the Professor*, 245.

97. Adam Smith to William Strahan, Kirkcaldy, Fifeshire, November 9, 1776, in Rasmussen, *Infidel and the Professor*, 247, 249.

98. Ibid., 248.

99. Quoted in pertinent part in Rasmussen, *Infidel and the Professor*, 228.

100. Smith to Strahan, in Rasmussen, *Infidel and the Professor*, 251.

10. KANT AND THE CLAIMS OF REASON

1. Immanuel Kant, *Prolegomena to Any Future Metaphysics*, trans. Paul Carus, 3rd ed. (Chicago: Open Court, 1912), 7. This chapter is adapted from my treatment of Kant in *Three Questions We Never Stop Asking* (Amherst, NY: Prometheus Books, 2010), chap. 3.

2. Immanuel Kant, *Critique of Pure Reason*, trans. Norman Kemp Smith, unabridged ed. (New York: St. Martin's, 1965), Axvii. Standard pagination for *Critique of Pure Reason* gives A citations (to the first German edition) and/or B citations (to the second German edition, to which Kant added substantial new material).

3. Ibid., A51, B75.

4. Ibid.

5. Ibid., Bxviii.

6. Ibid., A107 (emphasis added).

7. Ibid., B131–32.

8. Ibid., A116.

9. Ibid., B277.

10. Ibid., A111.

11. Ibid., B224.

12. Ibid., A246, B303 (italics omitted).

13. Ibid., A287, B344.

14. Ibid., Avii.

15. Ibid., A5, B8–9.

16. See Walter Isaacson, *Einstein: His Life and Universe* (New York: Simon & Schuster, 2007), 4.

17. Brian Greene, *The Fabric of the Cosmos: Space, Time, and the Texture of Reality* (New York: Knopf, 2004), 473.

18. Ibid., 487.

19. Ibid., 472.

20. Ibid., 20.

21. Ibid., 5 (italics omitted).

22. Kant, *Critique of Pure Reason*, A805, B833.

23. Ibid., Bxxxi.

24. Ibid., A595, B623.

25. Ibid., A600, B628.

26. Ibid., A620, B648.

27. Ibid., A622, B650.

28. Ibid., A623, B651.

29. Ibid., A630.

30. Immanuel Kant, *Critique of Judgement*, trans. James Creed Meredith (Oxford: Clarendon, 1952), pt. 2, 125.

31. Kant, *Critique of Pure Reason*, A569, B597 (italics omitted).

32. Immanuel Kant, *Critique of Practical Reason*, trans. Lewis White Beck (Indianapolis, IN: Bobbs-Merrill, 1956), 4.

33. Immanuel Kant, *Foundations of the Metaphysics of Morals*, trans. Lewis White Beck (Indianapolis, IN: Bobbs-Merrill, 1959), 16.

34. Ibid., 15.

35. Ibid., 6.

36. Ibid., 29.

37. Ibid., 31.

38. Ibid., 39.

39. Ibid., 47.

40. Ibid., 46.

41. Ibid., 71.

42. Ibid., 65.

43. Benedict de Spinoza, *Ethics*, ed. and trans. Edwin Curley (New York: Penguin Books, 1996), 4.P59, 147.

44. Kant, *Critique of Practical Reason*, 4.

45. Ibid., 130.

46. Ibid., 118.

47. Ibid., 127.

48. Ibid., 123.

49. Ibid., 129.

50. Ibid., 134.

51. Immanuel Kant, *Religion and Rational Theology*, ed. and trans. Allen W. Wood and George di Giovanni (Cambridge: Cambridge University Press, 1996), 190.

52. Ibid., 264 (italics omitted).

53. Ibid., 267.

54. Ibid., 186.

55. Ibid., 198.

56. Ibid., 193.

57. Ibid., 210 (italics omitted).

58. Ibid., 211n.

59. Ibid., 272.

60. Ibid., 180–81.

61. Ibid., 199.

62. See Kant, *Critique of Judgement*, pt. 2, 54.

63. Isaacson, *Einstein*, 393.

64. Ibid., 384, 387.

65. Ibid., 384–85, 389.

66. Ibid., 385.

67. Kant, *Critique of Practical Reason*, 166.

SUGGESTIONS FOR FURTHER READING

INTRODUCTION

Primary Sources

Bacon, Francis. *The New Organon.* Edited by Lisa Jardine and Michael Silverthorne. Cambridge: Cambridge University Press, 2000.

Hobbes, Thomas. *Leviathan.* With an introduction by Herbert W. Schneider. Indianapolis, IN: Bobbs-Merrill, 1958.

Montesquieu. *The Spirit of the Laws.* Edited and translated by Anne M. Cohler, Basia C. Miller, and Harold S. Stone. Cambridge: Cambridge University Press, 1989.

Smith, Adam. *The Wealth of Nations.* Edited by Edwin Cannan. New York: Modern Library, 2000.

Secondary Sources

Barzun, Jacques. *From Dawn to Decadence: 500 Years of Western Cultural Life, 1500 to the Present.* New York: HarperCollins, 2000.

Bergin, Joseph, ed. *The Seventeenth Century: Europe 1598–1715.* New York: Oxford University Press, 2001.

Berlin, Isaiah. *Against the Current: Essays in the History of Ideas.* Edited by Henry Hardy, with an introduction by Roger Hausheer. Harmondsworth, UK: Penguin Books, 1982.

Dolnick, Edward. *The Clockwork Universe: Isaac Newton, the Royal Society, and the Birth of the Modern World.* New York: HarperCollins, 2012.

Gay, Peter. *The Enlightenment: The Rise of Modern Paganism.* 1966. Reprint, New York: W. W. Norton, 1977.

Gay, Peter. *The Enlightenment: The Science of Freedom.* 1969. Reprint, New York: W. W. Norton, 1977.

Gribbin, John. *The Scientists: A History of Science Told Through the Lives of Its Greatest Inventors.* New York: Random House, 2003.

Hazard, Paul. *The Crisis of the European Mind, 1680–1715.* Translated by J. Lewis May, with an introduction by Anthony Grafton. New York: New York Review Books, 2012.

Israel, Jonathan I. *Radical Enlightenment: Philosophy and the Making of Modernity, 1650–1750.* New York: Oxford University Press, 2001.

Kline, Morris. *Mathematics and the Physical World.* New York: Dover, 1981.

McKenzie, A. E. E. *The Major Achievements of Science: The Development of Science from Ancient Times to the Present.* New York: Simon & Schuster, 1973.

Principe, Lawrence M. *The Scientific Revolution: A Very Short Introduction.* New York: Oxford University Press, 2011.

Winks, Robin W., and Thomas E. Kaiser. *Europe, 1648–1815: From the Old Regime to the Age of Revolution.* New York: Oxford University Press, 2004.

DESCARTES

Primary Sources

Descartes: Selected Philosophical Writings. Translated by John Cottingham, Robert Stoothoff, and Dugald Murdoch. Cambridge: Cambridge University Press, 1988.

The Philosophical Writings of Descartes. Translated by John Cottingham, Robert Stoothoff, and Dugald Murdoch. 2 vols. Cambridge: Cambridge University Press, 1985.

Secondary Sources

Ben-Yami, Hanoch. *Descartes' Philosophical Revolution: A Reassessment.* New York: Palgrave Macmillan, 2015.

Clarke, Desmond M. *Descartes: A Biography.* Cambridge: Cambridge University Press, 2012.

Gaukroger, Stephen. *Descartes: An Intellectual Biography.* New York: Oxford University Press, 1997.

Gottlieb, Anthony. *The Dream of Enlightenment: The Rise of Modern Philosophy.* Chap. 1. New York: Liveright, 2017.

Nadler, Steven. *The Philosopher, the Priest, and the Painter: A Portrait of Descartes.* Princeton, NJ: Princeton University Press, 2013.

Sorell, Tom. *Descartes: A Very Short Introduction.* New York: Oxford University Press, 2000.

Williams, Bernard. *Descartes: The Project of Pure Enquiry.* Harmondsworth, UK: Penguin Books, 1978.

MILTON

Primary Sources

Milton, John. *Paradise Lost.* Edited by Gordon Teskey. Norton Critical Editions. New York: W. W. Norton, 2005.

Milton's Selected Poetry and Prose. Edited by Jason P. Rosenblatt. Norton Critical Editions. New York: W. W. Norton, 2011.

Secondary Sources

Bush, Douglas. *John Milton: A Sketch of His Life and Writings.* New York: Collier Books, 1967.

Danielson, Dennis, ed. *The Cambridge Companion to Milton.* 1989. Reprint, Cambridge: Cambridge University Press, 1997.

Fish, Stanley. *Surprised by Sin: The Reader in "Paradise Lost."* 2nd ed. Cambridge, MA: Harvard University Press, 1998.

Forsyth, Neil. *John Milton: A Biography.* Oxford: Lion, 2008.

Frye, Northrop. *The Return of Eden: Five Essays on Milton's Epics.* 1965. Reprint, Toronto: University of Toronto Press, 1975.

John Milton's "Paradise Lost." Edited with an introduction by Harold Bloom. Modern Critical Interpretations. New York: Chelsea House, 1987.

Lewis, C. S. *A Preface to "Paradise Lost."* London: Oxford University Press, 1961.

Schwartz, Louis, ed. *The Cambridge Companion to "Paradise Lost."* New York: Cambridge University Press, 2014.

Wilson, A. N. *The Life of John Milton.* Oxford: Oxford University Press, 1984.

MOLIÈRE

Primary Sources

de La Rochefoucauld, François. *Maximes.* With an introduction by Jacques Truchet. Paris: Garnier-Flammarion, 1977.

Molière. *Don Juan.* Translated with an introduction by Richard Wilbur. San Diego, CA: Harcourt, 2001.

Molière: Four Comedies. Translated by Richard Wilbur. New York: Harcourt Brace Jovanovich, 1982.

Molière: Oeuvres Complètes. 4 vols. With an introduction by Georges Mongrédien. Paris: Garnier-Flammarion, 1965.

Molière. *"Tartuffe": A Verse Translation, Backgrounds and Sources, Criticism.* Edited by Constance Congdon and Virginia Scott, translated by Constance Congdon. New York: W. W. Norton, 2009.

Secondary Sources

Bradby, David, and Andrew Calder, eds. *The Cambridge Companion to Molière.* New York: Cambridge University Press, 2006.

Bulgakov, Mikhail. *The Life of Monsieur de Molière.* Translated by Mirra Ginsburg. New York: New Directions, 1986.

Gossman, Lionel. *Men and Masks: A Study of Molière.* Baltimore: Johns Hopkins Press, 1969.

Guicharnaud, Jacques. ed. *Molière: A Collection of Critical Essays.* Englewood Cliffs, NJ: Prentice-Hall, 1964.

Howarth, W. D. *Molière: A Playwright and His Audience.* Cambridge: Cambridge University Press, 1982.

Hubert, J. D. *Molière and the Comedy of Intellect.* Berkeley: University of California Press, 1973.

Picard, Raymond. *Two Centuries of French Literature.* Translated by John Cairncross. New York: McGraw-Hill, 1970.

Turnell, Martin. *The Classical Moment: Studies of Corneille, Molière and Racine.* 1948. Reprint, Westport, CT: Greenwood, 1975.

PASCAL

Primary Sources

Pascal, Blaise. *The Provincial Letters.* Edited by Paul A. Böer Sr., translated by Thomas M'Crie. N.p.: Veritatis Splendor, 2012.
Pascal's "Pensées." Translated by W. F. Trotter, with an introduction by T. S. Eliot. New York: E. P. Dutton, 1958.

Secondary Sources

Bishop, Morris. *Pascal: The Life of Genius.* Baltimore: Williams & Wilkins, 1936.
Blaise Pascal. Edited with an introduction by Harold Bloom. New York: Chelsea House, 1989.
Connor, James A. *Pascal's Wager: The Man Who Played Dice with God.* Oxford: Lion, 2007.
Hammond, Nicholas, ed. *The Cambridge Companion to Pascal.* Cambridge: Cambridge University Press, 2003.
O'Connell, Marvin R. *Blaise Pascal: Reasons of the Heart.* Grand Rapids, MI: Wm. B. Eerdmans, 1997.

SPINOZA

Primary Sources

Spinoza, Benedict de. *Ethics.* Edited and translated by Edwin Curley, with an introduction by Stuart Hampshire. New York: Penguin Books, 1996.
Spinoza, Benedict de. *Principles of Cartesian Philosophy.* Translated by Harry E. Wedeck, with a preface by Dagobert D. Runes. New York: Philosophical Library, 1961.
Works of Spinoza. Translated and with an introduction by R. H. M. Elwes. 2 vols. New York: Dover, 1955.

Secondary Sources

Garrett, Don, ed. *The Cambridge Companion to Spinoza.* Cambridge: Cambridge University Press, 1996.
Goldstein, Rebecca. *Betraying Spinoza: The Renegade Jew Who Gave Us Modernity.* New York: Schocken Books, 2006.
Hampshire, Stuart. *Spinoza: An Introduction to His Philosophical Thought.* 1951. Reprint, Harmondsworth, UK: Penguin Books, 1987.
Nadler, Steven. *A Book Forged in Hell: Spinoza's Scandalous Treatise and the Birth of the Secular Age.* Princeton, NJ: Princeton University Press, 2011.
Scruton, Roger. *Spinoza.* Oxford: Oxford University Press, 1986.

Stewart, Matthew. *The Courtier and the Heretic: Leibniz, Spinoza, and the Fate of God in the Modern World.* New York: W. W. Norton, 2006.

DEFOE AND SWIFT

Primary Sources

Defoe, Daniel. *A Journal of the Plague Year.* Mineola, NY: Dover, 2001.
Defoe, Daniel. *Robinson Crusoe.* Edited by Michael Shinagel. New York: W. W. Norton, 1994.
Defoe, Daniel. *The Storm.* Edited with an introduction and notes by Richard Hamblyn. London: Penguin Books, 2005.
The Essential Writings of Jonathan Swift. Edited by Claude Rawson and Ian Higgins. New York: W. W. Norton, 2009.
Swift, Jonathan. *Gulliver's Travels.* Edited by Albert J. Rivero. New York: W. W. Norton, 2002.

Secondary Sources

Brady, Frank, ed. *Twentieth Century Interpretations of "Gulliver's Travels."* Englewood Cliffs, NJ: Prentice-Hall, 1968.
Damrosch, Leo. *Jonathan Swift: His Life and His World.* New Haven, CT: Yale University Press, 2013.
Ellis, Frank H., ed. *Twentieth Century Interpretations of "Robinson Crusoe."* Englewood Cliffs, NJ: Prentice-Hall, 1969.
Modern Critical Views: Daniel Defoe. Edited with an introduction by Harold Bloom. New York: Chelsea House, 1987.
Modern Critical Views: Jonathan Swift. Edited with an introduction by Harold Bloom. New York: Chelsea House, 1986.
Stubbs, John. *Jonathan Swift: The Reluctant Rebel.* London: Penguin Books, 2017.
Watt, Ian. *The Rise of the Novel: Studies in Defoe, Richardson and Fielding.* 1957. Reprint, New York: Peregrine Books, 1983.
West, Richard. *Daniel Defoe: The Life and Strange, Surprising Adventures.* New York: Carroll & Graf, 2000.

VOLTAIRE

Primary Sources

Le Rond d'Alembert, Jean. *Preliminary Discourse to the Encyclopedia of Diderot.* Translated with an introduction and notes by Richard N. Schwab. Chicago: University of Chicago Press, 1995.
The Portable Voltaire. Edited with an introduction by Ben Ray Redman. New York: Penguin Books, 1977.
Voltaire. *Candide.* Edited by Nicholas Cronk, translated by Robert M. Adams. 3rd ed. New York: W. W. Norton, 2016.

Voltaire. *Philosophical Dictionary.* Edited and translated by Theodore Besterman. London: Penguin Books, 2004.

Voltaire. *Philosophical Letters: Or, Letters Regarding the English Nation.* Edited with an introduction by John Leigh, translated by Prudence L. Steiner. Indianapolis, IN: Hackett, 2007.

Voltaire: "Candide" and Other Stories. Translated with an introduction and notes by Roger Pearson. New York: Alfred A. Knopf, 1992.

Secondary Sources

Cronk, Nicholas, ed. *The Cambridge Companion to Voltaire.* Cambridge: Cambridge University Press, 2009.

Cronk, Nicholas. *Voltaire: A Very Short Introduction.* Oxford: Oxford University Press, 2017.

Davidson, Ian. *Voltaire: A Life.* New York: Pegasus Books, 2010.

White, R. J. *The Anti-Philosophers: A Study of the Philosophes in Eighteenth-Century France.* New York: St. Martin's, 1970.

JOHNSON

Primary Sources

Boswell, James. *Journal of a Tour to the Hebrides.* Preface and notes by Frederick A. Pottle and Charles H. Bennett. New York: Literary Guild, 1936.

Boswell, James. *The Life of Samuel Johnson.* Introduction by Edward G. Fletcher. 3 vols. New York: Heritage, 1963.

Johnson, Samuel. *The Rambler.* In *The Yale Edition of the Works of Samuel Johnson*, edited by W. Jackson Bate and Albrecht B. Strauss, vols. 3–5. New Haven, CT: Yale University Press, 1969.

Johnson, Samuel, and James Boswell. *A Journey to the Western Islands of Scotland* and *Journal of a Tour to the Hebrides.* Edited with an introduction and notes by Peter Levi. Harmondsworth, UK: Penguin Books, 1984.

Samuel Johnson: Selected Essays from the "Rambler," "Adventurer," and "Idler." Edited by W. Jackson Bate. New Haven, CT: Yale University Press, 1968.

Samuel Johnson: Selected Poetry and Prose. Edited with an introduction and notes by Frank Brady and W. K. Wimsatt. Berkeley: University of California Press, 1977.

Secondary Sources

Bate, W. Jackson. *The Achievement of Samuel Johnson.* Chicago: University of Chicago Press, 1978.

Bate, W. Jackson. *Samuel Johnson.* New York: Harcourt Brace, 1979.

Damrosch, Leo. *The Club: Johnson, Boswell, and the Friends Who Shaped an Age.* New Haven, CT: Yale University Press, 2019.

HUME

Primary Sources

Hume, David. *Dialogues Concerning Natural Religion.* Edited with an introduction and notes by Martin Bell. London: Penguin Books, 1990.

Hume, David. *Essays: Moral, Political, and Literary*, rev. ed. Edited with a foreword, notes, and glossary by Eugene F. Miller. Carmel, IN: Liberty Fund, 1987.

Hume, David. *An Inquiry Concerning Human Understanding.* Edited by Charles W. Hendel. Indianapolis, IN: Bobbs-Merrill, 1955.

Hume, David. *An Inquiry Concerning the Principles of Morals.* Edited by Charles W. Hendel. Indianapolis, IN: Bobbs-Merrill, 1957.

Hume, David. *The Natural History of Religion.* Edited with an introduction by H. E. Root. Stanford, CA: Stanford University Press, 1957.

Hume, David. *A Treatise of Human Nature.* Edited by L. A. Selby-Bigge. Oxford: Clarendon, 1888.

Secondary Sources

Harris, James A. *Hume: An Intellectual Biography.* New York: Cambridge University Press, 2015.

Herman, Arthur. *How the Scots Invented the Modern World.* New York: Broadway Books, 2001.

Norton, David Fate, ed. *The Cambridge Companion to Hume.* New York: Cambridge University Press, 1993.

Rasmussen, Dennis C. *The Infidel and the Professor.* Princeton, NJ: Princeton University Press, 2017.

KANT

Primary Sources

Kant, Immanuel. *Critique of Judgement.* Translated by James Creed Meredith. Oxford: Clarendon, 1952.

Kant, Immanuel. *Critique of Practical Reason.* Translated with an introduction by Lewis White Beck. Indianapolis, IN: Bobbs-Merrill, 1956.

Kant, Immanuel. *Critique of Pure Reason*, unabridged ed. Translated by Norman Kemp Smith. New York: St. Martin's, 1965.

Kant, Immanuel. *Foundations of the Metaphysics of Morals.* Translated with an introduction by Lewis White Beck. Indianapolis, IN: Bobbs-Merrill, 1959.

Kant, Immanuel. *Prolegomena to Any Future Metaphysics*, 3rd ed. Edited and translated by Paul Carus. Chicago: Open Court, 1912.

Kant, Immanuel. *Religion and Rational Theology.* Edited and translated by Allen W. Wood and George di Giovanni. Cambridge: Cambridge University Press, 1996.

316SUGGESTIONS FOR FURTHER READING

Secondary Sources

Cassirer, Ernst. *Kant's Life and Thought*. Translated by James Haden, with an introduction by Stephan Körner. New Haven, CT: Yale University Press, 1981.
Guyer, Paul. *Kant*. London: Routledge, 2006.
Körner, Stephan. *Kant*. Harmondsworth, UK: Penguin Books, 1955.
Kuehn, Manfred. *Kant: A Biography*. Cambridge: Cambridge University Press, 2001.
Scruton, Roger. *Kant: A Very Short Introduction*. New York: Oxford University Press, 1982.
Smith, Norman Kemp. *A Commentary to Kant's Critique of Pure Reason*. Atlantic Highlands, NJ: Humanities Press, 1962.
Strawson, P. F. *The Bounds of Sense*. London: Methuen, 1975.

INDEX

Adam and Eve, 47–52; Milton and, 26; Pascal and, 99; Voltaire and, 185–186
afterlife: Hume and, 239, 245–246; Kant and, 269–270; Milton and, 44–45; Spinoza and, 108, 129
Alice in Wonderland (Carroll), 133
"L'Allegro" (Milton), 30–31
Allen, Woody, 175
alternative geometries, Kant and, 261
altruism, Hume and, 236
analytic geometry, x, 2, 17
animals, nature of: Descartes and, 20–21; Spinoza and, 122; Voltaire and, 171–172
animal spirits, Descartes and, 19
Anne, queen of Great Britain, 136–137, 139, 142, 194
Anne of Austria, 90
Anselm of Canterbury, 117
a posteriori arguments, Hume and, 241
a priori arguments: Hume and, 233, 241; Kant and, 250, 253
Areopagitica (Milton), 36
arguments for existence of God, 117, 241–245; Descartes and, 13; Kant and, 264–270
Aristotle, x, 17, 18, 89–90, 144; Descartes and, 1, 2; Milton and, 44; Spinoza and, 127
Arouet, François-Marie. *See* Voltaire
arts, rational methodology and, xvii

astronomy: Descartes and, 8, 17; scientific revolution and, ix–x, xi
atheism, 163
Auerbach, Erich, 98, 106

Bach, Johann Sebastian, xvii
Bacon, Francis, x, 16, 170
Bate, W. Jackson, 206
The Battle of the Books (Swift), 141
Beeckman, Isaac, 7, 18
Béjart, Armande, 66
Béjart, Madeleine, 62, 63, 66
Berkeley, bishop, 215, 226, 248
Bible. *See* scriptures
biography, Boswell and, 193
Bishop, Morris, 87
Blake, William, 42
Boethius, 45, 117
Boswell, James, xxii, 193, 203, 205; on Edwards, 212; on Hume, 239, 245–246; on royalty, 202; and Scotland, 204–205; on sense impressions, 215; on Tetty, 197; on theater, 199; on truth, 209
Boyle, Robert, xi, 242
Brahe, Tycho, ix
Brobdingnag, 155–157
Bunyan, John, 143
Burke, Edmund, xiii, 203
Burman, Frans, 14
Byng, John, 188–189